WJEC/Eduqas
Religious Studies for A Level Year 2 & A2
Judaism

Helen Gwynne-Kinsey
Edited by Richard Gray

Published in 2018 by Illuminate Publishing Ltd, PO Box 1160, Cheltenham, Gloucestershire GL50 9RW

Orders: Please visit www.illuminatepublishing.com
or email sales@illuminatepublishing.com

© Helen Gwynne-Kinsey

The moral rights of the author have been asserted.

All rights reserved. No part of this book may be reprinted, reproduced or utilised in any form or by any electronic, mechanical, or other means, now known or hereafter invented, including photocopying and recording, or in any information storage and retrieval system, without permission in writing from the publishers.

British Library Cataloguing-in-Publication Data

A catalogue record for this book is available from the British Library

ISBN 978-1-911208-38-9

Printed by Ashford Colour Press, Gosport

05.19

The publisher's policy is to use papers that are natural, renewable and recyclable products made from wood grown in sustainable forests. The logging and manufacturing processes are expected to conform to the environmental regulations of the country of origin.

Every effort has been made to contact copyright holders of material reproduced in this book. If notified, the publishers will be pleased to rectify any errors or omissions at the earliest opportunity.

This material has been endorsed by WJEC/Eduqas and offers high quality support for the delivery of WJEC/Eduqas qualifications. While this material has been through a WJEC/Eduqas quality assurance process, all responsibility for the content remains with the publisher.

WJEC/Eduqas examination questions are reproduced by permission from WJEC/Eduqas

Series editor: Richard Gray
Editor: Geoff Tuttle
Design and Layout: EMC Design Ltd, Bedford

Acknowledgements

Cover Image: © Pedro Gutierrez/Shutterstock

Image credits:

p. 1 © Pedro Guiterrez; p. 6 Hendrickson Publishers, Peabody, Massachusetts. Used by permission. All rights reserved; p. 7 Paul Fearn / Alamy Stock Photo; p. 12 vadim kozlovsky; p. 15 ChameleonsEye / Shutterstock.com; p. 18 Rhonda Roth; p. 19 Public domain; p. 23 aradaphotography; p. 24 Alejo Miranda; p. 26 enterlinedesign; p. 29 Public domain; p. 32 artmig; p. 34 PhotoStock-Israel; p. 36 Public domain; p. 37 annalisa e marina durante; p. 38 neftali; p. 41 (top) Tyler Olson; p. 41 (bottom) Ververidis Vasilils; p. 43 Creative commons; p. 46 ChameleonsEye / Shutterstock.com; p. 48 SJ Travel Photo and Video; p. 51 Everett Historical; p. 52 Everett Historical; p. 53 Everett Historical; p. 54 Tashafuvango; p. 55 (top) Government Press Office; p. 55 (bottom) Frenklakh; p. 57 railway fx; p. 60 Andy Dean Photography; p. 62 Romolo Tavani; p. 64 (top) suns07butterfly; p. 64 (bottom) Igor Zh; p. 65 Inna_liapko; p. 66 Public domain; p. 68 Eddorov Artem; p. 69 M-SUR; p. 70 Mark Godden; p. 71 Liseykina; p. 73 Everett Historical; p. 76 donskarpo; p. 78 Rob / Alamy Stock Photo; p. 79 (top) Public domain; p. 79 (bottom) Public domain; p. 81 ChameleonsEye; p. 82 (top) Vladimir Melnik; p. 82 (bottom left) ungvar; p. 82 (bottom right) Stephen Rees; p. 84 CJCUC; p. 87 WENN UK / Alamy Stock Photo; p. 89 Renata Sedmakova / Shutterstock.com; p. 92 Creative commons; p. 93 Africa Studio; p. 94 Ganis; p. 95 Ekaterina Lin; p. 96 Nir Alon / Alamy Stock Photo; p. 98 Michael Ventura / Alamy Stock Photo; p. 99 Jewish Women's Archive; p. 100 Creative commons; p. 103 david156; p. 105 Agencja Fotograficzna Caro / Alamy Stock Photo; p. 108 KLBD; p. 109 Mike Abrahams / Alamy Stock Photo; p. 110 (top) menunierd; p. 110 (bottom) Serge75; p. 111 (top) ASAP / Alamy Stock Photo; p. 111 (bottom) pixinoo; p. 112 (top) Courtesy JCoSS; p. 112 (bottom) Hasmonean High School; p. 113 Courtesy Jewish Leadership Council; p. 116 John Yeadon / Cardiff Reform Synagogue; p. 120 Creative commons; p. 122 (top) Public domain; p. 122 (bottom) RusskyMaverick / Shutterstock.com; p. 124 DIMITRII A KUDASOV; p. 126 The Face of God after Auschwitz by Ignaz Maybaum; p. 128 enterlinedesign; p. 130 DyziO; p. 131 Afuta; p. 134 evantravels; p. 136 ChameleonsEye; p. 138 www.BibleLandPictures.com / Alamy Stock Photo; p. 139 david156 / Shutterstock.com; p. 140 By Winograd – Own work, Public Domain, https://commons.wikimedia.org/w/index.php?curid=21998901; p. 141 mikhail; p. 142 (left) Sharon Day; p. 142 (right) aga7ta; p. 143 Creative commons; p. 149 Eddie Gerald / Alamy Stock Photo; p. 151 Route55; p. 154 (top) ART Collection / Alamy Stock Photo; p. 154 (bottom) Alejo Miranda; p. 155 Public domain; p. 156 By Sonsaz (Own work) [GFDL (http://www.gnu.org/copyleft/fdl.html) or CC BY-SA 4.0-3.0-2.5-2.0-1.0 (https://creativecommons.org/licenses/by-sa/4.0-3.0-2.5-2.0-1.0)], via Wikimedia Commons; p. 158 (top) Public domain; p. 158 (bottom) Vadim Sadovski; p. 160 David Carillet; p. 162 Anneka; p. 165 Public domain; p. 166 Thoom; p. 169 (top) Phanie / Alamy Stock Photo; p. 169 (bottom) david156; p. 170 Juan Gaertner; p. 171 Anton_Ivanov; p. 173 Science History Images / Alamy Stock Photo; p. 174 (top) enterlinedesign; p. 174 (bottom) Courtesy of Yeshiva University; p. 175 Courtesy Clare Blackburn; p. 179 designer491; p. 181 Ideya

Contents*

About this book — 4

Theme 1: Religious figures and sacred texts — 6
- D: The structure and development of the Talmud and its importance within Judaism — 6
- E: Midrash in Judaism: the distinction between Halakhah and Aggadah — 22
- F: Rashi and Maimonides — 36

Theme 3: Significant social and historical developments in religious thought — YR 13 — 48
- A: The challenge of secularisation — 48
- B: The challenge of science — 64
- C: The development of Reform Judaism and Jewish attitudes to pluralism — 78

Theme 3: Significant social and historical developments in religious thought — YR 13 — 92
- D: Religion, equality and discrimination: Jewish family life and gender equality — 92
- E: Judaism and migration: the challenges of being a religious and ethnic minority in Britain — 107
- F: Holocaust theology — 120

Theme 4: Religious practices that shape religious identity — 138
- D: Beliefs and practices distinctive of Hasidic Judaism — 138
- E: Philosophical understandings of the nature of God and religious experience found in Kabbalah — 153
- F: Ethical debate within Judaism about embryo research — 169

Questions and answers — 183

Quickfire answers — 189

Glossary — 191

Index — 196

* The contents listed correspond to the Eduqas Full A Level Specification which matches equivalent WJEC A2 Specification as follows:

  Eduqas Theme 1: D,E,F = WJEC Theme 1: A,B,C
  Eduqas Theme 3: A,B,C = WJEC Theme 2: A,B & Theme 3: F
  Eduqas Theme 3: D,E,F = WJEC Theme 2: C & Theme 3: A,B
  Eduqas Theme 4: D,E,F = WJEC Theme 4: A,B,C

About this book

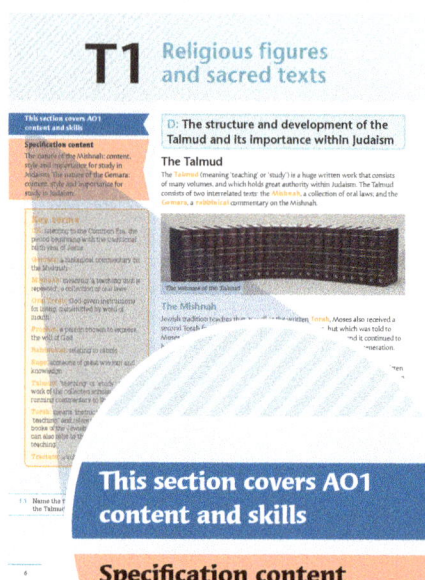

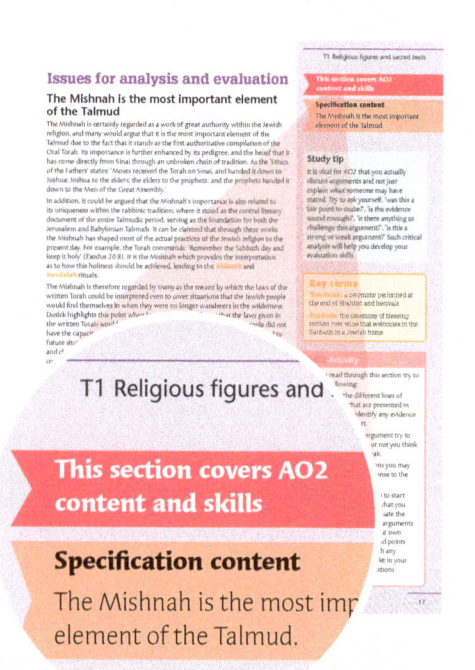

With the new A Level in Religious Studies, there is a lot to cover and a lot to do in preparation for the examinations at A Level. The aim of these books is to provide enough support for you to achieve success at A Level, whether as a teacher or a learner, and build upon the success of the Year 1 and AS series.

Once again, the Year 2 and A2 series of books is skills-based in its approach to learning, which means it aims to continue combining coverage of the Specification content with examination preparation. In other words, it aims to help you get through the second half of the course whilst at the same time developing some more advanced skills needed for the examinations.

To help you study, there are clearly defined sections for each of the AO1 and AO2 areas of the Specification. These are arranged according to the Specification Themes and use, as far as is possible, Specification headings to help you see that the content has been covered for A Level.

The AO1 content is detailed but precise, with the benefit of providing you with references to both religious/philosophical works and to the views of scholars. The AO2 responds to the issues raised in the Specification and provides you with ideas for further debate, to help you develop your own critical analysis and evaluation skills.

Ways to use this book

In considering the different ways in which you may teach or learn, it was decided that the books needed to have an inbuilt flexibility to adapt. As a result, they can be used for classroom learning, for independent work by individuals, as homework, and they are even suitable for the purposes of 'flipped learning' if your school or college does this.

You may be well aware that learning time is so valuable at A Level and so we have also taken this into consideration by creating flexible features and activities, again to save you the time of painstaking research and preparation, either as teacher or learner.

Features of the books

The books all contain the following features that appear in the margins, or are highlighted in the main body of the text, in order to support teaching and learning.

Key terms of technical, religious and philosophical words or phrases

> **Key terms**
> **Gemara:** a rabbinical commentary on the Mishnah

Quickfire questions simple, straightforward questions to help consolidate key facts about what is being digested in reading through the information

> **quickfire**
> 1.1 Name the two texts that make up the Talmud.

Key quotes either from religious and philosophical works and/or the works of scholars

> **Key quote**
> The study of Judaism, its history, ideas and ideals, begins now, as for the past fifteen centuries, in the pages of the Babylonian Talmud. **(Neusner)**

Study tips advice on how to study, prepare for the examination and answer questions

Study tip

When discussing the reasons for the greater authority of the Babylonian Talmud over the Jerusalem Talmud, make sure that you refer to the views of scholars/schools of thought in an accurate and effective way (L5 band descriptor AO1).

AO1 Activities that serve the purpose of focusing on identification, presentation and explanation, and developing the skills of knowledge and understanding required for the examination

AO1 Activity

Work in a group and identify five areas of modern life that would not have been relevant during the time of the giving of the Torah to Moses (e.g. cyber crime). When you have collated your list, find out through research online how Jews today have come to an understanding of each issue.

AO2 Activities that serve the purpose of focusing on conclusions, as a basis for thinking about the issues, developing critical analysis and the evaluation skills required for the examination

AO2 Activity

As you read through this section try to do the following:
1. Pick out the different lines of argument that are presented in the text and identify any evidence given in support.

Glossary of all the key terms for quick reference.

Specific feature: Developing skills

This section is very much a focus on 'what to do' with the content and the issues that are raised. They occur at the end of each section, giving 12 AO1 and 12 AO2 activities that aim to develop particular skills that are required for more advanced study at Year 2 and A2 stage.

The Developing skills for Year 2 and A2 are grouped so that each Theme has a specific focus to develop and perfect gradually throughout that Theme.

AO1 and AO2 answers and commentaries

The final section has a selection of answers and commentaries as a framework for judging what an effective and ineffective response may be. The comments highlight some common mistakes and also examples of good practice so that all involved in teaching and learning can reflect upon how to approach examination answers.

Richard Gray
Series Editor
2018

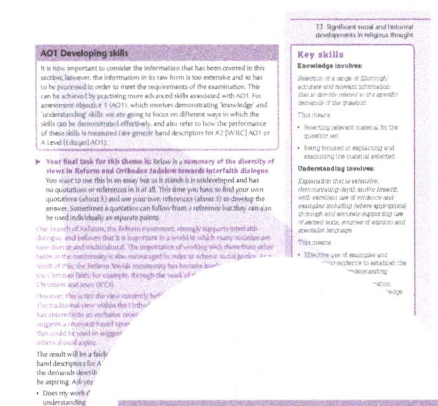

T1 Religious figures and sacred texts

This section covers AO1 content and skills

Specification content

The nature of the Mishnah: content, style and importance for study in Judaism. The nature of the Gemara: content, style and importance for study in Judaism.

Key terms

CE: referring to the Common Era; the period beginning with the traditional birth year of Jesus

Gemara: a rabbinical commentary on the Mishnah

Mishnah: meaning 'a teaching that is repeated'; a collection of oral laws

Oral Torah: God-given instructions for living, transmitted by word of mouth

Prophet: a person chosen to express the will of God

Rabbinical: relating to rabbis

Sage: someone of great wisdom and knowledge

Talmud: 'teaching' or 'study': the work of the collected scholars as a running commentary to the Mishnah

Torah: means 'instruction' or 'teaching' and refers to the first five books of the Jewish scriptures; it can also refer to the whole of Jewish teaching

Tractate: a volume of the Talmud

quickfire

1.1 Name the two texts that make up the Talmud.

D: The structure and development of the Talmud and its importance within Judaism

The Talmud

The **Talmud** (meaning 'teaching' or 'study') is a huge written work that consists of many volumes, and which holds great authority within Judaism. The Talmud consists of two interrelated texts: the **Mishnah**, a collection of oral laws; and the **Gemara**, a **rabbinical** commentary on the Mishnah.

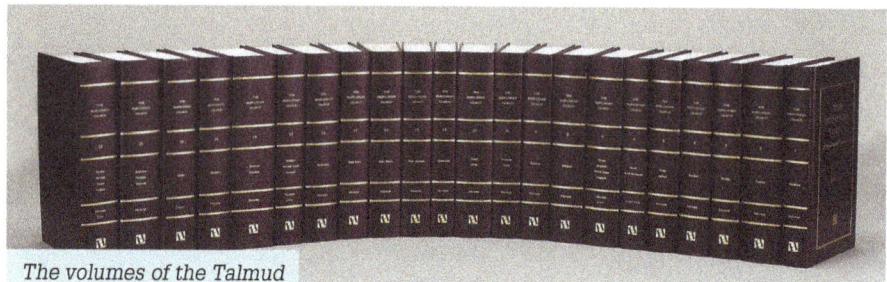

The volumes of the Talmud

The Mishnah

Jewish tradition teaches that as well as the written **Torah**, Moses also received a second Torah from God; one that was not written down, but which was told to Moses orally. This tradition became known as the **Oral Torah**, and it continued to be passed down, by word of mouth, to each new leader in each new generation.

Rabbi Wayne Dosick gives the reason for the existence of the Oral Torah by explaining that, according to tradition, God knew that the laws given in the written Torah would not be sufficient when the Jewish people were no longer wanderers in the desert:

'The laws of the written Torah did not cover situations that the people would face once they lived in towns and villages, once they were farmers or businessmen, instead of nomads; once they would set up permanent places of worship instead of portable tabernacles in the desert. However, the people did not have the capacity to look into and understand the future, and therefore they would not understand any laws given in their time and place that applied to a future time and place. So God told Moses the laws for the future, but they were not written down.'

Thus the Oral Torah was formulated and transmitted in memory, handed on from **prophets** to **sages**, from masters to pupils, from the time of Moses himself until it was eventually written down in the Mishnah, about 200 **CE**, and subsequently the Talmud.

This belief in an unbroken chain of tradition is expressed in the opening words of a **tractate** which was added to the Mishnah in about 250 CE. This tractate is known as 'Ethics of the Fathers' (Pirkei Avot). It begins: 'Moses received the Torah on Sinai, and handed it down to Joshua; Joshua to the elders; the elders to the prophets; and the prophets handed it down to the Men of the Great Assembly. They said three things: Be deliberate in judgement; raise up many disciples; and make a fence round the Torah.'

However, within this system, there existed a possibility of error due to the fact that the laws were transmitted orally to fallible human beings so that differing versions came into existence. These differing versions of the oral laws thus became the basis for the scholarly arguments, disputes, and debates that are to be found in later Jewish law literature. Dosick claims that: 'No longer would God's word be ascertained through prophecy, with individuals claiming Divine revelation. Instead, God's word would come only through the rabbis and the sages – who, according to their own proclamation, would be the sole inheritors and transmitters of God's continuing revelation.'

The early scholars and teachers (c.100 **BCE** to 100 CE) developed guidelines, known as **Halakhah** in order to ensure that the Jewish people were clear about how the **mitzvot** should be interpreted. Halakhah refers to the complete body of rules and practices that Orthodox Jews are bound to follow: the rules and regulations by which a Jew 'walks' through life. As has been mentioned earlier, this body of material developed orally, and because it was considered an oral tradition, Jews were prohibited from writing it down.

However, this attitude changed as a result of the Roman occupation of the Land of Israel in the early years of the first millennium. In 70 CE the Temple in Jerusalem, the centre of Jewish religious life, was destroyed. This, according to Wright, brought about a 'discernible change of emphasis in Jewish religion … In the absence of priestly sacrifice in the Temple, the sphere of Jewish holiness was extended. God was no longer seen as tied to a geographical location but could be found wherever the people of Israel were faithfully present.' Against this background, and coupled with the greater complexity of Halakhah, Jewish leaders realised the importance of **codifying** the expanding traditions in writing.

Dan Cohn-Sherbok claims that the most important scholar of this early rabbinic period was Judah Ha-Nasi, the head of the **Sanhedrin**, whose main achievement was the **redaction** of the Mishnah in the second century CE. Ha-Nasi compiled a volume of the discussions and rulings of the sages whose teachings had previously been transmitted orally.

The Mishnah includes lessons and quotations by sages from first-century rabbis such as Hillel and Shammai through to Judah Ha-Nasi. In all, it is believed that approximately 120 rabbinic scholars made a contribution, and they are referred to as the **Tannaim**.

Key quote

In the Judaism which emerged in the crucial centuries following the loss of the Temple, detailed guidance was offered for how every aspect of Jewish life was to be sanctified. The holy men providing this were called 'sages' and their first and principal work was the Mishnah, completed around 200 CE. The Mishnah's essential message is that the Jewish people, in spite of the absence of the Temple, retains its sanctity. **(Hoffman)**

Key quote

Rabbinic Judaism has served Judaism and the Jewish people well … by applying ongoing principles of adaptability and change to meet new and potentially threatening situations. **(Dosick)**

A meeting of the Sanhedrin

quickfire

1.2 What does the term 'Halakhah' refer to?

Key terms

BCE: Before the Common Era

Codifying: arranging laws or rules into a systematic code

Halakhah: literal meaning: 'the path that one walks'; Jewish law

Mitzvot: commandments

Redaction: to edit a text

Sanhedrin: Supreme rabbinical court

Tannaim: 'teachers' or 'repeaters'; term given to the contributors of the Mishnah

The Mishnah contains a collection of legal rulings and practices upon which Jewish tradition still depends; covering six principal areas of life. The content of the Mishnah is organised like a law book and is split into six basic orders, known as **sedarim**:

1. Seeds (**Zeraim**) – the laws relating to offerings for priests, gifts for the poor, and laws relating to agriculture
2. Holidays (**Moed**) – laws relating to the holy times of Sabbath and other festivals
3. Women (**Nashim**) – laws relating to marriage, divorce, incest, adultery and property
4. Damages (**Nezikin**) – laws regarding civil disputes, rabbinic courts, vows and punishments
5. Holy things (**Kodashim**) – Temple sacrifices, ritual slaughter and dietary laws
6. Purity (**Tohorot**) – ritual cleanliness and impurity.

The language of the Mishnah of today is Hebrew with a small number of **Aramaic** sentences. Within the six orders, the text is divided into volumes (tractates), chapters (**perek**), and paragraphs (**mishnayot**). Hence, as with Torah and Halakhah, the word Mishnah can refer to both the whole corpus and to a single unit within it.

The Mishnah teaches the oral tradition by example, meaning that it presents actual cases that have been brought to judgement, usually accompanied by details of the debate on the matter along with the judgement that was given by a notable rabbi (or rabbis) based upon Halakhah. In this way, its purpose is to bring to everyday reality the practice of the mitzvot as presented in the Torah.

However, while most discussions in the Mishnah concern the correct way to carry out the laws that are recorded in the Torah, it usually presents its conclusions without an explicit link to particular scriptural passages (although scriptural passages *do* occur in places). For this reason, it is arranged in order of topics rather than as a form of Biblical commentary.

Wright offers the following brief passage as an example of the type of content to be found in the Mishnah:

'From what time in the morning may the Shema be recited? As soon as one can distinguish between blue and white. R. Eliezer says: Between blue and green. And it should be finished before sunrise. R. Joshua says: Before the third hour: for so it is the way of kings, to rise up at the third hour. He that recites it from that time onward suffers no loss and is like to one that reads in the Law.' (M. Berakhot 1:1)

Different views on the issue are offered, and there is no clear answer given at the end of the debate. Wright accepts that this produces rather a cryptic effect, and can make the work seem impossible to understand for a student. However, she argues that it is unlikely that the Tannaim and their editors were being deliberately obscure. It may be that what has been preserved is not the full account of the rabbinic discussion on a matter, but a collection of 'tags' which could be used to prompt ancient students' memorised knowledge of a debate. This, says Wright, possibly fits in with some of the other characteristics of the Mishnah. For example, the Mishnah assumes that its readers will share its presuppositions and sphere of reference. There is no introduction or conclusion to outline or assess the contents for an 'outsider'. It is presumed that the reader will know these things, and much more concerning Jewish practice and belief. For example, in the discussion quoted above there is no definition or explanation of what the Shema is, nor any account of why one should bother to recite it.

The Mishnah itself also raises questions that are highlighted by Wright who asks: 'What is the rationale for the order in which the material is presented? Why are some chapters apparently misplaced within the thematic orders, for example, "Arot" (which deals with ethics) in Nezikin (damages)? Why (if the traditional story is unreliable) was the Mishnah written at all? If it really was an attempt

---

quickfire

1.3 Name the six basic orders of the Mishnah.

Key terms

Aramaic: a language used in the Near East from the 6th century BCE

Kodashim: 'holy things'; 5th of the six orders of the Mishnah

Mishnayot: a paragraph

Moed: 'holy times' or 'holidays'; 2nd of the six orders of the Mishnah

Nashim: 'women'; 3rd of the six orders of the Mishnah

Nezikin: 'damages'; 4th of the six orders of the Mishnah

Perek: chapter of the Mishnah

Sedarim: orders

Tohorot: 'purity'; 6th of the six orders of the Mishnah

Zeraim: 'seeds'; 1st of the six orders of the Mishnah

to reconstruct Judaism for a new post-Temple era, why is the majority of the Mishnah's content (in particular that in the orders Moed, Kodashim, and Tohorot) concerned with priestly purity and sacrificial procedure? All these are key questions for scholars of Jewish law during the Tannaitic period.'

Another area of debate for scholars relates to the purpose of the Mishnah. It appears to be a practical law manual that provides a guide to Halakhah, yet Jacob Neusner believes that there were other reasons for its completion. He too questions the inclusion of a large quantity of Temple-related material for a post-Temple Jewish society. Why place rules about the cult of the Temple, which could no longer be carried out, alongside rules about the conduct of agriculture, and family life, which were still possible? In doing so, Neusner contends that the Mishnah asserts that even though the Temple has been destroyed, the holiness of Israel still persists. The covenant between God and the Jews is eternal.

However, this is not the only argument that has been used in order to explain the inclusion of Temple-related material. It could be that Judah Ha-Nasi and his contemporaries saw the loss of the Temple as being only a temporary affair, and believed that it would, in time, be rebuilt. Alternatively, it may be that even at this early date, the study of the law was regarded as a **mitzvah** or religious duty. 'If this were the case' says Wright, 'then the Mishnah can be seen as an example of Torah study for its own sake, unconnected to solving the practical problems of everyday life.'

The Gemara

The Gemara is a vast Aramaic text which takes the form of a commentary on the Mishnah. It is a much longer work than the Mishnah, and presents the discussions of the later rabbis who were known as **Amoraim**.

It was feared that once the Mishnah was written down, it would no longer be able to meet the demands of the changing times. Academies of Jewish learning in Palestine and Babylonia grew up in order to counter this, and the rabbis from these centres of learning met to discuss new issues; arguing and debating upon concerns arising from the Mishnah, the Torah and other sources. These dialogues were ultimately recorded and became the Gemara. Whereas the Mishnah deals mainly with matters of Halakhah, the Gemara contains both Halakhah and non-legal narrative material that is known as **Aggadah**. The Mishnah, with the Gemara came to be known as the Talmud.

The Gemara is organised in the same way as the Mishnah in accordance with the six orders. However, within the Gemara the orders provide the starting place for the discussion of diverse topics that include such things as contemporary medical knowledge, superstitions and criminal law. The style is that of a continuous flow of ideas and uninterrupted thought, filled with meaningful tangents and digressions. Even though the Gemara deals with practical issues, it is a very academic text.

In its relationship to the Mishnah, the Gemara has multiple functions: it explains unclear words or phrasing; it provides precedents or examples in application of the law; it offers alternative opinions from sages of the Mishnah and their contemporaries. Significantly, whereas the Mishnah rarely cites biblical text, the Gemara introduces connections between the biblical text and the practices and legal opinions of its time for nearly every law discussed. It also extends and restricts applications of various laws, and even adds laws that have been left out of the Mishnah entirely such as those relating to the key observances of the festival of Hanukkah.

Key terms

Aggadah: all non-legal rabbinic literature, e.g. stories, legends, extracts from sermons

Amoraim: rabbinic interpreters of the third and fourth century whose discussions are recorded in the Talmud

Mitzvah: commandment

Key quote

… the Gemara consists largely of detailed and strenuously argued disagreements on the meaning and validity of both Mishnaic and Biblical laws, in which as much attention is paid to the arguments that are eventually overruled as to those that carry the day. For this reason, the close study of the Gemara has been regarded as an excellent mental training.
(De Lange)

Key terms

Amidah: the name of a daily prayer

Talmud Bavli: the Babylonian Talmud

Here is an example of how the Mishnah and Gemara work together. Its focus is that of a central Jewish prayer, the **Amidah** and how it should be recited. First, we have the rabbinic views as recorded in the Mishnah:

Mishnah: Rabbi Gamaliel says that everyone should pray the 'Eighteen' (Blessings) daily. Rabbi Yehoshua says that one should only pray an extract of the 18 blessings. Rabbi Akiva says that if one knows them clearly one should say all 18, otherwise one should pray the extract. Rabbi Eliezer says that whoever prays 'on automatic' isn't really praying at all.

Generations later, the rabbis reading this Mishnah wondered why there should be 18 blessings in the first place, and the Gemara serves to offer a solution.

Gemara: On what are these 'Eighteen Blessings' based? Rabbi Hillel, the son of Rabbi Shmuel Bar Nachmani, says that they are indicated by the 18 times the name of God is mentioned in Psalm 29. Rav Yosef bases it on the 18 times God's name is mentioned in the Shema. Rabbi Tanchum said in the name of Rabbi Yehoshua Ben Levy that the 18 blessings correspond to the 18 vertebrae in the human spine.

Another characteristic of the Gemara is that even though it appears from the text that the rabbis are actually in conversation with each other, this is not the case. In this particular instance Rabbi Hillel and Rav Yosef lived a century apart in the third and fourth century respectively.

Key quotes

Thus in two succeeding lines of a Gemara in the Talmud, two sages who lived hundreds of years apart seem to be arguing with and responding to each other over a particular issue. It is as if a book discussing principles of U.S. law had President Washington's and President Clinton's statements about a particular issue following one after the other, in seeming discussion and debate. **(Dosick)**

The writing of the Mishnah and of the Gemara were the rabbis' answer to the destruction of the Temple, the creation of a Judaism based on guidelines and norms of behaviour and practice that enabled the Jews to survive an even longer exile than the Babylonian one. **(Robinson)**

The Jerusalem and Babylonian Talmuds

There are two versions of the Talmud: the Jerusalem (or Palestinian) Talmud, and the Babylonian Talmud (**Talmud Bavli**), both named after the centres of Jewish learning where they developed. The Jerusalem Talmud was compiled at the end of the fourth century CE and the Babylonian Talmud during the sixth century CE.

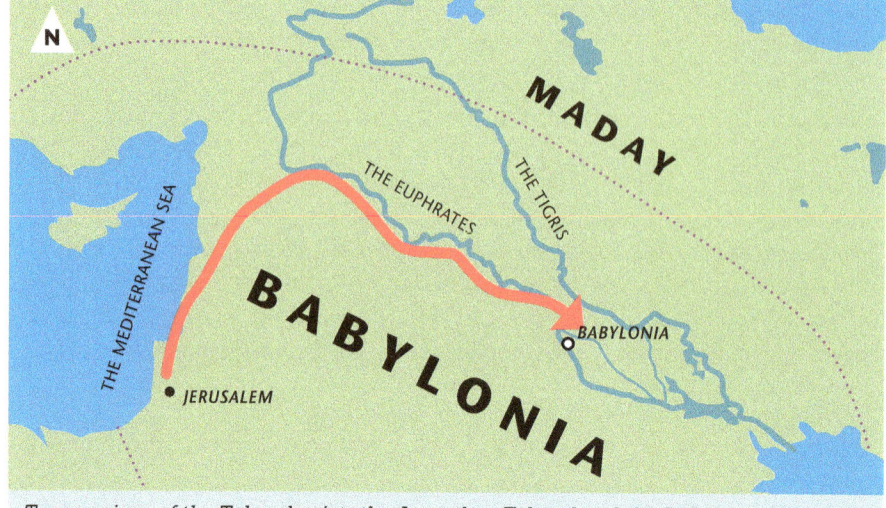

Specification content

The differences between the Jerusalem and Babylonian Talmuds.

Key quote

Because there are two Gemaras, one from the Land of Israel and one from Babylonia, there are two Talmuds. The Jerusalem Talmud, contains the Mishnah, along with the Gemara, from the Land of Israel. The Babylonian Talmud, contains the Mishnah, along with the Gemara, from Babylonia. **(Dosick)**

Two versions of the Talmud exist: the Jerusalem Talmud and the Babylonian Talmud.

The Jerusalem Talmud

Dan Cohn-Sherbok explains how the Jerusalem Talmud developed: From the first century BCE Palestinian rabbinic scholars had been engaged in the interpretation of scripture. The most important scholar of this early rabbinic period was Judah Ha-Nasi, the head of the Sanhedrin, whose main achievement was the redaction of the Mishnah in the second century CE. Ha-Nasi compiled a volume of the discussions and rulings of the sages whose teachings had previously been transmitted orally. By the first half of the fourth century, Jewish scholars in Israel had collected together the teachings of generations of rabbis in the academies of Tiberius, Caesarea and Sepphoris, and these extended discussions of the Mishnah became the Jerusalem Talmud. The views of these Palestinian teachers had an important influence on scholars in Babylonia, though this work never attained the same prominence as that of the Babylonian Talmud.

The Babylonian Talmud

The Babylonian Talmud was compiled around 500 CE. George Robinson points out that when the Jerusalem Talmud had reached its final form, the Babylonian scholars were still only at the early stage of debating the Mishnah in their academies. However, he notes that in the two hundred years that had elapsed between the editing of the two Talmuds: 'the weight of the Jewish world – in terms of population, prominence, and influence – had shifted to Babylonia'.

The growth in the importance of the centres of scholarship in Babylonia rather than in Palestine came about, explains Cohn-Sherbok, due to the decline of Jewish institutions in Israel. One of the reasons for this slump was that in the fourth century Christianity became the official religion of the Roman Empire, and rabbinic institutions in Galilee were closed.

The differences between the Jerusalem and Babylonian Talmuds

In addition to the differences in their places of origin, and their dates of compilation, a comparison of the Jerusalem and Babylonian Talmuds reveals that they are also very different in language, content and approach. As far as language is concerned, the Jerusalem Gemara is primarily written in Palestinian Aramaic, which is different from the Jewish dialect of the Babylonian region.

The Jerusalem Talmud is the shorter of the two versions, with content that is more focused and succinct, even though it contains longer narrative portions than the Babylonian Talmud. In addition, it is less standardised, and presents a looser collection of teachings and discussion. There is also the tendency to repeat large sections of material, and some scholars have suggested that the reason for the repetition is that the Jerusalem Talmud never underwent comprehensive editing; whilst others argue that the repetition was a deliberate stylistic choice, aimed at reminding the readers of connections between one section and another. The Babylonian Talmud is sophisticated and relatively uniform in style, suggesting to scholars that co-ordinated editorial work was carried out by a redactor, or team of redactors.

Both versions of the Talmud are composed of the Mishnah and the Gemara, and as far as the Mishnah is concerned, they are very much the same except for some variations in the text and order of the material. However, it is in the content and style of the Gemara where differences are evident. Neither Talmud contains Gemara on all seventy-three tractates of the Mishnah; however, the Jerusalem Talmud includes the first thirty-nine; and the Babylonian Talmud has Gemara on thirty-six-and-a-half non-consecutive tractates. Some scholars have suggested that this could be a reflection of the different priorities of each place; whilst others believe that parts of each Gemara had been lost, and as such, they were only able to work with what was available.

quickfire

1.4 Name the two versions of the Talmud.

Key quote

For a time Palestinian Jewry followed the Jerusalem Talmud while Babylonian Jewry followed the teachings and conclusions of the Babylonian Talmud. A major split in Judaism was averted because Jewish life in Palestine declined rapidly, while Jewish life in Babylonia flourished in the centuries following the redaction of the two Talmuds.
(Unterman)

> **Key terms**
>
> **Berakhot:** blessings
>
> **Halakhic:** relating to Jewish law; from 'halakhah' meaning 'the path that one walks'
>
> **Halakhot:** laws
>
> **Sukkah:** a 'booth' or 'hut'
>
> **Sukkot:** meaning 'booths' or 'huts'; the name of the festival commemorating the wandering of the Jews during their time in the wilderness
>
> **Talmud Yerushalmi:** the Jerusalem Talmud

The Jerusalem Talmud does, however, contain Gemara on the entire first order of Zeraim, the agricultural laws, which the Babylonian Talmud omits. Robinson explains that there is a logical reason for this state of affairs: '… the agricultural laws, by and large, apply mostly entirely to farming in the Land of Israel, even without the existence of the Temple, so it is not surprising that the Palestinian sages gave them a weight that the Babylonian sages did not. After all, they had a practical daily usage in Palestine.' However, the Babylonian Talmud does include Gemara on Tractate **Berakhot**, the first tractate in Zeraim; since that tractate covers the laws of prayer, which continued to be of importance in Babylonia.

The Jerusalem Talmud rarely includes debate of any great length, containing mostly legal (**Halakhic**) rulings; and this is in contrast to the Babylonian Talmud which is more discursive, containing detailed arguments, involving extensive explanation. The latter appears to be in accordance with the prescription of the sages: 'A person should divide his time between scripture, halakhah and erudition.' (Talmud, Sanhedrin 24a, Tosafot)

An example of the difference between the two can be seen in the way in which each Talmud discusses the following Mishnah relating to the festival of **Sukkot**:

'For all seven days (of Sukkot), one should turn one's **Sukkah** into one's permanent home, and one's house into one's temporary home …' (Sukkah 2:9)

The Babylonian Talmud (Talmud Bavli Sukkah 28b–29a) embarks upon a lengthy discussion of this requirement by debating the question 'How should one turn one's Sukkah into a permanent home?' The ensuing debate suggests that it can be done by bringing one's beautiful vessels and couch into the Sukkah, and by eating and sleeping in it. This is countered by a question: 'Is that really so? But did not Rava (one of the great Babylonian scholars) say that one should study Torah and Mishnah in the Sukkah, but Talmud outside of it?' And so the discussion continues, with the inclusion of stories from the lives of the rabbis that serve to act as exemplification for the particular argument being made.

In contrast, the Jerusalem Talmud includes very little discussion on the very same Mishnah: 'The Torah says, "You shall dwell in booths." "Dwell" always means "live" as it says, "you will inherit the land and dwell there" (Deuteronomy 17:14). This means that one should eat and sleep in the Sukkah and should bring one's dishes there.' (**Talmud Yerushalmi** Sukkah 2:10)

The way in which the information is set out also differs between the two Talmuds. In the Jerusalem Talmud, quoted sections of the Mishnah are labelled as '**Halakhot**'. Reference to the text is usually made by quoting tractate, chapter and Halakhah. Thus Sukkah 2:10 means Tractate Sukkah, Chapter 2, Halakhah 10.

Some editions of the Jerusalem Talmud are printed in folio pages, each side of which has two columns. Thus, citations from the Jerusalem Talmud also often include a reference to the page and column number (a, b, c, or d).

The Babylonian Talmud is printed on folio pages, and is referred to by page number and side (a or b). However, this particular difference is not related to choices made by the rabbinic communities in Jerusalem or Babylon, but due to a variation in early printing techniques and preferences.

A page from the Talmud

What must, however, be the most significant difference between the two Talmuds is that the Babylonian Talmud has the greater authority within Judaism. Indeed, when the term 'Talmud' is used, it is accepted without qualification that it refers to the Babylonian edition. Jacob Neusner highlights this when he says: 'The Babylonian Talmud is the primary source for Jewish law and theology.'

Robinson is also in accordance with this evaluation: 'With two major centres of study in the Jewish world, Gemara developed on parallel tracks and the result was two separate (and not equal) books … the Jerusalem Talmud, and the Babylonian Talmud.' This is despite the fact that the Jerusalem Talmud has its provenance in the Land of Israel. Why, therefore, does the Babylonian Talmud hold greater authority than that of its Jerusalem counterpart?

Robinson suggests that during the two hundred years that had elapsed between the editing of the two Talmuds, the weight of the Jewish world 'in terms of population, prominence and influence' had shifted to Babylonia. It is not surprising therefore that the heads of the Talmudic academies in Babylonia were looked to as the authorities and spiritual guides of the Jewish people, and that the Babylonian Talmud came to assume a greater importance in matters of Halakhah. These post-Talmudic rabbis were called **Geonim** (singular: **Gaon**), meaning 'pride', 'genius', or 'outstanding scholar' (based on a verse from Psalm 47: 'He chose our heritage for us, the pride of Jacob whom He loved.'), and they based their legal decisions upon the Babylonian text. As a result of this, the Jerusalem Talmud fell into disuse. The period of the Geonim lasted from approximately 600 CE to 1000 CE.

Michael Satlow also concurs that the Babylonian Talmud is far larger and more intricate as a result of the growth of the rabbinic movement in Babylonia: 'As the rabbis themselves consolidated, perhaps they felt a need to consolidate their past teachings.' He goes on to say that '… the Babylonian rabbinic academies developed such institutional prestige that they would eventually so heavy-handedly assert the superiority of the Babylonian over the Palestinian Talmud that, for all practical purposes, the latter was dropped from the rabbinic curriculum. Later rabbis adopted the principle that when the two Talmuds diverged, the Babylonian Talmud's opinion or version was always preferable. The "victory" of the Babylonian over the Jerusalem Talmud was to some extent due to politics, but even so it would never have succeeded unless the text was itself rich and complex enough to sustain interest.'

According to Maimonides, whose life began almost a hundred years after the era of the Geonim, all Jewish communities formally accepted the Babylonian Talmud as binding upon themselves. This authority extends to modern Jewish practice which follows the Babylonian Talmud's conclusions in all areas when the two Talmuds conflict.

The **Hasidim** also hold that the Babylonian Talmud is greater in authority than the Jerusalem Talmud. Eliezer Posner offers a reason for this. He makes reference to Rabbi Yirmiya, who claims that when the prophet Jeremiah said 'He causes me to dwell in darkness' (Lamentations 3:6), he was referring to the Babylonian Talmud. This poses a further question: if the Babylonian Talmud was written in the darkness of exile, while the Jerusalem Talmud was written in the light of the Land of Israel, closer to the time of the Temple, then why do we choose darkness over light?

According to Posner, the **Rebbe** discussed this question many times and explained it in this way: When a person searches in the light they find what they are looking for immediately. When the lights are dim, however, they are forced to search further, examining everything their hand touches; turning it again and again, struggling to understand, categorise and put the pieces together. In the long run, who understands deeper? Not the one who saw the truth at first glance, but the one who struggled to find it. As it turned out, the exile provided something that could not be achieved in the Land of Israel.

Key quote

The study of Judaism, its history, ideas and ideals, begins now, as for the past fifteen centuries, in the pages of the Babylonian Talmud. **(Neusner)**

Key terms

Gaon: meaning 'pride', 'genius', or 'outstanding scholar'

Geonim: name given to the heads of the two Babylonian academies in Sura and Pumbedita, which exercised great authority over the Jewish world in the seventh and eighth centuries

Hasidim: literally means 'the pious one'; an ultra-orthodox wing of Judaism

Rebbe: the title given to the spiritual leader of Hasidic Jewish communities

Key quotes

When the Talmud Yerushalmi disagrees with our Talmud, we disregard the Yerushalmi. **(Machzor Vitry)**

To the Orthodox Jew it (the Babylonian Talmud) is the authoritative text of Judaism, and its authority can only be denied at the risk of heresy. **(Unterman)**

Key quotes

There is nothing quite like the Babylonian Talmud ... It is a book of law that often refuses to make a decision about the law; an interpretation that frequently succeeds only in complicating the Mishnah; a set of rigorous arguments punctuated with light stories, jokes, and bizarre tangents ... It is a quintessentially dialogical text, at once in conversation with itself and encouraging dialogue with its readers and among them. It is very much a product of its age and place, exhibiting many similarities and parallels to Persian and Zoroastrian cultures and traditions, but as a literary work it is unique. **(Satlow)**

Talmud is studied for the practical applications of its laws; for its mind-expanding challenges in logic and reasoning; for its total immersion in Jewish concerns; for its wisdom and insights into the human experience; and for its own sake – for the simple love of learning and growing. **(Dosick)**

Key term

Shabbat: the seventh day of the week; the day of rest according to the Ten Commandments

quickfire

1.5 Give two reasons why the Talmud holds such great authority within Judaism.

The Rebbe developed this theme further in noting that the distinction between the two Talmuds is not just in content, but in approach. The Jerusalem Talmud focuses on content: i.e. what? Whilst the Babylonian Talmud is based upon process: i.e. why? In other words, the Jerusalem Talmud gets straight to the point and provides a clear ruling, whilst the Babylonian Talmud, as Posner puts it, 'is full of questions and doubts, often without any resolution'. In the long run, the Babylonian approach became the standard Jewish approach, and this is because 'Torah learning is much more about the experience of getting there than it is about what you find once you're there. That's one explanation why, even once we have the answer we were looking for, we preserve the entire discussion and study it again and again. Not only the destination, but the path itself is also Torah.' (Posner)

Dosick perhaps, sums up the debate about the authority of the Babylonian Talmud quite succinctly by pointing out that since the time of the compilation of the Talmuds, most Jews have lived outside the Land of Israel. The Babylonian Talmud is thus the more important of the two Talmuds because it deals with issues that have relevance to the majority of Jews.

Study tip

When discussing the reasons for the greater authority of the Babylonian Talmud over the Jerusalem Talmud, make sure that you refer to the views of scholars/ schools of thought in an accurate and effective way (L5 band descriptor AO1).

AO1 Activity

After reading the section on 'The differences between the Jerusalem and Babylonian Talmuds' create a mind map or comparison table in order to highlight the main differences between them.

The importance of the Talmud within Judaism

The Talmud is a work of great authority within Judaism, and remains one of its central texts. It represents an unbroken chain of tradition that reaches back to the transmission of the Oral Torah to Moses at Mount Sinai, and provides a comprehensive, written version of Jewish Oral Law and the subsequent commentaries on it. It has enabled guidelines in the form of Halakhah to be created, thus ensuring that the mitzvot that were transmitted from God to Moses can be interpreted correctly in order to remain relevant no matter how times and society have changed over the millennia.

AO1 Activity

Work in a group and identify five areas of modern life that would not have been relevant during the time of the giving of the Torah to Moses (e.g. cyber crime). When you have collated your list, find out through research online how Jews today have come to an understanding of each issue.

It is for this reason that the Talmud is regarded as being indispensable to understanding the laws and customs that are still practised today. For example, if a person wants to find out about the prohibitions relating to **Shabbat** they could refer to Tractate Shabbat and find there numerous laws and customs relating to that particular matter. It is a code which ensures that Jews continue to live a life of holiness in accordance with the terms of the eternal covenant that exists between God and the Jewish people.

Due to its size and complexity, the Talmud is not usually found in many Jewish homes. Moreover, as Nicholas De Lange points out, it is written in a mixture of Hebrew and Aramaic, and even Jewish people who are fluent in biblical Hebrew are unable to read it without further training. Yet, even though it is primarily the domain of rabbis and scholars, and is not readily accessible to the wider Jewish community, De Lange contends that: 'Its authority in traditional rabbinic Judaism is enormous, even outstripping that of the Bible in some respects ...'

Such is its importance that the Talmud remains the main focus of traditional Jewish education at the **yeshiva**. Robinson explains that: 'Judaism has always valued intellectual activity – study of sacred texts – as an end in itself, and never more than in Talmud study. As a way of understanding how Judaism took the shape it has, Talmud study is elucidating.'

The Talmud is usually studied in groups or pairs. This is because it is a collection of dialogues and was meant to be studied in that way. It is important therefore to have a study partner (**havruta**), and passages from the Talmud are discussed and debated aloud, and not concluded until the nuance of every word has been explored.

Thus the process of argument, discussion and persuasion is regarded to be just as important as the decision itself, based as it is upon the historical precedent set in the early rabbinic period: conclusions having been based upon the ability of one school of thought to persuade the community of rabbis that its point of view represented the best understanding of Torah and God's demands upon the Jewish people.

Indeed, such is its importance within the Jewish tradition that study of the Talmud also has a place on the syllabuses of contemporary Reform rabbinical colleges, even though the laws and regulations which make up a large piece of its subject matter, and have a great influence on Orthodox practice, are not considered binding in Reform Judaism.

Judah Ha-Nasi taught that God studies Talmud three hours a day. Therefore studying Talmud is merely one more example of '**imitatio dei**' (imitation of God). It is a code that enables holiness to remain at the centre of Jewish life.

Key terms

Havruta: a study partner (for Talmudic study)

Imitatio dei: meaning 'imitation of God'

Yeshiva: a Jewish academy for Talmudic study

Key quote

To learn Torah is to fully appreciate its quintessential infiniteness.
(Rav Moshe Taragin)

Study tip

Make sure that you are familiar with all the key terms and their correct definitions. This is especially relevant for this section. This will ensure that you are making 'thorough and accurate use of specialist language and vocabulary in context' (L5 band descriptor AO1).

Studying Talmud at yeshiva

Key skills Theme 1 DEF

This Theme has tasks that deal with the basics of AO1 in terms of prioritising and selecting the key relevant information, presenting this and then using evidence and examples to support and expand upon this.

Key skills

Knowledge involves:

Selection of a range of (thorough) accurate and relevant information that is directly related to the specific demands of the question.

This means:

- Selecting relevant material for the question set
- Being focused in explaining and examining the material selected.

Understanding involves:

Explanation that is extensive, demonstrating depth and/or breadth with excellent use of evidence and examples including (where appropriate) thorough and accurate supporting use of sacred texts, sources of wisdom and specialist language.

This means:

- Effective use of examples and supporting evidence to establish the quality of your understanding
- Ownership of your explanation that expresses personal knowledge and understanding and NOT just reproducing a chunk of text from a book that you have rehearsed and memorised.

As you work through each section of the book, the focus will be on a variety of different aspects associated with AO1 so that you can comprehensively perfect the overall skills associated with AO1.

AO1 Developing skills

It is now important to consider the information that has been covered in this section; however, the information in its raw form is too extensive and so has to be processed in order to meet the requirements of the examination. This can be done by practising more advanced skills associated with AO1. The exercises that run throughout this book will help you to do this and prepare you for the examination. For assessment objective 1 (AO1), which involves demonstrating 'knowledge' and 'understanding' skills, we are going to focus on different ways in which the skills can be demonstrated effectively, and also refer to how the performance of these skills is measured (see generic band descriptors for A2 [WJEC] AO1 or A Level [Eduqas] AO1).

▶ **Your task is this:** Below is a **summary of the differences between the Jerusalem and Babylonian Talmuds**. It is 200 words long. You are needed to use this for an answer but could not repeat all of this in an essay under examination conditions so you will have to condense the material. Discuss which points you think are the most important and then re-draft into your own summary of 100 words.

Jerusalem Talmud: originated in Palestine (4th century CE) as a compilation of the discussions and rulings of rabbis whose teachings had previously been transmitted orally; compiled by Judah Ha-Nasi; language is Palestinian Aramaic; the shorter Talmud; repetition is evident suggesting it wasn't edited; contains the first 39 tractates of the Mishnah; contains mostly Halakhic rulings, but rarely debates of great length; fell into disuse due to the fact that since its compilation most Jews have lived outside the Land of Israel, and therefore the issues contained within it are no longer entirely relevant to their needs.

Babylonian Talmud: originated in Babylon (6th century CE); written in Jewish dialect of the region; sophisticated in style which suggests editing; it contains Gemara on 36 ½ non-consecutive tractates; omits the first order of agricultural laws which were no longer relevant in Babylonia; content is more discursive, containing detailed arguments; holds the greatest authority within Judaism, with scholars suggesting that this is because Babylonia had become the centre of the Jewish world, and thus the Talmudic academies and scholars (Geonim) came to assume greater importance.

Information is set out differently in their printed versions, due mainly to variations in early printing techniques and preferences.

When you have completed the task, refer to the band descriptors for A2 (WJEC) or A Level (Eduqas) and, in particular, have a look at the demands described in the higher band descriptors towards which you should be aspiring. Ask yourself:

- Does my work demonstrate thorough, accurate and relevant knowledge and understanding of religion and belief?
- Is my work coherent (consistent or make logical sense), clear and well organised? **(WJEC band descriptor only but still important to consider for Eduqas)**
- Will my work, when developed, be an extensive and relevant response which is specific to the focus of the task?
- Does my work have extensive depth and/or suitable breadth and have excellent use of evidence and examples?
- If appropriate to the task, does my response have thorough and accurate reference to sacred texts and sources of wisdom?
- Are there any insightful connections to be made with other elements of my course?
- Will my answer, when developed and extended to match what is expected in an examination answer, have an extensive range of views of scholars/schools of thought?
- When used, is specialist language and vocabulary both thorough and accurate?

Issues for analysis and evaluation

The Mishnah is the most important element of the Talmud

The Mishnah is certainly regarded as a work of great authority within the Jewish religion, and many would argue that it is the most important element of the Talmud due to the fact that it stands as the first authoritative compilation of the Oral Torah. Its importance is further enhanced by its pedigree, and the belief that it has come directly from Sinai through an unbroken chain of tradition. As the 'Ethics of the Fathers' states: 'Moses received the Torah on Sinai, and handed it down to Joshua; Joshua to the elders; the elders to the prophets; and the prophets handed it down to the Men of the Great Assembly.'

In addition, it could be argued that the Mishnah's importance is also related to its uniqueness within the rabbinic tradition; where it stood as the central literary document of the entire Talmudic period, serving as the foundation for both the Jerusalem and Babylonian Talmuds. It can be claimed that through these works the Mishnah has shaped most of the actual practices of the Jewish religion to the present day. For example, the Torah commands: 'Remember the Sabbath day and keep it holy' (Exodus 20:8). It is the Mishnah which provides the interpretation as to how this holiness should be achieved, leading to the **kiddush** and **havdalah** rituals.

The Mishnah is therefore regarded by many as the means by which the laws of the written Torah could be interpreted even to cover situations that the Jewish people would find themselves in when they were no longer wanderers in the wilderness. Dosick highlights this point when he states that God knew that the laws given in the written Torah would not be sufficient for all time. However, the people did not have the capacity to understand how laws given in their time could be applied to future situations. The Mishnah therefore has an important role in supplementing and clarifying the commandments of the Torah, and this adds weight to the contention that it is the most important element of the Talmud.

However, some might claim that the Mishnah was much more important historically than it is in the present day. In order to pursue this argument, it is important to take account of the impact of the Roman occupation of the Land of Israel in the early years of the first millennium. In 70 CE the Temple in Jerusalem, the very centre of Jewish religious life, was destroyed thus bringing about a change of emphasis for the Jews. It was at this time of crisis that Jewish leaders realised the importance of codifying the oral tradition in writing. This led ultimately to a compilation of the discussions and rulings of the sages by Judah Ha-Nasi. The Mishnah emerged during this period, and the new environment in which the Jewish people found themselves gave rise to the formation of the Talmud. It could be argued that it would be difficult to deny the importance of the Mishnah at this particular time in Jewish history when it acted as the foundation for the Talmud itself.

Key quote

(The passage from 'Ethics of the Fathers') may be read by subsequent generations as presenting the Mishnah as directly linked to Judaism's foundational moment at Sinai. The role of the Tannaim or 'men of the Great Synagogue' is one of conservation. Their task is to build 'a fence around the Law', to clarify and extend the body of halakhah in order to ensure that the divine will for Israel will not be accidentally infringed. **(Wright)**

T1 Religious figures and sacred texts

This section covers AO2 content and skills

Specification content
The Mishnah is the most important element of the Talmud.

Study tip
It is vital for AO2 that you actually discuss arguments and not just explain what someone may have stated. Try to ask yourself, 'was this a fair point to make?', 'is the evidence sound enough?', 'is there anything to challenge this argument?', 'is this a strong or weak argument?' Such critical analysis will help you develop your evaluation skills

Key terms
Havdalah: a ceremony performed at the end of Shabbat and festivals

Kiddush: the ceremony of blessing recited over wine that welcomes in the Sabbath in a Jewish home

AO2 Activity
As you read through this section try to do the following:
1. Pick out the different lines of argument that are presented in the text and identify any evidence given in support.
2. For each line of argument try to evaluate whether or not you think this is strong or weak.
3. Think of any questions you may wish to raise in response to the arguments.

This Activity will help you to start thinking critically about what you read and help you to evaluate the effectiveness of different arguments and from this develop your own observations, opinions and points of view that will help with any conclusions that you make in your answers to the AO2 questions that arise.

17

WJEC / Eduqas Religious Studies for A Level Year 2 and A2 Judaism

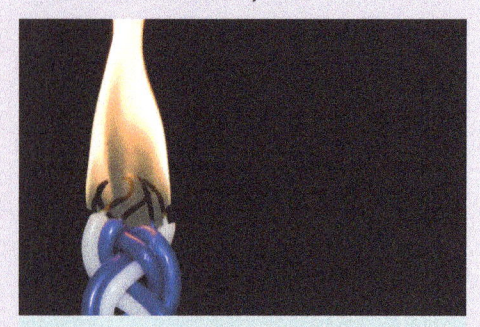

The lighting of the havdalah candle signifies that Shabbat has come to an end.

Key questions

Is the claim that the Mishnah represents an unbroken chain of tradition sufficient to argue that it is the most important element of the Talmud?

Has the Mishnah retained its importance in present-day Judaism?

How important is the Gemara in relation to the Mishnah within Judaism?

Key quote

Like all legal traditions, Jewish law has never been able to remain static. As new situations arise, societies develop, technologies advance, the Torah's meaning for new contexts has to be clarified … The halakhic text associated most closely with the destruction of the Temple and re-conceptualisation of Judaism is the Mishnah, a compendium of traditions normally attributed to the editorship of Rabbi Judah Ha-Nasi. **(Wright)**

AO2 Activity

List some conclusions that could be drawn from the AO2 reasoning from the above text; try to aim for at least three different possible conclusions. Consider each of the conclusions and collect brief evidence to support each conclusion from the AO1 and AO2 material for this topic. Select the conclusion that you think is most convincing and explain why it is so. Try to contrast this with the weakest conclusion in the list, justifying your argument with clear reasoning and evidence.

Many would argue, however, that despite its authoritative provenance, the Mishnah cannot be regarded in isolation within the Talmud. The Mishnah, for example, doesn't give definite rulings on problems and, as a result of this, additions to the corpus of religious law were inevitable. Wright points out that this is even true of codes such as the Mishnah which purports to be divine in association or origin.

This has led some to assert that the Gemara also has a valuable and important position within the Talmud. Evidence for this is based on the following line of argument: whilst most discussions found within the Mishnah concern the correct way to carry out the laws that are recorded in the Torah, it usually presents its conclusions without an explicit link to particular scriptural passages in all but a very few cases. This has been regarded by some as a significant omission. Nevertheless, the Gemara, acting as a commentary on the Mishnah, introduces the missing connections between the biblical text and the practices and legal opinions of its time for nearly every law discussed. It also extends and restricts applications of various laws, and even adds laws that have been left out of the Mishnah entirely such as those relating to the key observances of the festival of Hanukkah.

In addition, the Gemara also explains unclear words or phrasing, and provides precedents or examples in application of the law, and also offers alternative opinions from sages of the Mishnah and their contemporaries. The importance of the Gemara is such that there is great emphasis placed upon its study at yeshiva. This is because it trains the brain in deep and sharp thinking, and allows a basic understanding of the reasoning of the Talmud in order to bring about a proper understanding of Jewish law. It is claimed that Mishnah can be learned by studying Gemara, and so study of Gemara brings about a deeper understanding of the Mishnah. However, in the same vein, we should not forget that the Gemara acts as a companion to the Mishnah, and that it relies upon the Mishnah for its very existence.

Another area of debate for scholars that could be used to question the claim that the Mishnah is the most important element of the Talmud, relates to its purpose. We have already established its significance as a guide to Halakhah, and yet it also contains a large quantity of Temple-related material which raises queries as to why this is the case. Some critics have wondered why the Mishnah contains rules about the cult of the Temple which could no longer be carried out due to its destruction. Surely this lack of clarity of purpose detracts from its importance. Not so, claims Neusner, who asserts that even though the Temple has been destroyed, the holiness of Israel still persists, and the Mishnah acts as a reminder that the covenant between God and the Jews is eternal.

Other scholars have also proposed arguments that explain the inclusion of Temple-related materials. For example, it has been argued that Judah Ha-Nasi and his contemporaries saw the loss of the Temple as being only a temporary affair, and believed that it would, in time, be rebuilt. Alternatively, it may be that even at this early date, the study of the law was regarded as a mitzvah or religious duty. 'If this were the case' says Wright, 'then the Mishnah can be seen as an example of Torah study for its own sake, unconnected to solving the practical problems of everyday life.' Neither of these arguments detracts from the importance of the Mishnah within the Talmud.

In conclusion, there are clearly areas where we might question the claim that the Mishnah is the most important element of the Talmud. However, it cannot be denied that the Mishnah has played a decisive role in the religious life of the Jewish people; providing the means by which the Jews have been able to adapt and live according to God's commandments in whichever circumstance or place they have found themselves from the early days in exile to the present time.

T1 Religious figures and sacred texts

The relative importance of the Gemara

Specification content

The relative importance of the Gemara.

The very fact that the Gemara is one of only two texts that make up the Talmud underlines the assertion that it holds a position of authority and importance within the Jewish faith. However, its importance in relation to the Mishnah is the issue which needs to be investigated. What is its role within the Talmud, and does it supersede the Mishnah in terms of its importance?

The Mishnah is certainly regarded as a work of great authority within the Jewish religion, and many would argue that it is the most important element of the Talmud due to the fact that it stands as the first authoritative compilation of the Oral Torah. Its importance is further enhanced by its pedigree, and the belief that it has come directly from Sinai through an unbroken chain of tradition. As the 'Ethics of the Fathers' states: 'Moses received the Torah on Sinai, and handed it down to Joshua; Joshua to the elders; the elders to the prophets; and the prophets handed it down to the Men of the Great Assembly.'

However, despite its provenance, it could be argued that once the Mishnah was written down it was no longer able to meet the demands of changing times and circumstances. Neither did it give definitive rulings on specific problems. Rabbis continued to meet to discuss new issues; arguing and debating upon concerns arising from the Mishnah, the Torah and other sources. These dialogues were ultimately recorded and became known as the Gemara. As new questions arose, interpretations were offered, so that old summaries were supplemented or recast. It was the Gemara that provided a record for these further additions to the corpus of Jewish religious law. It is the Gemara, therefore, it could be asserted, which was key in bringing about a clearer understanding of how to live according to the mitzvot. And as such, might be said by some to surpass the Mishnah in its importance as the necessary element in bringing about a comprehensive understanding of the Talmud.

The following examples could be used as evidence to show how it is the Gemara rather than the Mishnah that has brought about a more coherent understanding of the Talmud: it explains unclear words or phrasing; it provides precedents or examples in application of law; it offers alternative opinions from sages of Mishnah. It can therefore be seen to be bringing clarity to the material in the Mishnah and aids understanding of the issues under discussion.

The Gemara also has a wider range of content than the Mishnah, and deals with non-Halakhic issues that relate to the practicalities of life such as medical knowledge, superstition and criminal law. It also extends and restricts applications of various laws, and even adds laws that have been left out of the Mishnah entirely such as those relating to the key observances of the festival of Hanukkah.

In addition, some might say that the Gemara plays a significant role in making the all-important connections between the biblical text and the practices and legal opinions of its time for nearly every law discussed. This is in contrast to the Mishnah which rarely does so.

Another line of argument could be that we must not forget the relationship between the two texts of the Talmud. By its very nature, the Gemara acts as a commentary on the Mishnah, and therefore relies upon the Mishnah for its existence. It cannot therefore be viewed in isolation; however, it could be argued that its content brings about a greater understanding and is therefore essential as a commentary upon the Mishnah. Furthermore, the Gemara is never printed independently, and will never be viewed with the same authority as its more important predecessor.

Hillel is associated with the development of the Mishnah and the Talmud.

AO2 Activity

As you read through this section try to do the following:

1. Pick out the different lines of argument that are presented in the text and identify any evidence given in support.
2. For each line of argument try to evaluate whether or not you think this is strong or weak.
3. Think of any questions you may wish to raise in response to the arguments.

This Activity will help you to start thinking critically about what you read and help you to evaluate the effectiveness of different arguments and from this develop your own observations, opinions and points of view that will help with any conclusions that you make in your answers to the AO2 questions that arise.

Key questions

Could the Mishnah alone have met the demands of changing times and circumstances within Judaism?

Does the Gemara bring about a clearer understanding of how to live according to the mitzvot?

To what extent does the Gemara rely upon the Mishnah?

Key quotes

The Talmud builds on the Mishnah in several ways that generally serve to investigate and clarify the second-century compilation. Sources for the Mishnah are investigated, and some problems settled – hence the Talmud's other name, Gemara or 'completion'. … Like the author(s) of m. Avot, the sages 'reported' in the Gemara want to build a fence around, or expand, the scope of the law so as to minimise the risk of it being infringed accidentally. **(Wright)**

… the Gemara consists largely of detailed and strenuously argued disagreements on the meaning and validity of both Mishnaic and Biblical laws, in which as much attention is paid to the arguments that are eventually overruled as to those that carry the day. For this reason, the close study of the Gemara has been regarded as an excellent mental training. **(De Lange)**

AO2 Activity

List some conclusions that could be drawn from the AO2 reasoning from the above text; try to aim for at least three different possible conclusions. Consider each of the conclusions and collect brief evidence to support each conclusion from the AO1 and AO2 material for this topic. Select the conclusion that you think is most convincing and explain why it is so. Try to contrast this with the weakest conclusion in the list, justifying your argument with clear reasoning and evidence.

In order to highlight the usefulness, and thus the importance of the Gemara in its relationship with the Mishnah, we should offer a practical example of the way in which the two texts complement each other. The focus of the following example is that of a central Jewish prayer, the Amidah, and how it should be recited as recorded in the Mishnah: Rabbi Gamaliel says that everyone should pray the 'Eighteen' (Blessings) daily. Rabbi Yehoshua says that one should only pray an extract of the 18 blessings. Rabbi Akiba says that if one knows them clearly one should say all 18, otherwise one should pray the extract. Rabbi Eliezer says that whoever prays 'on automatic' isn't really praying at all. It is an important issue, and yet generations later, the rabbis reading this Mishnah wondered why there should be 18 blessings in the first place.

It is here that the Gemara serves to offer a solution by asking and offering answers to the question 'On what are these "Eighteen" blessings based?' The explanation from the Gemara is as follows: Rabbi Hillel, the son of Rabbi Shmuel Bar Nachmani, says that they are indicated by the 18 times the name of God is mentioned in Psalm 29. Rav Yosef bases it on the 18 times God's name is mentioned in the Shema. Rabbi Tanchum said in the name of Rabbi Yehoshua Ben Levy that the 18 blessings correspond to the 18 verterbrae in the human spine.

Study tip

It is important for AO2 that you include the views of scholars and/or schools of thought when formulating your response to a particular contention. Any discussion of the Mishnah and Gemara would benefit from the views of the sages as well as from more current scholars. However, make sure that the views you use are relevant to the point that you are making. Your ability to use such views in an appropriate way would distinguish a high-level answer from one that is simply a general response.

Furthermore, the importance of the Gemara is such that great emphasis is placed upon Jewish students studying it at yeshiva. Even though the Gemara is organised in the same way as the Mishnah in accordance with the six orders, it acts as the starting place for the discussion of the aforementioned diverse topics, and allows for a contemporary viewpoint to be derived. The style is that of a continuous flow of ideas and uninterrupted thought, filled with meaningful tangents and digressions, and its inclusion in the curriculum is based upon the conviction that it trains the brain in deep and sharp thinking. This process, it has been argued, thus brings about a basic understanding of the reasoning of the Talmud which in turn can lead to a proper understanding of Jewish law. It has been said that studying Gemara will help each student to absorb the spirit of the Torah. However, on the reverse side of this, some have questioned the relevance of the Gemara for anyone other than the Talmudic scholars at yeshiva. It needs to be noted that the Gemara is a highly academic text, written in the Aramaic language, and would not be read in any great detail by the majority of Jews.

In conclusion, there are clearly aspects of the Gemara that can be used as evidence of its importance. However, it cannot be ignored that it depends entirely upon the Mishnah for its existence; the two texts are interrelated with the Talmud's discussions recorded in consistent form with the citing of a law from the Mishnah, followed by rabbinic deliberation on its meaning provided by the Gemara. It cannot therefore be judged on its own merit, and many would agree that the Mishnah is the text of greatest importance. However, by using the same rule of thumb, could it not be argued that neither can the Mishnah be regarded in isolation within the Talmud. As has been mentioned, the Mishnah doesn't give definitive rulings on problems, leading to the necessary formation of the Gemara.

AO2 Developing skills

It is now important to consider the information that has been covered in this section; however, the information in its raw form is too extensive and so has to be processed in order to meet the requirements of the examination. This can be done by practising more advanced skills associated with AO2. The exercises that run throughout this book will help you to do this and prepare you for the examination. For assessment objective 2 (AO2), which involves 'critical analysis' and 'evaluation' skills, we are going to focus on different ways in which the skills can be demonstrated effectively, and also refer to how the performance of these skills is measured (see generic band descriptors for A2 [WJEC] AO2 or A Level [Eduqas] AO2).

▶ **Your task is this:** Below is a **summary of two different points of view concerning the Mishnah as the most important element of the Talmud**. It is 150 words long. You want to use these two views and lines of argument for an evaluation; however, to just list them is not really evaluating them. Present these two views in a more evaluative style by firstly condensing each argument and then, secondly, commenting on how effective each one is (weak or strong are good terms to start with). Allow about 200 words in total.

The Mishnah is the first authoritative compilation of the Oral Torah having come directly from Sinai through an unbroken chain of tradition. It serves as the foundation for the two Talmuds. It has shaped most of the actual practices and beliefs of Judaism and continues to play a decisive role in the religious life of the Jewish people, providing the means by which they have been able to adapt and live according to God's commandments in whichever circumstances they have found themselves to the present time.

However, its importance might have been greater historically than in the present day. It doesn't give definitive rulings on matters and rarely makes explicit links to particular scriptural passages. It needs the Gemara to act as a commentary upon it. There are also questions about its purpose, e.g. why does it contain a large quantity of Temple-related material? Surely this detracts from its importance.

When you have completed the task, refer to the band descriptors for A2 (WJEC) or A Level (Eduqas) and, in particular, have a look at the demands described in the higher band descriptors towards which you should be aspiring. Ask yourself:

- Is my answer a confident critical analysis and perceptive evaluation of the issue?
- Is my answer a response that successfully identifies and thoroughly addresses the issues raised by the question set?
- Does my work show an excellent standard of coherence, clarity and organisation? **(WJEC band descriptor only but still important to consider for Eduqas)**
- Will my work, when developed, contain thorough, sustained and clear views that are supported by extensive, detailed reasoning and/or evidence?
- Are the views of scholars/schools of thought used extensively, appropriately and in context?
- Does my answer convey a confident and perceptive analysis of the nature of any possible connections with other elements of my course?
- When used, is specialist language and vocabulary both thorough and accurate?

T1 Religious figures and sacred texts

Key skills Theme 1 DEF
This Theme has tasks that deal with the basics of AO2 in terms of developing an evaluative style, building arguments and raising critical questions.

Key skills
Analysis involves:

Identifying issues raised by the materials in the AO1, together with those identified in the AO2 section, and presents sustained and clear views, either of scholars or from a personal perspective ready for evaluation.

This means:

- That your answers are able to identify key areas of debate in relation to a particular issue
- That you can identify, and comment upon, the different lines of argument presented by others
- That your response comments on the overall effectiveness of each of these areas or arguments.

Evaluation involves:

Considering the various implications of the issues raised based upon the evidence gleaned from analysis and provides an extensive detailed argument with a clear conclusion.

This means:

- That your answer weighs up the consequences of accepting or rejecting the various and different lines of argument analysed
- That your answer arrives at a conclusion through a clear process of reasoning.

As you work through each section of the book, the focus will be on a variety of different aspects associated with AO2 so that you can comprehensively perfect the overall skills associated with AO2.

WJEC / Eduqas Religious Studies for A Level Year 2 and A2 Judaism

This section covers AO1 content and skills

Specification content

The meaning and purpose of midrash. Midrashic method: peshat (plain, literal); remez (hint); derash (homily); sod (hidden).

E: Midrash in Judaism: the distinction between Halakhah and Aggadah

Midrash

Another important example of rabbinic literature is **Midrash**. Just as the Mishnah and Gemara developed as a way of addressing the unanswered questions of the Bible, Midrash also evolved as a body of literature that serves to interpret sacred texts in a thorough manner.

Key quote

Midrash represents the effort to seek truth in Scripture, in order to address current day questions to ancient, enduring revelation. **(Neusner)**

Neusner explains that the root of the word midrash is 'darash', a term used in Genesis 25:22 where Rebecca goes to 'inquire of the Lord'. In line with this usage, the purpose of midrash is to seek truth in scripture, and use it to address present-day issues which have no precedent in the Torah. The language of the Bible can be terse and ambiguous, and therefore interpretation is vital in order to seek out the significance of the text. The Greek word for such interpretation is **exegesis**, and the Hebrew word used for biblical exegesis by ancient Jewish authorities is midrash.

We need, however, to be aware that the word 'midrash' conveys several meanings. Neusner notes that in current usage it has three levels of meaning:

1. **The process**, that is, a particular way of reading and interpreting a verse of scripture. For example, we may say 'the ancient rabbis executed Midrash for Genesis 1:1'.
2. **The result** of that process, thus a given verse and its interpretation, as in 'the Midrash Genesis 1:1 says that …'.
3. **The collection** of the results of such a process: 'Genesis Rabbah is a compilation of Midrash exegesis of the book of Genesis'.

Midrash with a capital 'M' refers to the interpretation of the written Torah set down by the Rabbinic sages; midrash with a small 'm' is simply a fancy way of saying 'exegesis' or 'interpretation'.

There are two major collections of **midrashim**. The first is the **Mekhilta** (dating from c. 300 CE) on the book of Exodus, the **Sifra** (book) on Leviticus, and the **Sifrei** (books) on Numbers and Deuteronomy. The second is called the **Midrash Rabbah** (dating from the fifth century CE) which is a compilation of commentaries on each of the five books of the Jewish scriptures, and one on the **Megillot**.

Midrashic method

Robinson says that the sages claimed that every passage of the Torah has seventy aspects (a number that may reflect the fact that there were seventy sages who made up the Sanhedrin). The medieval commentators thus practised four principal methods of midrashic interpretation in order to come to a greater understanding of the text:

- Peshat – the 'plain' or 'literal' sense meaning of a passage.
- Remez – meaning 'hint' or allusive meaning.
- Derash – the **homiletical** meaning (from which the word 'midrash' is derived).
- Sod – the hidden, mystical reading.

Together these four terms form an **acronym** PaRDeS, a word of Persian origin meaning an area surrounded by a fence, and which is used in the Talmud to mean an orchard or garden.

quickfire

1.6 What is the purpose of midrash?

Key terms

Acronym: a word made from the first letters of other words

Exegesis: a critical explanation of a text, especially of scripture

Homiletical: relating to 'homily'; a sermon

Megillot: the five scrolls that are read on special holidays. They are Song of Songs, Ruth, Lamentations, Ecclesiastes and the book of Esther

Mekhilta: meaning 'rules of interpretation'; the name given to a particular collection of midrashim

Midrash: meaning 'to inquire' (from the Hebrew word' darash'); referring to the literature developed in classical Judaism that attempts to interpret Jewish Scriptures

Midrash Rabbah: meaning 'The Great Midrash'; the name given to a particular collection of midrashim

Midrashim: plural of midrash

Sifra: 'book'

Sifrei: 'books'

Peshat

This is the most basic way of reading the text for its 'plain sense' meaning; its literal, factual meaning. Peshat draws upon the context of the passage; its normal sense and the customary meaning for the words that are used. It also takes account of the passage's historical and cultural setting.

For example, this is how Rashbam, a twelfth-century commentator, gives a plain-sense reading of the passage from Genesis 49:7 in which Jacob says he will 'divide' his sons Simeon and Levi, and 'scatter them in Israel'. Rashbam understands the passage in its most literal historical context, that neither Simeon or Levi would have a tribe of their own, and that their peoples would be dispersed among the twelve tribes. The tribe of Simeon was subsequently absorbed into Judah, and Levi's was redefined as a priestly tribe, without a land of its own, and that's all there is to it.

Peshat readings are also able to accommodate metaphorical and figurative language. A good example of this is the instruction found in Deuteronomy 6:8: 'Bind them as a sign on your hand and let them serve as a symbol on your forehead.' This is understood by the sages to refer to the wearing of **tefillin** on the arm and head.

Peshat is regarded as the keystone of interpretation. It is claimed that if one discards peshat, one loses any real chance of gaining an accurate understanding of the text.

Remez

Remez is the Hebrew word for 'hint,' and as a method of Torah interpretation it seeks the **allegorical** meaning of the text, focusing on the philosophical implications contained within it. The most obvious example of such a reading would be the statement by Talmudic sages that Song of Songs is in reality about the relationship between the people of Israel and God rather than the highly erotic love song it first appears to be.

This interpretation represents the standard rabbinic view, and is the reason why Rabbi Akiva declared the Song of Songs to be 'the Holy of Holies', in which the 'lover' is God and the 'beloved' is the community of Israel. The Midrash Rabbah interprets the whole of the Song of Songs in this way. For example, 'Let him kiss me with the kisses of his mouth' (1:2) is interpreted as referring to the revelation at Sinai when Israel took it upon itself to keep the Torah and an angel was sent by God to kiss each Israelite. Another example is the verse 'Like a lily among thorns, is my darling among the young women.' (2:2) This is interpreted as referring to Israel's oppression by **secular** powers.

Maimonides also wrote in the same vein when discussing the love of God: 'What is the proper form of the love (of God)? It is that he should love the Lord with great, overpowering, fierce love to the extent that his soul is bound to the love of God and he dwells on it constantly, as if he were love-sick for a woman and dwells on this constantly, whether he is sitting or standing, eating or drinking … This concept was implied by Solomon when he stated as a metaphor "I am lovesick" … the totality of the Song of Songs is a parable describing (this love).'

The following final example can be used to show the difference between peshat and remez in interpreting Proverbs 20:10, for instance: 'False weights and false measures, both are an abomination to the Lord.' The peshat would be concerned that a merchant should use the same set of weights and scales in order to give fair measurements to all of his customers. The remez, however, implies that this proverb goes further and relates to the importance of being fair and honest in all aspects of a person's life.

Key quotes

No passage loses its peshat.
(Talmud)

And Jacob called his sons and said, 'Come together that I may tell you what is to befall you in days to come …
Simeon and Levi are a pair …
I will divide them in Jacob,
Scatter them in Israel.'
(Genesis 49: 1–7)

The levitical priests, the whole tribe of Levi, shall have no territorial portion with Israel. They shall live only off the Lord's offerings by fire as their portion, and shall have no portion among their brother tribes: the Lord is their portion, as He promised them.
(Deuteronomy 18:1–2)

Key terms

Allegorical: relating to a story or picture, for example, which can be interpreted to reveal a hidden meaning usually moral or spiritual in nature

Secular: relating to things which are not religious

Tefillin: two small leather boxes with compartments that contain passages from the Torah

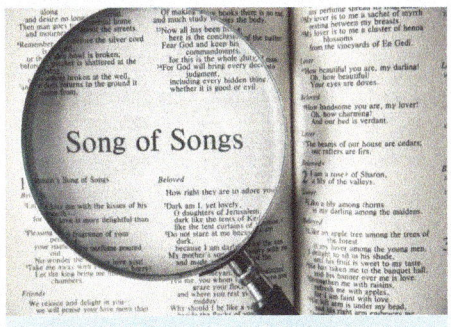

Song of Songs presents an allegory of the relationship between the people of Israel and God.

Key terms

Decalogue: the Ten Commandments

Gematria: numerology

Homily: a sermon

Kabbalah: Jewish mystical tradition

Notarikon: from a Greek word meaning 'shorthand writer'

Parable: a story used to illustrate a moral or spiritual lesson

Key quote

Sod posits that truth is beyond human sensory perception and cognition, and thus it cannot be expressed solely in words. (Eisenberg)

The Hebrew alphabet

Derash

Derash is derived from the verb 'darash' meaning 'to seek', and when found in the Bible it usually means to ask of a prophet. As an interpretative technique, however, derash uses **homily** and **parable** to reveal the underlying meaning of a text as opposed to its 'plain' meaning.

In Exodus Rabbah 50:3, Rabbi Levi uses derash to explain the meaning of the following text: 'They (the Israelites) came to Marah, but they could not drink the water of Marah because it was bitter; that is why it was named Marah' (Exodus 15:23). The water may indeed have been bitter, as slightly salty pools and wells are common in the desert; however, Rabbi Levi states that the deeper, truer meaning of this passage is that this particular generation of Hebrews was bitter in its deeds.

Another example of derash, highlighted by Robinson, deals with the aftermath of the destruction of Pharaoh and the Egyptian army in the Red Sea. The hosts of angels begin to sing as the last Egyptians disappear beneath the torrents, and God rounds on them angrily, saying; 'My children are dying and you sing?' This midrash underlines the delicate balance God walks throughout the Tanakh between stern judge and compassionate parent.

Sod

Sod is the method of biblical interpretation that seeks to find the mystical significance of the text, and it is this method of interpretation that is found throughout the **Kabbalah**.

Robinson explains that central to Jewish mysticism is the idea that the truth cannot be expressed solely in words. The scriptures are written in human language, but are of divine inspiration: 'Therefore, the mystics reason, the words must contain divine truth, but not when read in the way that humans normally read them. In some way, these divine words must symbolise truth beyond words. Reading for denotation and connotation will not uncover that truth.' (Robinson)

Instead the mystics read the scriptures as if the text is a codebook, using methods such as **gematria** and **notarikon** as a means of deciphering the deeper, mystical meaning.

Gematria is a system by which the letters of the Hebrew alphabet are each given a numerical value. A simple example of the way in which gematria works can be seen in connection with the Hebrew word 'chai', meaning 'life'. The word 'chai' is made up of two letters from the Hebrew alphabet whose total numerical value is that of 18. For many Jews it has become the practice to give gifts and donations to charity in multiples of 18, and this is known as 'giving chai'.

A more extensive example is taken from Numbers 6:5, a passage which describes the ritual obligations of a Nazirite. It illustrates the use of gematria to calculate the length of time for which a Nazirite's vow is valid: the Hebrew word 'yihyeh' is composed of two 'yods', each of which has a numerical value of ten, and two 'heys' each with a value of five. In Numbers 6:5, the phrase 'kadosh yihyeh' ('he shall be holy') is thus interpreted as the reason that a Nazirite's vows last for thirty days (yod [10] + hey [5] + yod [10] + hey [5] = 30).

Notarikon can be understood in two ways:

1. A word is understood as an acronym for its real meaning. Eisenberg uses the first word of the Ten Commandments, 'Anokhi', meaning 'I' as an example. He explains that it is actually an abbreviation for 'Ana Nafshi Ketavit Yahavit/I Myself wrote and gave [them]', so that there can be no doubt that the **Decalogue** is the word of God.

2. A word may be broken up into other words. For example, the name Reuben becomes re' u ben/see the son.

However, as Gershom Scholem, the great historian of Jewish mysticism, wryly observes, 'Explication of the level of sod, of course, had limitless possibilities, a classic illustration of which is Nathan Spira's Megillah Amukot (1637), in which Moses' prayer to God in Deuteronomy (3:23ff.) is explained in 252 different ways.'

Study tip
The Internet provides a multitude of opportunities for research into Jewish beliefs and practice, and the resources section of the specification provides a list of websites that are considered to be reliable. However, your research will almost certainly take you to other sites, and therefore it is advisable to cross-reference information in order to ensure that it is dependable and worthy of use in your examination answers.

quickfire
1.7 What are the four principal methods of midrashic interpretation?

AO1 Activity
Research and note down further examples that could be used to illustrate the four principal methods of midrashic interpretation. Present the examples to the other members of your class/study group and ask them to place each one in the correct category. Remember that you will need to be able to explain to the group why each one is to be found in a particular category should they be unable to do so correctly.

Halakhah and Aggadah – background information

The issues discussed by the sages fell into two categories, Halakhah and Aggadah. Halakhah is the legal rulings and the reasoning behind them that govern Jewish practice. Aggadah is anything found in rabbinic writings that isn't about legal discussions and decisions, and comprises a wide-ranging collection of legends, parables, folklore and stories that add depth of understanding and meaning to the Jewish experience.

Hayim Nathan Bialik, (a Jewish poet of the late 19th to the mid-20th century) who compiled one of the most comprehensive collections of Aggadic folklore, 'Book of Tales', wrote: 'Halakhah wears an angry frown; Aggadah, a broad smile. The one is the embodiment of the Attribute of Justice, iron-handed, rigorous and severe; the other is the embodiment of the Quality of Mercy, essentially lenient and indulgent, mild as a dove. The one promulgates coercive decrees and knows no compromise; the other presumes only to suggest and is sympathetically cognizant of man's shortcomings ... A living Halakhah is the embodiment of an Aggadah of the past and the seed of the future, and so it is also conversely; for the beginning and end of these two are indissolubly joined and linked with each other.'

Robinson further underlines the link between the two by explaining that: 'The ethical content of aggadah – and this material is always fundamentally didactic and moral in nature – informs the legal decisions of halakhah.'

Key quotes
Halakhah represents the body, the actual deed; Aggadah represents the soul, the content, the fervent motive. **(Bialik)**

Since the days of the Talmud, the answer to the question 'How do we follow the mitzvot?' has been 'halakhah'. **(Robinson)**

quickfire
1.8 What is the difference between Halakhah and Aggadah?

Halakhah and the 613 mitzvot

In order to discover the mitzvot, Jews refer to the Halakhah. Halakhah means Jewish law, although its literal meaning is 'the path that one walks'. It is a term which refers to the complete body of rules and practices that Orthodox Jews are bound to follow: the rules and regulations by which a Jew 'walks' through life. Halakhah is a means of regulating the 613 mitzvot, and it has its source in the Torah, rabbinic thought and long-standing traditions.

Specification content
The Halakhah and the 613 mitzvot.

WJEC / Eduqas Religious Studies for A Level Year 2 and A2 Judaism

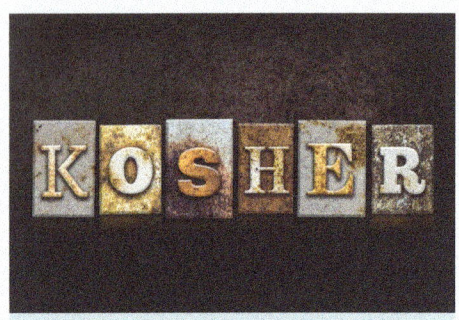

The kosher food laws have developed as a result of Halakhic interpretation.

quickfire

1.9 What is Midrash Halakhah?

Key terms

Gezerot: prohibitions against behaviour that seemingly break the mitzvot or could lead to transgressions

Kosher: food which a Jew is permitted to eat; food prepared in accordance with Jewish dietary laws

Specification content

Halakhah as the revealed will of God – Orthodox and Reform views.

Midrash Halakhah is the name given to the rabbinical method of interpreting the legal topics contained in scripture. The rabbis identified three categories of Halakhah. The first is that which derives logically and clearly from scriptural verse, such as the prohibition against eating pork. Leviticus 11:2–3 states: 'These are the animals which you may eat ... anything which has a completely split hoof and chews the cud, this you may eat ...' Pigs have split hooves, but do not chew the cud and therefore are not **kosher** animals. Secondly, there is Halakhah that has been obtained by interpreting a verse or verses according to prescribed methods. For example, Exodus 23:19 says, 'You must not boil a kid (young goat) in its mother's milk.' As a result of this prohibition, Jews who keep kosher homes do not eat meat and dairy products in the same meal. Finally, there is Halakhah that is derived from Moses at Sinai that consist of strongly held traditions that the rabbis believed were part of the original Oral Torah.

Midrash Halakhah thus attempts to clarify, specify or extend a law beyond its obvious reference points.

For example, Deuteronomy 6:6–9 states: 'These commandments that I give you today are to be on your hearts. Impress them on your children. Talk about them when you sit at home and when you walk along the road, when you lie down and when you get up. Tie them as symbols on your hands and bind them on your foreheads. Write them on the doorframes of your houses and on your gates.' This passage, along with Deuteronomy 11:13–21 and Numbers 15:37–41, have come to form a very important prayer within Judaism, and that is the Shema.

The ancient rabbis discussed and interpreted all aspects of this passage. For example, does the phrase 'these commandments' refer only to the commandments in this particular passage, or does it refer to the commandments that are to be found in the whole of the Torah? Likewise, does the phrase 'when you lie down and when you get up' refer to the physical position of prayer, or to the times at which one should pray (evening and morning)? The practices that have been derived from their deliberations and decisions are now firmly fixed in Orthodox Jewish practice: the tefillin boxes that are worn on the arm and forehead, and the mezuzah in its container that is fixed to the doorpost.

In order to make sure that the mitzvot were not broken unknowingly, the rabbis also issued prohibitions called **gezerot**. For example, the rabbis prohibited horseback riding on Shabbat, because one might violate the Sabbath by breaking off a branch to use as a whip.

The destruction of the Temple in Jerusalem in 70 CE deprived Judaism of its religious centre, thus meaning that the mitzvot which refer to the priestly system and sacrifice were no longer able to be carried out. However, Midrash Halakhah enabled the rabbis to fashion new practices which replaced the requirement for sacrificial worship, and to connect those practices to the words of the Torah. Jews therefore came to encounter many of the Torah's passages regarding law and practice in a different way in light of Halakhic midrashim.

It should be noted, however, that some of the sages, most prominently Maimonides, rejected the use of midrash as a source of Halakhah. They believed that Halakhah must be derived from the Oral Law and that, while midrash is important as a methodology for reconciling biblical text with legal doctrine, it does not represent actual evidence for Halakhic rulings.

Halakhah as the revealed will of God

Orthodox views

There is, however, diversity within Judaism regarding the notion that Halakhah is the revealed will of God. Orthodox Judaism is the traditional branch of the Jewish faith whose members accept literally that the Torah is the direct revelation of God.

As a result of this belief, Orthodox Jews consider it their duty to continue to obey the mitzvot which are contained within it. As De Lange explains: 'The rabbis maintained firmly that all rules of the halakhah, whether specially mentioned in the Torah or deduced by the rabbis themselves ... all originated with God at Sinai and are to be observed.'

Psalm 16:8 says: 'I have set the Lord always before me' and this expresses a cardinal principle of the Torah that is relevant to Orthodox Jews, that all actions should be filled with the awareness that they are being enacted in the presence of God. Therefore, every detail of one's actions is important.

Reform views

One of the defining characteristics of Reform Judaism is its attitude to the revelation of the Law on Mount Sinai as set out in clauses 3 and 4 of the Pittsburgh Platform:

> 'We recognise in the Mosaic legislation a system of training the Jewish people for its mission during its national life in Palestine, and today we accept as binding only the moral laws, and maintain only such ceremonies as elevate and sanctify our lives... We hold that all such Mosaic and rabbinical laws as regulate diet, priestly purity, and dress originated in ages and under the influence of ideas altogether foreign to our present mental and spiritual state... Their observance in our days is apt rather to obstruct than to further modern spiritual elevation... We consider ourselves no longer a nation, but a religious community, and therefore expect neither a return to Palestine, nor a sacrificial worship under the sons of Aaron, nor the restoration of any of the laws concerning the Jewish state.'

Although Reform Jews believe the Torah contains many divine truths, and that it remains the foundation of their religion, they consider it to be a product of human minds. In other words, they believe that God did reveal the Law to Moses, but that this revelation was not dictated word for word to him. Rather that the revelation from God inspired others to write. It follows that if the Torah is the word of God as interpreted by human beings, then humans can make mistakes. It is therefore important to re-evaluate the mitzvot in the light of each new situation in which the Jews find themselves.

Robinson tells us that in the early days of the Reform movement there were two approaches to Halakhah. On the one hand, Rabbi Abraham Geiger called for the reform of Halakhic procedure and practice and for a scientific use of tradition. The thinking behind this approach was to allow for a gradual evolutionary process whereby Halakhah would be brought in line with contemporary realities. On the other hand, Rabbi Samuel Holdheim rejected the Oral Law outright as 'the rigid hand of the Talmud'.

In modern times Halakhah functions differently for Reform Jews, and in order to understand how it works we need to take account of Reform **responsa**. Responsa are the Reform movement's own version of the questions and answers literature that rabbis have been composing for centuries. Indeed, they are in themselves Halakhic documents that give considered and learned answers to the questions that Jews ask. Moreover, they are written in the traditional Jewish style of legal reasoning. However, Reform responsa act in a very different way with the most significant difference being that they act in an advisory role and are not considered to be binding or obligatory. Final decisions are made by individuals or communities who take into account all the factors that are relevant to them at a particular time and place, and then they choose accordingly.

Reform Jews regard Halakhah as an on-going conversation in which the conversation cannot be brought to a premature end by a formal declaration. It is nevertheless difficult to generalise due to the **pluralistic** nature of Reform Judaism. Thus one can find congregations in which most men wear **kippot** during services, as well as congregations in which the wearing of kippot is prohibited.

Key quote

... the distinguishing mark of God's people Israel is that there is not a single thing in their lives that God through the Torah has not connected with a commandment. (Ludwig)

Key terms

Kippot: plural of 'kippah', a skull cap

Pluralistic: relating to 'pluralism', the existence of variety within a group

Responsa: answers to questions on Halakhah given by Jewish scholars on topics addressed to them

quickfire

1.10 How do Reform responsa differ from the more traditional Jewish responsa?

Robinson says: 'Reform Judaism has always been a response to halakhic guidelines ... On the one hand, Reform continues to reject the authority of such Orthodox texts as the **Shulchan Arukh** and the right of the rabbinate to issue normative rulings that would be binding on congregations and individual Jews. On the other hand, the very existence of Reform responsa, going back to the earliest days of the movement suggests that the relation between Reform Judaism and halakhah is more complicated and less adversarial than originally thought.'

> ### AO1 Activity
> Use your knowledge of Reform views towards the Halakhah to complete the following task:
>
> A non-Jew has visited a number of different Reform synagogues and has noticed that in one all the men were wearing kippot; in another both men and women were wearing kippot; and in a third no one was wearing kippot at all. Imagine that you are a Reform rabbi: how would you explain such variation in practice to that person?
>
> This practices the AO1 skill of being able to show an accurate understanding of religious belief.

Key quote
For the Reform Jew, individual conscience, often guided by a four-thousand-year-old heritage, informs ethical decisions. Thus halakhah still is not Revealed Truth, yet neither is it to be dismissed any longer. **(Robinson)**

Specification content
The purpose and role of Aggadah in midrash.

Key terms
Aggadot: plural of Aggadah

Didactic: intending to teach or instruct

Ethical: to live according to a set of moral principles

Shabbatot: plural of Shabbat

Shulchan Arukh: the Code of Jewish Law

Tanakh: Hebrew name for the Bible

The purpose and role of Aggadah in midrash

The key collections of Aggadic midrashim date from the 4th to the 6th centuries CE. For example, Genesis Rabbah, Leviticus Rabbah and Lamentations Rabbah each contain interpretative material on the book of the **Tanakh** whose name they bear. Another example, Pesikta de Rav Kahana is a homiletic midrash on the festivals and the special **Shabbatot**.

Joseph Heinemann suggests that there are three broad categories of Aggadah (although he also notes that neither the names nor boundaries of these categories are firmly fixed): **Aggadot** that are inextricably linked to the biblical narrative; historical Aggadot which tell of post-biblical personalities and events and **ethical**/**didactic** Aggadot which offer guidance and outline principles in the area of religious and ethical thought. However, in relation to the last category, it should be noted that Aggadot of all types are generally intended to teach some kind of lesson.

Robinson seeks to explain how midrash Aggadah works by first disclosing that it is not representative of a conventional method of literary interpretation. For example, it often takes its reading of the Tanakh not from the actual text but from interpretations that have already been made. It sometimes also interprets individual words that have been removed from their original context. He cites an example of an interpretation from Lamentations Rabbah that he describes as being 'diametrically opposed to the meaning of the original passage'. The opening verse of Lamentations, 'She (Jerusalem) is become like a widow' is read as an optimistic statement. Jerusalem has become '*like* a widow', not *actually* a widow. The midrash says 'rather as a woman whose husband has gone abroad but who intends to return to her'.

In other cases, the rabbis strove to explain inconsistencies found in biblical narrative. One famous midrash explains an apparent inconsistency in the Book of Genesis, in which both man and woman are created in the first chapter, but then man is suddenly alone in the second chapter. A midrash says the first woman was named Lilith, but Adam couldn't get along with her. He complained bitterly to God: 'We can't agree on anything. She never listens to me!' So, according to that midrash, God banished Lilith and replaced her with Eve, with whom Adam could better relate.

On a deeper, more theological level, Aggadic midrashim can also be used to reconcile issues that appear to be irreconcilable. For example, how can God be both a ruthless judge and a loving parent? An extract from Genesis Rabbah 12:15 offers a solution:

There was once a king who had some fragile goblets. He said, 'If I put hot water in them, they will shatter; if I put cold water into them, they will crack.' So the king mixed cold and hot water together and poured it in, and they were not damaged. Similarly, God said, 'If I create the world with the attribute of mercy, sin will multiply; if I create it with the attribute of justice, how can it endure? I shall create it with both together, then it will endure.'

Aggadic midrashim also serve to supplement the biblical texts in order to make them easier to understand, whilst also making the characters more human. The result is a method of teaching the Bible 'in a simple, folksy way, to tell stories and offer moral lessons. They were the sermons – the ethical lessons drawn from the biblical text – of their time' (Dosick). An example of this can be illustrated by a famous midrashic tale from Genesis Rabbah concerning Abraham when he was a boy:

Abraham and the incident of the smashed idols.

Abraham's father was an idol salesman, with a shop full of stone statues of various gods. One day he put Abraham in charge of the shop and went out. Abraham, however, took a stick and began to smash all the idols except for the largest one, into whose hands he placed the stick. His father came back, saw the destruction and cried 'What happened?' Abraham replied, 'The biggest idol smashed all of the others to pieces.' His father was angry and rounded upon his son. 'Do you take me for a fool?' he shouted, 'these are nothing but stone idols and are incapable of such destruction.' And Abraham replied, 'you are correct father, idols are powerless, so why do you continue to sell them?'

Aggadic midrashim provide great quantities of material for sermons; indeed, notes De Lange, much of it is drawn from sermons in the first place, as its frequent parables and exhortations remind us. In this way, meanings can be drawn from the simple, concise text. He concludes by suggesting that if one seeks philosophical answers to questions about God from this method, then a person may be dissatisfied. However, '… in the immediacy and intuitiveness of its apprehensions and the way it extracts multiple and often surprising answers from a close reading of texts it often seems remarkably modern'. (De Lange)

Study tip

Your ability to show thorough, accurate and relevant knowledge and understanding of religion and belief is one of the keys to achieving the highest possible level in your answers. In order to do this, you need to ensure that you don't show confusion in your understanding of the purpose and role of the 'mishnah' and 'midrash', for example.

Key quote

The imaginative nature of aggadah can be seen in the way in which a number of second-century rabbis interpret the phrase 'the spirit of God' in Genesis 1:2. One takes it to mean 'wind', another 'Adam' and another 'Messiah'. All three interpretations are included with no attempt to adjudicate. The test of their 'rightness' lies entirely in their poetic force. Thus aggadah is important for providing what lies behind the practice, not in the sense of formal doctrine … but in terms of vitality and inspiration. **(Hoffman)**

WJEC / Eduqas Religious Studies for A Level Year 2 and A2 Judaism

Key skills

Knowledge involves:

Selection of a range of (thorough) accurate and relevant information that is directly related to the specific demands of the question.

This means:

- Selecting relevant material for the question set
- Being focused in explaining and examining the material selected.

Understanding involves:

Explanation that is extensive, demonstrating depth and/or breadth with excellent use of evidence and examples including (where appropriate) thorough and accurate supporting use of sacred texts, sources of wisdom and specialist language.

This means:

- Effective use of examples and supporting evidence to establish the quality of your understanding
- Ownership of your explanation that expresses personal knowledge and understanding and NOT just reproducing a chunk of text from a book that you have rehearsed and memorised.

AO1 Developing skills

It is now important to consider the information that has been covered in this section; however, the information in its raw form is too extensive and so has to be processed in order to meet the requirements of the examination. This can be done by practising more advanced skills associated with AO1. For assessment objective 1 (AO1), which involves demonstrating 'knowledge' and 'understanding' skills, we are going to focus on different ways in which the skills can be demonstrated effectively, and also refer to how the performance of these skills is measured (see generic band descriptors for A2 [WJEC] AO1 or A Level [Eduqas] AO1).

▶ **Your next task is this:** Below is a **summary of midrashic method**. You want to explain this in an essay but they are your teacher's notes and so to write them out is simply copying them and not demonstrating any understanding. Re-write your teacher's notes but you need to replace the words used (apart from key religious or philosophical terminology) with different words so that you show that you understand what is being written and that you have your own unique version.

PaRDeS is an acronym which is used to refer to the following four methods of midrashic interpretation:

Peshat is known as the 'plain' or 'literal' sense meaning of a passage and is the most basic way of reading the text for its literal, factual meaning.

Remez is the Hebrew word for 'hint,' and as a method it seeks the allegorical meaning of the text, focusing on the philosophical implications contained within it. For example, it discerns that the Song of Songs is a text describing the relationship between the people of Israel and God rather than the highly erotic love song that it appears to be on the surface.

Derash is derived from the verb 'darash' meaning 'to seek'. As an interpretative technique derash uses homily and parable to reveal the underlying meaning of a text as opposed to its 'plain' meaning.

Sod is the method of biblical interpretation that seeks to find the mystical significance of the text, and it is this method of interpretation that is found throughout the Kabbalah. The scriptures are read as if the text is a codebook, using methods such as gematria and notarikon as a means of deciphering the deeper, mystical meaning.

When you have completed the task, refer to the band descriptors for A2 (WJEC) or A Level (Eduqas) and, in particular, have a look at the demands described in the higher band descriptors towards which you should be aspiring. Ask yourself:

- Does my work demonstrate thorough, accurate and relevant knowledge and understanding of religion and belief?
- Is my work coherent (consistent or make logical sense), clear and well organised?
- Will my work, when developed, be an extensive and relevant response which is specific to the focus of the task?
- Does my work have extensive depth and/or suitable breadth and have excellent use of evidence and examples?
- If appropriate to the task, does my response have thorough and accurate reference to sacred texts and sources of wisdom?
- Are there any insightful connections to be made with other elements of my course?
- Will my answer, when developed and extended to match what is expected in an examination answer, have an extensive range of views of scholars/schools of thought?
- When used, is specialist language and vocabulary both thorough and accurate?

Issues for analysis and evaluation

The importance of Halakhah versus the importance of Aggadah for Judaism

There is undoubtedly a strong and vital relationship between Halakhah and Aggadah, and such is the strength of that relationship that it makes it difficult on the one hand to argue for the importance of one over the other. Robinson, for example, defines the relationship in the following way: 'The ethical content of aggadah – and this material is always fundamentally didactic and moral in nature – informs the legal decisions of halakhah.' Furthermore, Bialik, a prominent writer and compiler of one of the most comprehensive collections of Aggadic folklore, 'Book of Tales', claimed that: 'A living Halakhah is the embodiment of an Aggadah of the past and the seed of the future, and so it is also conversely; for the beginning and end of these two are indissolubly joined and linked with each other.' It cannot be denied that both scholars, through the strength and clarity of their words, are placing equal value on both aspects of midrash.

Moreover, the issues discussed by the sages of old appear to have fallen naturally into these two categories, thus providing a balance between Jewish behaviour as set down according to the legal rulings of Halakhah; and the meaning Jews find in those behaviours that are contained in the wide-ranging collection of legends, parables, folklore and stories of the Aggadah that add depth of understanding and meaning to the Jewish experience. To put it more succinctly, Halakhah deals with the law, and Aggadah with the meaning of the law. When Heschel claimed that 'Halakhah without Aggadah is dead, Aggadah without Halakhah is wild', he is expressing the fact that both are equal in importance, with each acting as a tempering force upon the other.

A further example of the importance that is attached to both Halakhah and Aggadah in the same measure can be found in an interpretation of Genesis 27:28. When Isaac blessed Jacob he said: 'May God give you the dew of heaven and the fat of the earth, and plenty of new grain and wine.' The Midrash interprets this verse in the following way: 'Dew of heaven is Scripture, the fat of the earth is Mishnah, new grain is halakhah, wine is aggadah.' There appears to be no suggestion here that one is of greater importance than the other.

However, some might claim that it is Midrash Halakhah that should be held in a position of greater importance due to the role it has played throughout the history of Judaism. Its literal meaning, 'the path that one walks', denotes its function as the means by which the 613 mitzvot continue to be regulated, thus ensuring that they remain relevant in society. In order to discover the mitzvot, a Jew must refer to Halakhah. Midrash Halakhah thus attempts to clarify, specify or extend a law beyond its obvious reference points. It has its sources in the Torah, rabbinic thought and long-standing traditions.

Even so, it might be argued that even within Halakhah some aspects are more important than others, and in order to analyse this contention we need to look at the three categories of Halakah that were identified by the rabbis.

Firstly, there is that which derives logically and clearly from a scriptural verse, such as the command to eat only the meat from animals that have both a split hoof and who chew the cud. Secondly, there is Halakhah that has been obtained by interpretation, and which results in practices that are now an established part of Judaism. Finally, there is Halakhah that is derived from Moses at Sinai that consist of strongly held traditions that the rabbis believed were part of the original Oral Torah. Perhaps it is the latter which holds greater authority.

Another aspect of Halakhah that might be used to argue for its superiority over Aggadah is the inclusion of prohibitions, or gezerot. Such prohibitions were added in an attempt to ensure that the mitzvot were not broken unknowingly, and their purpose has been described as 'building a fence around the law'. In addition, some

---

T1 Religious figures and sacred texts

This section covers AO2 content and skills

Specification content
The importance of Halakhah versus the importance of Aggadah for Judaism.

AO2 Activity

As you read through this section try to do the following:

1. Pick out the different lines of argument that are presented in the text and identify any evidence given in support.
2. For each line of argument try to evaluate whether or not you think this is strong or weak.
3. Think of any questions you may wish to raise in response to the arguments.

This Activity will help you to start thinking critically about what you read and help you to evaluate the effectiveness of different arguments and from this develop your own observations, opinions and points of view that will help with any conclusions that you make in your answers to the AO2 questions that arise.

Key quote

Aggadah deals with man's ineffable relations to God, to other men, and to the world. Halakhah deals with details, with each commandment separately; aggadah with the whole of life, with the totality of religious life. Halakhah deals with the law; aggadah with the meaning of the law. Halakhah deals with subjects that can be expressed literally; aggadah introduces us to a realm that lies beyond the range of expression. **(Heschel)**

Orthodox Jews believe that God revealed the Law to Moses on Mount Sinai.

Key questions

Is there an indissoluble link between Halakhah and Aggadah?

Can Halakhah claim greater importance due to its role in maintaining the relevance of the 613 mitzvot?

Does the Reform view of Halakhah dilute its importance in any way?

What are the strengths of Aggadah?

AO2 Activity

List some conclusions that could be drawn from the AO2 reasoning from the above text; try to aim for at least three different possible conclusions. Consider each of the conclusions and collect brief evidence to support each conclusion from the AO1 and AO2 material for this topic. Select the conclusion that you think is most convincing and explain why it is so. Try to contrast this with the weakest conclusion in the list, justifying your argument with clear reasoning and evidence.

---

might say that Midrash Halakhah ultimately enabled the rabbis to fashion new practices which replaced the requirement for sacrificial worship when the destruction of the Temple in Jerusalem deprived Judaism of its religious centre. In doing this, Midrash Halakhah connected those new practices to the words of the Torah.

However, it needs to be recognised as part of this analysis that there is diversity within Judaism regarding the notion that Halakhah is the revealed will of God. Orthodox Jews accept literally that the Torah is the direct revelation of God, whereas Reform Jews believe that God did reveal the Law to Moses, but consider the Torah to be a product of human minds. Halakhah therefore functions differently for Reform Jews, who base their decisions upon responsa. Responsa are themselves Halakhic documents that give considered answers to the questions that Jews ask; however, they act in an advisory role and are not considered to be binding or obligatory. Perhaps the issue here is the question as to whether or not this diversity within Judaism regarding attitudes to Halakhah dilutes its importance in any way.

Study tip

It is vital for AO2 that you present a response that successfully identifies and thoroughly addresses the issues raised by the question set. In order to do this, you need to make sure that you have a clear understanding of the statement in question. Take time to read the statement thoroughly a number of times, and note down in your own words what you think it is claiming. This method will help to ensure that you focus on the relevant points.

It is also important to weigh up the perceived strengths and weaknesses of the Aggadah in order to judge its importance in relation to Halakhah. In the first instance, the Midrash Aggadah does not appear to be representative of a conventional method of literary interpretation, a fact that might be used by some to suggest that it lacks the integrity afforded to Halakhah. For example, it often takes its understanding of the Tanakh from interpretations that have already been made rather than from the text itself. However, in other areas it can be seen to play an important role in explaining inconsistencies in biblical text. For example, a famous midrash explains how, in the Book of Genesis, both man and woman are created in the first chapter, but then man is suddenly alone in the second chapter. It is also important on a deeper, more theological level when used to reconcile issues that appear to be irreconcilable. For example, how can God be both a ruthless judge and a loving parent?

A further strength of Aggadic midrashim is their ability to supplement biblical texts in order to make them easier to understand, whilst also making the characters more human. The result of this, as Dosick describes, is a method of teaching the Bible 'in a simple, folksy way, to tell stories and offer moral lessons. They were the sermons – the ethical lessons … of their time'. An example of this can be illustrated by a famous midrashic tale from Genesis Rabbah concerning Abraham smashing the idols in his father's shop. This story is so well known that many Jews have grown up thinking that it was actually written in Genesis. Perhaps this serves to show that Aggadah is not inferior to Halakhah, just that it fulfils a completely different purpose.

In conclusion, it is perhaps comforting to know that even the rabbis of old struggled to decide which was the most important. As Heschel says: 'Our task is to learn how to maintain a harmony between the demands of Halakah and the spirit of Aggadah.'

Key quote

It is impossible to decide whether in Judaism supremacy belongs to halakhah or to aggadah, to the lawgiver or to the Psalmist. The rabbis may have sensed the problem. Rav said: 'The world was created for the sake of David, so that he might sing hymns and psalms to God.' Samuel said: 'The world was created for the sake of Moses, so that he might receive the Torah.' **(Heschel)**

Whether or not Midrash is an imprecise science

Midrash has been described by Satlow as 'a rule-driven form of interpretation'. Some might argue that this very definition suggests that Midrash is a precise skill or technique by which some kind of systematic observation is applied in order to gain an insight into the deeper meaning of the Torah. Indeed, the fact that Midrash presents a method that has been accepted, and which holds an important position within the canon of Jewish sacred texts could be used as evidence for this particular contention. The four methods of midrashic interpretation may be different in approach: ranging from peshat which seeks the 'plain' or 'literal' sense of the meaning of a passage, to sod, which searches for the hidden, mystical reading; but all are accepted as a means of encountering the will of God through the Torah.

Nevertheless, some might suggest that by virtue of the fact that Midrash is a method of *interpretation*, it is therefore open to a variety of opinions, and thus not as precise as it could be. Evidence for this can be offered by drawing attention to the fact that collections of midrashim contain two or more rabbinical opinions on the same subject, sometimes often diametrically opposed to each other. For example, a passage that can be used to illustrate this characteristic is to be found in the Jerusalem Talmud which preserves a midrashic debate over the question of what is the most important verse in the Torah. Rabbi Akiva claims that it is 'You shall love your neighbour as yourself' from Leviticus 19. Ben Azzai disagrees, maintaining that Genesis 5 provides an even greater principle: 'This is the record of Adam's line. When God created man, He made him in the likeness of God.' Akiva uses self and self-interest as the key precept whereas Ben Azzai uses the image of God as the key principle of human existence. There follows no precise conclusion as to which of the two is indeed the most significant; rather it is left up to the readers to decide for themselves which principle they prefer. There are no right answers here, only opportunities for further discussion.

Another line of argument might take account of the fact that there are two distinct elements within the Midrash: Halakhah and Aggadah. In order to understand the mitzvot, Jews refer to Halakhah, a term which refers to the complete body of rules and practices that Orthodox Jews are bound to follow: the rules and regulations by which a Jew 'walks' through life. Halakhah is a means of regulating the 613 mitzvot, and has its source in the Torah, rabbinic thought and long-standing traditions. It could be argued that this particular aspect of the Midrash shows evidence of greater precision in its interpretation of that which is considered to be the word of God. For example, the clear and undisputed practices within Orthodox Judaism of wearing tefillin boxes on the arm and forehead, as well as the mezuzah in its container that is fixed to the doorpost, have arisen from the interpretation of the verses from Deuteronomy 6:4–9 that state: 'These commandments that I give you today are to be on your hearts ... Tie them as symbols on your hands and bind them on your foreheads. Write them on the doorframes of your houses and on your gates.'

Key quote

Biblical narrative is often elliptical, fragmented. Midrash is one way of filling in the gaps. The Bible served the rabbis as an ur-text to be elaborated on, filled out with more stories that refined the metaphors that the Bible was meant to be. **(Robinson)**

It should be noted, however, that some of the sages, most prominently Maimonides, rejected the use of midrash as a source of Halakhah. They believed that Halakhah must be derived from the Oral Law and that while midrash is important as a methodology for reconciling biblical text with legal doctrine, it does not represent actual evidence for Halakhic rulings. This could be used to suggest that it is not as precise as the sages would hope for.

T1 Religious figures and sacred texts

Specification content

Whether or not Midrash is an imprecise science.

Key questions

Can the midrashic method be regarded as a precise means of scriptural interpretation?

Is Halakhah more precise than Aggadah?

Does the Midrash serve its purpose regardless of its imprecision or otherwise?

AO2 Activity

As you read through this section try to do the following:

1. Pick out the different lines of argument that are presented in the text and identify any evidence given in support.
2. For each line of argument try to evaluate whether or not you think this is strong or weak.
3. Think of any questions you may wish to raise in response to the arguments.

This Activity will help you to start thinking critically about what you read and help you to evaluate the effectiveness of different arguments and from this develop your own observations, opinions and points of view that will help with any conclusions that you make in your answers to the AO2 questions that arise.

Key quote

… midrash, like the Talmud, is part of a 'book' that is never finished, one that continues to grow as we bring new historical understanding and new historical contexts to our own reading of the sacred texts. Midrash continued to be written after the great compilations of the rabbinic era. Midrash continue to be written today. Indeed, any time we gloss a biblical text ourselves, we are creating new midrashim. **(Robinson)**

Tefillin boxes are worn on the arm and on the forehead in response to the interpretation of Deuteronomy 6:8: 'Tie them as symbols on your hands and bind them on your foreheads.'

AO2 Activity

List some conclusions that could be drawn from the AO2 reasoning from the above text; try to aim for at least three different possible conclusions. Consider each of the conclusions and collect brief evidence to support each conclusion from the AO1 and AO2 material for this topic. Select the conclusion that you think is most convincing and explain why it is so. Try to contrast this with the weakest conclusion in the list, justifying your argument with clear reasoning and evidence

---

In contrast, Midrash Aggadah might not be regarded as being as precise in its method. Robinson, for instance, discloses that it is not a conventional method of literary interpretation. His opinion might not equate to an admittance of imprecision, but the fact that it often takes its reading of the Tanakh from interpretations that have already been made, and also occasionally interprets individual words that have been removed from their original context might suggest differently. Notwithstanding it may begin its exploration with a word or passage from the Tanakh, but Jewish tradition allows for a broad range of opinion and interpretation from an Aggadic text. It provides the opportunity for a greater freedom of speculation than Halakhic explanation which is aimed at determining legal principles.

Furthermore, some Aggadic midrashim contain fantastic legends centred upon previous rabbis or biblical figures. The story of Abraham smashing the idols in his father's shop in order to illustrate their impotence is just such an example. Aggadah also strives to explain inconsistencies found in the biblical narrative, creating a tale to explain an apparent inconsistency in the Book of Genesis in which both man and woman are created in the first chapter, but then man is suddenly alone in the second chapter. There is no precise link to such an account in the Tanakh, and yet the story is so well known that many Jews have grown up thinking that it was actually written in the Book of Genesis.

Study tip

You need to be able to recognise the difference between knowledge and understanding (AO1) and evaluation (AO2). Make sure that you don't lose your focus. If your answer to an AO2 questions is not evaluative then it will not reach the required A level standard.

Some Aggadic passages soar into the realms of mystical ecstasy and theological speculation on subjects such as angels, demons, paradise and hell. However, Aggadic stories are not meant to be taken at face value, and perhaps the point of them is not that they provide a precise interpretation, but rather that they offer a means by which to illustrate a moral or ethical point to listeners as part of a sermon, for example. The rabbis wrote in a style that was probably never meant to be taken literally, but they wrote great tales of fiction that were designed to make a point. It might be said that whereas the Halakhah is an obligation and therefore needs to be precise, the Aggadah does not face the same constraints.

De Lange recognises that if a person seeks philosophical answers to questions about God from this method then they may be dissatisfied. However, '… in the immediacy and intuitiveness of its apprehensions and the way it extracts multiple and often surprising answers from a close reading of texts it often seems remarkably modern'. (De Lange) It has been said that Jews in general do not look for perfect, definitive answers to their questions about scripture. In discussion they rarely ask, 'What does it mean?' Instead they ask, 'What *could* it mean?' But that's not the end of it, for as soon as an answer is given another will ask, 'What *else* could it mean?' This approach is summed up in the old adage which states 'Two Jews, three opinions'.

Overall, perhaps the issue is not whether Midrash is an imprecise science or not, but rather whether or not it has been successful in its purpose to 'seek truth in Scripture' as Neusner defines. Seen in this light, it could be argued that it has played its part successfully due to the way in which it has continued to seek answers to contemporary problems, and to craft new stories that continue to make connections between the Jewish way of life and the unchanging Torah.

AO2 Developing skills

It is now important to consider the information that has been covered in this section; however, the information in its raw form is too extensive and so has to be processed in order to meet the requirements of the examination. This can be done by practising more advanced skills associated with AO2. For assessment objective 2 (AO2), which involves 'critical analysis' and 'evaluation' skills, we are going to focus on different ways in which the skills can be demonstrated effectively, and also refer to how the performance of these skills is measured (see generic band descriptors for A2 [WJEC] AO2 or A Level [Eduqas] AO2).

▶ **Your next task is this:** Below is a brief **summary of two different points of view concerning the importance of Halakhah versus the importance of Aggadah for Judaism**. You want to use these two views and lines of argument for an evaluation; however, they need further reasons and evidence for support to fully develop the argument. Re-present these two views in a fully evaluative style by adding further reasons and evidence that link to their arguments. Aim for a further 100 words.

The Halakhah could claim superiority due to its function in ensuring that the 613 mitzvot continue to be regulated. It is through Midrash Halakhah that the mitzvot have remained relevant in an ever-changing world. It also includes prohibitions to ensure that the mitzvot are not broken unknowingly, and their purpose has been described as 'building a fence around the Law'. It also has its sources in the Torah.

However, the fact that there is a strong relationship between Halakhah and Aggadah could make it difficult to argue for the greater merit of one over the other. Scholars such as Robinson have explained the relationship as one in which the ethical content of Aggadah informs the legal decisions of Halakhah. It is also the case that the issues discussed by the sages appear to have fallen naturally into the two categories, which may suggest that the two are of equal importance.

When you have completed the task, refer to the band descriptors for A2 (WJEC) or A Level (Eduqas) and, in particular, have a look at the demands described in the higher band descriptors towards which you should be aspiring. Ask yourself:

- Is my answer a confident critical analysis and perceptive evaluation of the issue?
- Is my answer a response that successfully identifies and thoroughly addresses the issues raised by the question set?
- Does my work show an excellent standard of coherence, clarity and organisation?
- Will my work, when developed, contain thorough, sustained and clear views that are supported by extensive, detailed reasoning and/or evidence?
- Are the views of scholars/schools of thought used extensively, appropriately and in context?
- Does my answer convey a confident and perceptive analysis of the nature of any possible connections with other elements of my course?
- When used, is specialist language and vocabulary both thorough and accurate?

Key skills

Analysis involves:

Identifying issues raised by the materials in the AO1, together with those identified in the AO2 section, and presents sustained and clear views, either of scholars or from a personal perspective ready for evaluation.

This means:

- That your answers are able to identify key areas of debate in relation to a particular issue
- That you can identify, and comment upon, the different lines of argument presented by others
- That your response comments on the overall effectiveness of each of these areas or arguments.

Evaluation involves:

Considering the various implications of the issues raised based upon the evidence gleaned from analysis and provides an extensive detailed argument with a clear conclusion.

This means:

- That your answer weighs up the consequences of accepting or rejecting the various and different lines of argument analysed
- That your answer arrives at a conclusion through a clear process of reasoning.

WJEC / Eduqas Religious Studies for A Level Year 2 and A2 Judaism

This section covers AO1 content and skills

Specification content

Rashi's importance in the history of Talmudic study. Rashi's approach to midrash: close reading, forensic exegesis and the goal of clarity through peshat (literal interpretation).

Rashi (Rabbi Solomon ben Isaac)

Key terms

Chumash: a printed text containing the Five Books of Moses

Philologist: a person who studies literary texts

Rashi: an acronym for Rabbi Solomon ben Isaac

quickfire

1.11 Which approach to midrash is Rashi particularly known for?

F: Rashi and Maimonides

Rashi's importance in the history of Talmudic study

Key quote

His (Rashi's) lips were the seat of wisdom, and thanks to him the Law, which he examined and interpreted, has come to life again. **(ben Nathan)**

Rabbi Solomon ben Isaac (1040–1105), better known as **Rashi**, was a prominent medieval Jewish scholar who was born in Troyes, a town in north-eastern France. As a young man Rashi spent a period of about fifteen years studying in Worms and Mainz (both situated in what is now modern-day Germany). On returning to Troyes, which had itself become a centre of Jewish learning, Rashi acted as both rabbi and judge for the Jewish community in his home town. However, as these were unpaid roles he also worked with his family in the vineyards. He was to remain in Troyes for the rest of life and ultimately die there. However, his influence upon Talmudic study was to extend over the centuries to the present day. Indeed, such is his influence that he is considered to be one of the most important medieval scholars; and no Jew who studies the Torah or Talmud does so without Rashi's influence.

It is during the medieval period in which Rashi lived that the practice of commenting on passages from Jewish scripture really began. Its advance came from the need to explain the text and to counter any contemporary views that were not in accord with orthodox rabbinic teaching. Rashi wrote many works, but his commentaries on the whole of the Hebrew Bible and the Talmud are the ones upon which his fame rests. Robinson describes Rashi as '… one of those extraordinary minds that humanity throws up periodically, a Torah scholar unequalled in the thoughtfulness of his commentaries, fluent in many languages, an accomplished poet, and a skilled **philologist**. Most Jews who have had even a fleeting acquaintance with biblical commentary knows the phrase "**Chumash** with Rashi" – a copy of the Five Books of Moses that include Rashi's commentaries.'

Rashi's approach to midrash

Rashi's biblical commentaries are characterised by their reliance on peshat, the 'plain' or 'literal' sense meaning of a passage. Rashi has been described as a traditionalist in his approach of close reading, forensic exegesis and the goal of clarity through peshat (literal interpretation). Unlike the exegesis found in midrashic literature, which is not tied closely to the text but wanders far from its literal meaning, Rashi's commentary preserves rabbinic interpretations of the plain meaning of the Bible. He writes in clear, concise, and readable Hebrew prose, drawing on a wide range of knowledge that includes the seeming trivia of agricultural life. However, this should not come as a surprise considering that he himself was an agricultural worker. His considerable knowledge of Hebrew grammar is another strong point of the books, and grammatical explanations are to be found interspersed in his commentary.

At the same time his writings are rich in derash, midrashic folklore and homilies that illustrate his points with charm and wit. This aspect of his writing, claims Robinson, is undoubtedly one of the attractions that has made his biblical commentaries a perennial favourite.

Furthermore, 'The midrashim which Rashi quotes became the common heritage of the ordinary Jew who knew them from his acquaintanceship with Rashi rather than from any contact with midrashic literature. Traditional Jewish Bible study was invariably accompanied by Rashi's commentary, which attained an almost sacrosanct status, and was commented on in turn by literally hundreds of super-commentaries. Rashi also influenced Christian students of the Bible in the Middle Ages.' (Unterman)

Here follow two examples of Rashi's approach to midrash.

Rashi on Exodus 23:19

According to Exodus 23:19, 'You shall not boil a kid in its mother's milk.' In the Talmudic period the rabbis had already noted that this injunction appears three times in the Torah and derived from this repetition a blanket prohibition against eating milk and dairy products together. On this verse Rashi comments:

'"You shall not boil a kid": "Kid" includes a calf or a sheep, for the word "kid" signifies a tender young (animal, i.e. not a specific species). And you find this in many places in the Torah where it is written "kid", it is necessary to specify after it "flock". For example, "I will send a kid of the flock" (Genesis 38:17). "Go to the flock and fetch me two choice kids" (Genesis 27:9). (These verses) teach you that where it is written simply "kid", even a cow or sheep is to be understood. And in three places (this verse) is written in the Torah: One (teaches) the prohibition of eating (milk and meat products together), one the prohibition of deriving benefit (from eating milk and meat products together), and one the prohibition of cooking (milk and meat products together, even if you do not eat them).'

'You shall not boil a kid in its mother's milk' doesn't just prohibit the eating of goat meat with dairy products, but applies to all meat.

What Rashi is saying here is that the Torah doesn't simply prohibit the eating of goat meat with dairy products, but that it applies to all meat. A kid, he argues, is a word that includes other species. He argues that the Torah supports this understanding by drawing attention to the fact that in other verses 'kid' is paired with the word 'flock' to specify livestock generally. It follows therefore that even when the word 'flock' does not appear in conjunction with 'kid' it should be understood as such. What we see here is the way in which Rashi supports the rabbinic interpretation of the verse by applying a rigid linguistic analysis.

Rashi on Leviticus 24:19–20

Leviticus 24:19–20 states: 'If anyone maims his fellow, as he has done so it shall be put in him; fracture for fracture, eye for eye, tooth for tooth. The injury he inflicted on another shall be inflicted on him.' Rashi explains what this means:

'"It shall be put in him:" Our rabbis have explained that this does not mean putting a real disfigurement on him, but that he should be compensated for the injury with money. This is done by assessing the injury as one would with a slave who has been hurt. The proof for this is to be found in the word "put" which implies that something, namely money, is "put" from one hand into another.'

Both examples are characteristic of the way in which Rashi takes the student through the text phrase by phrase, explaining the discussion. His skill is built upon a masterful grasp of biblical language as well as knowledge and understanding of the generations of scholars who have gone before him. This has allowed him to make a clear distinction between what the Bible actually said (the peshat), and what has been read into it (derash) by tradition.

Equally important is Rashi's commentary on the Talmud. Solomon says: 'He (Rashi) is the commentator, *par excellence*, on the Talmud. His gift of anticipating the reader's questions and of brief, clear explanation, make you feel that he is in the room with you, expounding the text, guarding you firmly from error.' And such is the success of his approach that his commentary on the Talmud continues to be acknowledged as the definitive explanation to the present day.

Study tip

When answering a question on Rashi's approach to midrash, make sure that you include specific examples from his work, and can present his conclusions in a logical and accurate way.

AO1 Activity

After reading the section on Rashi, note down evidence and examples that could be used to illustrate his significance in Judaism. This could help you to achieve the best possible AO1 level in an examination answer (B5 AO1 level descriptors).

WJEC / Eduqas Religious Studies for A Level Year 2 and A2 Judaism

Specification content

Maimonides' significance in the history of Jewish studies. The approach taken by Maimonides to midrash: philosophy and reason.

Key terms

Rambam: an acronym for Rabbi Moses ben Maimon

Yigdal: meaning 'magnify'; a synagogue hymn containing the Thirteen Principles of Faith

quickfire

1.12 Which of Maimonides' works contains a list of Jewish beliefs?

Maimonides (Rabbi Moses ben Maimon)

Key quotes

3. I believe with perfect faith that God does not have a body. Physical concepts do not apply to Him. There is nothing whatsoever that resembles Him at all. **(The Thirteen Principles of Faith)**

7. I believe with perfect faith that all the prophecy of Moses is absolutely true. He was the chief of all prophets, both before and after him. **(The Thirteen Principles of Faith)**

13. I believe with perfect faith that the dead will be brought back to life when God wills it to happen. **(The Thirteen Principles of Faith)**

Maimonides

Rabbi Moses ben Maimon (1135–1204), better known as Maimonides or simply as **Rambam**, was a prominent medieval Jewish intellectual, theologian and philosopher. He was born in the Spanish city of Cordoba, and was the son of the city's rabbinical judge. In 1148, however, the family was forced to flee as a result of Muslim persecution. Maimonides first settled in Fez, Morocco in 1160 where he received his training in medicine, but then moved to Egypt where he became the leader of Cairo's Jewish community.

Maimonides is a significant figure within Judaism, but especially within the Orthodox tradition where his 'Thirteen Principles of Faith' are now widely held as obligatory beliefs. Robinson describes him as: '… one of the giants of Jewish thought … He wrote the definitive study of the 613 mitzvot, some of the most incisive commentaries on Talmud and Torah, and the most distinguished work on explicitly Jewish philosophy until this century.'

Robinson divides the works of Maimonides into two groups: the Halakhic and the philosophical. The writings on Halakhah include his Commentary to the Mishnah, which he wrote whilst in his youth, and which contains the aforementioned Thirteen Principles of the Jewish Faith. His work also includes numerous letters and responsa that were written in answer to queries from Jewish communities throughout the Mediterranean at a time when these communities were under great pressures to maintain their Jewish identity.

Key quote

Maimonides is perhaps the most famous and resplendent figure of medieval Judaism. His fame is as a direct result of the quality and quantity, scope and originality, magnetism and fascination of his writings. **(Isadore Twersky)**

In order to come to an understanding of his significance within Judaism, as well as his particular approach to midrash, it is worthwhile considering three of his most significant works: The Thirteen Principles of Faith, The Mishneh Torah, and The Guide for the Perplexed.

The Thirteen Principles of Faith

De Lange attests that Maimonides is associated particularly with one of the best-known answers to the question 'what must a Jew believe?' In his commentary on the Mishnah he lists thirteen 'principles of our pure Torah and its foundations'. This list, now known as The Thirteen Principles of Faith, has come to be regarded as the most famous list of the principles of Judaism. They are perhaps best seen as a sort of unofficial Jewish creed, and have made their way into the prayer book in two forms, as a creed beginning 'I believe with perfect faith that …' and as a hymn. The hymn, called **Yigdal** (meaning 'magnify') is sung as part of the opening of the morning service and also as part of the close of the evening service at the synagogue.

The Thirteen Principles had their origin as a result of the need to create a clear statement of faith in order to defend Judaism against heretical views. Epstein notes that in Maimonides' case, several of his principles were specifically meant to challenge Christianity. For example, the third principle was meant to challenge the Christian view that God took bodily form. However, issues regarding the status of Moses as the highest in rank of all the prophets (number 7) and a belief in the resurrection of the dead (number 13), for example, all contribute to sum up the essential tenets of Judaism.

Key quote

A statement of belief so concise and compelling that it was incorporated into the weekday morning service. **(Robinson)**

T1 Religious figures and sacred texts

Mishneh Torah

The **Mishneh Torah** is considered to be the ultimate manual of Jewish law. It was written in order to update the law of the Talmud and to make it clear and concise for the Jews of the time. Gathering its substance from the Tanakh, the two Talmuds and midrashic literature, Maimonides' goal was to take these difficult texts, and to condense them into something that almost anyone could read. In the introduction to the work he wrote: 'Hence, I have entitled this work Mishneh Torah, for the reason that a person who first reads the Written Law and then this compilation, will know from it the whole of the Oral Law, without having occasion to consult any other book between them.'

The Mishneh Torah consists of fourteen books, each one dealing with a separate subject in the Jewish legal system. The contents of the fourteen books can be grouped into four major subject headings: on God and humankind; on the life of the individual; on religion and ritual law; and on civil and criminal law. Unterman describes the work as 'a major, some would say the major, contribution to the field of Jewish law'.

Maimonides' contribution to the history of Jewish studies is also significant for his belief that philosophical investigation should be an integral part of the Jewish faith. The Mishneh Torah was very different in style to what had gone before. Solomon claims that its most remarkable feature is the way in which Maimonides expounds Halakhah in terms of his ethical and philosophical convictions, for instance by interpreting the commandment to love God as including a call to engage in natural science and comprehend the wonders of creation. Furthermore, Solomon describes the short sections on **cosmology** and medicine as 'masterpieces of what nowadays would be thought of as popular science writing'. Maimonides also rejected rabbinic laws that he considered to be based on superstition, belief in demons and magic, and was particularly outspoken in his rejection of astrology.

Twersky reasons that, 'Maimonides is not constrained by Midrashic explanations; he ranges freely and imaginatively in aligning laws with the ethical-intellectual goals he has defined or in correlating them with the historical-sociological conditions he has reconstructed.'

The Guide for the Perplexed

The Guide for the Perplexed was written as an attempt to help those Jews who had become bewildered by the teachings of Greek philosophy and who did not know how they could be reconciled with Jewish belief. Maimonides was convinced that if Judaism was not open to investigation and philosophical reflection then it would be likely to contain heretical ideas. As Unterman puts it: 'To believe in Judaism without investigating one's beliefs is, for Maimonides, to believe only in a superficial and mechanical way.' The result was the blending of the philosophical methods of **Aristotelianism** with biblical revelation. This shocked some conservative scholars, as it seemed to them that Maimonides was exalting the teachings of Aristotle above the spiritual traditions of the rabbinic sages. Even today, notes Solomon, the Orthodox tradition which venerates his Mishneh Torah as the height of Halakhic writing, is puzzled by many of the doctrines in the guide. They either ignore, or read mystical interpretations into it which would probably have alarmed its author. Nevertheless, Solomon describes The Guide for the Perplexed as Maimonides' 'philosophical masterpiece'.

Maimonides' philosophic stance can be seen in his conviction that 'it is through wisdom, in an unrestricted sense, that the rational matter we receive from the Law through tradition is demonstrated' (Guide, III, ch.54). And it is this real wisdom that is the goal towards which every person should aim. Maimonides held firm to the view that, 'The opinions (of the Torah) should first be known as being received through tradition, then they should be demonstrated.' In his mind belief is not just assent to a body of truth, but 'belief is the affirmation that what has been represented is outside the mind just as it has been represented in the mind' (Guide, I, ch. 50).

quickfire

1.13 What was Maimonides' goal in writing the Mishneh Torah?

Key terms

Aristotelianism: a school or tradition of ancient Greek philosophy that takes its defining inspiration from the work of the philosopher Aristotle

Cosmology: a theory that explains the nature of the universe

Mishneh Torah: meaning 'Repetition of the Torah'

Key quotes

On these grounds, I, Moses the son of Maimon, bestirred myself, and, relying on the help of God … intently studied all these works, with the view of putting together the results obtained from them … all in plain language and terse style, so that the entire Oral Law might become systematically known to all. **(Introduction to Mishneh Torah)**

For him (Maimonides) philosophy was not alien to religion but identical with it, for truth was, in the end, the sole issue. Faith is a form of knowledge; philosophy is the road to faith. **(Neusner)**

Study tip

When answering a question on the approach taken by Maimonides to midrash, take care that you don't get bogged down by merely listing the contents of his major works. Rather, use your knowledge of his significant texts in order to illustrate his particular style of reasoning.

Key terms

Adonai: meaning 'Lord'

Bereshith: literal meaning 'at the head of' or 'in the beginning (of)'

De novo: (creation) from pre-existing matter

Plurality: a large number or variety

Specification content

A comparison of the views of Rashi and Maimonides concerning an understanding of the creation text of Genesis 1.

Key quote

The Torah, which is the law book of Israel, should have commenced with the verse 'This month shall be unto you the first of the months,' which is the first commandment given to Israel. What is the reason, then, that it commences with the account of the creation? Because of the thought expressed in the text (Psalm 111:6) 'He revealed to His people His powerful works, in giving them the heritage of the nations.' **(Rashi)**

quickfire

1.14 How did Rashi translate Genesis 1:1?

At the very centre of The Guide for the Perplexed is Maimonides' conception of God. The Shema includes the phrase 'God is one' but what is meant by this statement? Maimonides argued that God is a perfect unity, having no parts, either literally or figuratively.

Therefore, God has no arms or legs; neither does God have a beginning or an end. It follows that, in Aristotelian terms, one cannot actually say 'God is ...' and proceed to describe the attributes of God. To describe God in such a way is to admit a division between subject and predicate, in other words, a **plurality**: 'Those who believe that God is One and that He has many attributes declare the unity with their lips and assume the plurality in their thoughts' (Guide, ch. 50). Therefore, concluded Maimonides, one cannot discuss God in terms of positive attributes.

On the other hand, one *can* describe what God is *not*. God is not corporeal; does not occupy space; does not experience birth, decay and death. This method of reasoning is usually described as 'negative theology'. Maimonides concludes by stating, 'All we understand is that God exists ... is a being to whom none of **Adonai**'s creatures is similar, who has nothing in common with them, who does not include plurality ...'

Thus he allowed his Jewish readers the opportunity to reconcile Aristotle with Torah, 'to adhere to the faith of their ancestors while still embracing the rationalism that a man of science, like Maimonides, embraced willingly'. (Robinson)

The views of Rashi and Maimonides concerning an understanding of the creation text of Genesis 1

Rashi on Genesis 1

Rashi's great skill as a grammarian can be seen in his interpretation of the creation text as found in Genesis 1:1. He uses peshat and focuses on traditional exegesis through language and grammar in order to analyse the text.

The Book of Genesis begins with the Hebrew word '**Bereshith**', which has been understood as meaning 'In the beginning'. Rashi begins his analysis by suggesting that the question might well be posed: why doesn't the Torah start where the law begins, half-way through Exodus? He continues by pointing out that Israel's status as the Land of the Jews depends upon the existence of God and his creation of the world. If it was not the will of God that this people occupy Israel, it is not their land other than by force of arms. The Torah starts at the creation to show the Jewish occupation of Israel in a just light.

Rashi continues by analysing the words 'Bereshith bara' meaning 'in the beginning God created'. And it is at this point that he indicates his intention to proceed by means of peshat when he says: 'If, however, you wish to explain it in its plain sense, explain it thus: At the beginning of the creation of heaven and earth when the earth was without form and void and there was darkness, God said, Let there be light. The text does not intend to point out the order of the acts of Creation – to state that these (heaven and earth) were created first; for if it intended to point this out, it should have been written Barishona bara, "At first God created ..."'

The first sentence of Genesis is often translated as, 'In the beginning God created the heavens and earth.' Rashi, however, presents it as: 'In the beginning of God's creation of the heavens and the earth, the earth was unformed and void, darkness was on the face of the deep, and the spirit of God hovered over the face of the waters.' Rashi's understanding of Genesis 1:1 thus proposes creation '**de novo**' (creation from pre-existing matter). The world was already a formless void, lying in readiness for God to say something and to breathe life into it. In Rashi's words: 'The Spirit of God was hovering on the face of the waters, and Scripture had not yet disclosed when the creation of the waters took place... consequently you must learn from this that the creation of the waters preceded that of the earth. And a further proof that the heavens and the earth were not the first thing created is that the heavens were created from fire and water, from which it follows that fire and water were in existence before the heavens. Therefore you must needs admit that the text teaches nothing about the earlier or later sequence of the acts of creation.'

Maimonides on Genesis 1

Analysis of Genesis 1:1 appears to present the reader with two different ways of interpreting the act of creation. On the one hand, the text suggests an act that constitutes the first instant of time, and on the other suggests an act in which God shapes the world from a pre-existent and formless matter. As Maimonides indicates in The Guide for the Perplexed, rabbinic commentary had reached no definite conclusion on the matter. His approach was to undertake an investigation based upon philosophical argument. Maimonides never doubts that the creation of the world depends upon God, but the question is how? In Guide 2:13 he suggests three ways, based upon the theories of Moses, Plato and Aristotle.

Moses: God created the world out of nothing in a free and spontaneous act that constituted the first moment in history. This is referred to as creation '**ex nihilo**' and creation 'de novo'.

Plato: the world was created 'de novo' from pre-existing matter. This has been likened to the way in which a potter shapes clay, and imposes form on pre-existent material.

Aristotle: creation is neither 'de novo' nor 'ex nihilo'. Rather the world is eternal and its existence is best understood as an eternal emanation. The consequence of this view is that the world has always existed and will always exist in the form in which it is now.

Scholars generally agree that Maimonides' treatment of creation is one of his greatest achievements, and yet there is very little agreement on the exact nature of his view on this subject. Maimonides spent most of his time discussing the Aristotelian view; however, he concedes that his restricted knowledge of God means that he is unable to claim certainty about how God is responsible for the world. By his own admission, all one can do is tip the balance in favour of the account offered by Moses.

Seeskin concludes: 'Though some people fault Maimonides for not coming up with a stronger argument on behalf of Moses, he would reply by saying that given the limits of our knowledge, this is the strongest argument we can expect. Although Maimonides is often seen as part of the Aristotelian tradition, and often expresses praise for Aristotle, his account of creation indicates that he is willing to depart from Aristotle when he thinks the arguments lead in that direction.'

AO1 Activity

It is vital that you are able to make thorough and accurate use of specialist language and vocabulary in context. Test your knowledge of the following terms/names/phrases by putting each in a sentence using your own words. Make sure however, that each sentence is relevant to the issues that have been studied in this particular unit:

Adonai; Aristotle; Bereshith; Chumash; Cosmology; 'de novo'; 'ex nihilo'; Mishneh Torah, philologist; plurality; Rambam; Yigdal.

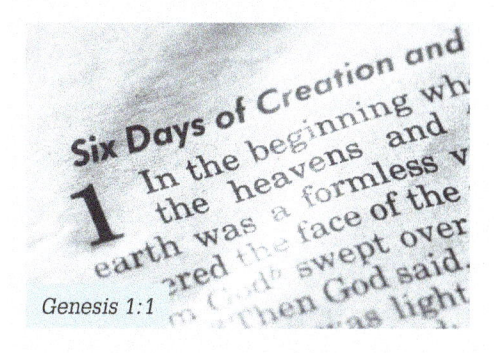

Genesis 1:1

Key term

Ex nihilo: (of creation) out of nothing

quickfire

1.15 What do the terms 'ex nihilo' and 'de novo' mean?

Key quote

God's bringing the world into existence does not have a temporal beginning, for time is one of the created things. **(Maimonides)**

Aristotle

WJEC / Eduqas Religious Studies for A Level Year 2 and A2 Judaism

Key skills

Knowledge involves:

Selection of a range of (thorough) accurate and relevant information that is directly related to the specific demands of the question.

This means:

- Selecting relevant material for the question set
- Being focused in explaining and examining the material selected.

Understanding involves:

Explanation that is extensive, demonstrating depth and/or breadth with excellent use of evidence and examples including (where appropriate) thorough and accurate supporting use of sacred texts, sources of wisdom and specialist language.

This means:

- Effective use of examples and supporting evidence to establish the quality of your understanding
- Ownership of your explanation that expresses personal knowledge and understanding and NOT just reproducing a chunk of text from a book that you have rehearsed and memorised.

AO1 Developing skills

It is now important to consider the information that has been covered in this section; however, the information in its raw form is too extensive and so has to be processed in order to meet the requirements of the examination. This can be done by practising more advanced skills associated with AO1. For assessment objective 1 (AO1), which involves demonstrating 'knowledge' and 'understanding' skills, we are going to focus on different ways in which the skills can be demonstrated effectively, and also refer to how the performance of these skills is measured (see generic band descriptors for A2 [WJEC] AO1 or A Level [Eduqas] AO1).

▶ **Your next task is this:** Below is a brief **summary of Rashi's approach to midrash**. You want to explain this in an essay but as it stands at present it is too brief. In order that you demonstrate more depth of understanding, develop this summary by providing examples that will help you explain it further. Aim for 200 words in total.

Rashi relied upon peshat in order to come to the 'plain' or 'literal' sense of a passage from scripture. He was also an expert in Hebrew grammar and his grammatical explanations aid the clarity of his interpretations. Derash and midrashic folklore are also evident in his writings, which he used to illustrate his commentary. An example of his approach can be seen in the way in which he explains how the prohibition of Exodus 23:19 relates to all animals and not just to baby goats by arguing that the word 'kid' is a word that includes other species.

When you have completed the task, refer to the band descriptors for A2 (WJEC) or A Level (Eduqas) and, in particular, have a look at the demands described in the higher band descriptors towards which you should be aspiring. Ask yourself:

- Does my work demonstrate thorough, accurate and relevant knowledge and understanding of religion and belief?
- Is my work coherent (consistent or make logical sense), clear and well organised?
- Will my work, when developed, be an extensive and relevant response which is specific to the focus of the task?
- Does my work have extensive depth and/or suitable breadth and have excellent use of evidence and examples?
- If appropriate to the task, does my response have thorough and accurate reference to sacred texts and sources of wisdom?
- Are there any insightful connections to be made with other elements of my course?
- Will my answer, when developed and extended to match what is expected in an examination answer, have an extensive range of views of scholars/schools of thought?
- When used, is specialist language and vocabulary both thorough and accurate?

Issues for analysis and evaluation

The relative importance of Rashi and Maimonides for understanding Hebrew scriptures

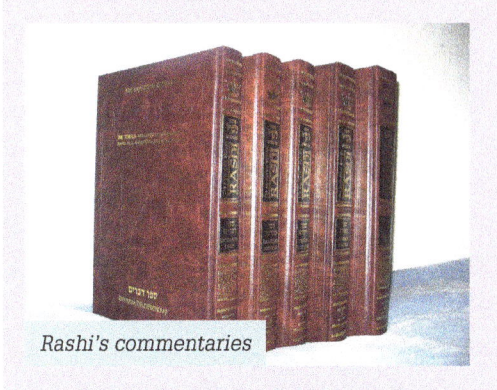

Rashi and Maimonides, two of the most renowned scholars from the history of the Jewish religion, have both had a significant influence upon the way in which Jews have come to an understanding of the Hebrew scriptures. It is their legacies, however, that need to be taken into account when evaluating their relative importance.

Rashi, the earlier of the two scholars, lived during the period when the practice of commenting on passages from Jewish scripture really began. Rashi wrote many works, but his commentaries on the whole of the Hebrew Bible and the Talmud are the ones upon which his fame rests. His influence can be highlighted by the fact that it has been claimed that no Jew who studies the Torah or Talmud does so without his influence. We can deduce from this therefore that Rashi's importance for understanding Hebrew scriptures is significant. Evidence for his influence comes from Jacobs who says: 'Few books can surpass those of Rashi. His writings circulated with great rapidity, and his commentary on the Talmud greatly extended the knowledge of the subject, thus increasing the number of Talmudic schools in France.' We now need to establish the reason why this was the case, and to deduce how he came to hold such an important role in the history of Talmudic study.

Scholars note that Rashi has been acclaimed for his ability to present the basic meaning of a text in a manner that is clear and concise, and it is for this reason that his work is accessible to both rabbis and students alike. For example, Rashi's biblical commentaries are characterised by their reliance on peshat, the 'plain' or 'literal' sense meaning of a passage. Rashi has also been described as a traditionalist. Unlike the exegesis found in midrashic literature, which is not tied closely to the text but wanders far from its literal meaning, Rashi's commentary preserves rabbinic interpretations of the plain meaning of the Bible. He writes in clear, concise, and readable Hebrew prose, drawing on a wide range of knowledge that includes the seeming trivia of agricultural life. His considerable knowledge of Hebrew grammar is another strong point of the books, and grammatical explanations are to be found interspersed in his commentary. It could be suggested that it is for these reasons that his commentaries on the Talmud became the textbook for established scholars and students alike, and his explanation on the Pentateuch the common study for the people. Without Rashi's commentary on the Talmud, it is likely that it would have remained inaccessible to any but the most experienced Jewish scholars. Yet any student who has been introduced to Talmudic study by a teacher is able to continue learning on their own, deciphering its language and meaning with the aid of Rashi.

It is for this reason that Robinson describes Rashi as '… one of those extraordinary minds that humanity throws up periodically, a Torah scholar unequalled in the thoughtfulness of his commentaries, fluent in many languages, an accomplished poet, and a skilled philologist. Most Jews who have had even a fleeting acquaintance with biblical commentary knows the phrase "Chumash with Rashi" – a copy of the Five Books of Moses that include Rashi's commentaries.' And it should be noted that his writings are also rich in derash, midrashic folklore and homilies that illustrate his points with charm and wit. This aspect of his writing claims Robinson, is undoubtedly one of the attractions that has made his biblical commentaries a perennial favourite. However, Rashi has not been without his critics and Jacobs claims that his 'lack of scientific method, unfortunately prevents his occupying the rank in the domain of exegesis merited by his other qualities'.

T1 Religious figures and sacred texts

This section covers AO2 content and skills

Specification content
The relative importance of Rashi and Maimonides for understanding Hebrew scriptures.

Rashi's commentaries

AO2 Activity

As you read through this section try to do the following:

1. Pick out the different lines of argument that are presented in the text and identify any evidence given in support.
2. For each line of argument try to evaluate whether or not you think this is strong or weak.
3. Think of any questions you may wish to raise in response to the arguments.

This Activity will help you to start thinking critically about what you read and help you to evaluate the effectiveness of different arguments and from this develop your own observations, opinions and points of view that will help with any conclusions that you make in your answers to the AO2 questions that arise.

Key quotes

Rashi's wonderful commentary on the Talmud, composed in the 11th century, made that text approachable. (Halbertal)

Even if his (Rashi's) work is inferior in creative power to some productions of Jewish literature, it has exercised a far wider influence than any one of them. His is one of the masterminds of rabbinic literature on which he has left the imprint of his predominant characteristics – terseness and clearness. His work is popular among all classes of Jews because it is intrinsically Jewish. (Jacobs)

Key questions

Is the fact that Rashi's commentaries are based upon peshat the reason for his continuing influence in Biblical studies?

Does Maimonides' philosophical approach to midrash take anything away from his importance?

Is it possible to compare the approaches of Rashi and Maimonides in an objective way?

AO2 Activity

List some conclusions that could be drawn from the AO2 reasoning from the above text; try to aim for at least three different possible conclusions. Consider each of the conclusions and collect brief evidence to support each conclusion from the AO1 and AO2 material for this topic. Select the conclusion that you think is most convincing and explain why it is so. Try to contrast this with the weakest conclusion in the list, justifying your argument with clear reasoning and evidence.

Among Jews, however, his reputation has not suffered, and his works on the Hebrew scriptures continue to carry weight and authority.

There is no doubt either that Maimonides too holds a position of great authority especially within Orthodox Judaism, and scholars have suggested that his fame is based upon the quality, quantity, scope and originality of his writings. However, one obvious distinction between the two scholars is that it is generally agreed that Rashi's ideas are accessible to most Jews, and are the substance, for example, of sermons at the synagogue; whilst Maimonides, on the other hand, appeals more to the intellectuals, and is frequently misunderstood. Nevertheless, it cannot be denied that Maimonides has exerted such an influence on the understanding of the Hebrew scriptures that it has led to him being described as one of the most outstanding giants of Jewish thought.

Evidence for his scholarship and influence can be offered in the form of one of his works known as the Mishneh Torah. It is considered to be the ultimate manual of Jewish law, and Maimonides' reason for writing it was in order to update the law of the Talmud to make it clear and concise for the Jews of the time. The fact that Orthodox Jews regard his Mishneh Torah as the pinnacle of Halakhic writing, and that Unterman describes the work as 'a major, some would say *the* major, contribution to the field of Jewish law', adds weight to the argument that Maimonides has played an important role in bringing about a greater understanding of the Hebrew scriptures.

Study tip

When you are required to draw a comparison between two things or people, i.e. the relative importance of Rashi and Maimonides, make sure that you do not give only half an answer by failing to provide a balanced response that considers both.

However, it also needs to be noted that the Mishneh Torah was very different in style to what had gone before in the field of Jewish scholarship. This is due to the fact that Maimonides' contribution to the understanding of Hebrew scriptures is based upon his belief that philosophical investigation should be an integral part of the Jewish faith. Evidence for this can be seen in the Mishneh Torah where he expounds Halakhah in terms of his ethical and philosophical convictions, and in doing so he stepped outside the traditional parameters of Jewish scholarship. Maimonides received criticism for his approach, and even though he was admired as a legal authority, some Jewish scholars were troubled by his views which they believed were out of line with traditional doctrine: for example, his beliefs about the physical resurrection; and that knowledge of God should be based upon Aristotelian principles. He held the view that nothing in the Jewish sacred writings should require people to take anything on faith and was willing to re-interpret rabbinic and even biblical teachings so that they conformed to the truths of reason. This was not characteristic of traditional Jewish scholarship and was therefore considered by some as being sacrilegious.

Overall, perhaps it is not entirely possible to assess the relative importance of Rashi and Maimonides for understanding Hebrew scriptures in a wholly objective manner. It may be that the best solution is just to acknowledge that they are both important in their own way. Certainly, even though they had very different approaches, they both aimed to make the Talmud coherent and approachable. It is also difficult to compare them when they existed almost a century apart; indeed Maimonides' work contains not one quotation from or reference to so central a work as Rashi's commentary on Talmud. Furthermore, such is the nature of rabbinic scholarship that both scholars continue to take centre stage when matters of law are under discussion.

The extent to which Maimonides is the most complete Jewish scholar

There is no doubt that Maimonides holds a position of great authority especially within Orthodox Judaism, and scholars have suggested that his fame is based upon the quality, quantity, scope and originality of his writings. However, in order to decide whether or not he can be called the most complete Jewish scholar, it is necessary to analyse some of his major works and evaluate their impact upon Jewish beliefs and practice.

In the first instance it should be noted that Maimonides is associated with one of the best-known answers to the question 'what must a Jew believe?' In his commentary on the Mishnah he lists what he calls thirteen principles of our pure Torah and its foundations. This list, now known as The Thirteen Principles of Faith has come to be regarded as the most famous list of the principles of Judaism. They are perhaps best seen as a sort of unofficial Jewish creed, and have made their way into the prayer book in two forms, as a creed beginning 'I believe with perfect faith that ...' and as a hymn, called Yigdal which is sung as part of the opening of the morning service and also as part of the close of the evening service at the synagogue. It could be argued that such is the longevity and continued acceptance of this particular work of his, that it must surely place him within the ranks of the most illustrious scholars of Jewish history. However, perhaps he went even further than others in identifying the need to create a clear statement of faith in order to defend Judaism against heretical views.

Another work of his, known as the Mishneh Torah, can also be used as evidence of his scholarship. It is considered to be the ultimate manual of Jewish law, and Maimonides' reason for writing it was in order to update the law of the Talmud to make it clear and concise for the Jews of the time. In doing so, Maimonides used his skills as a scholar to gather its substance from the Tanakh, the two Talmuds and midrashic literature. It is a work of great scope and its fourteen volumes can be grouped into four major subject headings: on God and humankind; on the life of the individual; on religion and ritual law; and on civil and criminal law. The fact that Orthodox Jews regard his Mishneh Torah as the pinnacle of Halakhic writing, and that Unterman describes the work as 'a major, some would say *the* major, contribution to the field of Jewish law', adds weight to the argument that Maimonides is deserving of the accolade of the most complete Jewish scholar.

However, it also needs to be noted that the Mishneh Torah was very different in style from what had gone before in the field of Jewish scholarship. This is due to the fact that Maimonides' contribution to the history of Jewish studies is also significant for his belief that philosophical investigation should be an integral part of the Jewish faith. In the Mishneh Torah he expounds Halakhah in terms of his ethical and philosophical convictions. Twersky reasons that 'Maimonides is not constrained by midrashic explanations; he ranges freely and imaginatively in aligning laws with the ethical-intellectual goals he has defined or in correlating them with the historical-sociological conditions he has reconstructed.' On the face of it this could be used as evidence to suggest that Maimonides has stepped outside the traditional parameters of Jewish scholarship, and as such, could be used to raise an objection concerning the claim that he is the most compete Jewish scholar. Indeed, he was not without his critics. Even though he was admired as a legal authority, some Jewish scholars were troubled by his views, which they believed were out of line with traditional doctrine: for example, his beliefs about the physical resurrection; and that knowledge of God should be based upon Aristotelian principles. He held the view that nothing in the Jewish sacred writings should require people to take anything on faith and was willing to re-interpret rabbinic and even biblical teachings so that they conformed to the truths of reason. This was not characteristic of traditional Jewish scholarship and was therefore considered by some as being sacrilegious.

T1 Religious figures and sacred texts

Specification content
The extent to which Maimonides is the most complete Jewish scholar.

AO2 Activity
As you read through this section try to do the following:

1. Pick out the different lines of argument that are presented in the text and identify any evidence given in support.
2. For each line of argument try to evaluate whether or not you think this is strong or weak.
3. Think of any questions you may wish to raise in response to the arguments.

This Activity will help you to start thinking critically about what you read and help you to evaluate the effectiveness of different arguments and from this develop your own observations, opinions and points of view that will help with any conclusions that you make in your answers to the AO2 questions that arise.

Key quotes

'Original' is not a word often used in connection with a code of Jewish law. In general, the rule tends to be that if it's true it isn't new, and if it's new it isn't true. But 'original' is precisely the right word to use in connection with Moses Maimonides' law code in the Mishneh Torah … (Sacks)

There are eight degrees in alms-giving, one lower than the other. Supreme above all is to give assistance to a fellowman who has fallen on evil times by presenting him with a gift or loan, or by entering into a partnership with him or procuring him work, thereby helping him to become self-supporting. (Maimonides)

Key questions

Are the works of Maimonides indicative of a complete Jewish scholar?

Is Maimonides' approach so different that it has taken him outside the traditional parameters of Jewish scholarship?

Are there other Jewish scholars who are equally worthy of the accolade?

AO2 Activity

List some conclusions that could be drawn from the AO2 reasoning from the above text; try to aim for at least three different possible conclusions. Consider each of the conclusions and collect brief evidence to support each conclusion from the AO1 and AO2 material for this topic. Select the conclusion that you think is most convincing and explain why it is so. Try to contrast this with the weakest conclusion in the list, justifying your argument with clear reasoning and evidence.

Furthermore, at one point he was seen as such a threat to Judaism and rabbinic learning that there was an attempt to prevent the study of 'The Guide for the Perplexed' as well as the philosophical sections of the Mishneh Torah. And yet, even though his philosophical approach made him stand out as different from the sages of his time and after his death, it is significant to note that he had not been the first Jewish philosopher. Maybe the fact that such opposition was made to his works in particular is indicative of the fact that his impact had been much greater than those philosophical Jewish scholars who had gone before.

Study tip

An understanding of some of the characteristics that might be attributed to a Jewish scholar would help in your assessment of the extent to which Maimonides fits the description. Do not expect to find a definitive list, but highlight what you consider to be some of the more significant attributes.

Another line of argument could be that we must not forget that there are other notable Jewish scholars who continue to have an impact upon Jewish beliefs and practices. Some might consider Rashi, for instance, to be the most complete Jewish scholar for it is his commentaries on the Tanakh and Talmud that are still at the foundation of Jewish education to this day. Unterman notes that it is the midrashim which Rashi quotes that has become what he calls 'the common heritage of the ordinary Jew'. He also draws attention to the fact that traditional Jewish Bible study is invariably accompanied by Rashi's commentary. We can also use evidence from Robinson's evaluation of Rashi to highlight the high standing that he holds within Judaism: '… one of those extraordinary minds that humanity throws up periodically, a Torah scholar unequalled in the thoughtfulness of his commentaries …'

Jewish scholarship is characterised by Torah and Talmud study.

One obvious difficulty that we have in attempting to decide whether or not Maimonides is representative of the most complete Jewish scholar is that we don't have a definitive list of characteristics to which we can compare his achievements. We can only proceed by suggesting that Maimonides fits the description by taking account of the influence that he has had in the wider Jewish field of Jewish belief and practice. For example, his identification and discussion of eight different stages of charity that are to be found in the Mishneh Torah continue to have an influence upon Jewish practices concerning giving to those members of the community who are in need. And even in discussions about the nature and characteristics of God do we find the voice and opinion of Maimonides, with his famous insistence that only God's actions can be known, and even those only tell us what God is *not* like, rather than what God *is* like.

Notwithstanding the contradictions that have been raised, it cannot be ignored that Maimonides' contributions have influenced Jewish and non-Jewish scholars alike. Taking all of these things into account, it might confidently be asserted that he therefore deserves to be regarded as a complete Jewish scholar in the history of the faith. Current-day scholars would concur, having described him as one of the most outstanding giants of Jewish thought.

AO2 Developing skills

It is now important to consider the information that has been covered in this section; however, the information in its raw form is too extensive and so has to be processed in order to meet the requirements of the examination. This can be done by practising more advanced skills associated with AO2. For assessment objective 2 (AO2), which involves 'critical analysis' and 'evaluation' skills, we are going to focus on different ways in which the skills can be demonstrated effectively, and also refer to how the performance of these skills is measured (see generic band descriptors for A2 [WJEC] AO2 or A Level [Eduqas] AO2).

▶ **Your next task is this:** Below is an **argument concerning the extent to which Maimonides is the most complete Jewish scholar**. You need to respond to this argument by thinking of three key questions you could ask the writer that would challenge their view and force them to defend their argument.

Maimonides holds great authority within Orthodox Judaism, and his influence is as a direct result of the quality, quantity, scope, originality, and fascination of his writings, all of which are indicative of a good Jewish scholar.

Maimonides is associated with one of the best-known answers to the question 'what must a Jew believe?' 'The Thirteen Principles of Faith' are widely held as a list of obligatory beliefs. Moreover, they have become an integral part of Orthodox worship and are sung in the morning and evening services.

The Mishneh Torah can also be used as evidence of his scholarship. His purpose in writing it was to bring about an understanding of the Talmud, and it is this work perhaps that has made him stand out above the rest. He wrote it in order to update the law of the Talmud and to make it clear and concise for Jews of the time. Orthodox Jews regard his Mishneh Torah as the pinnacle of Halakhic writing.

Wide-ranging views of his have become a part of contemporary Judaism: his beliefs about the nature of God; charity. This influence offers more evidence that can be used to argue in favour of his scholarly prowess.

When you have completed the task, refer to the band descriptors for A2 (WJEC) or A Level (Eduqas) and, in particular, have a look at the demands described in the higher band descriptors towards which you should be aspiring. Ask yourself:

- Is my answer a confident critical analysis and perceptive evaluation of the issue?
- Is my answer a response that successfully identifies and thoroughly addresses the issues raised by the question set?
- Does my work show an excellent standard of coherence, clarity and organisation?
- Will my work, when developed, contain thorough, sustained and clear views that are supported by extensive, detailed reasoning and/or evidence?
- Are the views of scholars/schools of thought used extensively, appropriately and in context?
- Does my answer convey a confident and perceptive analysis of the nature of any possible connections with other elements of my course?
- When used, is specialist language and vocabulary both thorough and accurate?

T1 Religious figures and sacred texts

Key skills

Analysis involves:

Identifying issues raised by the materials in the AO1, together with those identified in the AO2 section, and presents sustained and clear views, either of scholars or from a personal perspective ready for evaluation.

This means:

- That your answers are able to identify key areas of debate in relation to a particular issue
- That you can identify, and comment upon, the different lines of argument presented by others
- That your response comments on the overall effectiveness of each of these areas or arguments.

Evaluation involves:

Considering the various implications of the issues raised based upon the evidence gleaned from analysis and provides an extensive detailed argument with a clear conclusion.

This means:

- That your answer weighs up the consequences of accepting or rejecting the various and different lines of argument analysed
- That your answer arrives at a conclusion through a clear process of reasoning.

T3 Significant social and historical developments in religious thought

This section covers AO1 content and skills

Specification content

The origins of Religious Zionism with reference to Amos 9:14–15 and 'Zion theology' found in the Hebrew Bible.

A: The challenge of secularisation

AO1 Activity

As you read through this theme, note down significant dates and their corresponding events. When you have done so, create a chronological timeline so that you have a clear idea of what happened when and why.

The origins of Religious Zionism

Zion is one of the biblical names for Jerusalem which has also come to refer to Israel as a whole. Jews have always held the belief that the Land of Israel (**Eretz Yisrael**) is the place that God promised them as part of the covenant relationship made with Abraham. The sign of the covenant was to be circumcision, and in return God promised Abraham: 'I will give to you and to your descendants after you … all the land of Canaan, for an everlasting possession.' (Genesis 17:7–8)

The promise to Abraham was passed to his son, Isaac, and then to his grandson, Jacob. Jacob and his sons settled in the land of Egypt, but were enslaved there. Moses led them through the wilderness back towards Canaan, and during the course of the journey he received the Torah on Mount Sinai. According to the Book of Deuteronomy, Moses declared: 'The Lord commanded me at that time to teach you the laws and rules, that you might do them in the land which you are going to possess.' (Deuteronomy 4:14)

In the years that followed, the Jews did establish themselves in the land that God had promised them, and Jerusalem came to be a place of great significance when King David made it his capital and eventually the location where all sacrificial worship was centralised. One of the hills on which the city was set was Mount Zion, and thus the name came to signify the whole land. Hoffman says: 'That this physical arena was to enable the covenant people to live out God's requirements is reflected in the term **Eretz Hakodesh** (The Holy Land).'

Key terms

Eretz Hakodesh: meaning 'The Holy Land'

Eretz Yisrael: meaning 'Land of Israel'

Zion: one of the names for Jerusalem; also used as a name for all of Israel

The holy city of Jerusalem

T3 Significant social and historical developments in religious thought

However, residence in the Holy Land was not to be permanent, and when many of its people were exiled in Babylon, their longing and desire to return to their homeland became evident in scripture: 'By the rivers of Babylon, there we sat, sat and wept, as we thought of Zion.' (Psalm 137:1)

Nevertheless, hope remained that the Land of Israel would be restored to them, and this finds its expression in the words of the prophet Amos: '"I will restore my people Israel. They shall rebuild ruined cities and inhabit them; they shall plant vineyards and drink their wine; they shall till gardens and eat their fruits. And I will plant them upon their soil, nevermore to be uprooted from the soil I have given them," says the LORD your God.' (Amos 9:14–15)

Such is the importance of Zion that beliefs which have developed around it have been given expression in the term 'Zion theology'. The prophecies of Isaiah in particular relate to the belief that there will be a future re-grouping of Jewish exiles who will return to Zion and experience the restoration of God's city. For Isaiah foretells that Zion will be restored in such a way as to become the 'glorious crown' which will be 'renowned on earth'. (Isaiah 62:1–8)

Furthermore, Zion will become a light to all nations: 'Arise, shine, for your light has dawned ... And nations shall walk by your light' (Isaiah 60:1–3) and because the nations of the world will come to recognise and fear God they too will bring tribute to Zion. Central to the book of Isaiah is the theme that Zion will become the central place on earth, and that all nations will live in peace and justice under God's rule:

'In the days to come,

The Mount of the Lord's House

Shall stand firm above the mountains

And tower above the hills;

And all the nations

Shall gaze on it with joy.'

(Isaiah 2:2)

The book of the prophet Jeremiah also places great emphasis upon the importance of Zion. On the one hand, he perceives his calling to be one in which he announces judgement against a nation that has turned away from God; whilst on the other, he looks to a future time in which God's people will have repented: 'Turn back, rebellious children declares the Lord ... I will take you one from a town and two from a clan, and bring you to Zion.' (Jeremiah 3:14) Zion becomes a symbol of the restoration of the Jewish nation in which future leaders will be appointed by God; leaders who will rule with justice and fairness: 'I will raise up a true branch of David's line. He shall reign as king and shall prosper, and he shall do what is just and right in the land.' (Jeremiah 23:5)

From very early times, the connection between the Jews and the Holy Land was preserved in the **liturgy**, and the return to the Land of Israel is a recurring theme within worship. The Amidah, for example, contains the following references:

No. 10 'Sound the great horn for our freedom. Raise the banner to rally our exiles, and gather us in from the four corners of the earth. Blessed are you, O Lord, who gathers the dispersed of his people Israel.'

Key quote

Upon your walls, O Jerusalem,
I have set watchmen,
Who shall never be silent
By day or by night ...
Take no rest
And give no rest to Him,
Until he establishes Jerusalem
And make her renowned on earth.
(Isaiah 62:6–7)

Key term

Liturgy: the set form of words or ritual used in worship

quickfire

3.1 Name three prophets whose prophecies make reference to a return to Zion.

Key quote

I will build you firmly again,
O Maiden Israel ...
Again you shall plant vineyards
On the hills of Samaria ...
For the day is coming when watchmen
Shall proclaim ...
Come, let us go up to Zion,
To the LORD our God.
(Jeremiah 31:4–6)

No. 14 'To Jerusalem, your city, return in mercy, and dwell in it, as you have promised. Rebuild it soon in our days as an everlasting structure, and swiftly establish it in the throne of David. Blessed are you, O Lord, who rebuilds Jerusalem.'

No. 17 'O Lord our God, receive with pleasure your people Israel and their prayers … May our eyes witness your return in mercy to Zion. Blessed are you, O Lord, who brings back his **Shekinah** to Zion.'

And at Passover, when many Jews gather as a family to commemorate the escape from slavery in Egypt, the meal ends with the words 'Next year may we be in Jerusalem; next year may we be free.' Wherever they are in the world, Jews look forward to a time when they will return to Zion, where the Temple will be rebuilt, and where all the nations will gather to worship God.

Some might argue that the religious idea of a return to the Promised Land is the true origin of Zionism. However, as Hoffman observes, 'The term "Zionism" could thus be used of these beliefs and hopes. What it has come to denote, however, is something altogether more political. It denotes an identification of State with land, of Zionism with Judaism, and is the source of much conflict and confusion. The whole weight of the biblical promise, with the collective hope of ingathering, lies behind the Jewish association with Israel, the land. "The Holy Land" is one to which you make **aliyah** ('ascent'), the term used generally now of "immigration" to Israel. But any line of continuity with what is now understood as Zionism in terms of Israel, the State, is not a straight one.'

Key terms

Aliyah: meaning 'ascent' or 'going up'; also used in the sense of 'immigration' to the Land of Israel

Anti-Semitism: hostility to and/or discrimination against Jews

Nationalism: a movement which seeks to preserves a nation's culture

Shekinah: means 'dwelling' or 'settling' and denotes the divine presence of God in the world

Study tip

Make sure that you are able to make thorough and accurate reference to relevant examples from the Jewish scriptures when discussing Zion theology.

The rise of nationalism in response to anti-Semitism in the 19th century

Specification content

The rise of nationalism in response to anti-Semitism in the 19th century.

Europe in the 1870s was an unsettled place. Newly independent nations emerged, and each wished to preserve a distinctive national identity. People began to take a renewed interest in their own history, literature and music. This culminated in the desire to recreate nation states where people would live together as one race, and with one common language. This led to the rise of **nationalism** and as a result of this, minority groups of all kinds were persecuted because they were seen as a threat to the ruling majority.

The term '**anti-Semitism**' was first coined by a German journalist, Wilhelm Marr, in the 1870s. Previously, hatred of the Jews had been based upon a religious justification in that they were seen as being responsible for putting Jesus to death. The concept changed in the 1870s when Marr claimed that the Jews were a biologically alien people who could never be assimilated into European society because they were of a different and foreign race. He claimed that the Jews had corrupted all standards, banned idealism from society, had come to dominate commerce, and ruled cultural life. Furthermore, it was being claimed that the Jews were in control of the financial institutions and were thus responsible for the difficult economic conditions of the time. This argument proved to be very attractive to many shopkeepers, skilled workers, and clerks. And in 1881 it was being claimed publicly by philosopher and economist Eugen Dühring that the Jewish physical type posed a threat to the pure-bred German nation. A petition was organised to prevent any further immigration and achieved around 225,000 signatories.

Cohn-Sherbok plots the growing rise of anti-Semitism: '(The petition) was followed in 1882 by an international anti-Semitic congress. In the next decade anti-Semitic parties elected sixteen deputies to the German Reichstag. At the end of the century

Key quote

… when a number of other dependent and oppressed nationalities have been allowed to regain their independence, we, too, must not sit even one moment longer with folded hands; we must not admit that we are doomed to play on in the future the hopeless role of the 'wandering Jews' … it is our bounden duty to devote all our remaining moral force to re-establish ourselves as a living nation, so that we may finally assume a more fitting and dignified role. **(Pinsker)**

anti-Semitism was utilised by Karl Lueger to foster the creation of the first political party in Europe which obtained power on the basis of anti-Jewish feeling.'

The wave of anti-Semitism spread through Europe and in Russia an outbreak of vicious **pogroms** began in 1881, bringing about the death and destruction of 160 Jewish communities. This was followed by the introduction of the May Laws which placed restrictions upon Jewish businesses. Unable to function, and facing certain economic ruin, many Jews realised that their only hope of survival was to leave Europe. Most went to the United States, but many looked to Palestine where groups known as Lovers of Zion (**Hovovei Zion**) were already supporting settlements.

In the early days of the settlements there was no particular political agenda, simply a desire to set up communities. However, Leon Pinsker, an eminent Russian physician, published a book called *Autoemancipation* in which he argued that the liberation of the Jews could only be achieved by the establishment of a Jewish homeland. He did not specify where he thought this homeland should be, but reasoned that if the Jews had their own land like other nations then there would be no further need for anti-Semitism. Lovers of Zion approved of his sentiments and the momentum grew for the establishment of a Jewish homeland.

Key quotes

German culture has proved itself ineffective and powerless against this foreign power. This is a fact; a brute inexorable fact. State, Church, Catholicism, Protestantism, Creed and Dogma, are all brought low before the Jewish tribunal. **(Marr)**

For the living, the Jew is a dead man; for the natives, an alien and a vagrant; for property holders, a beggar; for the poor, an exploiter and millionaire; for patriots, a man without a country, for all classes, a hated rival. **(Pinsker)**

Political Zionism

Anti-Semitism was also on the rise in France at the end of the nineteenth century, and is best illustrated by reference to what has become known as the Dreyfus Affair. Alfred Dreyfus was a high-ranking French army officer, and also a Jew. In 1894 he was accused of high treason, and although he protested his innocence, he was sentenced to life imprisonment. France was divided on the issue. Many believed that he was part of a Jewish conspiracy to undermine the stability of France, whilst others believed that a miscarriage of justice had taken place.

It was later discovered that the documents which had been used to convict him had been forged, but nonetheless he was tried again in 1899 and found guilty. The affair caused a sensation, and he was eventually pardoned by the French president, but not formally pardoned until some years later in 1906. For the Jews of France, this case highlighted the fact that anti-Semitism was at the heart of the nation. The Dreyfus Affair was to have a profound effect upon an Austrian journalist, Theodor Herzl, who has come to be recognised as the father of the political Zionist movement.

The trial of Alfred Dreyfus

T3 Significant social and historical developments in religious thought

quickfire

3.2 In which decade was the term 'anti-Semitism' first used?

Key terms

Hovovei Zion: meaning 'lovers of Zion'; organisations established with the aim of supporting Jewish settlement in the Land of Israel

Pogroms: the organised persecutions or massacres of Jews

Specification content

Political Zionism and the developing idea of a national identity amongst Jews with reference to: the Dreyfus affair; the work of Herzl and the international Zionist movement.

Theodor Herzl

Theodor Herzl and the establishment of the Zionist Movement

Theodor Herzl (1860–1904) was an Austrian journalist who had been born into an **assimilated** Jewish family in Vienna. He was sent to Paris to cover the trial of Dreyfus, and the whole event made a huge impression upon him. As he himself said: 'I became a Zionist because of the Dreyfus trial which I attended in 1894 … the wild screams of the street mob at the building where it was ordered that Dreyfus be deprived of his rank still resounds in my ears.'

In his and many other Jewish minds, the whole affair demonstrated that the problem of anti-Semitism in Europe was simmering beneath the surface ready to boil over. In a tract written after the Dreyfus Affair, entitled '**Der Judenstaat**' (The Jewish State) Herzl argued that even though Jews may seek to integrate into the societies in which they live, they will never be truly accepted or treated as equals. He came to the conclusion that anti-Semitism would only cease being a problem if the Jewish people had a land of their own.

Key quote

I therefore address my first words to those Jews who are strong and free of spirit … I am introducing no new idea; on the contrary, it is a very old one. It is a universal idea … old as the people, which never, even in the time of bitterest calamity, ceased to cherish it. This is the restoration of the Jewish state. **(Herzl)**

The First Zionist Conference, 1897

With this in mind, Herzl convened a meeting which became known as the First Zionist Conference. It took place in Basel, Switzerland in 1897, and called for a national home for Jews based upon international law. It set out the goals of the Zionist movement:

> 'Zionism seeks to establish a home for the Jewish people in Eretz Israel secured under public law. The Congress contemplates the following means to the attainment of this end:
> 1. The promotion by appropriate means of the settlement in Eretz Israel of Jewish farmers, artisans, and manufacturers.
> 2. The organisation and uniting of the whole of Jewry by means of appropriate institutions, both local and international, in accordance with the laws of each country.
> 3. The strengthening and fostering of Jewish national sentiment and national consciousness.
> 4. Preparatory steps toward obtaining the consent of governments, where necessary, in order to reach the goals of Zionism.'

And so the World Zionist Organisation was formed with Herzl as its first president. A diary extract of his from 1897 illustrates his feelings: 'Were I to sum up the Basel Congress in a word – which I shall guard against pronouncing publicly – it would be this: At Basel I founded the Jewish State. If I said this out loud today I would be greeted by universal laughter. In five years perhaps, and certainly in fifty years, everyone will perceive it.'

From then on he embarked upon a series of meetings with heads of state and other influential people in an attempt to gain their support for his ideas. He was prepared to consider sites other than the traditional Promised Land in Palestine as a homeland for the Jews. Parts of Turkey, Cyprus, and even an area of Uganda were considered. The last was given approval by the British government, but it aroused such protest at the Sixth Zionist Congress that Herzl had to make a commitment to Palestine as the only possible site. Herzl died in 1904, and it is probable that the strain of these negotiations finally undermined his health.

quickeire

3.3 Name the tract written by Herzl as a result of the Dreyfus affair.

Specification content

The First Zionist Conference in 1897 and the establishment of political and legal claims.

Key terms

Assimilated: to have become part of a larger group especially when they are of a different race or culture

Der Judenstaat: meaning 'The Jewish State'; a pamphlet written by Herzl in 1896

Key quote

And what glory awaits those who fight unselfishly for the cause! Therefore I believe that a wondrous generation of Jews will spring into existence … The Jews who wish for a State will have it. We shall live at last as free men on our own soil, and die peacefully in our own homes. **(Herzl)**

Labour Zionism and the development of kibbutz

After Herzl's death, the presidency of the Zionist movement was taken over by David Wolffsohn. Under his leadership, socialist Jews became members of the movement through the Labour Zionist Party. Labour Zionism believed in founding the Jewish national home on Jewish labour. By the beginning of the twentieth century, there had been a significant migration of Jews to Palestine. The majority settled in the cities, but a small minority were determined to become farmers. They came not only to return to their ancient homeland, but also to forge a new way of life. They succeeded in developing farming communities which came to play a significant role in the establishment and building of the State of Israel.

These farming communities took the form of **kibbutzim**. The first **kibbutz** was established in 1909. A kibbutz is a society dedicated to mutual aid and social justice; a socioeconomic system based on the principle of joint ownership of property; equality and co-operation of production, consumption and education. It was a revolutionary idea in which Labour Zionism sought to achieve Jewish national and social fulfilment by fusing Zionism with socialism.

The revival of the Hebrew language in its modern spoken form

The new settlers in Palestine were determined to create a society based upon the Hebrew language and culture, and the name that is synonymous with the revival of the Hebrew language in particular is Eliezer Ben Yehuda. Ben Yehuda was a philologist who felt most strongly that along with a return to the Holy Land, the Jewish people should also begin to speak their own language once more. Ben Yehuda therefore went to Palestine taking with him his ideas for bringing about a revival of the Hebrew language.

Fellman tells us that Ben Yehuda adopted several plans of action: 'The main ones were three-fold, and they can be summarised as "Hebrew in the Home", "Hebrew in the School" and "Words, Words, Words."' As far as 'Hebrew in the Home' was concerned, Ben Yehuda decided to speak only Hebrew with every Jew he met. He realised that it was possible to converse at a simple level, with some mistakes, but it was his aim that Hebrew would ultimately become the dominant, first language of Palestine.

Fellman proposes, however, that it was 'Hebrew in the School' that was the most important step in bringing about the revival of the Hebrew language. Jewish immigrants had arrived in Palestine from all over Europe, bringing with them a variety of native tongues. However, Ben Yehuda proposed that the younger generation would speak only Hebrew in school; it would become the common language of the classroom, and subsequently, the language of the home.

Key quote

The Hebrew language will go from the synagogue to the house of study, and from the house of study to the school, and from the school it will come into the home and … become a living language. **(Ben Yehuda)**

Notwithstanding the problems presented by a lack of trained teachers, textbooks and resources, Ben Yehuda gained the support of the community around him and as time went on, these linguistic problems were solved, 'and a young all-Hebrew speaking generation did emerge and develop, thus ensuring beyond anything else that the revival would be a success'. (Fellman)

T3 Significant social and historical developments in religious thought

Specification content
Revival of Hebrew language in its modern spoken form. Labour Zionism and the development of kibbutz.

Key terms
Kibbutz: a communal settlement
Kibbutzim: plural form of kibbutz

Workers on a kibbutz in Palestine in the early years of the 20th century

Ben Yehuda's aim was to make Hebrew the dominant language of Palestine.

Hebrew newspapers followed, and Fellman claims that by the end of the nineteenth century it was possible for most people to read and understand a Hebrew newspaper without too much difficulty. However, Ben Yehuda was aware that there were objects and concepts which did not have an equivalent word in Hebrew: terms such as 'doll' and 'ice-cream' for example. The 'Words, Words, Words' part of his action plan thus came about by Ben Yehuda also using his newspaper as the means by which to introduce new terms. He also produced a Hebrew dictionary so as to be able to record these new Hebrew words with precision and accuracy; and to help him with this endeavour he founded the Hebrew Language Council, which was the forerunner of the modern-day Hebrew Language Academy, the foremost authority on all matters relating to the Hebrew language.

However, as Fellman notes, Ben Yehuda did not revive the Hebrew language entirely on his own as the new settlers were receptive to his ideas and were willing to speak Hebrew on arrival in Palestine. Such was the success of the revival that in 1922, Hebrew was recognised as the official language of the Jews in Palestine.

> **Specification content**
>
> The development of the Zionist Movement and the establishment of the secular state of Israel.

The development of the Zionist Movement

From the earliest days of Zionism, there have been various different parties within the movement. The political wing and the World Zionist Organisation were essentially secular in their aims and aspirations. Herzl himself believed that a Jewish state was a political necessity if Jews were to escape from recurrent outbursts of anti-Semitism. On the other hand, some early members attempted to justify a return to Zion on religious grounds, but they were in the minority. In general, Herzl's movement ignored the religious aspects of Judaism and emphasised the political needs of the people of Israel.

At the Fifth Zionist Conference in 1901, some Western European delegates adopted an anti-religious stance, and in response to this, Rabbi Isaac Reines formed the Mizrachi party which became the religious wing of the Zionist Movement. The motto of Mizrachi was 'The Land of Israel to the People of Israel according to the Law of Israel'.

The Mizrachi ideal was to secure the future of the Jewish people through study of the Torah, observance of the mitzvot and return to the ancient homeland. In 1920 the Mizrachi moved its headquarters to Jerusalem and the World Zionist Organisation made it responsible for Jewish education in Palestine. The Mizrachi party fought long and hard against the secular Zionists to preserve the Jewish character of the State of Israel. Due to its efforts, Shabbat remains an official day of rest, where public transport is suspended. Jewish law also covers issues of marriage and divorce for example.

Other Zionists emphasised the cultural nationalism of the nation, based upon the belief that Jewish existence was grounded not in the Jewish religion but in Jewish civilisation.

The establishment of the secular state of Israel

Cohn-Sherbok notes that: 'The **Holocaust** and the establishment of the State of Israel were organically related events – the death of millions of Jews in the Second World War profoundly affected Jewry throughout the world.' By the end of the Second World War, there was an urgent need to resettle thousands of Holocaust survivors, and many of them tried to make their way to Palestine. Indeed, the tragic events served to emphasise the need for a safe, secure, free, and independent Jewish homeland. It was against this background that the work of political Zionism intensified. Dosick says: 'Zionists were largely responsible for rallying public opinion and creating the political atmosphere that moved the world towards the Zionist cause and moved the United Nations toward the vote that set the stage for the establishment of the modern State of Israel.'

> **Key term**
>
> **Holocaust:** the term used to denote the murder of nearly 6 million Jews by Germany between 1933 and 1945

In order to bring about the creation of a Jewish state, the Jewish community had to persuade the allies of the merit of their plan. In 1917 the British government had pledged its support for a Jewish homeland in Palestine through the Balfour Declaration. However, in 1939 a government report rejected this proposal leading to the British forces in Palestine restricting immigration and turning back refugee ships.

A struggle against the British ensued, and in 1944 an extremist group called the Stern Gang murdered Lord Moyne, the British Minister for Middle East Affairs. Jewish resistance movements continued to attack British military targets, and the Arabs, who did not want large-scale Jewish immigration, also joined the fray.

In 1946, the British government handed over the Palestinian problem to the United Nations although Britain did not withdraw from the country straight away. Once the British announced their intention to leave, the US President Harry Truman argued for the creation of a Jewish state. In May 1947 the United Nations discussed the Palestinian problem, and they voted to partition Palestine into separate Jewish and Arab states. On 14 May 1948 the Jews of Palestine proclaimed the State of Israel.

Key quote

The Land of Israel was the birthplace of the Jewish people. Here their spiritual, religious and national identity was formed … Accordingly, we, the members of the National Council, representing the Jewish people in Palestine and the Zionist movement of the world … hereby proclaim the establishment of the Jewish State in Palestine, to be called Israel. **(Proclamation of the State of Israel)**

Migration to Israel

The Proclamation of the Establishment of the State of Israel declared: 'The State of Israel will be open for Jewish immigration and the ingathering of the exiles …' And so the repopulation of the free and independent Jewish state began.

After Israel had been declared a state, a quarter of a million Holocaust survivors made their way to settle in the Jewish homeland. This was followed by other groups who came from all over the world, including nearly all of the Jewish communities of Libya, Yemen and Iraq. Throughout the existence of the modern State of Israel, more than 1.5 million Jews have come to 'make aliyah', to come and live in what Doscik describes as 'the ancient and renewed Jewish land'.

This was followed in 1950 by the **Knesset** (Israel's Parliament) passing a piece of legislation known as the Law of Return. This legislation gave Jews, those of Jewish ancestry, and their spouses, the right to migrate, settle in Israel and gain citizenship without having to undergo a formal naturalisation procedure. It gave a legal basis for one of the objectives of the Zionist Movement which was to provide a solution to the Jewish people's problem by re-establishment of a home for the Jewish people in Eretz Israel.

The Law of Return allowed Jews from all over the world to gain citizenship in Israel.

T3 Significant social and historical developments in religious thought

Key quote

His Majesty's Government view with favour the establishment of a national home for the Jewish people, and will use their best endeavours to facilitate the achievement of this object …' **(Balfour Declaration)**

On 14 May 1948 David Ben Gurion declared the State of Israel.

quickfire

3.4 In which year was the State of Israel established?

Specification content
Migration to Israel; the challenge of secularisation with reference to the specific response by Haredi Judaism.

Key term
Knesset: the Parliament of modern Israel

Key quote

May the lord bless you from Zion;
may you share the prosperity of Jerusalem
all the days of your life,
and live to see your children's children.
May all be well with Israel!
(Psalm 128:5–6)

55

> **quickfire**
>
> **3.5** Name the legislation passed by the Knesset that gave Jews the right to Israeli citizenship.

> **Key terms**
>
> **Haredi:** meaning 'fearful'; a member of a Jewish group characterised by strict adherence to the traditional form of Jewish law, and rejection of modern secular culture
>
> **Haredim:** plural form of Haredi
>
> **Messianic:** relating to the Messiah, the 'anointed one'; one who will usher in a new era for humanity, which will be established under the rule of God
>
> **Redemption:** the act of being saved

Yet, as Dosick cautions, 'it has been – and continues to be – no easy task to meld Jews from such wide varieties of backgrounds and cultures ... into one modern nation-state'. For example, the Law of Return has been amended a number of times to meet changing circumstances. In 1970 the amendment stated that a Jew is one born to a Jewish mother or who has been converted to Judaism. However, in subsequent years, there have been many attempts by the religious parties to amend the Law of Return so that only those who have been converted according to Halakhah are deemed Jewish and thereby eligible to settle in the State of Israel. If accepted, this would mean that all conversions undertaken by the Conservative or Reform rabbinate would be invalid.

The challenge of secularisation with reference to the specific response by Haredi Judaism

De Lange explains that traditional Judaism today, particularly in Israel, is often designated by the Hebrew epithet '**haredi**', meaning 'fearful' in the sense of maintaining an attitude of awe or veneration to God: according to Isaiah 66:5 those who 'tremble' before the Lord. **Haredim** have a distinctive style of dress: the men wear beards and side locks and black coats and hats, while married women have shaven heads, covered by a wig or headscarf, and wear modest clothing that hides most of their bodies.

Haredim in Israel are opposed to secular Zionism due to the concern that secularisation will replace the Jewish faith and observance of religion. This is based upon the belief that although the Torah teaches that it is the duty of all pious Jews to pray for the return to Zion, this must be preceded by **messianic redemption**. Only when God has sent the long-promised 'anointed one' will the exiles of Israel return to the Holy Land and all nations will turn to Jerusalem to learn of the One God. It was taught that it was forbidden to accelerate divine deliverance as this would happen in God's good time. The Holy Land was given to the Jewish people on the condition that they observe the Torah and its commandments. When they failed to do this, their sovereignty over the land was taken from them, and they went into exile. And likewise, in the future, God will grant the Jews a land of their own because they have served God properly and kept to their side of the covenant.

Another objection is that the State of Israel set up as a political body does not have the Torah and the mitzvot at its heart, and is therefore a secular society. Haredi Jews maintain that Jewish nationality is not like that of other people, whose ties to their homeland are based on historical association with that land and through sharing a common language and culture with those who live there. Jewish nationality was ordained by God. It should not be the Jews, led by the Zionists, who had chosen to settle in the Holy Land; settlement should come about as part of God's plan. The Zionist movement was therefore seen as an evil conspiracy against God's will.

T3 Significant social and historical developments in religious thought

Haredi Jews are opposed to the State of Israel.

Key quote

Hear the word of the LORD, you who tremble at his word … (Isaiah 66:5)

Notwithstanding their opposition to the State of Israel, it has been calculated that currently 10% of the population of Israel is made up of Haredi Jews. They at first refused even to consider settling in Israel, but the rising tide of anti-Semitism in Europe in the 1930s put paid to that, and they sought refuge in Palestine.

In modern-day Israel, Haredi Jews have refused to assimilate, and live in closed communities. Nevertheless, the Israeli government has reached out to them through the areas of education and army membership. For example, The Council for Higher Education has invested a considerable amount of money in establishing frameworks for the education of Haredim. The government has also in the past granted exemption for Haredi Jews from compulsory military service, although recent legislation has sought to bring an end to this exemption. However, in spite of these concessions, De Lange claims that Haredim in Israel are increasingly violent in their hostility to modernising trends, and particularly to secular Zionism.

AO1 Activity

Haredi protests within the State of Israel are still common occurrences. Search newspaper articles online for evidence of the protests of the Haredim in Israel.

Study tip

It is important in this section that you have a clear understanding of the distinction between religious Zionism and political Zionism. Your ability to differentiate between the two will allow you to access one of the higher levels in the band descriptors for AO1.

Key quote

For the sake of Zion I will not be silent,
For the sake of Jerusalem I will not be still,
Till her victory emerge resplendent
And her triumph like a flaming torch.
Nations shall see your victory,
And every king your majesty.
(Isaiah 62:1–2)

Key quote

(In Israel), with its Jewish majority, the problems of religion and state are far from being solved, and Jewish identity and religious observance are at the forefront of the political agenda … there are Jewish political parties, enjoying small but significant support, and Jewish issues not infrequently lead to violent clashes. In addition, the issues in question have a direct bearing on the rights of the non-Jewish minorities, and on relations between Jews and non-Jews, as well as the status of the progressive Jewish movements. (De Lange)

WJEC / Eduqas Religious Studies for A Level Year 2 and A2 Judaism

Key skills Theme 3ABC

This Theme has tasks that concentrate on a particular aspect of AO1 in terms of using quotations from sources of authority and in the use of references.

AO1 Developing skills

It is now important to consider the information that has been covered in this section; however, the information in its raw form is too extensive and so has to be processed in order to meet the requirements of the examination. This can be achieved by practising more advanced skills associated with AO1. The exercises that run throughout this book will help you to do this and prepare you for the examination. For assessment objective 1 (AO1), which involves demonstrating 'knowledge' and 'understanding' skills, we are going to focus on different ways in which the skills can be demonstrated effectively, and also refer to how the performance of these skills is measured (see generic band descriptors for A2 [WJEC] AO1 or A Level [Eduqas] AO1).

▶ **Your next task is this:** Below is an outline of **the origins of Religious Zionism**. At present it has no quotations at all to back up the points made. Underneath the outline are two quotations that could be used in the outline in order to improve it. Your task is to rewrite the outline but make use of the quotations. Such phrases as 'according to ...', 'the scholar ... argues', or, 'it has been suggested by ...' may help.

Zion is a biblical name for Jerusalem which has also come to refer to Israel as a whole. It is regarded by Jews as the land God promised them as part of the covenant relationship made with Abraham. In the years that followed, the Jews established themselves in the land that God had promised them, and Jerusalem came to be a place of great significance when King David made it his capital and eventually the location where all sacrificial worship was centralised. One of the hills on which the city was set was Mount Zion, and thus the name came to signify the whole land. However, residence in the Holy Land was not to be permanent, and when many of its people were exiled in Babylon, their longing and desire to return to their homeland became evident in scripture. Such is the importance of Zion that beliefs which have developed around it have been given expression in the term 'Zion theology'.

> 'That this physical arena was to enable the covenant people to live out God's requirements is reflected in the term Eretz Hakodesh (The Holy Land).' (Hoffman)

> 'I will give to you and to your descendants after you ... all the land of Canaan, for an everlasting possession.' (Genesis 17:7–8)

When you have completed the task, try to find another quotation that you could use and further extend your answer.

Key skills

Knowledge involves:

Selection of a range of (thorough) accurate and relevant information that is directly related to the specific demands of the question.

This means:

- Selecting relevant material for the question set
- Being focused in explaining and examining the material selected.

Understanding involves:

Explanation that is extensive, demonstrating depth and/or breadth with excellent use of evidence and examples including (where appropriate) thorough and accurate supporting use of sacred texts, sources of wisdom and specialist language.

This means:

- Effective use of examples and supporting evidence to establish the quality of your understanding
- Ownership of your explanation that expresses personal knowledge and understanding and NOT just reproducing a chunk of text from a book that you have rehearsed and memorised.

Issues for analysis and evaluation

The validity and strength of the links between Zionism and Judaism — learn

Zion is one of the biblical names for Jerusalem which has also come to refer to the Land of Israel as a whole. Jews have always held the belief that the Land of Israel is the place that God promised them as part of the covenant relationship made with Abraham: 'I will give to you and to your descendants after you … all the land of Canaan, for an everlasting possession.' (Genesis 17:7–8)

However, after gaining the Promised Land, they subsequently lost it again when they were exiled due to historical events. Nevertheless, the promise of a return is a recurring theme both within the Jewish scriptures and as part of the liturgy. For example, the prophet Amos declared: '"I will restore my people Israel. They shall rebuild ruined cities and inhabit them; they shall plant vineyards and drink their wine; they shall till gardens and eat their fruits. And I will plant them upon their soil, nevermore to be uprooted from the soil I have given them", says the LORD your God.' (Amos 9:14–15) On the one hand therefore, it might appear that the goal of Zionism to return to the Land of Israel and to establish the Jewish nation once more after many hundreds of years of exile is exactly the same as that of religious Jews. This might therefore suggest that there is a strong link between Zionism and Judaism. However, this might not actually be the case as we shall see.

In the first instance we need to take into consideration the fact that Zionism and Judaism differ in their motives. Political Zionists saw Zion as a solution to anti-Semitism rather than as a religious movement; whereas Judaism is centred on a personal relationship with God rather than the establishment of a political state. Nevertheless, both Zionists and Jews wanted a 'land of their own' even though this desire was based upon different criteria: for Zionists under the guidance of Herzl, it would bring about an end to anti-Semitism which had developed in the nineteenth century. It is at this point that it is significant to note that in the early days of the Zionist movement, Herzl was prepared to consider sites other than the traditional Holy Land in Palestine as a homeland for the Jews, with parts of Turkey, Cyprus and even an area in Uganda under consideration. However, his proposal didn't go down well at the Sixth Zionist Congress, and such a protest ensued that Herzl was forced to make a commitment to Palestine as the only acceptable site. This, it could be argued, is evidence of a deep-rooted link between Zionism and Judaism: that there is to be no compromise over the place where the Jewish nation should be established, as set down in the Torah.

Notwithstanding the desire to establish a Jewish state in the traditional Holy Land, historically Zionism has been a movement dominated by secularist Jews. Herzl and the majority of his colleagues were assimilated Jews who no longer practised the requirements of the Torah. Many Zionists saw no place for the mitzvot in modern-day society, and this immediately put them at odds with the basic tenets of the Jewish faith. Herzl was focused not on the religious aspects of Judaism, but in emphasising the political needs of the people of Israel. Yet, as has already been noted, the very essence of the Zionist idea, that Jews should return to the Holy Land and establish a government there is not inherently secular. We can offer other evidence which displays the fact that the Zionist movement *did* have members who were of a religious persuasion even though they were in the minority. At the Fifth Zionist Conference in 1901, some Western European delegates adopted an anti-religious stance, and in response to this, Rabbi Isaac Reines formed the Mizrachi party which became the religious wing of the Zionist Movement. The motto of Mizrachi was 'The Land of Israel to the People of Israel according to the Law of Israel'.

T3 Significant social and historical developments in religious thought

This section covers AO2 content and skills

Specification content
The validity and strength of the links between Zionism and Judaism.

Key quote
We have honestly striven everywhere to merge ourselves in the social life of surrounding communities … in vain are we loyal patriots, in some places, our loyalty running to extremes … Distress binds us together, and thus united, we suddenly discover our strength. Yes, we are strong enough to form a state, and a model state. We possess all human and material resources necessary for the purpose. (Herzl)

AO2 Activity
As you read through this section try to do the following:
1. Pick out the different lines of argument that are presented in the text and identify any evidence given in support.
2. For each line of argument try to evaluate whether or not you think this is strong or weak.
3. Think of any questions you may wish to raise in response to the arguments.

This Activity will help you to start thinking critically about what you read and help you to evaluate the effectiveness of different arguments and from this develop your own observations, opinions and points of view that will help with any conclusions that you make in your answers to the AO2 questions that arise.

WJEC / Eduqas Religious Studies for A Level Year 2 and A2 Judaism

Key questions

Do the differing motives of Zionism and Judaism suggest that there are no links between them at all?

Has religious Zionism had any impact upon political Zionism?

Are all Jews in agreement about the future hope of the in-gathering of Jewish exiles in the Holy Land?

Not all Jewish groups share the same beliefs about a return to the Promised Land.

Key quote

Many haredim are fundamentally opposed to a secular, modern, pre-messianic Jewish state … to this day, Agudot Israel members run for election and sit in the Knesset, but they refuse to accept any official ministerial post in the Israeli cabinet, and remain steadfast in their anti-Zionist ideology. **(Weiss)**

AO2 Activity

List some conclusions that could be drawn from the AO2 reasoning from the above text; try to aim for at least three different possible conclusions. Consider each of the conclusions and collect brief evidence to support each conclusion from the AO1 and AO2 material for this topic. Select the conclusion that you think is most convincing and explain why it is so. Try to contrast this with the weakest conclusion in the list, justifying your argument with clear reasoning and evidence.

We see here a palpable link between Zionism and Judaism: the Mizrachi ideal was to secure the future of the Jewish people through study of the Torah, observance of the mitzvot and return to the ancient homeland. The Mizrachi party fought long and hard against the secular Zionists to preserve the Jewish character of the State of Israel. Due to its efforts, Shabbat remains an official day of rest, where public transport is suspended. Jewish law also covers issues of marriage and divorce. This is quite a compromise with what Herzl initially envisaged, and shows the strength of the religious branch of the Zionist movement. However, there also remained other Zionists who emphasised the cultural nationalism of the nation, based upon the belief that Jewish existence was grounded not in the Jewish religion but in Jewish civilisation.

Another aspect of this issue which needs consideration is the fact that there is even a difference of opinion about the return to Israel within Judaism itself. For Orthodox Jews, Israel would be re-established in the Promised Land as the result of meeting the conditions of observing the Torah and its commandments. Haredim in Israel are totally opposed to secular Zionism, and can see no link whatsoever between a State, which is not based upon the teachings of the Torah, and Judaism. Furthermore, Haredi Jews believe that although the Torah teaches that it is the duty of all pious Jews to pray for the return to Zion, this return must be preceded by messianic redemption, and only then will the exiles of Israel return to the Holy Land.

Study tip

It is important to make good use of transition words when writing your response to an AO2 issue. Transition words help the reader to understand the direction that your argument is taking. Try to avoid over-use of the phrases 'on the one hand … on the other hand;' they have their uses, but aim to expand your vocabulary by using a variety of transition words such as 'consequently', 'moreover', 'nevertheless', for example.

The stance of the Haredim is in contrast to Reform Jews who generally reject totally the idea that Jews would re-create a Jewish state in their ancestral homeland. They rejected the notion that there would be a Messiah, and the belief that they were in exile. Instead they suggested that the fact that Jews were dispersed across the world was a necessary thing, and that they had been chosen to spread the truth of God to all nations. In this instance they also differ greatly from the aims of the Zionist movement, and are not linked to a common goal. Rather than being linked, Reform Jews asserted that the political aspirations of Zionism went against the universalistic spirit of Judaism because it called into the question the loyalty of Jews to the countries in which they lived.

Overall, it seems to be the case that there are too many differences between Zionism and Judaism to be able to argue for any real strong and valid links between the two. There is also the problem that any conclusion depends upon one's understanding of the term Zionism, which is ambiguous even within Judaism. As Hoffman observes: 'The term "Zionism" … has come to denote … something altogether more political and an identification of State with land … (and the relationship between) Zionism with Judaism is the source of much conflict and confusion.' However, that is not to decry Zionism, as Dosick notes that it is largely down to the Zionists that the United Nations moved towards the vote that set the stage for the establishment of the modern State of Israel.

✱ Whether or not Zionism is specifically a Jewish movement — *important*.

The term 'Zionism' is usually understood as one that relates to the movement which was instigated by Theodor Herzl in response to the rising tide of anti-Semitism in Europe at the end of the nineteenth century. In this way it could be argued that Zionism *is* specifically a Jewish movement, as it focused on the need to establish a political state, which would act as a solution to the problem of discrimination against the Jews which was widespread during this particular period in history. However, it is important to note at this point that although Herzl himself was a Jew, he came from a family that had successfully assimilated into Viennese society. He was not therefore concerned with the creation of a state that would be based upon the requirements of the Torah; which might lead some to argue to the contrary, that based upon this criterion Zionism is not specifically a Jewish movement at all.

However, perhaps it should be established whether or not there is any common ground between what might be called political Zionism and religious Zionism. One line of argument suggests that political Zionism has its foundation in Zion theology. Zion is one of the biblical names for Jerusalem which has also come to refer to the Land of Israel as a whole. Jews have always held the belief that the Land of Israel is the place that God promised them as part of the covenant relationship made with Abraham: 'I will give to you and to your descendants after you … all the land of Canaan, for an everlasting possession.' (Genesis 17:7–8)

However, after gaining the Promised Land, they subsequently lost it again when they were exiled due to historical events. Nevertheless, the promise of a return is a recurring theme both within the Jewish scriptures and as part of the liturgy. For example, the prophet Amos declared: '"I will restore my people Israel. They shall rebuild ruined cities and inhabit them; they shall plant vineyards and drink their wine; they shall till gardens and eat their fruits. And I will plant them upon their soil, nevermore to be uprooted from the soil I have given them", says the LORD your God.' (Amos 9:14–15) On the one hand therefore, it might appear that the goal of Zionism to return to the Land of Israel and to establish the Jewish nation once more after many hundreds of years of exile is exactly the same as that of religious Jews. This might therefore add weight to the argument that Zionism is specifically a Jewish movement. The **diaspora**, it could be suggested, weakens Judaism, whereas Zionism promotes Jewish unity and national identity. Furthermore, it strengthens the Jewish faith in Israel so that every Jew should look upon Zionism with a positive outlook.

Another consideration that needs to be included in this discussion is that there is no clear-cut way by which to define Jewishness. For some it is to be born to a Jewish mother, being brought up in the Jewish faith and identifying with Jewish history. For others it is a national identity which does not necessarily go hand-in-hand with religious observance. For the latter, there is possibly a closer alliance with political Zionism; for the former it does not automatically mean that political Zionism has any relevance at all, and yet both can legitimately claim to be Jewish.

Key quote

The Land of Israel was the birthplace of the Jewish people. Here their spiritual, religious and national identity was formed. Here they achieved independence and created a culture of national and universal significance … Exiled in Palestine, the Jewish people remained faithful to it in all the countries of their dispersion, never ceasing to pray and hope for their return and the restoration of their national freedom. **(Proclamation of the State of Israel)**

T3 Significant social and historical developments in religious thought

Specification content
Whether or not Zionism is specifically a Jewish movement.

Key term
Diaspora: the term used to denote the Jews who live outside Israel

AO2 Activity

As you read through this section try to do the following:

1. Pick out the different lines of argument that are presented in the text and identify any evidence given in support.
2. For each line of argument try to evaluate whether or not you think this is strong or weak.
3. Think of any questions you may wish to raise in response to the arguments.

This Activity will help you to start thinking critically about what you read and help you to evaluate the effectiveness of different arguments and from this develop your own observations, opinions and points of view that will help with any conclusions that you make in your answers to the AO2 questions that arise.

Study tip

Ensure that you reflect the differing views of the various groups that are to be found in Judaism where relevant. Steer clear of making sweeping statements such as 'All Jews believe that ...'

Key questions

Are there any common links between Zionism and Judaism?

Could it be claimed that Zionism has strengthened the Jewish faith in Israel?

Is the definition of what makes a person Jewish of any significance in relation to this issue?

'I will restore my people Israel ... they shall plant vineyards ... never more to be uprooted from the soil I have given them.' (Amos 9:14–15)

AO2 Activity

List some conclusions that could be drawn from the AO2 reasoning from the above text; try to aim for at least three different possible conclusions. Consider each of the conclusions and collect brief evidence to support each conclusion from the AO1 and AO2 material for this topic. Select the conclusion that you think is most convincing and explain why it is so. Try to contrast this with the weakest conclusion in the list, justifying your argument with clear reasoning and evidence.

However, not all Jews accept that Zionism is a Jewish movement, and many view it as a secular rather than a religious organisation. For example, Orthodox Jews would not ally themselves with political Zionism due to their belief that Israel will only be re-established in the Promised Land as the result of meeting the conditions of observing the Torah and its commandments. Haredim in Israel are totally opposed to secular Zionism, and can see no link whatsoever between a State, which is not based upon the teachings of the Torah, and Judaism. Furthermore, Haredi Jews believe that although the Torah teaches that it is the duty of all pious Jews to pray for the return to Zion, this return must be preceded by messianic redemption, and only then will the exiles of Israel return to the Holy Land.

Neither do Reform Jews identify with Zionism. The Pittsburgh Platform brought about a total rejection of the idea that Jews would re-create a Jewish state in their ancestral homeland. They reject the notion that there will be a Messiah, and the belief that they are in exile. Instead they suggest that the fact that Jews are dispersed across the world is a necessary thing, and that they have been chosen to spread the truth of God to all nations. In this instance they also differ greatly from the aims of the Zionist movement, and are not linked to a common goal. Rather than being linked, Reform Jews asserted that the political aspirations of Zionism went against the universalistic spirit of Judaism because it called into the question the loyalty of Jews to the countries in which they lived. This is a strong argument for rejecting the notion that Zionism is specifically a Jewish movement.

Key quote

Once we were Pharaoh's slaves in Egypt, and Yahweh brought us out from Egypt with a mighty hand ... Us he brought out from there so that he might bring us in, to give us the land which he promised by oath to our ancestors. (Deuteronomy 6:21–23)

It would be inaccurate, however, to suggest that there are no connections between political Zionism and religious Zionism, and the Mizrachi party is a case in point. At the Fifth Zionist Conference in 1901, some Western European delegates adopted an anti-religious stance, and in response to this, Rabbi Isaac Reines formed the Mizrachi party which became the religious wing of the Zionist Movement. The motto of Mizrachi was 'The Land of Israel to the People of Israel according to the Law of Israel'. This may not be an argument that is strong enough to suggest that Zionism is specifically a Jewish movement in the religious sense of the term, but it does show that the Jewish faith continues to have an impact upon the Zionist movement. It could well be claimed that without the intervention of the religious wing of the party, Judaism as a faith would have been weakened due to the main focus upon secular and political aims. However, the Mizrachi party acted as a tempering factor whose ideal was to secure the future of the Jewish people in their homeland based upon study of the Torah and living life according to the mitzvot. It is thanks to them that the Jewish character of the State of Israel has been preserved. Due to their efforts, Shabbat remains an official day of rest, where public transport is suspended. The legal system of the State of Israel also defers to Jewish law on the matter of marriage and divorce, for example.

Overall, it could be concluded that there is such a difference between the political and religious recognition of the State of Israel that Zionism could never be said to be described as a specific Jewish movement. It could also be argued that there is no need for such a link anyway as Israel as a secular state is vindicated on this basis alone without Judaism. Neither is the continued existence of the Jewish faith hindered by the belief that only God will usher in the legitimate return to the Promised Land.

AO2 Developing skills

It is now important to consider the information that has been covered in this section; however, the information in its raw form is too extensive and so has to be processed in order to meet the requirements of the examination. This can be achieved by practising more advanced skills associated with AO2. The exercises that run throughout this book will help you to do this and prepare you for the examination. For assessment objective 2 (AO2), which involves 'critical analysis' and 'evaluation' skills, we are going to focus on different ways in which the skills can be demonstrated effectively, and also refer to how the performance of these skills is measured (see generic band descriptors for A2 [WJEC] AO2 or A Level [Eduqas] AO2).

▶ **Your next task is this:** Below is an **evaluation of the view that there may be links between Zionism and Judaism, but that they differ in their motives**. At present it has no quotations at all to support the argument presented. Underneath the evaluation are two quotations that could be used in the outline in order to improve it. Your task is to rewrite the outline but make use of the quotations. Such phrases as 'according to …', 'the scholar … argues', or, 'it has been suggested by …' may help.

The promise of a return to the Land of Israel is a recurring theme both within the Jewish scriptures and as part of the liturgy. When Herzl spoke of just such a return, it could be argued that it suggests that there is a strong link between Zionism and Judaism. However, we need to consider the fact that they differed in their motives. Political Zionists saw Zion as a solution to anti-Semitism rather than as a religious relationship with God; whereas Judaism is centred on a personal relationship with God rather than the establishment of a political state.

Such was Herzl's desire to create a homeland that he was prepared to consider sites other than the Holy Land in Palestine. However, this proposal didn't gain acceptance at the Sixth Zionist Congress and he was forced to make a commitment to Palestine alone. This, it could be argued, is evidence of a deep-rooted link between Zionism and Judaism: that there is to be no compromise over the place where the Jewish nation should be established, as set down in the Torah.

'I will restore my people Israel. They shall rebuild ruined cities and inhabit them; they shall plant vineyards and drink their wine; they shall till gardens and eat their fruits. And I will plant them upon their soil, nevermore to be uprooted from the soil I have given them,' says the LORD your God. (Amos 9:14–15)

'I am introducing no new idea; on the contrary, it is a very old one. It is a universal idea … old as the people, which never, even in the time of bitterest calamity, ceased to cherish it. This is the restoration of the Jewish state.' (Herzl)

When you have completed the task, try to find another quotation that you could use and further extend your evaluation.

T3 Significant social and historical developments in religious thought

Key skills Theme 3ABC
This Theme has tasks that concentrate on a particular aspect of AO2 in terms of using quotations from sources of authority and in the use of references in supporting arguments and evaluations.

Key skills
Analysis involves:

Identifying issues raised by the materials in the AO1, together with those identified in the AO2 section, and presents sustained and clear views, either of scholars or from a personal perspective ready for evaluation.

This means:

- That your answers are able to identify key areas of debate in relation to a particular issue
- That you can identify, and comment upon, the different lines of argument presented by others
- That your response comments on the overall effectiveness of each of these areas or arguments.

Evaluation involves:

Considering the various implications of the issues raised based upon the evidence gleaned from analysis and provides an extensive detailed argument with a clear conclusion.

This means:

- That your answer weighs up the consequences of accepting or rejecting the various and different lines of argument analysed
- That your answer arrives at a conclusion through a clear process of reasoning.

63

WJEC / Eduqas Religious Studies for A Level Year 2 and A2 Judaism

This section covers AO1 content and skills

Specification content
Diversity of responses within Judaism to the philosophical issues relating to both the nature of God and to the creation event with reference to bereshith (in the beginning).

Jews believe that God created the universe.

Key quote
Creation ends the unity of the reality that existed before the cosmos. After creation, there is a non-God part of reality. **(Epstein)**

God said, 'Let there be light'; and there was light. (Genesis 1:3)

Key terms
Ani Ma'amin: a poetic form of Maimonides' 'Thirteen Principles of Faith' which is recited every day after morning prayers at the synagogue

Celestial: relating to heaven

Cosmogony: a theory regarding the origins of the universe

quickfire
3.6 What does Midrash Konen say about the creation of the world?

B: The challenge of science

Creation

It is a basic and traditional Jewish belief that God is the creator of the universe. The Book of Genesis begins with the Hebrew word 'Bereshith', which has been understood as meaning 'In the beginning'. According to Genesis 1:1 'In the beginning God created the Heaven and the Earth' and the centrality of this belief is such that it has influenced the liturgy of the synagogue in many ways. For example:

- In the synagogue hymn that comes before the reading from the Psalms, God is depicted as the creator of everything: 'Blessed be He who spoke, and the world existed; Blessed be He; Blessed be He who was the Master of the world in the beginning.'
- Another synagogue hymn expresses a similar view: 'You are the same before the world was created; You have been the same since the world was created.'
- The first principle of the Jewish faith, as expressed in the **Ani Ma'amin** prayer, attests: 'I believe with perfect faith that the creator, blessed be His name is the Author and Guide of everything that has been created, and that He alone has made, does make, and will make all things.'

And yet, queries Epstein, why did God create the cosmos? 'If God is a perfect Being, why was it necessary to add to God's existence? If perfect, God didn't need a world.' The only seeming response to this question, poses Epstein, is that God created the cosmos for a purpose; and that ultimately the purpose involved human beings who needed somewhere to live. 'Given this purpose', wrote Epstein, 'God's creation of the world could not just be an artistic, creative endeavour. There was an ultimate moral plan.' Epstein uses the word 'cosmos' as synonymous with the universe, and includes within its meaning all of material reality that there is in this universe.

A **cosmogony** is a theory about the origin of the universe, and Epstein indicates that the Bible's cosmogony rests on two stories at the beginning of Genesis. The Torah opens with the first creation story in Genesis 1:1–2:4: 'In the beginning of God's creation of the heavens and the earth, the earth was unformed and void, darkness was on the face of the deep, and the spirit of God hovered over the face of the waters. God said, "Let there be light"; and there was light.' The second story is found in Genesis 2:4–24 in which God forms human beings from the dust of the earth. Epstein notes that there are pre-existing elements in the world; God didn't create the cosmos out of nothing but from the chaos of earth and water. In later times, creation from nothing came to be called creation 'ex nihilo'.

Early Christianity developed a new cosmogony that there was no material in the world prior to creation. That became part of Islamic theology, and through it creation from nothing found its way into medieval Jewish theology.

Cohn-Sherbok informs us that much speculation about the nature of the creative process is to be found in rabbinic literature, with Genesis Rabbah providing numerous examples of debates and conjecture on the matter. For example, the idea of the world as a pattern in the mind of God is expressed in relation to the belief that God looked into the Torah and created the world. Here the Torah is conceived of as a type of architectural blueprint for the creation of the world; according to Midrash Konen (2:24), God drew three drops of water and three drops of fire from the **celestial** Torah, and from them made the world.

However, with respect to the order of creation, there is some disagreement with the School of Shammai stating: 'The heavens were created first and then the earth', following Genesis 1:1; whilst the School of Hillel, in contrast, argues that they were both created simultaneously in accordance with Genesis Rabbah 1:9.

Genesis Rabbah also contains reference to a philosopher who said to Rabbi Gamaliel: 'Your God is a great craftsman, but He found good materials to help him in the work of creation, namely unformed (space), void, darkness, water, wind, and the deep.' Rabbi Gamaliel, however, argued that all of these materials were explicitly described as being created by God and were not pre-existent.

In the third century, Rabbi Yohanan argued that God took two coils, one of fire and the other of snow, wove them into each other, and created the world.

According to another rabbinic source, all things were formed at the same time on the first day of creation, but appeared at the other six days just as figs are gathered simultaneously in one basket but each selected individually (Gen. R. 12:4). And again in Genesis Rabbah the sages stressed that God created several worlds, but destroyed them before creating this one (Gen. R. 9:2).

Cohn-Sherbok also makes reference to the Ethics of the Fathers which says that: 'The goal of creation is summed up in the rabbinic claim that whatever the Holy One, blessed be He, created in his world, He created for His glory.'

Analysis of Genesis 1:1 appears to present the reader with two different ways of interpreting the act of creation. On the one hand, the text suggests an act that constitutes the first instant of time, and on the other, an act in which God shapes the world from a pre-existent and formless matter.

Rashi's translation of Genesis 1:1 reads as: 'In the beginning of God's creation of the heavens and the earth, the earth was unformed and void, darkness was on the face of the deep, and the spirit of God hovered over the face of the waters.' This understanding of the verse thus proposes creation 'de novo' (creation from pre-existing matter). The world was already a formless void, lying in readiness for God to say something and to breathe life into it. In Rashi's words: 'The Spirit of God was hovering on the face of the waters, and Scripture had not yet disclosed when the creation of the waters took place … consequently you must learn from this that the creation of the waters preceded that of the earth. And a further proof that the heavens and the earth were not the first thing created is that the heavens were created from fire and water, from which it follows that fire and water were in existence before the heavens.'

As far as Maimonides is concerned, he indicates in The Guide for the Perplexed, that rabbinic commentary had reached no definite conclusion on the matter. His approach was to undertake an investigation based upon philosophical argument. Maimonides never doubted that the creation of the world depended upon God, but the question was, how? In Guide 2:13 he suggests three ways, based upon the theories of Moses, Plato and Aristotle:

- **Moses:** God created the world out of nothing in a free and spontaneous act that constituted the first moment in history. This is referred to as creation 'ex nihilo' and creation 'de novo'.
- **Plato:** the world was created 'de novo' from pre-existing matter. This has been likened to the way in which a potter shapes clay, and imposes form on pre-existent material.
- **Aristotle:** creation is neither 'de novo' nor 'ex nihilo'. Rather the world is eternal and its existence is best understood as an eternal **emanation**. The consequence of this view is that the world has always existed and will always exist in the form in which it is now.

A basket of figs provides an analogy in explanation of all things being formed on the first day of creation.

Key quote

Said R. Nehemiah: They were like those who gather figs, when each appears in its own time. R. Berekiah observed in confirmation of this view … and the earth brought forth implies something which is already stored in it. (Gen. R. 12:4)

Key term

Emanation: something that issues or proceeds from something else

WJEC / Eduqas Religious Studies for A Level Year 2 and A2 Judaism

Saadia (882–942), who has been described as the first great Jewish thinker of the medieval period, argued for a deity who is alive, powerful, and wise and who created the world 'ex nihilo,' who pre-existed the world and who is separate from the world. And that creator is one, a unity and not a plurality. Robinson explains that Saadia argues: '... if God has a plurality of attributes, this implies that the Creator is composite in nature. Therefore, we can only understand the various supposed attributes of "God-ness" as implications imposed on God by our limited understanding of the Almighty's nature, rather than actual attributes of the Deity. The only reason we **anthropomorphise** God is that we lack both the comprehension to delineate God's true nature and the language with which to express it. God is the cause of all **corporeal** existence, yet is not corporeal, for if the Creator were corporeal there would have to be something that caused God to come into being.'

Saadia Gaon (882–942)

Saadia anticipates Maimonides in his discussion of creation, arguing that God created the world not from any necessity but out of free will. He also harkens back to Akiva in his reliance on what philosophers have come to call 'the argument from design' for the existence of God. The argument from design proposes that all parts of the world fit together in a skilful pattern; all levels of creation fit and reflect this design; it is impossible to expect that such design could have come about without the planning of a Supreme Being. Therefore, someone must have created the world and everything in it, and that someone must have pre-existed the world in order to have created it. As Robinson concludes: 'All the facets of God that were enumerated above can be derived logically from this single fact.'

Furthermore, much of the worldview that Saadia established proceeds from the argument for design. It is reasonable to give thanks to one's creator; therefore, all human beings should follow the commandments as an expression of gratitude. At the same time, the commandments were given to the people of Israel by God so that humanity could live a fulfilling life. For Saadia, observing the mitzvot is a form of self-fulfilment as well as a way of thanking God for the bounty of creation.

In the Middle Ages, a number of Jewish theologians believed that God created the universe 'ex nihilo'. However, the Kabbalists interpreted the doctrine of 'ex nihilo' in a special sense. Cohn-Sherbok explains: 'God, they maintained, should be understood as the Divine Nothing because as He is in and of himself, nothing can be predicated. The Divine is beyond human understanding. Creation 'ex nihilo' thus refers to the creation of the universe out of God, the Divine Nothing.' This occurred, they argued, through a series of divine emanations. For the Kabbalists the first verse of Genesis alludes to the process within the Godhead prior to the creation of the universe. In **Lurianic Kabbalah** the ideal of God creating and destroying worlds before the creation of this world is viewed as referring to spiritual worlds. Thus the 'void' in Genesis denotes the stage of God's self-revelation known as 'world of the void', which precedes 'world of perfection.' In later Kabbalistic thought it was maintained that the void in Genesis is the primordial void remaining after God's withdrawal to make room for the universe. On this understanding, God's decree 'Let there be light' (Genesis 1:3) means that God caused light to be emanated from the divine being into the void in order to provide sustaining power required for the worlds which were later to be formed.

quickfire

3.7 What reason has been given to explain why people anthropomorphise God?

Key quote

Saadia upholds the absolute unity of God, and argues firmly for creation 'ex nihilo'. *(Stanford Encyclopedia of Philosophy)*

Key terms

Anthropomorphise: to attribute human form/behaviour/characteristics to God

Corporeal: having a bodily form

Lurianic Kabbalah: a school of Kabbalah named after Rabbi Isaac Luria who developed it

An early cosmological text, **Sefer Yezirah** or Book of Creation, appears at first to be a book of primitive science. Alexander describes it thus: 'In broad outline its teaching is clear; it offers an "atomic" theory of nature, i.e. it accounts for the diverse phenomena which go to make up the world in terms of varying combinations of a small number of irreducible elements or "atoms".' However, it is not without its problems as a major issue of interpretation arises from the fact that it appears to present two separate cosmologies; and furthermore, it fails to present a clear link between the two.

Alexander explains that the first cosmology is based upon the first ten numbers of the decimal system, which the text calls the ten Sefirot. It appears to suggest that creation took place in three phases:

Phase 1 sees the emergence of the first four Sefirot, which correspond to the 'Spirit of the Living God', and the basic elements of Air, Water and Fire. This process is characterised by a process of emanation (although the word itself is not used) and the text is noticeably reserved about deriving the 'Spirit of the Living God' from God.

Phase 2 takes place within the sphere of the three basic elements and is characterised by the verbs 'engrave' and 'hew out'. In the element of Air, God 'engraves and hews out' the twenty-two fundamental letters of the Hebrew alphabet. In the element of Water, God 'engraves and hews out' the primordial chaos from which the physical world emerged. In the element of Fire, God 'engraves and hews out' the **Merkavah**, the heavenly world of the Throne of Glory and the angels.

Phase 3 involves the fundamental letters and is characterised by the verb 'to seal'. God takes three of the letters and by arranging them in a variety of combinations establishes in infinite space the boundaries of the universe. The last six Sefirot correspond to the six dimensions of finite space. And so, the author of the work concludes, three principles were involved in the creation of the world: limit, letter and number.

The second cosmology treats the twenty-two letters of the Hebrew alphabet as the building blocks of the universe. The reasoning follows that language is composed of words, which in turn are composed of letters, and therefore speech 'is not only a means of communication but also an operational agent destined to produce being – it has an ontological value. This value, however, does not extend to every form of language; it belongs to the Hebrew language alone' (Vajda). In other words, speech does not merely name things; it calls them into being. This idea was probably suggested by the prominence which Genesis gives to God's speech in the process of creation.

> ### AO1 Activity
> Create a mind map that summarises facts about (a) God's nature and (b) God's actions, in relation to creation. This helps with the ability to select and present the key, relevant features of the material you have read.

Study tip

It is vital that you have a clear understanding of the various philosophical issues that relate to both the nature of God and to the creation event. When answering questions on this topic, make sure that you do not get confused.

T3 Significant social and historical developments in religious thought

quickfire

3.8 Name the early cosmological text that, according to Alexander, offers an 'atomic' theory of nature.

Key terms

Merkavah: meaning 'chariot'; a school of early Jewish mysticism, drawn from the Book of Ezekiel, signifying a mystical vision of divinity

Sefer Yezirah: Book of Creation; an early cosmological text

Key quotes

The Sefer Yezirah teaches us the existence of a Single Divine Power ... **(Ha-Levi)**

The twenty-two sounds and letters are the Foundation of all things. **(Sefer Yezirah)**

The challenge of science

Until the end of the fourteenth century or thereabouts, religion and science were in much closer agreement with each other, and it is an irony that science was born out of the work of both theologians and philosophers. Indeed, until the sixteenth century, the theologians and philosophers *were* the scientists. At that time, the religious and scientific worldviews agreed with each other because they acknowledged that scientific explanation always included a reference to God. The beginnings of modern science in the sixteenth century, however, led to a major change in the way in which people understood God's place in the universe and the divine relationship with human beings. This change resulted in a gradual separation of science and religion, so that it became possible to accept scientific principles without reference to God.

As a result of this shift, Epstein maintains that most modern thinkers have abandoned what traditionalists still believe: that God gave the Torah to Moses at Mount Sinai. As such, a modern contemporary view is that the Bible is not cosmology but literature, using stories, traditions and poetic devices such as **metaphor** to provide a narrative for the Jewish people. 'As such, its purpose is to discuss folk beliefs, not science, and to transmit a moral vision, a sense of personal and communal values, not provide a literal description, including offering a poetic description of the creation of the world.' (Epstein)

Many people consider religion and science to be in direct opposition to each other. On closer study, however, we can see that they have some things in common. For example, both seek to understand the world in which we live, as well as our place within that world. Furthermore, it doesn't mean that someone who believes that God created the world has to accept only the biblical account. It is possible that God used scientific laws to create the universe and all that it contains; and whilst creation is a religious and not a physical doctrine, physical laws become subsumed under religious ones. For example, the idea that God brought natural laws into existence to create the natural world is consistent with traditional Judaism: 'Thus said the Lord: As surely as I have established My covenant with day and night – the laws of heaven and earth – so I will never reject the offspring of Jacob and My servant David.' (Jeremiah 33:25–26)

Maimonides acknowledged the relationship between religion and science, and he was convinced that if Judaism was not open to investigation and philosophical reflection then it would be likely to contain heretical ideas. Furthermore, he was not averse to introducing scientific knowledge into his formulations of Jewish law. In the introduction to The Guide for the Perplexed he argues that Torah must be grounded in reason, and that divine science (metaphysics) can only be successfully undertaken after studying the natural sciences (physics). Maimonides wrote that if science and Torah were misaligned, it was either because science was not understood or that the Torah had been misinterpreted. It therefore followed that if science proved a point, then the finding should be accepted and scripture should be interpreted accordingly.

Key quote

… it is through wisdom, in an unrestricted sense, that the rational matter we receive from the Law through tradition is demonstrated. **(Maimonides)**

Key term

Metaphor: a thing regarded as representative or symbolic of something else

Some accept that it is possible that God used scientific laws to create the universe.

Jewish responses to the theory of evolution

As far as evolutionary concepts and ideas are concerned, in ancient times they had primarily been based on philosophical arguments rather than on **empirical** data. However, the advent of Charles Darwin's theory of evolution, which argued that life began with very simple cells and later developed into what we see today through a process of natural selection, brought about a discussion within the Jewish community regarding the relationship between the accepted principles of the faith and modern scientific findings. The scientific theory of evolution seems to contradict the biblical account of creation. Whilst the Bible claims that God created the world in six days, culminating with the creation of humanity, the theory of evolution asserts that humanity evolved over billions of years. How do Jews approach this contradiction?

Key quote

Judaism, as a religion, and certainly Conservative Judaism, sees creation as a purposeful process directed by God; however, each individual defines the Divine. This is clearly in consonance with the theory of Intelligent Design. What Darwin sees as random, we see as the miraculous and natural unfolding of God's subtle and beautiful plan. **(Schwab)**

Many ultra-Orthodox Jews reject the theory of evolution entirely. This is because they accept the Bible as embodying eternal truths. As a result of this, there is an unwillingness to re-interpret scripture in order to bring about a reconciliation with a scientific theory that, in their view, may be overhauled at some time in the future. Some ultra-Orthodox groups even go so far as to place a ban upon any Jewish books on evolution. For example, in 2005, a few ultra-Orthodox rabbis banned Natan Slifkin's books on science and Torah which seem to support evolutionary theory. Those who banned his books believed that he was challenging Jewish religious authority and thereby undermining the Jewish faith.

On the other hand, some Jews reject the biblical account of creation because it contradicts the theory of evolution. They see the Bible as an ancient human document that can no longer provide a meaningful understanding of the beginning of the universe for a person living in the twenty-first century. They therefore look to modern science to explain the origin of the world. Indeed, Pinker argues that the theory of natural selection best explains the origins of complex life, and no God could possibly have created a world that has so many faults in its design.

Another approach is to strive to integrate the biblical account with the findings of modern science. Some Orthodox Jewish scientists read evolutionary theory into the Bible, arguing that the Bible and modern scientific theory describe the same process using different language. A case in point is Gerald Schroeder, an Israeli physicist, who used Einstein's theory of relativity to explain how God's six days of creation are equivalent to fifteen billion years of scientific evolution.

Other Jewish thinkers such as Mordecai Kaplan and Yeshayahu Leibowitz, reconcile the biblical account and evolutionary theory by rejecting literal understandings of the Bible in favour of metaphorical or allegorical readings. They argue that the Bible is not meant to provide an accurate scientific description of the origins of the world; rather it is a spiritual account of *why* the world came into being and what the role of humankind is in it. These thinkers follow a long tradition of Jewish commentators who view the Bible non-literally, from rabbis of the Talmudic era to Maimonides.

T3 Significant social and historical developments in religious thought

Specification content
Evolution and different Jewish understandings of the creation process.

Key term
Empirical: based on experimental, observation or experience rather than on theory

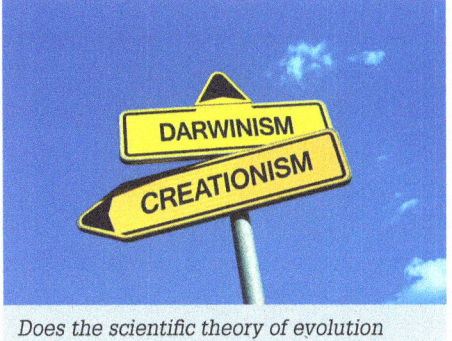

Does the scientific theory of evolution contradict the biblical account of creation?

WJEC / Eduqas Religious Studies for A Level Year 2 and A2 Judaism

> **Key term**
>
> **Palaeontology:** the branch of science concerned with fossil animals and plants

Key quotes

Conservative Judaism has always been premised on the total embrace of critical enquiry and science. More than being compatible with Conservative Judaism, I would say that it is a mitzvah to learn about the world and the way it works to the best of our abilities, since that is to marvel with awe at God's handiwork. To not do so is sinful. **(Fine)**

We have frameworks built into our system to integrate the findings of science into our religious and theological beliefs. This is because we believe that the natural world, and the way it works, was created by God and therefore its workings must be consistent with our religious beliefs. **(Schwab)**

Fossils are evidence of previous 'worlds' as described in some Kabbalistic texts.

Some Kabbalists also embrace many aspects of evolutionary theory as they hold that they corroborate their understanding of the origins of the world and its development. Rabbi Abraham Issac Kook, one of the Chief Rabbis of Israel, saw evolutionary theory as support for the Kabbalistic ideas of the unity of life and the progressive unfolding of natural history. In the 1800s Rabbi Lipschitz gave a famous lecture on Torah and **palaeontology** in which he said that the Kabbalistic texts teach that the world has gone through many cycles of history, each lasting for many tens of thousands of years. He linked this to the finding of dinosaur skeletons and the remains of woolly mammoths and concluded that: 'From all this, we can see that all the Kabbalists have told us for so many centuries about the fourfold destruction and renewal of the Earth has found its clearest possible confirmation in our time.' The ancient fossils were the remains of dinosaurs and other animals that had perished in the previous 'worlds' as described in some Kabbalistic texts.

By the early to mid-1900s, the majority of Conservative and Reform Jews came to accept the existence of evolution as a scientific fact, and interpreted Genesis and related Jewish teachings in the light of this information. For example, Conservative Judaism supports the use of science as the proper way to learn about the physical world in which we live, and encourages its members to understand evolution in a way that does not contradict the accepted scholarly findings of the scientists. However, Professor Ismar Schorsch writes that: 'The Torah's story of creation is not intended as a scientific treatise ... The note it strikes in its sparse and majestic narrative offers us an orientation to the Torah's entire religious worldview and value system. Creation is taken up first not because the subject has chronological priority but rather to ground basic religious beliefs in the very nature of things. And I would argue that their power is quite independent of the scientific context in which they were first enunciated.'

And Rabbi David J. Fine offers a commonly held Conservative view on the subject: 'Many of the people who accept evolution, even many scientists, believe in what is called "theistic evolution", that is, that behind the billions of years of cosmic and biological evolution, there is room for belief in a creator, God, who set everything into motion, and who stands outside the universe as the cause and reason for life.'

However Conservative Judaism has not yet developed a unified, official response to the subject, and therefore a broad range of views is evident.

> ### AO1 Activity
>
> After reading the section 'Jewish responses to the theory of evolution', close the book and finish off the following statements. You may need to write more than a sentence in order to give a coherent understanding of each point of view:
>
> 1. Ultra-Orthodox Jews reject the theory of evolution entirely because ...
> 2. Some Jews reject the biblical account of creation because ...
> 3. Some Orthodox Jews strive to integrate the biblical account with the findings of modern science because ...
> 4. Some Jewish thinkers reject literal understandings of the Bible in favour of metaphorical or allegorical readings because ...
> 5. Kabbalists embrace many aspects of evolutionary theory because ...
>
> Compare and discuss your sentences with someone else who has also completed the task. This will help to provide you with a summary of the relevant facts about Jewish responses to the theory of evolution.

The debate about the age of the universe

One of the most noteworthy contradictions between Torah and science is the age of the universe. According to the accepted Jewish calendar, the universe has been in existence for almost 6,000 years. It starts with the year 1 dated from the creation of the universe in the Book of Genesis. This timescale, however, stands in contradiction to scientific data that currently assumes that it was formed many billions of years ago.

Steinburg addresses this discrepancy by suggesting that it can be reconciled in two ways: 'either by endorsing the standard calculation of the Jewish calendar, and interpreting the scientific data differently; or by endorsing the scientific calculation and explaining the Jewish calendar differently'. He continues by claiming: 'Both are possible with no hard evidence to the contrary, either by science or by Judaism.' What he means by this is that even the scientific calculations concerning the age of the universe are based upon certain assumptions that the universe started from zero and that the laws of nature have never changed. Neither of these assumptions has been experimentally proven, and are therefore based upon belief and logic only.

According to classical rabbinic tradition, the view is that God created the world almost 6,000 years ago. This view has its basis in a chronology that was developed in a midrash named **Seder Olam**, which is based upon a literal reading of the Book of Genesis. However, there are also many other Jewish sources that provide evidence to suggest that the universe is older than scripture would have us believe. For example:

- Midrash Genesis Rabbah 3:7 notes that other worlds were created and destroyed before this present one was decided upon as the permanent one.

- Talmud Chaggiga 13b–4a states that there were 974 generations before God created Adam: 'R. Simeon the Pious said: These are the 974 generations who pressed themselves forward to be created.'

- Midrash Psalms 90:4 suggests that the first 'week' of creation as described in Genesis may not have been the same as the time reckoning we know today. The 'week' may have lasted for an extremely long period of time, suggesting that the kind of time spoken of is imaginary and conceptual rather than actual. Or indeed, it might well be understood as to be suggesting that human time is in an entirely different scale from divine time.

Psalm 90 might be suggesting that human time is in an entirely different scale from divine time.

Based upon these examples as well as scientific evidence, most modern rabbis accept that the universe is much older than that suggested by the Jewish calendar.

Study tip

There are many opportunities in this topic to show that you can use an extensive range of scholarly views/schools of thought. It is important, however, that you are accurate in their usage. Rather than just learning names, test yourself further by writing a short paragraph in connection with each one that summarises the viewpoint/argument that they have made.

T3 Significant social and historical developments in religious thought

Specification content
The debate about the age of the universe.

quickfire
3.9 Approximately how old is the universe according to the accepted Jewish calendar?

Key quotes

The biblical calendar age of the universe is calculated by adding up the generations since Adam. This reaches a number slightly under 6,000 years. **(Schroeder)**

The world may be only some 6,000 years old. God could have put the fossils in the ground and juggled the light arriving from distant galaxies to make the world appear to be billions of years old. There is absolutely no way to disprove this claim. **(Schroeder)**

For in Your sight a thousand years are like yesterday that has passed, like a watch of the night. **(Psalm 90:4)**

Key term

Seder Olam: meaning 'order (or chronology) of the world'; a text that contains a chronology of the Jewish people from the creation of the universe to the construction of the Second Temple in Jerusalem

quickfire
3.10 Name three Jewish sources that suggest that the universe is older than scripture would have us believe.

Key skills

Knowledge involves:

Selection of a range of (thorough) accurate and relevant information that is directly related to the specific demands of the question.

This means:

- Selecting relevant material for the question set
- Being focused in explaining and examining the material selected.

Understanding involves:

Explanation that is extensive, demonstrating depth and/or breadth with excellent use of evidence and examples including (where appropriate) thorough and accurate supporting use of sacred texts, sources of wisdom and specialist language.

This means:

- Effective use of examples and supporting evidence to establish the quality of your understanding
- Ownership of your explanation that expresses personal knowledge and understanding and NOT just reproducing a chunk of text from a book that you have rehearsed and memorised.

AO1 Developing skills

It is now important to consider the information that has been covered in this section; however, the information in its raw form is too extensive and so has to be processed in order to meet the requirements of the examination. This can be achieved by practising more advanced skills associated with AO1. For assessment objective 1 (AO1), which involves demonstrating 'knowledge' and 'understanding' skills, we are going to focus on different ways in which the skills can be demonstrated effectively, and also refer to how the performance of these skills is measured (see generic band descriptors for A2 [WJEC] AO1 or A Level [Eduqas] AO1).

▶ **Your next task is this:** Below is a **summary of the debate about the age of the universe**. At present it has no references at all to support the points made. Underneath the summary are two references to the works of scholars, and/or religious writings, that could be used in the outline in order to improve the summary. Your task is to rewrite the summary but make use of the references. Such phrases as 'according to ...', 'the scholar ... argues', or, 'it has been suggested by ...' may help. Usually a reference included a footnote but for an answer in an A Level essay under examination conditions this is not expected, although an awareness of which book your evidence refers to is useful (although not always necessary).

One of the most noteworthy contradictions between Torah and science is the age of the universe. According to the accepted Jewish calendar, the universe has been in existence for almost 6,000 years. This timescale, however, stands in contradiction to scientific data that currently assumes that it was formed many billions of years ago. One attempt to explain this discrepancy is to integrate the biblical account with the findings of modern science. Some Orthodox Jewish scientists read evolutionary theory into the Bible, arguing that the Bible and modern scientific theory describe the same process using different language.

The majority of Conservative and Reform Jews have, however, come to accept the existence of evolution as a scientific fact, and have thus interpreted Genesis and related Jewish teachings in the light of this information. Conservative Judaism, for example, supports the use of science as the proper way to learn about the physical world in which we live, and encourages its members to understand evolution in a way that does not contradict the accepted scholarly findings of the scientists.

'The biblical calendar age of the universe is calculated by adding up the generations since Adam. This reaches a number slightly under 6,000 years.' (Schroeder)

'Many of the people who accept evolution, even many scientists, believe in what is called "theistic evolution", that is that behind the billions of years of cosmic and biological evolution, there is room for belief in a creator, God, who set everything into motion, and who stands outside the universe as the cause and reason for life.' (Fine)

When you have completed the task, try to write another reference that you could use and further extend your answer.

Issues for analysis and evaluation

The success of Judaism in meeting the challenges posed by science

It has been argued that the emergence of what we now call modern science has led to a major change in the way in which people have come to understand God's place in the universe as well as God's relationship with humanity. This change has resulted in a gradual separation of science and religion, so that it has become possible to accept scientific principles without any reference to God whatsoever. It would therefore appear that one of the most basic principles of the Jewish faith, that God created the universe and everything in it, has been challenged by scientific investigation that deals only with hard facts that are visible, demonstrable, provable and verifiable.

Such is the central place of the belief that God is the creator of the universe within Judaism, that it might well be assumed that the Jewish faith provides a unified theory about the act of creation; however, this is not the case. There is evidence of much speculation about the nature of the act of creation to be found even within rabbinic literature. Genesis Rabbah provides numerous examples of debate on this matter. With respect to the order of creation, for example, there is disagreement between the School of Shammai and the School of Hillel. The former states that the heavens were created first, followed by the earth; whereas the latter argues in contrast that they were both created simultaneously in accordance with Genesis Rabbah 1:9. Other sources propose that God created the universe from materials that were pre-existent; whereas Rabbi Gamaliel argued that all of these materials were explicitly described as being created by God and were therefore not in existence beforehand. Such diversity of opinion, it could be argued, would suggest that Judaism does not hold a strong position that could be used successfully as a response to the challenges posed by science.

An alternative area for debate could be to suggest that science doesn't actually pose any challenge to Judaism at all, thus negating the question as to whether or not Judaism has been successful in responding to scientific findings. In order to illustrate this particular viewpoint, reference can be made to evolutionary theory. In ancient times, evolutionary concepts and ideas had primarily been based on philosophical arguments rather than on empiric data. However, the advent of Charles Darwin's theory of evolution, which argued that life began with very simple cells and later developed into what we see today through a process of natural selection, brought about a discussion within the Jewish community regarding the relationship between the accepted principles of the faith and modern scientific findings. The scientific theory of evolution presented a major challenge to the biblical account of creation. Whilst the Bible claims that God created the world in six days, culminating with the creation of humanity, the theory of evolution asserts that humanity evolved over billions of years. Notwithstanding scientific verification, many ultra-Orthodox Jews rejected, and continue to reject, the theory of evolution entirely. This is because they accept the Bible as embodying eternal truths. As a result of this, there is an unwillingness to re-interpret scripture in order to bring about a reconciliation with a scientific theory that, in their view, may be overhauled at some time in the future. Some ultra-Orthodox groups even go so far as to place a ban upon any Jewish books on evolution. For example, Natan Slifkin's books on science and Torah, which seem to support evolutionary theory, were banned by a number of ultra-Orthodox rabbis on the grounds that he was challenging Jewish religious authority and thereby undermining the Jewish faith. Thus we see that for this particular group within Judaism, science has posed no particular challenge other than how to deal with those who suggest that evolutionary theory actually does have a place within the Jewish worldview.

T3 Significant social and historical developments in religious thought

This section covers AO2 content and skills

Specification content
The success of Judaism in meeting the challenges posed by science.

Darwin's theory of evolution presented a major challenge to the biblical account of creation.

AO2 Activity

As you read through this section try to do the following:

1. Pick out the different lines of argument that are presented in the text and identify any evidence given in support.
2. For each line of argument try to evaluate whether or not you think this is strong or weak.
3. Think of any questions you may wish to raise in response to the arguments.

This Activity will help you to start thinking critically about what you read and help you to evaluate the effectiveness of different arguments and from this develop your own observations, opinions and points of view that will help with any conclusions that you make in your answers to the AO2 questions that arise.

Key quotes

Man is descended from a hairy, tailed quadruped, probably **arboreal** in its habits. **(Darwin)**

I have called this principle, by which each slight variation, if useful, is preserved, by the term of Natural Selection. **(Darwin)**

Key term

Arboreal: denoting an animal that lives mainly in trees

Study tip

In order to ensure that you have a clear understanding of the relationship between the religious and scientific responses to creation that have been mentioned in this section, make a comparison between the creation model according to Judaism and the evolutionary model for the origin of life.

Key questions

Does science pose a challenge to the Jewish belief that God created the universe and everything in it?

How have some Jews responded to Darwin's theory of evolution?

Is it acceptable to suggest that there is a positive relationship between science and religious belief for some Jews?

AO2 Activity

List some conclusions that could be drawn from the AO2 reasoning from the above text; try to aim for at least three different possible conclusions. Consider each of the conclusions and collect brief evidence to support each conclusion from the AO1 and AO2 material for this topic. Select the conclusion that you think is most convincing and explain why it is so. Try to contrast this with the weakest conclusion in the list, justifying your argument with clear reasoning and evidence.

Likewise, Maimonides did not acknowledge that science posed a problem to the Jewish faith. He accepted that there was a valid relationship between religion and science, and he was convinced that if Judaism was not open to investigation and philosophical reflection then it would be likely to contain heretical ideas. Furthermore, he was not averse to introducing scientific knowledge into his formulations of Jewish law. In the introduction to The Guide for the Perplexed he argues that Torah must be grounded in reason, and that divine science (metaphysics) can only be successfully undertaken after studying the natural sciences (that which we now call physics). Maimonides wrote that if science and Torah were misaligned, it was either because science was not understood or that the Torah had been misinterpreted. It therefore followed that if science proved a point, then the finding should be accepted and scripture should be interpreted accordingly.

To continue with the same line of argument, Epstein for instance indicates that a standard contemporary view within Judaism is that the Bible is not cosmology but literature which uses stories, traditions and metaphor to provide a narrative for the Jewish people. As such its purpose is not scientific, but acts as the means by which to transmit a moral vision, a sense of personal and communal values. It does not therefore provide a literal description but rather more offers a poetic depiction of the creation of the world and doesn't bring science into conflict with religious belief at all.

Furthermore, some assert that it is possible that God used scientific laws to create material reality and that while creation is a religious and not a physical doctrine, physical laws become subsumed under religious ones. Epstein suggests that the idea that God brought natural laws into existence to create the natural world in some sense corresponds with Jewish beliefs: 'Thus said the Lord: As surely as I have established My covenant with day and night – the laws of heaven and earth – so I will never reject the offspring of Jacob and My servant David.' (Jeremiah 33:25–26)

Key quote

It turns out that the world is not a riddle but a mystery. A riddle, after all, has an answer. We never learn the answer to the world. We learn only the limits of our knowledge, not the finished facts of the world. Facts can be confined by language or mathematical representations. The world's mystery eludes such confinements, making writing about the world particularly challenging. **(Epstein)**

The position held by the majority of Conservative and Reform Jews also provides confirmation that science does not pose a major threat to Jewish beliefs about the creation of the universe. Conservative Judaism, for example, supports the use of science as the proper way to learn about the physical world in which we live, and encourages its members to understand evolution in a way that does not contradict the accepted scholarly findings of the scientists. And Rabbi David J. Fine offers a commonly held Conservative view on the subject: 'Many of the people who accept evolution, even many scientists, believe in what is called "theistic evolution", that is, that behind the billions of years of cosmic and biological evolution, there is room for belief in a creator, God, who set everything into motion, and who stands outside the universe as the cause and reason for life.'

In conclusion, some might suggest that the very fact that Jewish beliefs about the creation of the universe still retain their relevance in contemporary society must surely bring us to the conclusion that Judaism has been successful in meeting the challenges posed by scientific discovery. Indeed, it could also be said that there are still many unanswered questions regarding the creation of the universe that science brings us no further along in understanding than religion.

Whether or not Judaism is compatible with science

A common view of the general relationship between Judaism and science is that the two are incompatible. On the one hand, science deals with hard facts that are visible, demonstrable, provable and verifiable. The Jewish faith, on the other hand, is concerned with values and beliefs that are subjective rather than objective; is based on things which are apparently unverifiable and not even visible; is based on faith and allowing no room for scientific principles which conflict with the basic beliefs of the faith.

Furthermore, as modern science progressed, its findings brought about a change in the way in which people came to understand God's place in the world. Science and the Jewish faith moved even further apart as it became possible to accept things without reference to God. For example, the universe was seen more as a 'machine' rather than the living creation of God, and there no longer remained the need to refer to God in order to explain how the world worked. Darwin's theory of evolution in particular can be seen to have undermined traditional Jewish views by proposing that life on earth developed in small steps over a long period of time, and that all living things were not in their final form at the time of creation. In relation to the theory of evolution, it could be argued that as far as the ultra-Orthodox branch of the Jewish faith is concerned, Judaism can never be compatible with science. This is because they reject the theory entirely based upon their acceptance of the Bible as embodying eternal truths. As a result of this, there is an unwillingness to re-interpret scripture in order to bring about reconciliation with a scientific theory. Such is the gulf between science and religion in this instance that in very recent times, Natan Slifkin's books on science and Torah, which seem to support evolutionary theory, were banned by a number of ultra-Orthodox rabbis on the grounds that he was challenging Jewish religious authority and thereby undermining the Jewish faith.

Another noteworthy contradiction between Torah and science regards the age of the universe. According to the accepted Jewish calendar, the universe has been in existence for almost 6,000 years. It starts with the year 1 dated from the creation of the universe in the Book of Genesis. This timescale, however, stands in contradiction to scientific data that currently assumes that it was formed many billions of years ago and suggests incompatibility with the beliefs of the Jewish faith. However, perhaps there is some compatibility after all, as there are also Jewish sources that provide evidence to suggest that the universe is actually older than scripture would have us believe. For example, Midrash Genesis Rabbah contains a reference to the fact that other worlds were created and destroyed before this present one was decided upon as the permanent one. A Talmudic reference also states that there were 974 generations before God created Adam. Interestingly, Midrash Psalms 90:4 suggests that the first 'week' of creation as described in Genesis may not have been the same as the time reckoning we know today. The 'week' may have lasted for an extremely long period of time, suggesting that the kind of time spoken of is imaginary and conceptual rather than actual. Or indeed, it might well be understood as to be suggesting that human time is in an entirely different scale from divine time. Whichever way one interprets it, it could be used to suggest that Judaism and science are not as far apart as has been assumed.

Key quote

Human genetics does not provide as poetic or simple a story as the biblical tale of Adam and Eve. And the Bible has a deliberate moral dimension that science does not include. **(Epstein)**

T3 Significant social and historical developments in religious thought

Specification content

Whether or not Judaism is compatible with science.

AO2 Activity

As you read through this section try to do the following:

1. Pick out the different lines of argument that are presented in the text and identify any evidence given in support.
2. For each line of argument try to evaluate whether or not you think this is strong or weak.
3. Think of any questions you may wish to raise in response to the arguments.

This Activity will help you to start thinking critically about what you read and help you to evaluate the effectiveness of different arguments and from this develop your own observations, opinions and points of view that will help with any conclusions that you make in your answers to the AO2 questions that arise.

Key quote

Because the Big Bang created time, the related question, What caused the Big Bang? also has no answer. There was no such entity as causation, which is a time-related phenomenon … A modern Jew might define God as identical to the Big Bang, but, like an identification of God with nature … such an identity has lost touch with Judaism's crucial understanding of the cosmos having a moral dimension. **(Epstein)**

Is it fair to say that Judaism is compatible with science?

Key questions

Does the debate about the age of the universe suggest that Judaism is totally incompatible with science?

Do all Jewish groups deny the validity of scientific findings?

How is it possible to reconcile the teachings of the Torah with the findings of modern science?

AO2 Activity

List some conclusions that could be drawn from the AO2 reasoning from the above text; try to aim for at least three different possible conclusions. Consider each of the conclusions and collect brief evidence to support each conclusion from the AO1 and AO2 material for this topic. Select the conclusion that you think is most convincing and explain why it is so. Try to contrast this with the weakest conclusion in the list, justifying your argument with clear reasoning and evidence.

Further evidence that Judaism has long been considered to be compatible with science can be offered with reference to Maimonides. In medieval times he accepted that there was a valid relationship between religion and science. He proposed that if Jews did not open their minds to investigation and philosophical reflection then they were in danger of absorbing heretical ideas. Furthermore, he was not averse to introducing scientific knowledge into his formulations of Jewish law. In the introduction to The Guide for the Perplexed he argues that Torah must be grounded in reason, and that divine science (metaphysics) can only be successfully undertaken after studying the natural sciences (that which we now call physics). Maimonides wrote that if science and Torah were misaligned, it was either because science was not understood or that the Torah had been misinterpreted. It therefore followed that if science proved a point, then the finding should be accepted and scripture should be interpreted accordingly.

It is also evident that it is possible for Judaism to be compatible with science without recourse to abandoning the Torah. Just as scientists are open to change, and are willing to discard theories when a new theory emerges, so too can we see a similar process in relation to the Torah amongst Reform Jews. Reform Jews believe in God's revelation and that the Torah contains many divine truths, but they attribute the authorship of the Torah to divinely inspired humans. Reform Jews accept the possibility that there is no guarantee that the writers were equally inspired in everything they wrote, and as a consequence of this, it is possible to re-interpret the mitzvot in order to meet changing circumstances.

Study tip

Research the concept of deism and the 'God of the gaps' theory in order to gain a deeper insight into the ways in which religion has responded to scientific findings that have changed our understanding of God's relationship with the world.

Additionally, it could be argued that the perceived, irreconcilable differences between the Torah and scientific findings are not in fact contradictory at all, and that it's all down to the way in which texts from the Torah are interpreted. One approach is to strive to integrate the biblical account with the findings of modern science by accepting that they are both describing the same process but by using different language. Jewish thinkers such as Kaplan and Leibowitz have brought about a reconciliation between the biblical account and evolutionary theory by rejecting literal understandings of the Bible in favour of metaphorical or allegorical readings. They argue that the Bible is not meant to provide an accurate scientific description of the origins of the world; rather it is a spiritual account of *why* the world came into being and what the role of humankind is in it. These thinkers follow a long tradition of Jewish commentators who view the Bible non-literally, from rabbis of the Talmudic era to Maimonides.

To continue with the same line of argument, Epstein for instance, indicates that a standard contemporary view within Judaism is that the Bible is not cosmology but literature which uses stories, traditions and metaphor to provide a narrative for the Jewish people. As such, its purpose is not scientific, but acts as the means by which to transmit a moral vision, a sense of personal and communal values. It does not therefore provide a literal description but rather more offers a poetic depiction of the creation of the world and doesn't bring science into conflict with religious belief at all.

In conclusion, although there will always be Jews who consider religion and science to be totally irreconcilable, there are also many who realise, and accept, that they are compatible in so many ways. And perhaps the most noteworthy issue that combines the two is that both seek to understand the world in which we live, as well as our place in that world.

AO2 Developing skills

It is now important to consider the information that has been covered in this section; however, the information in its raw form is too extensive and so has to be processed in order to meet the requirements of the examination. This can be achieved by practising more advanced skills associated with AO2. For assessment objective 2 (AO2), which involves 'critical analysis' and 'evaluation' skills, we are going to focus on different ways in which the skills can be demonstrated effectively, and also refer to how the performance of these skills is measured (see generic band descriptors for A2 [WJEC] AO2 or A Level [Eduqas] AO2).

▶ **Your next task is this:** Below is an **evaluation of the argument that science does not necessarily pose a problem to the Jewish faith**. At present it has no references at all to support the arguments presented. Underneath the evaluation are two references made to the works of scholars, and/or religious writings, that could be used in the evaluation in order to improve it. Your task is to rewrite the evaluation but make use of the references. Such phrases as 'in his/her book … (scholar) argues that …', 'an interesting argument in support of this is made by … who suggests that …', or, 'the work of (scholar) has made a major contribution to the debate by pointing out …' may help. Usually a reference included a footnote but for an answer in an A Level essay under examination conditions this is not expected, although an awareness of which book your evidence refers to is useful (although not always necessary).

Maimonides argued that there was a valid relationship between religion and science. His belief was based upon the conviction that if Judaism were to remain closed to the findings of scientific investigation and philosophical reflection, it would be more likely to contain heretical ideas. Furthermore, he was not averse to introducing scientific knowledge into his formulations of Jewish law. * Maimonides believed that if science and Torah were misaligned, it was either because science was not understood or that the Torah had been misinterpreted. It therefore follows, he argued, that if science proved a point, then the finding should be accepted and scripture should be interpreted accordingly.

Furthermore, some assert that it is possible that God used scientific laws to create material reality and that while creation is a religious and not a physical doctrine, physical laws become subsumed under religious ones. *

Introduction to The Guide for the Perplexed

Jeremiah 33:25–26

When you have completed the task, try to write another reference that you could use and further extend your evaluation.

T3 Significant social and historical developments in religious thought

Key skills
Analysis involves:

Identifying issues raised by the materials in the AO1, together with those identified in the AO2 section, and presents sustained and clear views, either of scholars or from a personal perspective ready for evaluation.

This means:

- That your answers are able to identify key areas of debate in relation to a particular issue
- That you can identify, and comment upon, the different lines of argument presented by others
- That your response comments on the overall effectiveness of each of these areas or arguments.

Evaluation involves:

Considering the various implications of the issues raised based upon the evidence gleaned from analysis and provides an extensive detailed argument with a clear conclusion.

This means:

- That your answer weighs up the consequences of accepting or rejecting the various and different lines of argument analysed
- That your answer arrives at a conclusion through a clear process of reasoning.

WJEC / Eduqas Religious Studies for A Level Year 2 and A2 Judaism

This section covers AO1 content and skills

Specification content
The role of the Pittsburgh Platform.

C: The development of Reform Judaism and Jewish attitudes to pluralism

The development of Reform Judaism

Solomon indicates that different forms of Judaism have existed side by side from as far back as the first century CE, with each group claiming to be the one which was based upon the original Torah. 'Unfortunately,' he says, 'we cannot go back to some "pure, authentic Torah" received and handed on by Moses' in order to find out who was correct. However, the rabbis believed that the Torah was preserved in its original form by earlier rabbis who passed on the information from generation to generation.

During the Middle Ages, the Jews confronted those who committed **heresy** by excommunicating them from the Jewish community for thirty days or more if the need arose. Such excommunication (the **herem**) would be followed by hardship, as exclusion meant that the ejected individual would suffer severe social and economic consequences as they would be unable to earn a living, and would no longer have a place in society. This meant therefore that people rarely questioned the accepted Jewish way of life.

However, things began to change in the eighteenth century when a significant number of Jews in Western European countries began to acquire **civil rights**. As a result of this, the traditional elders and rabbis lost some control over the way of life lived by the Jews in their communities. Questions and differences of opinion could no longer be suppressed, and many Jews started to perceive that aspects of traditional Jewish community life were becoming out-of-date. By the end of the eighteenth century, notes Solomon, three options remained for Western European Jews, particularly those living in Germany and France:

1. They could assimilate, which would result in the loss of Jewishness.
2. They could maintain their traditions unchanged, which would bring about alienation and the loss of civil rights.
3. They could change or modernise Judaism in order to gain social acceptance without abandoning their Jewish identity.

And it is from the third option that we see the emergence of the group that was to become known as Reform Judaism. 'It was not, at first, intended to be a separate movement. Only when the proposed changes were rejected by the traditionalists was Reform, as a distinct movement, born, and only then was the label "Orthodox" firmly attached to those who opposed the radical change.' (Solomon)

In the early nineteenth century, German Reformers acted to bring changes to areas such as public worship in an attempt to bring back those Jews who had abandoned the faith in order to gain social acceptance in the wider secular society. The Reformers felt that Jews who were falling away from the faith might be more drawn to attend services which were more contemporary in style. They aimed to make worship more beautiful and relevant by cutting out things which were no longer really applicable such as references to sacrifice. Prayers were said in German rather than in Hebrew, and organ music was introduced together with mixed choirs. After some opposition, the first Reform Temple to be successful was erected in 1818.

Key terms

Civil rights: the rights of all citizens to political, social and religious freedom and equality

Herem: ban; excommunication

Heresy: belief or opinion contrary to the authorised teachings of the faith

Laymen: people who do not hold religious office; i.e. in the Jewish faith, people who are not rabbis

Piety: being religiously sincere

Key quote

The pioneers of the Reform Movement were influential German **laymen** who sought to win back for Judaism those who were drifting away from it. Clearly, with so many Jews turning away from the faith, something had to be done to close the gap between the people and the traditional **piety**. (Close)

A Jewish choir, where young women and men sing together.

Modernisation of the liturgy, however, led to the need to re-evaluate Jewish theology, and the early principles of Reform Judaism were formulated by Rabbi Abraham Geiger (1810–1874). Geiger's philosophical deliberations regarding the revealed will of God led to the concept of Progressive Revelation which has become the basic principle of Reform Judaism. Progressive Revelation proposes that as society changes, then so must Judaism's response to such developments be modified in order to remain relevant. As Close puts it: 'Judaism then is evolutionary, a living faith which must change and grow. Each generation must question, re-examine, re-interpret its heritage for itself, i.e. in the light of its own needs and insights. What has been taught in the past is important and must be respected, but it is not necessarily the way forward for the future.' However, it is important to note that Geiger never saw himself as offering a new Judaism, rather it was the Judaism of the past brought up to date. He argued that the essence of Judaism was ethical monotheism, and that many traditional doctrines and practices no longer had any meaning or validity in the light of this opinion.

Rabbi Abraham Geiger (1810–1874)

This approach also led to a re-evaluation of the Torah as the divine revelation of God. Although Reform Jews believe that the Torah contains many divine truths, and that it remains the foundation of their faith, they attribute its authorship to divinely inspired human beings. As a consequence of this, it is possible to re-interpret the mitzvot according to the current needs or situation of the individual. Nevertheless, this does not detract from the importance of the Torah, which is still instructional, inspiring and a necessary resource.

The role of the Pittsburgh Platform

Although Reform Judaism had been established in Europe, it ultimately became a strong force in the United States. The first signs of Reform Judaism appeared in the United States in 1824 when a small group of congregants in Charlestown, South Carolina, attempted to introduce some of the reforms of Germany's Hamburg Temple into synagogue worship. As more Jewish migrants arrived in the United States, many settled in New York and founded communities for worship. Among those who arrived from Germany were a number of Reform rabbis who sought to establish the movement in the new country. Rabbi Isaac Mayer Wise (1819–1900), in particular, has been credited with guiding Reform Judaism to a position of great strength. Wise published a new Reform prayer book, as well as several Jewish newspapers. He was also responsible for establishing the Union of American Hebrew Congregations, the Hebrew Union College for the education of Reform rabbis, and the Central Conference of American Rabbis.

However, it wasn't until 1885 when a group of Reform rabbis met in Pittsburgh that the principles of American Reform Judaism were formally set down. The result of their deliberations is a list that has come to be known as the Pittsburgh Platform. Neusner notes that the Pittsburgh Platform takes up each component of the Reform system in turn:

1. Who is Israel?
2. What is its way of life?
3. How does it account for its existence as a distinct, and distinctive, group?

Neusner explains: 'Israel once was a nation but today is not a nation. It once had a set of laws that regulate diet, clothing, and the like. These no longer apply, because Israel is not now what it was then. Israel forms an integral part of Western civilisation.

T3 Significant social and historical developments in religious thought

Key terms

Ethical monotheism: God is the source of one standard of morality and requires that people act decently toward each other

Israel: used in this particular context as a term for the Jewish people

Progressive Revelation: the concept that old laws of the Bible are no longer applicable in modern society in which new ethical, moral and spiritual values have been 'revealed'

Theology: the study of God, religious belief and revelation

quickfire

3.11 Where was the first Reform Temple erected in 1818?

Key quotes

The Talmud, and the Bible too, that collection of books, most of them so splendid and uplifting, perhaps the most exalting of the literature of human authorship, can no longer be viewed as of Divine origin. (Geiger)

The defining characteristic of Reform Judaism is its attitude to the Revelation at Mount Sinai. (Romain)

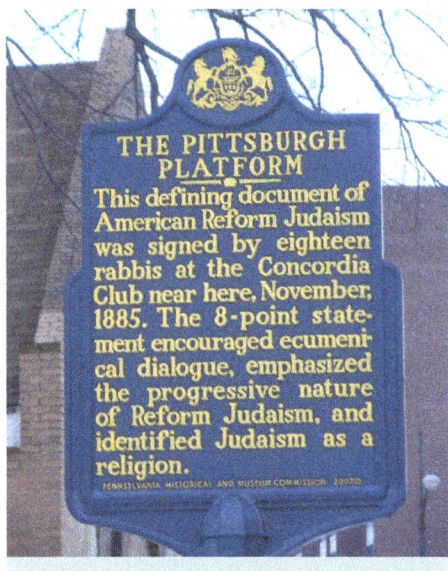

A plaque in commemoration of the Pittsburgh Platform.

WJEC / Eduqas Religious Studies for A Level Year 2 and A2 Judaism

quickfire

3.12 In which country did Reform Judaism become a strong force?

The reason to persist as a distinctive group was that the group has its work to do, a mission – to serve as a light to the nations. That meant, namely, to realise the messianic hope for the establishment of a kingdom of truth, justice, and peace. For that purpose, Israel no longer constitutes a nation. It now forms a religious community.'

Key quote

We recognise in the Mosaic legislation a system of training the Jewish people for its mission during its national life in Palestine, and today we accept as binding only the moral laws, and maintain only such ceremonies as elevate and sanctify our lives... We hold that all such Mosaic and rabbinical laws as regulate diet, priestly purity, and dress originated in ages and under the influence of ideas altogether foreign to our present mental and spiritual state ... Their observance in our days is apt rather to obstruct than to further modern spiritual elevation ... We consider ourselves no longer a nation, but a religious community, and therefore expect neither a return to Palestine, nor a sacrificial worship under the sons of Aaron, nor the restoration of any of the laws concerning the Jewish state. **(Pittsburgh Platform)**

The role of the Pittsburgh Platform can therefore be seen as that of providing an authoritative statement that established the principles of Reform Judaism. The statement called for the following things:

- Instead of a 'nation', Jews are to be regarded as a 'religious community' within whichever country they find themselves to be living.
- A rejection of laws which have a ritual rather than a moral basis. An example of this is a rejection of the Jewish dietary laws.
- That there is no longer a need to dress in a specific way.
- For Jews to live in different nations is a necessary thing, as they have been chosen to spread the monotheistic truth and morality over all the earth, and to be an example to others.

The legacy of the Pittsburgh Platform

Specification content

The legacy of the Pittsburgh Platform with reference to: attitudes towards liberationist thought (concern for the poor) and Tikkun Olam (repair of the world).

Reform Judaism has historically emphasised the need to fight for social justice; to work tirelessly for the rights of the downtrodden; and to create a just society on earth. This aim is set out clearly in the final clause of the Pittsburgh Platform which states: 'In full accordance with the spirit of the Mosaic legislation, which strives to regulate the relations between rich and poor, we deem it our duty to participate in the great task of modern times, to solve, on the basis of justice and righteousness, the problems presented by the contrasts and evils of the present organisation of society.'

In order to work towards this aim, the mission of Israel is to stand as an example of the highest standards of ethics and morals, and to bring the world to an awareness of, and commitment to, ethical monotheism. Satlow encapsulates this ideal in his summation of the Pittsburgh Platform: 'Here is a vision of a rational, universalistic Judaism rooted in its enduring preservation of the highest human religious truths, the God-idea, whose divine mission is to bring social justice to the world.'

Liberationist thought (concern for the poor) and Tikkun Olam (repair of the world)

Key term

Tikkun Olam: meaning 'repair of the world'; used in relation to social action and the pursuit of social justice

Liberationist thought is a term that is used to describe the movement which attempts to address the problems of poverty and injustice in the world; and social action is at its heart. Concern for the poor within liberationist thought lies within the broader category of **Tikkun Olam** (repair of the world). Tikkun Olam has its roots in classical rabbinic literature; however, since the 1950s it has come to denote the concept of repairing the world through human actions and the pursuit of social justice. This sentiment is echoed in the Pittsburgh Platform, as well as the Jewish prayer book which emphasises the fact that the Jews have a sacred mission to: 'perfect the world under the Kingdom of God'. (**Alenu**)

Dosick explains the background to the concept of Tikkun Olam: 'Created in the image of God, Jews – and all human beings who follow the Jewish model – are not to be mere spectators, mere bystanders, in the unfolding process of creation and daily existence ... Rather, we are here on earth to be active participants, partners with God, in the task of building up the world and making it into the best place that it can be.' The Jewish mission is thus to use the resources that God has provided in order to work to combat the injustices that are evident in the world; to bring the world closer to transformation and perfection.

Social action is thereby the means by which one's ethical thoughts are transformed into deeds and campaigns. Examples of such actions can be seen within the Jewish concepts of **tzedakah** and **gemilut hasadim**.

The Hebrew word tzedakah is usually translated as 'charity'; however, its literal meaning is 'justice' or 'righteousness'. When a Jewish person carries out a charitable act, they are undertaking one of the most basic requirements of the mitzvot: that of providing for those who are unable to provide for themselves. Thus, for Jews, charitable acts are more than just showing a kindness by making a donation to a worthy cause; they are considered to be right actions which are just as important as any other mitzvot. The Torah says 'There will always be poor people in the land. Therefore I command you to be open-handed toward your fellow Israelites who are poor and needy.' (Deuteronomy 15:11)

One of the ways in which a Jewish person can give to charity on a regular basis is through a **tithe** (which is the giving of a tenth of their income, after taxes have been taken, to charity). Judaism sees this act as moving some way towards redressing the balance between those who are fortunate and those who are not.

However, tzedakah is not only about giving money to worthy causes. The Talmud says: 'Just as God visits the sick, feeds the hungry and clothes the naked, so you do the same.' It is important to show kindness and mercy to those who are in difficulty and who need support. This can be done best by giving up one's time to help someone.

Giving of one's own time and effort is called gemilut hasadim, which literally means 'the giving of loving kindness', and is all about doing good deeds. An important aspect of gemilut hasadim is that it is something which anyone can do; both rich and poor alike, and it is done without expecting anything in return.

Social action in the shape of Tikkun Olam is undoubtedly a vast area in a world where there are so many causes that deserve attention. Dosick addresses this challenge: 'The task seems overwhelming, impossible for any one person in any one generation. And it is. That is why an ancient sage taught, "It is not your task to complete the work, but you are not free to desist from it".' (Pirkei Avot 2:21)

AO1 Activity

Undertake an online research task in order to find actual examples of Jewish social action campaigns. Synagogue websites are a good place to start, but using the terms gemilut hasadim and tzedakah might also be helpful.

Study tip

The writings of Maimonides concerning the 'ladder of tzedakah' also give an important insight into concern for the poor. It would be helpful to remind yourself of what he had to say on this matter.

T3 Significant social and historical developments in religious thought

Key terms

Alenu: the prayer that marks the end of all three daily prayer services at the synagogue

Gemilut hasadim: 'the giving of loving kindness'; doing good deeds

Tithe: the giving of a tenth of one's income, after taxes have been taken, to charity

Tzedakah: 'charity'; literal meaning is 'justice' or 'righteousness'

quickfire

3.13 What does the term 'liberationist thought' refer to?

Charitable deeds are acts of devotion

Key quotes

Reform Jews are committed to social justice ... Like the prophets, we never forget that God is concerned about the everyday and that the blights of society take precedence over the mysteries of heaven. A Reform synagogue that does not alleviate the anguish of suffering is a contradiction in terms. **(Yoffie)**

To do what is right and just is more desired by the Lord than sacrifice. **(Proverbs 21:3)**

One who is gracious to a poor man lends to the Lord, and God will repay him for his good deed. **(Proverbs 19:17)**

Whosoever has not pity upon his fellow man is no child of Abraham. **(Talmud)**

Specification content

Attitudes towards other religions; the diversity of views in Reform and Orthodox Judaism towards interfaith dialogue.

Reform Judaism accepts the validity of other religious traditions in addition to its own.

Attitudes towards other religions

Key quote

(Reform Jews) have also accepted the fundamentally post-modern concept of religious pluralism – the view that different or contradictory forms of Judaism (and non-Jewish) belief and practice can (or even should) coexist. (Wright)

Religious pluralism is the view that no one religion can claim to be the sole and exclusive source of truth. Religious pluralism thus recognises that some level of truth and value exists in other religious traditions too. Reform Judaism accepts the validity of other religions, and clause 1 of the Pittsburgh Platform is unequivocal on this matter: 'We recognise in every religion an attempt to grasp the Infinite, and in every mode, source or book of revelation held sacred in any religious system the consciousness of the indwelling of God in man.'

This pluralistic outlook was in contrast to what had gone before. Previously, Jewish thinkers had argued that Judaism contains God's fullest revelation to humankind. Thus it is the superior religion, surpassing all rivals. Even the most liberal thinkers maintained that all human beings will eventually acknowledge the truth of Jewish monotheism.

In 1999, just over a century after the first Pittsburgh Platform declaration, the Central Conference of American Rabbis returned to the city, and addressed familiar themes. However, whereas the first Platform recognised 'in every religion an attempt to grasp the Infinite', the new statement advocates that Reform Jews 'seek dialogue and joint action with people of other faiths in the hope that together we can bring peace, freedom and justice to our world.'

Cohn-Sherbok explains the impact of this declaration on Jewish beliefs about God's revelation:

> 'Instead of declaring that God uniquely disclosed his word to the Jewish people in the Hebrew Scriptures as well as through the teachings of rabbinic scholars, Jews should recognise that their Holy Writ is simply one record among others. Both the Written and the Oral Torah have particular significance for Jewry, but this does not imply that these writings contain a uniquely true and superior divine disclosure. Instead, the Torah as well as rabbinic literature should be conceived as a record of the spiritual life of the nation and testimony of its religious quest. As such, it should be viewed in much the same light as the New Testament, the Qur'an, the Bhagavad Gita, and the Vedas. For the Jewish people, their own sacred literature has special significance, but it should not be regarded as possessing truth for all humankind.'

Reform Jews acknowledge that their sacred literature is one record among others.

Reform Jewish attitudes to pluralism also included a revision of the doctrine of the Jews as the chosen people of God. As Cohn-Sherbok explains: 'In fact, however, there is simply no way of determining if a single group stands in a unique relationship with God ... other traditions have proposed a similar view of both general and special providence, yet maintain that God's action in the world has taken an entirely different course ... such differences in interpretation highlight the subjective nature of all belief systems.'

The Reform attitude to pluralism is also evident in the liturgy. For example, the Alenu has been altered by changing one of the daily blessings that praises God for 'not making me a Gentile'. This negative statement in the original implies that there is something wrong with being a non-Jew. Instead of praising God for not being a gentile, the prayer now thanks God 'who made me a Jew'. This modification allows worshippers to continue to celebrate their heritage, and yet it is done in a positive way without expressing a negative evaluation of others who are not of the Jewish faith.

Diversity of views in Reform and Orthodox Judaism towards interfaith dialogue

The Pittsburgh Platform of 1999 advocates that Reform Jews 'seek dialogue and joint action with people of other faiths in the hope that together we can bring peace, freedom and justice to our world'. This indicates a clear openness towards the promotion of interfaith dialogue. Reform Jews today believe that such dialogue is important because many societies are now diverse and multicultural. The Torah also supports interfaith partnerships by teaching that it is important to accept others without prejudice: 'You shall not take vengeance or bear a grudge against your countrymen. Love your fellow as yourself.' (Leviticus 19:18)

The importance of working with those from other faiths in the community is also encouraged in order to achieve social justice. The Talmud says: 'In a city where there are both Jews and Gentiles, the collectors of alms collect from both Jews and Gentiles; they feed the poor of both, visit the sick of both, bury both and restore the lost goods of both, for the sake of peace.' To this end, the Reform Jewish community has become involved with those of the Christian faith, for example, through the work of the International Council of Christians and Jews (ICCJ). The mission statement of the ICCJ states that its purpose is to:

- Promote understanding and cooperation between Jews and Christians based on respect for each other's identity and integrity
- Address issues of human rights
- Counter all forms of prejudice and discrimination
- Recognise the integrity and 'otherness' of each other's faith
- Coordinate worldwide activities in order to examine current issues across national and religious boundaries
- Encourage research and education in order to promote inter-religious understanding
- Perform outreach in regions that have little or no Jewish-Christian dialogue
- Provide a platform for wide-ranging theological debate in order to bring a religious choice to the contemporary search for answers to existential and ethical challenges.

T3 Significant social and historical developments in religious thought

quickfire

3.14 What does the term religious pluralism mean?

quickfire

3.15 Which prayer in Judaism has been altered by Reform Judaism from 'not making me a Gentile' to 'who made me a Jew'?

Key terms

Alms: donations of food, money, etc., for the poor

Existential: relating to human existence

Gentile: the term used for a person who is not a Jew

Key terms

Particularism: the doctrine that God has chosen to have a relationship with one particular group (in this case, the Jews) rather than a relationship which is open to everyone

Universal: relating to all people, and not just to one particular group

Key quote

Both these universalistic and particularistic elements co-exist side by side within Judaism, and perhaps not always perceived from within as separate, and in some ways conflicting perspectives. **(Unterman)**

CJCUC

Key quote

The time will soon be with us when a theologian who attempts to work out his position unaware that he does so as a member of a world society in which other theologians equally intelligent, equally devout … are Hindus, Buddhists, Muslims … is as out of date as is one who attempts to construct an intellectual position unaware that Aristotle has thought about the world … **(Smith)**

However, this is not the view currently held within Judaism as a whole, and as such there is diversity of opinion within the faith regarding the need for interfaith dialogue. The traditional view within the Orthodox tradition, for instance, is that God has entered into an exclusive covenant with the Jews. When Moses ascended Mount Sinai, God called to him and promised to stay with the Jews, never to abandon them, because they were now a divinely chosen people: 'Now if you obey me fully and keep my covenant, then out of all nations you will be my treasured possession.' (Exodus 19:5) On the one hand, this suggests a covenant based upon **particularism**; a belief that Judaism is the one true faith.

However, the Torah begins with God creating a covenant first with Adam, and then with Noah. These covenants had both been **universal** in nature, and it could be argued that when they failed, God's role for Abraham was to lead his descendants both spiritually and literally to the establishment of a nation. This was to be done in such a way as to show the *whole world* that God was the one and only all-powerful God, whom people should follow and worship. Reference to this universalistic perspective can be found within classical rabbinic literature: 'The Holy One, blessed be He, exiled Israel among the nations only in order that they should add converts to their number.' (Rabbi Eleazer ben Pedat) This can also be interpreted as suggesting that Judaism is the one true faith to which all should aspire.

Rabbi Joseph Soloveitchik and Rabbi Moshe Feinstein, both principal Orthodox Rabbinic leaders, recorded their opinions on interfaith dialogue in response to Pope Paul XXIII who had extended a hand of friendship to the Jews in an attempt to mend relations with them. Soloveitchik wrote: 'We are a totally independent faith community. We do not revolve as a satellite in any orbit. Nor are we related to any other faith community as "brethren" even though "separated".' He acknowledged the historical relationship between Judaism and Christianity since the latter grew out of the former. However, he argued against legitimising the relationship for fear that it would lead to the affirmation of the Church that Judaism's sole purpose was to pave the way for Christianity.

Meanwhile, it appears from Feinstein's deliberations that interfaith dialogue is Halakhically prohibited, based upon the concern that Jews might be enticed by the faith and values of other religions.

However, not all Orthodox Jews disparage interfaith dialogue; for example, a public statement entitled 'To Do the Will of Our Father in Heaven: Toward a Partnership between Jews and Christians' was published on the website of the Centre for Jewish-Christian Understanding and Cooperation (CJCUC). It was signed by 30 Orthodox rabbis and recognised the need for a common mission between Jews and Christians to perfect the world under the sovereignty of God.

AO1 Activity

Write down five key points you have learned about the role and legacy of the Pittsburgh Platform.

This will help in selecting relevant information for an answer to a question that expects knowledge and understanding of the development of Reform Judaism.

Study tip

When answering a question on Jewish attitudes to pluralism, make sure to remember that the focus in the specification is on how Judaism interacts with other faiths: '… attitudes towards other religions …'

AO1 Developing skills

It is now important to consider the information that has been covered in this section; however, the information in its raw form is too extensive and so has to be processed in order to meet the requirements of the examination. This can be achieved by practising more advanced skills associated with AO1. For assessment objective 1 (AO1), which involves demonstrating 'knowledge' and 'understanding' skills, we are going to focus on different ways in which the skills can be demonstrated effectively, and also refer to how the performance of these skills is measured (see generic band descriptors for A2 [WJEC] AO1 or A Level [Eduqas] AO1).

▶ **Your final task for this theme is:** Below is a **summary of the diversity of views in Reform and Orthodox Judaism towards interfaith dialogue**. You want to use this in an essay but as it stands it is undeveloped and has no quotations or references in it at all. This time you have to find your own quotations (about 3) and use your own references (about 3) to develop the answer. Sometimes a quotation can follow from a reference but they can also be used individually as separate points.

One branch of Judaism, the Reform movement, strongly supports interfaith dialogue, and believes that it is important in a world in which many societies are now diverse and multicultural. The importance of working with those from other faiths in the community is also encouraged in order to achieve social justice. As a result of this, the Reform Jewish community has become involved with those of the Christian faith; for example, through the work of the International Council of Christians and Jews (ICCJ).

However, this is not the view currently held within Judaism as a whole. The traditional view within the Orthodox tradition, for instance, is that God has entered into an exclusive covenant with the Jews. On the one hand, this suggests a covenant based upon particularism, and presents an interpretation that could be used to suggest that Judaism is the one true faith to which all others should aspire.

The result will be a fairly lengthy answer and so you could then check it against the band descriptors for A2 (WJEC) or A Level (Eduqas) and in particular have a look at the demands described in the higher band descriptors towards which you should be aspiring. Ask yourself:

- Does my work demonstrate thorough, accurate and relevant knowledge and understanding of religion and belief?
- Is my work coherent (consistent or make logical sense), clear and well organised?
- Will my work, when developed, be an extensive and relevant response which is specific to the focus of the task?
- Does my work have extensive depth and/or suitable breadth and have excellent use of evidence and examples?
- If appropriate to the task, does my response have thorough and accurate reference to sacred texts and sources of wisdom?
- Are there any insightful connections to be made with other elements of my course?
- Will my answer, when developed and extended to match what is expected in an examination answer, have an extensive range of views of scholars/schools of thought?
- When used, is specialist language and vocabulary both thorough and accurate?

T3 Significant social and historical developments in religious thought

Key skills

Knowledge involves:

Selection of a range of (thorough) accurate and relevant information that is directly related to the specific demands of the question.

This means:

- Selecting relevant material for the question set
- Being focused in explaining and examining the material selected.

Understanding involves:

Explanation that is extensive, demonstrating depth and/or breadth with excellent use of evidence and examples including (where appropriate) thorough and accurate supporting use of sacred texts, sources of wisdom and specialist language.

This means:

- Effective use of examples and supporting evidence to establish the quality of your understanding
- Ownership of your explanation that expresses personal knowledge and understanding and NOT just reproducing a chunk of text from a book that you have rehearsed and memorised.

WJEC / Eduqas Religious Studies for A Level Year 2 and A2 Judaism

This section covers AO2 content and skills

Specification content
The effectiveness of Jewish responses to pluralism.

Issues for analysis and evaluation

The effectiveness of Jewish responses to pluralism

It could be argued that religious pluralism, the view that no one religion can claim to be the sole and exclusive source of truth, appears initially to present an outlook that is in contradiction to the traditional standpoint of the Jewish faith. Those who claim that this is the case would argue that it is Judaism alone that contains God's exclusive revelation to humanity. According to the Orthodox tradition, when Moses ascended Mount Sinai, God called to him and promised to stay with the Jews, never to abandon them, because they were now a divinely chosen people: 'Now if you obey me fully and keep my covenant, then out of all nations you will be my treasured possession.' (Exodus 19:5) On the one hand this suggests a covenant based upon particularism, and as such, renders a discussion about the effectiveness of Jewish responses to pluralism as invalid.

Some, however, have pointed out that the Torah actually begins with God creating a covenant first with Adam, and then with Noah, and that these covenants had both been universal in nature. This interpretation could therefore be used as evidence to suggest that Judaism does not hold the singular position in God's relationship with humanity; and indeed might indicate that pluralism is a standpoint that is relevant within the faith. However, even though this universalistic perspective can also be found within the classical rabbinic tradition, it has been interpreted as implying that Judaism is the one true faith to which the whole world should aspire. This understanding can be seen in the writing of Rabbi Eleazer ben Pedat, for example: 'The Holy One, blessed be He, exiled Israel among the nations only in order that they should add converts to their number.'

However, not all Jewish denominations have denied the existence of religious pluralism outright as have many within Orthodox Judaism. Reform Judaism stands out in particular as being totally accepting of the validity of other religions. Indeed clause 1 of the Pittsburgh Platform is unequivocal on this matter: 'We recognise in every religion an attempt to grasp the Infinite, and in every mode, source or book of revelation held sacred in any religious system the consciousness of the indwelling of God in man.' It could therefore reasonably be argued that because Reform Judaism accepts the validity of other world faiths, it, amongst other Jewish groups, presents us with the best opportunity of assessing the effectiveness or otherwise of responses to pluralism.

Some would begin by perceiving that the attitude that Reform Jews have accepted with regard to pluralism has been effective in bringing about significant changes in the way in which Jews from this particular group have come to view their relationship with God, as well as their place and role in the world. For example, as Cohn-Sherbok points out, the very fact that Reform Jews accept that the Torah is simply one record amongst others leads them to accept that the writings of other faiths such as the New Testament, the Qur'an and the Bhagavad Gita, and the Vedas, for example, should all be held in the same regard. However, this in no way implies that the importance of the Torah has been diluted in any way, shape, or form. For Reform Jews, their own sacred literature continues to hold special significance, but they hold that it should not be regarded as possessing the truth for all of humanity.

Reform Jewish attitudes to pluralism have also been effective in bringing about a revision of the doctrine of the Jews as the chosen people of God. Instead of a 'nation', Reform Jews now regard themselves as a 'religious community'. Further evidence of the pluralistic nature of Reform Judaism is also evident in the liturgy.

For example, the Alenu has been altered by changing one of the daily blessings that praises God for 'not making me a gentile'. This negative statement in the original implies that there is something wrong with being a non-Jew. Instead of praising

Key quote

Both Jews and Christians have a common covenantal mission to perfect the world under the sovereignty of the Almighty, so that all humanity will call on His name and abominations will be removed from the earth. We understand the hesitation of both sides to affirm this truth and we call on our communities to overcome these fears in order to establish a relationship of trust and respect.
(Orthodox Rabbinic Statement on Christianity, CJCUC)

AO2 Activity

As you read through this section try to do the following:

1. Pick out the different lines of argument that are presented in the text and identify any evidence given in support.
2. For each line of argument try to evaluate whether or not you think this is strong or weak.
3. Think of any questions you may wish to raise in response to the arguments.

This Activity will help you to start thinking critically about what you read and help you to evaluate the effectiveness of different arguments and from this develop your own observations, opinions and points of view that will help with any conclusions that you make in your answers to the AO2 questions that arise.

God for not being a gentile, the prayer now thanks God 'who made me a Jew'. This modification allows worshippers to continue to celebrate their heritage, and yet it is done in a positive way without expressing a negative evaluation of others who are not of the Jewish faith.

Study tip

It is important to have a clear understanding of the concepts of 'particularism' and 'universalism' so that you are able to use them accurately when analysing the ways in which different denominations within Judaism view pluralism.

Many would argue that an assessment of the effectiveness of Jewish responses to pluralism should include an analysis of the ways in which Jews interact with other faith communities. One area which lends itself to such analysis concerns the matter of interfaith dialogue. Once again, it could be claimed, it is principally Reform Judaism that has been effective in this area. Evidence for this assertion can be found in the Pittsburgh Platform of 1999 which advocates that Reform Jews 'seek dialogue and joint action with people of other faiths in the hope that together we can bring peace, freedom and justice to our world'. However, perhaps the effectiveness of this declaration can only fully be judged by the actions that have emerged from it.

It can certainly be acknowledged that the Reform Jewish community has become involved with those of the Christian faith, for example, through the work of the International Council of Christians and Jews. This partnership has been established not only to bring about a greater understanding of each other's faiths, but also in order to address issues of human rights with a view to achieving social justice. On the other hand, it could be argued, however, that interfaith dialogue has been somewhat limited to that between the Jewish and the Christian traditions because there are already strong links between these two faiths. In this particular instance it could therefore be suggested that even though the effectiveness of the Jewish response to pluralism is evident in its work with Christianity, there is still much more to be done as far as other world faiths are concerned.

Interfaith dialogue exists between Judaism and Christianity.

In addition, the conventional Orthodox position is that interfaith dialogue is not relevant. Evidence for this can be cited in the words of Rabbi Soloveitchik who wrote: 'We are a totally independent faith community'. He further argued that legitimising a relationship between Judaism and Christianity would lead to the affirmation of the Church that Judaism's sole purpose was to pave the way for Christianity. Furthermore, Feinstein judged interfaith dialogue to be Halakhically prohibited, based upon the concern that Jews might be enticed by the faith and values of other religions.

In conclusion, some might say that pluralism has been effective in cases where working to ensure social action in partnership with another faith has brought about discernible and positive results. However, it is also evident that attitudes are changing towards pluralism within the Orthodox tradition. For example, 30 Orthodox rabbis recently signed a public statement that recognises the need for a common mission between Jews and Christians to perfect the world under the sovereignty of God. This suggests that there is a spiritual value to pluralism which transcends religious differences. Although we all come from Adam, the Mishnah proposes that human difference testifies to God's glory. If so, then it could be argued that Jews should celebrate the human diversity that is to be found within different religious traditions.

T3 Significant social and historical developments in religious thought

Key questions

Does the universalistic aspect of the Jewish covenant relationship necessarily mean that there should be acceptance of other religious faiths?

To what extent has accepting the validity of other faiths brought about significant changes to the way in which Reform Jews view their own relationship with God and their role in the world?

Is it acceptable to say that the Jewish faith has been successful in working in partnership with a great variety of world faiths?

Key quote

Our partnership in no way minimises the ongoing differences between the two communities and two religions. We believe that G-d employs many messengers to reveal His truth, while we affirm the fundamental ethical obligations that all people have before G-d that Judaism has always taught through the universal Noachide covenant.
(Orthodox Rabbinic Statement on Christianity, CJCUC)

AO2 Activity

List some conclusions that could be drawn from the AO2 reasoning from the above text; try to aim for at least three different possible conclusions. Consider each of the conclusions and collect brief evidence to support each conclusion from the AO1 and AO2 material for this topic. Select the conclusion that you think is most convincing and explain why it is so. Try to contrast this with the weakest conclusion in the list, justifying your argument with clear reasoning and evidence.

WJEC / Eduqas Religious Studies for A Level Year 2 and A2 Judaism

> **This section covers AO2 content and skills**

> **Specification content**
> The effectiveness of the Pittsburgh Platform in relation to the plight of the poor.

The effectiveness of the Pittsburgh Platform in relation to the plight of the poor

There is no doubt that Reform Judaism has always emphasised the need to fight for social justice and the plight of the poor. Nowhere is this aim more clearly delineated than in the Pittsburgh Platform of 1885 which states: 'In full accordance with the spirit of the Mosaic legislation, which strives to regulate the relations between rich and poor, we deem it our duty to participate in … (and) to solve, on the basis of justice and righteousness, the problems presented by the … present organisation of society.' However, in order to judge the effectiveness of this particular clause from the Pittsburgh Platform, it is necessary to discern whether or not it was more than merely a statement of intent. In other words, have its principles been effectively applied in relation to the plight of the poor?

Some might argue, however, that concern for the plight of the poor has always been an important aim within Judaism, and that the Pittsburgh Platform has brought nothing new to the Jewish faith on this account. The basis of this particular contention can be found in the concept of Tikkun Olam which has its roots in classical rabbinic literature. As Rabbi Jonah said: 'It is not written "Happy is he who gives to the poor," but "Happy is he who considers the poor".'

Other references from the Hebrew Scriptures can also be used as evidence to indicate that acts of kindness have always been required as a means by which to perfect or repair the world. One example among many is that from Proverbs 31:20 which notes: '(A capable woman) gives generously to the poor; her hands are stretched out to the needy.' Thus it is evident that the concept of Tikkun Olam has always been significant within the Jewish religion, and that it was seen as an effective means of ensuring a safeguard to those in society who may have been at a disadvantage.

Furthermore, examples of such actions are evident within the Jewish concepts of tzedakah and gemilut hasadim which have been fundamental within the Jewish faith since its inception. For example, the concept of tzedakah relates to the carrying out of a charitable act, and when a Jewish person undertakes such an act they are undertaking one of the most basic requirements of the mitzvot: that of providing for those who are unable to provide for themselves. The Torah says (in Deuteronomy 15:11): 'There will always be poor people in the land. Therefore I command you to be open-handed toward your fellow Israelites who are poor and needy.' Giving to the poor on a regular basis has also been an integral part of tzedakah, with many Jews contributing a tenth of their income to charity. Likewise, gemilut hasadim, the giving of one's time to help others, has been, and continues to be, one of the important means by which to address the plight of those in need throughout all branches of Judaism.

Key quote

How we give Tzedakah is as important as what we give. 'Do not humiliate a beggar', the Talmud warns us. 'God is beside him'. Rabbi Eleazar said, 'The reward that is paid for giving charity is directly related to the kindness with which it is given.' Deuteronomy 15:10 cautions, 'Your heart should not be grieved when you give'. (Robinson)

> **AO2 Activity**
> As you read through this section try to do the following:
> 1. Pick out the different lines of argument that are presented in the text and identify any evidence given in support.
> 2. For each line of argument try to evaluate whether or not you think this is strong or weak.
> 3. Think of any questions you may wish to raise in response to the arguments.
>
> This Activity will help you to start thinking critically about what you read and help you to evaluate the effectiveness of different arguments and from this develop your own observations, opinions and points of view that will help with any conclusions that you make in your answers to the AO2 questions that arise.

T3 Significant social and historical developments in religious thought

Key quote

We bring Torah into the world when we strive to fulfil the highest ethical mandates in our relationships with others and with all of God's creations. Partners with God in Tikkun Olam, repairing the world, we are called to help bring nearer the messianic age. We seek dialogue and joint action with people of other faiths in the hope that together we can bring peace, freedom and justice to our world. (Pittsburgh Platform 1999)

However, some might claim that the Pittsburgh Platform brought a new impetus to the need to address the plight of the poor; and that it gave the new movement its own particular identity. Thus the Pittsburgh Platform served to highlight the Reform movement's mission as that of standing as an example of the highest standards of ethics and morals, in order to bring the world to an awareness of, and commitment to, ethical monotheism. Feldman illustrates this contention when he says: 'It has become axiomatic that to be a Jew is to care about the world around us. To be a Reform Jew is to hear the voice of the prophets in our head; to be engaged in the ongoing work of Tikkun Olam; to strive to improve the world in which we live.' Feldman thereby acknowledges the heritage of Tikkun Olam within Judaism as a whole when he writes of the 'ongoing work'; however, it is significant that he continues by making a particular connection between Reform Judaism and the prophets of the Hebrew Scriptures. Amos, for example, expressed his concern for the poor: 'I loathe, I spurn your festivals, I am not appeased by your solemn assemblies ... But let justice well up like water, righteousness like an unfailing stream.' (Amos 5:21–24) In other words, the passion for social justice in relation to the plight of the poor is to be exemplified by action rather than ritual.

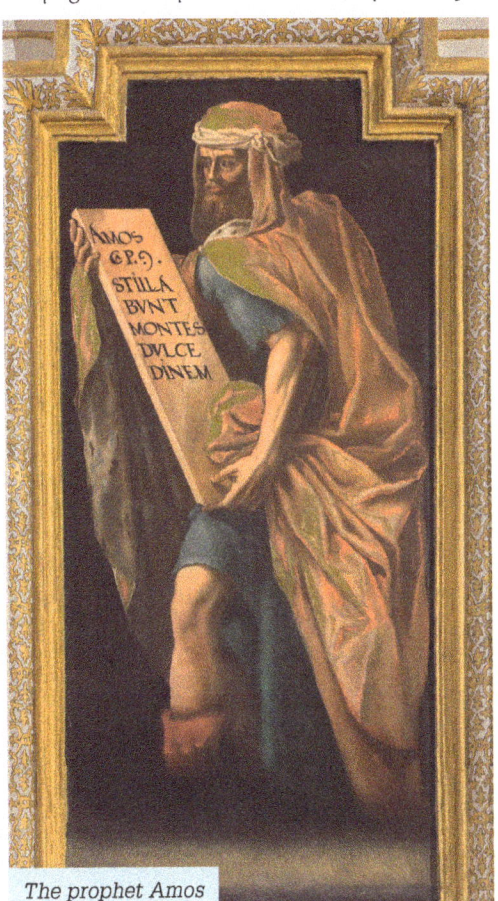

The emphasis upon social justice and the plight of the poor is also taken up by Reform Rabbi Yoffie, and, it is claimed, serves equally well to illustrate this particular line of argument: 'Reform Jews are committed to social justice ... Like the prophets, we never forget that God is concerned about the everyday and that the blights of society take precedence over the mysteries of heaven. A Reform synagogue that does not alleviate the anguish of suffering is a contradiction in terms.' Reform Jews believe that taking action to relieve those who are most vulnerable in society is the modern manifestation of the requirement in Leviticus 19 to leave the corners of the fields for the poor and needy to harvest. The Pittsburgh Platform has therefore been effective in underlining the importance for them to work individually and collectively towards a better and redeemed world.

The prophet Amos

Key quote

When you reap the harvest of your land, you shall not reap all the way to the edges of your field, or gather the gleanings of your harvest. You shall not pick your vineyard bare, or gather the fallen fruit of your vineyard; you shall leave them for the poor and the stranger: I the LORD am your God. (Leviticus 19:9–10)

Key questions

- Can it be argued that Judaism has always been concerned with addressing the plight of the poor?
- Has the Pittsburgh Platform brought anything new to the way in which Jews address the plight of the poor?
- Is it possible to measure the effectiveness of the Pittsburgh Platform in relation to the plight of the poor?

Key quote

We are obligated to pursue tzedek, justice and righteousness, and to narrow the gap between the affluent and the poor … We affirm the mitzvah of tzedakah, setting aside portions of our earnings and our time to provide for those in need. These acts bring us closer to fulfilling the prophetic call to translate the words of the Torah into the works of our hands. **(Pittsburgh Platform 1999)**

Study tip

Take note that reference has been made here to two versions of the Pittsburgh Platform. Make sure that you are aware of the differences between them, especially as far as content is concerned, so that you can use them in the correct context.

Furthermore, the Pittsburgh Platform of 1999 advocates joint action against poverty and social injustice through interfaith alliance by stating that Reform Jews: 'seek dialogue and joint action with people of other faiths in the hope that together we can bring peace, freedom and justice to our world'. This, it has been argued, is important as we now live in societies that are diverse and multicultural. Some might consider that this directive in the newer Pittsburgh Platform has enabled Reform Jews to forge relationships that have enabled the movement to make even greater progress in relation to the plight of the poor. For instance, the Reform Jewish community has become involved with those of the Christian faith through the work of the International Council of Christians and Jews. This association has resulted in, amongst other things, a mission to address issues of human rights.

In conclusion, it is clearly evident that Jews of all denominations believe that it is their duty to use the resources that God has provided in order to work to combat the injustices that are evident in the world. Notwithstanding, the Pittsburgh Platform of 1885 set out a clear definition of Reform Judaism, which, it has been claimed was more than merely a set of statements. Under the leadership of numerous rabbis, its ideals were applied to the society in which it was created. It is impossible to quantify the effectiveness of the Pittsburgh Platform in relation to the plight of the poor, nevertheless it is surely possible to illustrate how it has spurred Reform Jews into action with the result that commitment to social justice is a hallmark of the movement; a commitment that has inspired congregations to pursue a wide range of activities designed to 'repair the world'. And in any case, as an ancient sage taught, 'It is not your task to complete the work, but you are not free to desist from it.' (Pirkei Avot 2:21)

AO2 Activity

List some conclusions that could be drawn from the AO2 reasoning from the above text; try to aim for at least three different possible conclusions. Consider each of the conclusions and collect brief evidence to support each conclusion from the AO1 and AO2 material for this topic. Select the conclusion that you think is most convincing and explain why it is so. Try to contrast this with the weakest conclusion in the list, justifying your argument with clear reasoning and evidence.

Key quote

As Reform Jews we make a collective effort to bring our progressive values to bear in the community at large … We speak out on behalf of the vulnerable. And we seek justice for all. **(Feldman)**

AO2 Developing skills

It is now important to consider the information that has been covered in this section; however, the information in its raw form is too extensive and so has to be processed in order to meet the requirements of the examination. This can be achieved by practising more advanced skills associated with AO2. For assessment objective 2 (AO2), which involves 'critical analysis' and 'evaluation' skills, we are going to focus on different ways in which the skills can be demonstrated effectively, and also refer to how the performance of these skills is measured (see generic band descriptors for A2 [WJEC] AO2 or A Level [Eduqas] AO2).

▶ **Your final task for this theme is:** Below is an **evaluation of the effectiveness of the Pittsburgh Platform in relation to the plight of the poor**. You want to use this in an essay but as it stands it is a weak argument because it has no quotations or references in it at all as support. This time you have to find your own quotations (about 3) and use your own references (about 3) to strengthen the evaluation. Remember, sometimes a quotation can follow from a reference but they can also be used individually as separate points.

Some might argue that concern for the poor has always been an important aim within Judaism, and that the Pittsburgh Platform has brought nothing new to the Jewish faith on this account. For example, it is evident that the concept of Tikkun Olam has always been significant within the Jewish religion, and that it was seen as an effective means of ensuring a safeguard to those in society who may have been at a disadvantage. Furthermore, examples of such actions are evident within the Jewish concepts of tzedakah and gemilut hasadim, which have always been a fundamental part of the Jewish faith. For instance, the concept of tzedakah relates to the carrying out of a charitable act, and when a Jewish person undertakes such an act they are undertaking one of the most basic requirements of the mitzvot: that of providing for those who are unable to provide for themselves.

The result will be a fairly lengthy answer and so you could then check it against the band descriptors for A2 (WJEC) or A Level (Eduqas) and in particular have a look at the demands described in the higher band descriptors towards which you should be aspiring. Ask yourself:

- Is my answer a confident critical analysis and perceptive evaluation of the issue?
- Is my answer a response that successfully identifies and thoroughly addresses the issues raised by the question set?
- Does my work show an excellent standard of coherence, clarity and organisation?
- Will my work, when developed, contain thorough, sustained and clear views that are supported by extensive, detailed reasoning and/or evidence?
- Are the views of scholars/schools of thought used extensively, appropriately and in context?
- Does my answer convey a confident and perceptive analysis of the nature of any possible connections with other elements of my course?
- When used, is specialist language and vocabulary both thorough and accurate?

T3 Significant social and historical developments in religious thought

Key skills

Analysis involves:

Identifying issues raised by the materials in the AO1, together with those identified in the AO2 section, and presents sustained and clear views, either of scholars or from a personal perspective ready for evaluation.

This means:

- That your answers are able to identify key areas of debate in relation to a particular issue
- That you can identify, and comment upon, the different lines of argument presented by others
- That your response comments on the overall effectiveness of each of these areas or arguments.

Evaluation involves:

Considering the various implications of the issues raised based upon the evidence gleaned from analysis and provides an extensive detailed argument with a clear conclusion.

This means:

- That your answer weighs up the consequences of accepting or rejecting the various and different lines of argument analysed
- That your answer arrives at a conclusion through a clear process of reasoning.

T3 Significant social and historical developments in religious thought

This section covers AO1 content and skills

Specification content
The role of the family and the Jewish home as foundational for Jewish principles.

D: Religion, equality and discrimination: Jewish family life and gender equality

The role of the family and the Jewish home as foundational for Jewish principles

Such is the importance of the home within the Jewish faith that the sages referred to it as **mikdash me'at**, a small sanctuary: 'Our Rabbis taught that the home is considered to be a mikdash me'at ... like the ... **Tabernacle**, that God commanded the Israelites to build in the wilderness. God's intention is to dwell with us in our own "small sanctuaries", accompanying us "when we lie down, when we rise up", and along the way. The home, where we raise our children and where we feed our own spiritual hunger is not the ... Tabernacle, but a mikdash me'at, a small sanctuary that serves a similar purpose.' (Lyon)

Robinson considers the reasons why the Jewish home rose to such prominence, and indicates that the roles of both synagogue and home changed following the destruction of the Temple in 586 BCE and the enforced exile of the Jews in Babylon. 'Where else would the values of the faith be handed down besides the family?' he asks; and continues: '... the Jewish home is the place where children, adolescents, and even young adults receive their most important training in ... "Jewishness". It is in the family, in the home, that the principal celebrations of life-cycle events take place in Judaism.'

Key quote
Synagogues, study houses, and even homes are called mikdash me'at, a small temple. According to the Talmud, God will dwell in the holy spaces we create, for they are the Temple in miniature. **(Sinclair)**

Key terms
Chanukat habayit: the ceremony of dedication for a new Jewish home

Consecration: making something sacred; setting it apart for holy use

Mezuzah: a small parchment scroll fixed to the right-hand doorpost of every room in a Jewish house (except bathroom and toilet)

Mikdash me'at: meaning 'a small sanctuary/temple'

Tabernacle: the portable sanctuary in which the Jews housed the Ark of the Covenant

When a Jewish person or family moves into a new home, the dwelling undergoes **consecration** and dedication. This is because a Jewish home is not just a place where people live, but it is a place where people live according to the faith, traditions and values of the Jewish religion. The name given to the ceremony of dedication for the new home is **chanukat habayit**, and its central ritual is the affixing of a **mezuzah** to the doorpost of the house. This is in accordance with the commandment in the Torah: 'Hear, O Israel ... You shall love the Lord your God with all your heart and with all your soul and with all your strength ... Write them on the doorframes of your houses and on your gates.' (Deuteronomy 6:4–9) This particular ritual is significant therefore in that it denotes identity with, and commitment to, the Jewish faith.

The central ritual of chanukat habayit is the affixing of a mezuzah to the doorpost.

quickfire
3.16 What is the central ritual of chanukat habayit?

Study tip
In order to gain a greater understanding of the significance of chanukat habayit, it would be a good idea to research the ceremony in greater detail.

T3 Significant social and historical developments in religious thought

According to the prophet Ezekiel, God's presence remains with the Jewish people in the home in whichever place they find themselves: '... and I have become to them a small sanctuary (mikdash me'at) in the countries whither they have gone.' (Ezekiel 11:16) And, like the synagogue, the home continues to carry out various traditions of the Temple. For example, at Shabbat, the candles that are lit recall the Temple **menorah**, and the dining table is representative of the altar. Since the study of sacred texts is also a core value of Judaism, most observant Jewish families own a printed version of the Torah (Chumash), as well as a Tanakh and a prayer book.

The Jewish religion is also practised in the home through prayer and festivals. For example, at the beginning of Shabbat, **kiddush** is recited over wine prior to the evening meal. Kiddush consists of two sections: the blessing over the wine and the blessing of the day. A special cup is usually used for this purpose in honour of the blessing, and after kiddush has been recited, the cup is passed around the table so that everyone present can take a sip from it. Kiddush is also said on other important Jewish holidays such as at Passover and Rosh Hashanah.

A blessing over food is also recited before meals on other days of the week. Over food the blessing is: 'who brings forth bread from the earth'; over fruit: 'who creates the fruit of the tree'; over vegetables: 'who creates the fruit of the ground'. In addition, grace following meals is recited in the form of a prayer known as **Birkat Hamazon**. Thus the very act of eating becomes a holy event.

The cycle of the Jewish year provides a great variety of opportunities for worship at home. For example, at Passover, the **Haggadah** is read at the **Seder** and special symbolic foods are prepared which recall the slavery and exodus of the Israelites from Egypt.

At the festival of Sukkot, it is customary to commemorate the trek of the Israelites through the desert by building a sukkah against the wall of the house and living there for the week-long duration of the festival.

During Hanukkah, a nine-branched candelabrum in the home is representative of the miracle of the lamp that continued to burn in the Temple even though there was only enough oil to burn for one day. Nowadays it is customary to light a candle on the first night of the festival followed by an additional candle for each night until the last one when eight candles will be burning.

The lighting of the hanukkiah

Key quotes

A Jewish home has been described as a miniature sanctuary, and the table from which food is eaten has been called a miniature altar. **(Dosick)**

Praise to You, Adonai our God, Sovereign of the universe, Creator of the fruit of the vine. Praise to you, Adonai our God, Sovereign of the universe who finding favour with us, sanctified us with mitzvot ... You have given us Your holy Shabbat as an inheritance. Praise to You, Adonai, who sanctifies Shabbat. **(Kiddush)**

quickfire

3.17 Which prophet stated that God's presence remains with the Jewish people in the home?

Key terms

Birkat Hamazon: blessing said after a meal

Haggadah: means 'telling', the text recited at the Seder meal

Kiddush: a ceremony of prayer and blessing over wine to sanctify Shabbat and Jewish festivals

Menorah: a seven-branched candelabrum

Seder: the ritual service and ceremonial dinner which takes place in the Jewish home at Passover

93

Key terms

Bar mitzvah: 'son of the commandment'; the coming of age ceremony for a Jewish boy at 13 years of age

Bat mitzvah: 'daughter of the commandment'; the coming of age ceremony for a Jewish girl at 12 years of age

Minyan: a group of ten males over the age of 13 required before an act of communal prayer can take place

Shiva: the seven-day period following burial

Key quotes

(The family) is where one generation passes on its values to the next and ensures the continuity of a civilisation. **(Sacks)**

Children are the Jews' greatest treasure and blessing. They guarantee both the physical and spiritual survival of Judaism. **(Trepp)**

Honour your father and your mother. **(Exodus 20:12)**

Each of you must respect your mother and father. **(Leviticus 19:3)**

However, most significantly, it is within the home that family life is sanctified. At the birth of a male child, for example, a festive meal takes place at home on the Friday night after the birth. Similarly, bar mitzvah and bat mitzvah occasions are times of festivity in the home. In order to complete the life cycle, at times of mourning following the death of a family member, visitors come to the house to pay their respects during shiva, where a minyan recites the morning and evening prayers.

The raising of a family is a sacred duty within Judaism, and it is in the home that children, the next generation, learn from the example set by their parents. This is where they start their journey, living as a Jew, by practising the traditions and carrying out the mitzvot. As the Tanakh says: 'Teach a child how he should live, and he will remember it all his life.' (Proverbs 22:6) Jewish parents are thus expected to raise their children to be moral people. Sometimes it is necessary to punish a child, and the Talmud gives advice on which form this should take: 'Do not threaten a child. Either punish straight away or let the matter drop.'

Parents have a variety of obligations to their children apart from showing them how to live as Jews. For example, they must ensure that their children will be able to support themselves in adult life. As the Talmud says: 'Teach your son a trade, or you teach him to become a robber.' The Talmud also stresses that parents teach their children basic survival skills as for Jews, this too, is a religious obligation.

Children in return are expected to carry out the commandment to honour (Exodus 20:12) and respect (Leviticus 19:3) their parents. In practical terms, the Talmud refers to honour as providing parents with food, drink, clothing and transportation: 'See that they eat and drink and take them where they need to go.' Respect requires that a child does not sit in their parent's seat, does not interrupt them, and takes their side in a dispute. The Talmud praises such behaviour: 'There are three partners in man, the Holy One, blessed be He, the father, and the mother. When a man honours his father and mother, the Holy One blessed be He, says, "I will ascribe (merit) to them as though I had dwelt among them and they had honoured me."' Judaism also states that if parents do wrong then their children should point this out to them in a tactful way without hurting their feelings or being disrespectful.

Cohn-Sherbok highlights the fact that the Jewish tradition teaches that domestic harmony is the ideal of home life. The Talmud offers guidelines for attaining this goal: 'A man should spend less than his means on food, up to his means on clothes, and more than his means in honouring wife and children because they are dependent on him.' Such harmony depends upon compromise on the part of all members of the family as well as through the observance of Jewish rituals which serve to unify the family. Cohn-Sherbok says that the Jewish home is permeated with sanctity when the family lives in accordance with God's commandments.

Jewish coming of age ceremonies are times of great celebration within the Jewish home.

AO1 Activity

After reading the section on 'The role of the family and the Jewish home as foundational for Jewish principles' identify and list examples which show Jewish belief in practice in the home.

This practises the AO1 skill of being able to show a thorough, accurate and relevant knowledge and understanding of religion and belief.

T3 Significant social and historical developments in religious thought

The changing role of men and women in Judaism with reference to family life

In traditional Orthodox Jewish families there are distinct roles for men and women. The primary duty of the man in a family is to take care of his wife. He makes a promise to do this by signing the **ketubah** at their wedding. The ketubah ensures that he undertakes to support his wife 'even if I have to sell the coat from off my back'. The ketubah also ensures that the wife receives maintenance should the couple divorce or if the husband should die before her.

Traditionally, the father is also expected to ensure that his son is circumcised as a way of carrying out the mitzvah. Also, he should teach the Torah to his children and be an example to them.

It is generally accepted within Orthodox Judaism that the role of the wife is to bear children and take responsibility for family life. In the past, therefore, the life of a Jewish woman was centred totally around the home and family. This is because Judaism teaches that marriage and motherhood are important for a woman's own personal development. According to Halakhah, womanhood is a separate status with its own specific set of rules, obligations and responsibilities. Cohn-Sherbok notes that: 'In terms of religious observance, women were ... excluded from the study of the Torah and segregated from men ... In general they were exempted from time-bound commands; as a result they were not obliged to fulfil those commandments which must be followed at a particular time (such as the recitation of prayer). The purpose of these restrictions was to ensure that their attention and energy be directed toward completing their domestic duties.'

Within the Hasidic movement, the roles of men and women continue to be sharply defined and are separated into public male, and private female activities. As such, men are required to pray daily in a minyan, and to undertake study of the scriptures. Women, on the other hand, are focused upon the mitzvot relating to the home, and are responsible for keeping house, and ensuring that the children adhere to the prescribed religious precepts.

In other branches of the Jewish faith, however, the roles of men and women with reference to family life are changing. Reform Judaism is totally committed to gender equality, and although many women still have an important role in the family, and see it as a privilege, they also take on work and responsibilities outside the family. Nevertheless, the role of the mother is still considered to be vitally important for a successful Jewish family. Authority is given to the mother, because it is through her lineage that children are accepted to be Jewish; and also due to her important role in bringing up the children by teaching and demonstrating Jewish values and traditions. Traditionally, it is the mother who prepares kosher food, maintains a kosher kitchen and prepares for the festivals and Shabbat. She is also responsible for teaching her daughters what they will need to know when they have homes and a family of their own. Today, however, as a result of changing attitudes towards gender roles, and the influence of the wider world, the role of the father and mother interweave together and there is greater equality and co-operation.

The role and status of women in Judaism with reference to feminism

Women in the Orthodox Jewish tradition have always held a valued role in the home, but have been marginalised in religious public life. For example, in Orthodox synagogues men and women are seated separately, with the women sitting either in the balcony or behind a partition or screen. However, not only are they physically separated from the men, but they are also separated from the important ritual of worship. The reading of the portion of the Torah scroll from the reading desk, for example, is enacted within the male domain and is thus denied to the female members of the congregation.

Specification content
The changing role of men and women in Judaism with reference to family life.

Key term
Ketubah: marriage contract

Key quote
What a rare find is a capable wife! Her worth is far beyond that of rubies. (Proverbs 31:10)

A ketubah

Specification content
The role and status of women in Judaism with reference to feminism.

Key terms

Challah: a special loaf of bread used on Shabbat and festivals

Shul: a term used for synagogue

Taking challah: when making challah, a small piece of dough is separated and either burned or disposed of in a respectful way in accordance with the command in Numbers 15:18–21

quickfire

3.18 What are the three positive commandments that are designed for women according to Robinson?

Key quotes

When you enter the land to which I am taking you and you eat of the bread of the land, you shall set some aside as a gift to the LORD … You shall make a gift to the LORD from the first yield of your baking, throughout the ages. **(Numbers 15:18–21)**

The celebration of Rosh Chodesh as a woman's holiday … one of the earliest and most tenacious feminist rituals, represents both a restoration of a traditional women's observance and an opportunity to experiment with new spiritual forms. **(Plaskow)**

A woman may pray in the synagogue at specific times, but she is not obliged to; and due to of this lack of obligation it thus follows that she may not count in a minyan; nor may she lead others who are fulfilling their obligation. There are laws of modesty which some say are the reason why women are not allowed to lead the prayers in the synagogue: the thought being that a woman's voice and appearance might distract a man from his own prayers. Being a rabbi or a cantor has also been ruled out for this reason within Orthodox Judaism.

Robinson points out that the response of Orthodox pre-feminist women to this marginalisation was to develop rituals of their own that took place in the home. He notes that although there are only three positive commandments that are designed for women – lighting Shabbat candles, **taking challah**, and keeping the laws of ritual purity – women have throughout the years devised ways of making the ordinary household chore a sacred ritual as well. 'But these tasks, like women in an Orthodox **shul**, are invisible to men. And that didn't change, even in the Reform and Conservative worlds, for a very long time.' (Robinson)

Such restrictions have led some to claim that Jewish women lack equality with men within the Jewish faith, and that they have been assigned a subordinate role. However, this has been countered by the affirmation within the Orthodox tradition that men and women have complementary, yet different roles in religious life, resulting in differing obligations.

However, not all groups within Judaism have retained the traditional male/female roles that are evident in Orthodox communities. A case in point is the stance taken by the Reform movement which generally holds that the various differences between the roles of men and women in traditional Jewish law are not relevant to modern conditions and, as such, are not applicable today. Total equality between the sexes has always been an important principle in Reform Judaism and has enabled women to perform many rituals traditionally reserved for men, such as publicly reading the Torah; being part of the minyan; acting as cantor; and wearing tallit and tefillin. Furthermore, in a Reform synagogue there is no balcony or screen for women to sit separately from the men. And since 1975 in Britain, women have been able to serve in their communities as rabbis.

The second half of the twentieth century, however, saw the development of the Jewish feminist movement, which has had a considerable theological impact. Robinson notes that some of the changes are self-evident, such as liturgy being adjusted to reflect the idea that God is neither male nor female; or both male and female. However, Plaskow offers examples that show that liturgy and ritual have been particularly important areas for what she terms as 'Jewish feminist inventiveness'. For example, Jewish women are rediscovering elements of worship

Total equality between men and women is an important principle in Reform Judaism.

such as the ceremonies for the festival of **Rosh Chodesh**. Rosh Chodesh is celebrated as a woman's holiday because on this day, women would traditionally stop their work early in the day and meet together to study and celebrate. Today, many women have reclaimed the spirit of Rosh Chodesh as a celebration of, and for, women by writing new prayers and liturgies, and gathering together in prayer and study groups to mark the monthly observance. There has also been the development of a feminist liturgy for Passover that puts women's liberation at the centre of the festival.

Another area of note, according to Plaskow, has been the creation of a liturgy for the birth ceremonies of girls. She says: 'These are rooted in neither historical nor a continuing ritual but in a desire to assert and celebrate the value of daughters, welcoming them into the community with a ceremony parallel to **Brit milah**.'

The change in the role and status of Jewish women has also been aided by the rise of the **Havurah** movement (a small worship circle, based upon the principle of equality, and led by lay people rather than a rabbi), which has allowed them to take a more active part in worship and education. Changes are also evident within Orthodox Judaism where it is becoming more common for women to attend university, and to embark upon careers even though they claim no allegiance to feminism. Some Orthodox women also attend yeshiva where they are able to study the Talmud. Orthodox feminist, Blu Greenberg, believes that it is inevitable that the Orthodox community will eventually **ordain** women as rabbis, as she believes that: 'Learning is the road to ordination, and you can't close the last gates of the path.'

Debates about agunah (chained) and minyan

Halakhah has been an area in which many objections have been raised by Jewish feminists regarding the role and status of women; and debates about **agunah** and membership of the minyan are two areas of significance.

Agunah

Jewish feminists have focused great attention upon the difficult problem of divorce. The opening verses of Deuteronomy chapter 24 give the husband the right to divorce his wife by writing her a bill of divorce, known as a **get**. As a result of this passage from the Torah, Orthodox Jews will only allow a man to divorce his wife. It is thus a nonreciprocal arrangement, with a wife unable to instigate divorce proceedings as she is not allowed to give her husband a get.

Apart from denying equality to women, this situation can lead to unfortunate circumstances for the wife of a husband who refuses to give her a divorce, as without a get she is unable to remarry. Moreover, if the husband disappears, but is not known to have died, his abandoned wife, unable to divorce him, can never remarry. A woman in this particular situation falls into the category of 'agunah' or 'chained wife'.

There are many Jews today (and not only those who support the feminist movement) who agree that this inequality regarding divorce is unacceptable. A number of ways of dealing with the problem have been implemented. Liberal Jews, for example, have sought to rectify the disparity between the situation of the man and the woman in traditional divorce proceedings by doing away with the get altogether. Divorce has thereby become a civil matter rather than a religious one, and either the husband or wife can bring about an end to the marriage.

The Conservative movement has found a solution by inserting a clause into the ketubah which states that a husband who disappears for a period of several years, and who does not communicate with his wife during that time allows her to be divorced from him.

T3 Significant social and historical developments in religious thought

Key quotes

A man takes a wife … he writes her a bill of divorce, hands it to her, and sends her away from his house. **(Deuteronomy 24:1)**

Jewish marriages are created and sanctified 'according to the law of Moses and Israel'. The issue of the get, the Jewish divorce document, is the way to terminate Jewish marriages, according to Jewish law, with the same dignity and the same sanctity. **(Dosick)**

quickfire

3.19 How has the Havurah movement aided the change in the role and status of Jewish women?

Specification content

Debates about agunah (chained); debates about minyan.

Key terms

Agunah: meaning 'chained' and referring to a woman whose husband is missing but not known to be dead

Brit milah: circumcision

Get: a document of divorce

Havurah: meaning 'fellowship' or 'companionship'

Ordain: to appoint as a rabbi

Rosh Chodesh: meaning 'head of the month'; the first day of the month, marked by the birth of the new moon

Reform Jews follow a Talmudic principle: 'the law of the land is the law'. This states that in such matters, the secular law of the country will take precedence, and thus a divorce can be granted. Consequently, a couple who receive a civil divorce will also be divorced legally in the eyes of the Reform rabbinate.

Dosick explains that some couples sign a prenuptial agreement or have a clause written into the ketubah stating that if the marriage ends in divorce, the husband promises to grant his wife a Jewish divorce within a certain time after the civil divorce decree. If he refuses, or fails to do so, the **bet din** will act on his behalf to grant the divorce, citing his agreement to the prenuptial contract or to the clause in the ketubah as indicative of his agreement to the divorce.

Another practice is to insert a clause into the civil divorce settlement stating that the husband agrees to grant his wife a Jewish divorce within six months of the civil divorce decree. If he fails to do so, he can be held in contempt of court.

Minyan

The minyan is a group of ten men over the age of 13, which is needed before an act of communal prayer at the synagogue can take place. However, the idea that prayer is the expressed duty of men only is starting to change. Even within the Orthodox tradition, many women are declaring their right not just to be part of the congregation who sit in their own section of the synagogue praying, but to be active in leading the services. This has led to the rise of what are known as 'partnership **minyanim**'. A 'partnership minyan' is a prayer group that is both committed to maintaining Halakhic standards and practices and also to including women in ritual leadership roles to the fullest extent possible within the boundaries of Jewish Law. This means that the minyan must include at least ten men, and the traditional liturgy is used. 'Partnership minyanim' allow for women to lead prayers that are otherwise conducted only by men. They sit behind a curtain, as in many ultra-Orthodox synagogues, but nevertheless share many parts of conducting the worship. In some synagogues, women are able to participate fully in the Torah readings, and chanting the text.

This practice has raised many objections within the Orthodox tradition, even though the services themselves are totally Orthodox with no changes to the liturgy. Rabbi Daniel Sperber, a professor of Talmud, believes that there is no reason to ban women from participating in services: 'That is an old tradition, but it is not in the Torah. The reason women were banned dates back to the day when they were mainly uneducated and so it was considered an insult to the male congregations if they were led by women. That no longer applies. Many of our women are more educated than men.'

Not all Jewish communities share the same Orthodox practices concerning the minyan. Reform Judaism has done away with the requirement completely: thus prayers may be said with any number present. Conservative rabbis, seeking to redress the lack of gender equality, have included adult women to be counted within the minyan.

The reading of the Torah is no longer restricted to men in some synagogues.

Key terms

Bet din: meaning 'house of judgement'; a rabbinical court

Minyanim: plural of 'minyan'

The contributions of Judith Plaskow and Margaret Wenig to Jewish feminism

Judith Plaskow

Judith Plaskow

Key quote
'Standing again at Sinai' made a huge impact when it was first published, providing a new framework for understanding Jewish texts and conventions, and prompting new conversations about gender impact upon Judaism that were not part of the mainstream. **(Cohen)**

In 1990, Judith Plaskow (b. 1947) published what is considered to be the first book of Jewish feminist theology. In 'Standing Again at Sinai – Judaism from a feminine perspective' Plaskow created what has been described as a distinctly Jewish theology that has made a considerable contribution to Jewish women's theological discussions.

In 'Standing Again at Sinai' she describes what was to become a defining moment in her life as a Jew and as a feminist. She and her husband were chatting before going in for a Sabbath service when a member of the congregation came out and urged her husband to come in to make the minyan. Plaskow wrote: 'While I had attended services regularly for a year and a half and my husband was a relative newcomer, I could stay outside all day; my purpose was irrelevant for the purpose for which we had gathered … (it was) an enormously important click moment.' It was to lead her to the conclusion that: 'Excluded from prayer and study, women are excluded from the heart and soul of traditional Judaism.'

For Plaskow, feminism was more than merely attaining equal rights for women in religious or social structures: 'Feminism is a process of coming to affirm ourselves as women/persons – and seeing that affirmation mirrored in religious and social institutions.' (Plaskow)

In the chapter on Israel, Plaskow explores creating a community in which women would be present, equal and responsible; and when considering Torah, she argues for the use of feminist historical methodologies to uncover Jewish women's history. In her discussion on the traditional images of God, she begins by underlining what she describes as 'the unyielding maleness of the dominant Jewish picture of God', arguing that if God is viewed as a dominating male then human institutions are likely use this as a model and become male-dominated too.

Debra Cohen notes that since Plaskow wrote 'Standing Again at Sinai' women have gained a more active role within even Orthodox communities, such as in 'partnership minyanim', for example. Plaskow wrote of the challenge facing those women who wanted a more active role in Jewish religious life, and, it has been claimed, her work has enabled the changes in scholarship and liturgy that have brought about a growth in women's Torah exegesis. Examples from within the Reform movement include 'The Torah: A Women's Commentary', and there are also new publications from within other Jewish groups that reflect and value the female perspective. Cohen also describes how new Jewish rituals such as women's Seders and welcoming ceremonies for baby girls have since become mainstream.

T3 Significant social and historical developments in religious thought

Specification content
The contributions of Judith Plaskow and Margaret Wenig to Jewish feminism.

Key quotes
The project of creating a feminist Judaism fits into a larger project of creating a world in which all women, and all people, have both the basic resources they need to survive, and the opportunity to name and shape the structures of meaning that give substance to their lives. In the Jewish context, this means re-forming every aspect of tradition so that it incorporates women's experience … only then will Judaism become a religion that includes all Jews … will it truly be a Judaism of women and men. **(Plaskow)**

These problems with traditional images of God generate a need for new language that can better express the meaning of God for a pluralistic and responsible community. **(Plaskow)**

quickfire
3.20 Which publication is considered to be the first book of Jewish feminist theology?

Margaret Wenig

One of the first major theological topics to be addressed by Jewish feminists was the centrality of the male imagery for God in the Jewish tradition. In 1976, whilst at university, Margaret Wenig and fellow student Naomi Janowitz sought to address this matter by producing a new feminist version of the Sabbath prayer book that referred to God throughout using female pronouns and imagery. 'Siddur Nashim: A Sabbath Prayer Book for Women' presented God partly as: 'the traditional deity in feminine garb and partly a more thoroughly transformed divinity' (Plaskow).

The 'Siddur Nashim' addresses God as the 'blessed and glorified, exalted and honoured, magnified and praised ... Holy One, blessed is She.' God was also presented as a mother, giving birth to the world and protecting it with her womb:

'Blessed is She who spoke and the world came to be ...

Blessed is She who in the beginning, gave birth ...

Blessed is She whose womb covers the earth ...

Blessed is She whose womb protects all creatures.'

Plaskow considers that the liturgy of the 'Siddur Nashim' has weathered well over the years, but adds that it now demonstrates the incompleteness of its exploration. She says: 'The very accumulation of female pronouns in certain prayers is a glorious celebration of women's power ... but ... it does not address the nature of God as a dominating Other.' Nevertheless, Wenig can be considered to have initiated a process of examination about the transformation of religious language.

Wenig is also noted for her contribution to gender equality, and, as an openly gay woman, she was ordained as a rabbi in 1984 when there were very few female rabbis, let alone gay ones. Wenig and student rabbi Margaret Holub were responsible for proposing a resolution that a committee on 'Homosexuality and the Rabbinate' should be formed. The ensuing report, issued in 1990 declared that 'all rabbis, regardless of sexual orientation (should) be accorded the opportunity to fulfil the sacred vocation that they have chosen'. The committee also endorsed the view that 'all Jews are religiously equal regardless of their sexual orientation'. The report was ratified by The Central Conference of American Rabbis very soon afterwards.

In an interview given to *The New York Times* in 2009, Wenig reflected upon the fact that within the Reform tradition, congregations and rabbinical students no longer assume that a rabbi has to be a he or heterosexual. She also reports that she has seen a significant rise in the number of women who now attend seminaries of the Reform movement such as at the Hebrew Union College – Jewish Institute of Religion where she teaches. She is particularly well-known for a sermon that was published in 1990 entitled 'God Is a Woman and She is Growing Older', which portrays the deity as a loving, long-suffering mother who wonders why her children have lost touch: 'God would prefer that we come home. She is waiting for us, ever patiently until we are ready. God will not sleep. She will leave the door open and the candles burning waiting patiently for us to come home. Perhaps one day ... we will be able to look into God's ageing face and say "Avinu Malkeinu, our Parent, our Ruler, we have come home".'

Margaret Wenig

Study tip

Reading the actual texts by Plaskow and Wenig (such as 'Standing Again at Sinai' and 'God Is a Woman and She is Growing Older') will enable you to gain a greater understanding of the views of these two particular feminist scholars.

AO1 Activity

Explain how a Jew might respond to the following view: 'The feminist movement within Judaism has brought about significant changes regarding the role and status of women in the Jewish faith.'

Explain your answer using evidence and examples from what you have read.

AO1 Developing skills

It is now important to consider the information that has been covered in this section; however, the information in its raw form is too extensive and so has to be processed in order to meet the requirements of the examination. This can be achieved by practising more advanced skills associated with AO1. The exercises that run throughout this book will help you to do this and prepare you for the examination. For assessment objective 1 (AO1), which involves demonstrating 'knowledge' and 'understanding' skills, we are going to focus on different ways in which the skills can be demonstrated effectively, and also refer to how the performance of these skills is measured (see generic band descriptors for A2 [WJEC] AO1 or A Level [Eduqas] AO1).

▶ **Your task is this:** Below is a **summary of the contribution of Judith Plaskow to Jewish feminism**. It is 150 words long. There are three points highlighted that are key points to learn from this extract. Discuss which further two points you think are the most important to highlight and write up all five points.

'Standing Again at Sinai' by Plaskow is considered to be the first book of Jewish feminist theology, and in writing it, ==Plaskow has made a considerable contribution to Jewish women's theological discussions==. In her discussion on the traditional images of God, she argues that ==if God is viewed as a dominating male then human institutions are likely use this as a model and become male-dominated too==. She claimed: 'Feminism is a process of coming to affirm ourselves as women/persons – and seeing that affirmation mirrored in religious and social institutions.' Plaskow wrote of the challenge facing those women who wanted a more active role in Jewish religious life, and, it has been claimed, her work has enabled the changes in scholarship and liturgy that have brought about a growth in women's Torah exegesis. ==New Jewish rituals such as women's Seders and welcoming ceremonies for baby girls have also since become mainstream.==

Now make the five points into your own summary (as in Theme 1 Developing skills) trying to make the summary more personal to your style of writing.

1. ....
2. ....
3. ....
4. ....
5. ....

T3 Significant social and historical developments in religious thought

Key skills Theme 3DEF

This Theme has tasks that deal with the basics of AO1 in terms of prioritising and selecting the key relevant information, presenting this in a personalised way (as in Theme 1) and then using evidence and examples to support and expand upon this (as in Theme 3ABC).

Key skills

Knowledge involves:

Selection of a range of (thorough) accurate and relevant information that is directly related to the specific demands of the question.

This means:

- Selecting relevant material for the question set
- Being focused in explaining and examining the material selected.

Understanding involves:

Explanation that is extensive, demonstrating depth and/or breadth with excellent use of evidence and examples including (where appropriate) thorough and accurate supporting use of sacred texts, sources of wisdom and specialist language.

This means:

- Effective use of examples and supporting evidence to establish the quality of your understanding
- Ownership of your explanation that expresses personal knowledge and understanding and NOT just reproducing a chunk of text from a book that you have rehearsed and memorised.

WJEC / Eduqas Religious Studies for A Level Year 2 and A2 Judaism

This section covers AO2 content and skills

Specification content

Family life as the main strength of Judaism.

Issues for analysis and evaluation

Family life as the main strength of Judaism

It cannot be denied that the Jewish religion places great emphasis upon the importance of family life. Sacks further emphasises this contention when he claims that it 'is where one generation passes its values to the next and ensures continuity of a civilisation'. Indeed, the raising of a family is considered to be a sacred duty within the Jewish tradition as it is within the home that the next generation learns from the examples set by their parents. It is within the family unit that Jewish children start out on their journey, living as Jews, abiding by the traditions of the faith, and learning how to apply the mitzvot to their everyday lives. Further evidence of the importance placed upon the parents in cultivating religious devotion is to be found in the Tanakh which states: 'Teach a child how he should live, and he will remember it all his life.' (Proverbs 22:6) Jewish parents are thus expected to raise their children to be moral people.

In addition, the Jewish scriptures offer clear guidance about how parents and children are to conduct themselves within the family group. The Talmud, for instance, sets out the requirement that parents should ensure that their children will be able to support themselves in adult life: 'Teach your son a trade, or you teach him to become a robber.' It also stresses that parents teach their children basic survival skills as, for Jews, this too is a religious obligation. The requirements in Exodus to 'Honour your father and your mother', and Leviticus to 'respect your mother and father' display a reciprocal arrangement in which children also have a part to play. It could be argued that family life, lived in accordance with Jewish principles, provides a strong physical and emotional foundation; the likes of which will be passed on to future generations.

Moreover, many of the key events in life are celebrated or enacted within the family group. For example, the birth of a male child is celebrated with a festive meal which takes place at home on the Friday night after the birth. Another example of festivity in the home takes place when a Jewish boy or girl marks their coming of age at their bar or bat mitzvah. And to complete the life cycle, it is to the home that visitors come to mourn on the death of a family member.

Furthermore, the importance of the home as a place of worship is synonymous with the sanctity of family life within Judaism. Such is its significance that the sages referred to it as mikdash me'at, a small sanctuary: 'Our Rabbis taught that the home is considered to be a mikdash me'at ... like the ... Tabernacle, that God commanded the Israelites to build in the wilderness.' (Lyon) Subsequently, on moving to a new dwelling place, the home will undergo a ceremony of consecration and dedication which indicates that it is not merely a place to live, but that it is also the place where people live according to the traditions and values of the Jewish faith. Robinson is in accord with this when he ponders 'Where else would the values of the faith be handed down besides the family? ... the Jewish home is the place where children, adolescents, and even young adults receive their most important training in ... "Jewishness".'

Another line of argument might be to suggest that even though in theory family life appears to be the main strength of Judaism, there are other issues that might impinge upon its success. Consider, for example, living as a Jewish family in a secular society. There is a great likelihood in this situation that some kind of tension might arise concerning the differences between the two ways of life. Young Jewish adolescents in particular may find themselves at odds with the perceived constraints placed upon them such as being unable to meet with friends on a Friday evening due to Shabbat regulations, for example. The requirement to abide by the kosher food laws might also place a strain on family relationships should the young Jewish person feel that it is more important that they disregard

AO2 Activity

As you read through this section try to do the following:

1. Pick out the different lines of argument that are presented in the text and identify any evidence given in support.
2. For each line of argument try to evaluate whether or not you think this is strong or weak.
3. Think of any questions you may wish to raise in response to the arguments.

This Activity will help you to start thinking critically about what you read and help you to evaluate the effectiveness of different arguments and from this develop your own observations, opinions and points of view that will help with any conclusions that you make in your answers to the AO2 questions that arise.

the rules in order to fit in with the friends around them who are not of the Jewish faith. Likewise, for a working Jewish parent when the requirements of their job means that they are unable to partake in the Shabbat evening meal during the winter because they have not been able to leave work early. For Haredi Jews, who live within a closed society, family life is unhindered by such problems; but not so for other Jews who find themselves sometimes at odds with the demands of a secular society.

Study tip

Take care when writing your conclusion that you make an evaluative judgement as opposed to merely repeating the main strands of the arguments that you have used in your answer.

Another area for consideration is the suggestion that it is the synagogue that is the main strength of Judaism rather than family life. As an institution, it provides the location for all aspects of Jewish life as well as for prayer and worship. A typical synagogue is also the venue for the Jewish community's **bet midrash** which provides a place for the study of the scriptures and the learning of Hebrew. Major events in life are also marked in the synagogue as well as within the family home. For example, the reading from the Torah scrolls at bar/bat mitzvah ceremonies is symbolic of the young person reaching the age when they can take personal responsibility for keeping the mitzvot. This is acknowledged and witnessed by the wider Jewish community; a community that can provide future support for the individual should it be required.

The Friday night celebration of Shabbat is an important part of Jewish family life.

It could also be argued that the celebration of festivals is one of the main strengths of Judaism. Support for this contention could be based upon the fact that even those Jews who are usually non-observant, and who do not attend the synagogue on a regular basis, make a special effort to be present at certain times of the year such as at Yom Kippur. Other festivals such as Pesach and Rosh Hashanah could also be said to strengthen Jewish identity through reminding Jews of their relationship with God and indirectly, or directly, with the covenants that are at the very foundation of the Jewish faith. Festivals also provide the opportunity for Jews to meet with fellow believers, and thus to be reminded of the common themes which underpin Jewish identity.

The mitzvot too could be acknowledged as a strength of Judaism, with their purpose being to give moral and ethical guidance on the way in which God requires a Jew to live. They allow each individual to cultivate their relationship with God at all levels of daily life: in their relationships with other people; and what they eat. They can therefore be seen as an effective aid to spiritual development and the basis upon which Jewish lifestyle has been created.

In conclusion, it could be argued that there is no one particular thing that acts as the main strength of Judaism, but rather that it is a combination of a variety of elements. However, such is the influence of the family, especially upon young children, that we cannot deny it has an important part to play in the creation of the next generation of Jews.

T3 Significant social and historical developments in religious thought

Key quotes

… there is a universal recognition among Jewry that the home is central to Jewish existence and survival. **(Cohn-Sherbok)**

The idea that the survival of the Jewish community depends entirely on transferring the faith effectively is as true today as it has ever been, and the part played in this by the family remains vitally important. **(Hoffman)**

It's a great relief to know that God is available to us not only in the synagogue. It's a great relief to know that when we come home at the end of the day to a quiet house, we're not really alone at all, because God is there. **(Lyon)**

Key questions

What evidence do you think could be used to suggest that Jewish family life is the main strength of the faith?

Does living in a secular society present a threat to traditional Jewish family life?

To what extent do other elements within the Jewish faith act as its strength?

Key term

Bet midrash: house of study

AO2 Activity

List some conclusions that could be drawn from the AO2 reasoning from the above text; try to aim for at least three different possible conclusions. Consider each of the conclusions and collect brief evidence to support each conclusion from the AO1 and AO2 material for this topic. Select the conclusion that you think is most convincing and explain why it is so. Try to contrast this with the weakest conclusion in the list, justifying your argument with clear reasoning and evidence.

Whether or not women can be equal to men in Judaism

It could be argued that within certain Jewish groups such as the more Orthodox traditions, for example, the restrictions placed upon women suggest that equality is not possible for females in Judaism. Evidence for this viewpoint can be illustrated by reference to a number of practices, which, in secular society would certainly be regarded by many as exemplifying inequality. As far as divorce is concerned, for example, the Orthodox tradition only allows a man to divorce his wife. This practice is in accordance with the opening verses of Deuteronomy 24 which state that: 'A man takes a wife ... he writes her a bill of divorce, hands it to her, and sends her away from his house.' Consequently, as it is only the husband who has the right to instigate divorce proceedings, a woman is prohibited from following the same course of action should she be unhappy in her marriage. Furthermore, if a husband disappears, but is not known to have died, his abandoned wife, unable to divorce him can never remarry. A woman in this particular situation falls into the category of 'agunah' or 'chained wife'.

Other practices which can be used to exemplify inequality between men and women within Judaism are evident in relation to worship at the synagogue. In Orthodox synagogues men and women are seated separately, with the women sitting either in the balcony or behind a partition or screen. However, not only are they physically separated from the men; they are also separated from the important ritual of worship. The reading of the portion of the Torah scroll from the reading desk, for example, is enacted within the male domain and is thus denied to the female members of the congregation. Accordingly, women are also denied membership of the minyan, thus suggesting a role that is subordinate to men.

However, the development of the Jewish feminist movement in the latter part of the twentieth century suggests that women are taking action in order to bring about equality where it doesn't yet exist. The need for such a movement implies strongly that women are not yet equal to men in Judaism, yet advocates actions that will act to challenge, and ultimately to change, the imbalance. For example, through the development of small worship groups led by lay people rather than rabbis. This has been one way in which women in the more Orthodox traditions have been able to start taking an active part in worship. In addition, statistics show that there has been an increase in women attending yeshivot in contrast to the traditional view that prohibited women from the study of Talmud and Torah. Granted, this does not represent total equality by any means, but it does illustrate that an evolutionary process is taking place.

It is important to note, however, that not all groups within Judaism apply the same distinction between the roles of women and men. Indeed, practices from the Reform movement can be presented as evidence to show that women and men are already treated as equals. This state of affairs is based upon the premise that Halakhah is not the sole, legitimate form of decision making. Reform Jews consider their conscience and apply the ethical principles which are also an important part of the Jewish tradition when deciding upon a particular course of action. Reform Jews agree that the traditional distinction between the role of women and men goes against the principles of the faith. This has enabled women in Reform communities to gain equal access to all aspects of religious life. Women are therefore to be found serving their communities as cantors and rabbis; reading the Torah publicly in worship; wearing tallit and tefillin. Reform Judaism has also done away with the minyan completely.

Specification content
Whether or not women can be equal to men in Judaism.

Key quote
You could say that Jews invented the phrase, 'A woman's place is in the home'. Orthodox Jewish teaching has always declared that the primary religious responsibility of women is to keep the family together, to maintain the rituals of the faith, while praying is the expressed duty of men ... This is starting to change. **(Freedland)**

AO2 Activity
As you read through this section try to do the following:

1. Pick out the different lines of argument that are presented in the text and identify any evidence given in support.
2. For each line of argument try to evaluate whether or not you think this is strong or weak.
3. Think of any questions you may wish to raise in response to the arguments.

This Activity will help you to start thinking critically about what you read and help you to evaluate the effectiveness of different arguments and from this develop your own observations, opinions and points of view that will help with any conclusions that you make in your answers to the AO2 questions that arise.

Key quote

We too had a covenant; we too were there – women are seeking to transform Jewish ritual so that it acknowledges our existence and experience. In the ritual moment, women's history is made present. **(Plaskow)**

Study tip

Practise using relevant quotations from scholars in your AO2 answers. However, make sure that the quotations you use are relevant to the point or points that you are making.

Another line of argument is to suggest that it is not the case that women lack equality with men in the Orthodox tradition. This particular viewpoint is based upon the assertion that whereas women may not be full participants in matters of formal worship, they do, in fact, hold an equally important role which is based within the Jewish family. According to Halakhah, womanhood is a separate status with its own specific set of rules, obligations and responsibilities. Cohn-Sherbok explains that their exemption from taking part in formal worship should not perhaps be regarded as suggesting that they are inferior to men; but more in the sense of them being granted freedom from time-bound commandments such as the recitation of prayers in order that they might be able to concentrate on completing their important duties within the home and family. This is because Judaism teaches that marriage and motherhood are important for a woman's own personal development.

In addition to this, it might be argued that as the Jewish religion is based upon matrilineal descent, a mother holds great authority as it is through her lineage that her children are accepted to be Jewish. Women also have a significant role in teaching and demonstrating Jewish values and traditions to their children. For example, traditionally it is the mother who prepares kosher food, maintains a kosher kitchen and prepares for the festivals and Shabbat. She is also responsible for teaching her daughters what they will need to know when they have homes and a family of their own. Some might further assert that modest dress, and a regular time of separation for a woman during her menstrual cycle are critical examples of Jewish women being highly respected and honoured within the religion.

In conclusion, when addressing the issue of whether or not women can be equal to men in Judaism it is important not to make sweeping statements that only serve to suggest that the Jewish faith as a whole denies women equality. There are many examples which show that even if equality is not wholesale, there have certainly been changes in many areas which serve to provide women with equal opportunities. There are many Jews today, for example, who agree wholeheartedly that inequality regarding divorce is unacceptable. In order to counter this, Reform Jews follow a Talmudic principle: 'the law of the land is the law'. This states that in such matters, the secular law of the country will take precedence, and thus a divorce can be granted. Consequently, a couple who receive a civil divorce will also be divorced legally in the eyes of the Reform rabbinate.

It should also be noted that women are receiving greater recognition through the creation of new liturgy. For example, Plaskow notes the creation of a liturgy for the birth ceremonies of girls. She admits that such a ceremony has neither historical nor liturgical roots, and yet it is important in that it is a means by which to assert and celebrate the value of daughters by welcoming them into the community with a ceremony parallel to that of brit milah. And even Orthodox feminist, Blu Greenberg, believes that it is inevitable that the Orthodox community will eventually ordain women as rabbis, as she believes that the increase in Jewish women attending yeshivot signifies a transformation in the future. In her words: 'Learning is the road to ordination, and you can't close the last gates of the path.'

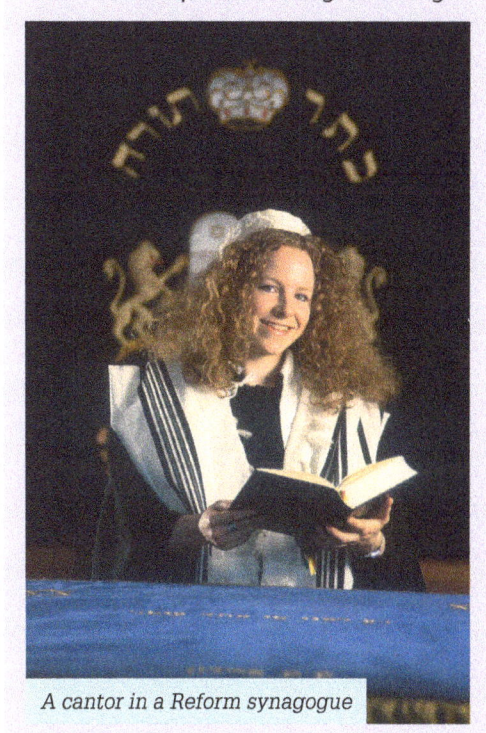

T3 Significant social and historical developments in religious thought

A cantor in a Reform synagogue

Key questions

What evidence do you think could be used to suggest that women are regarded as subordinate to men within Judaism?

Can it be argued successfully that gender inequality has been eradicated totally in some Jewish denominations?

To what extent is the move towards equality between women and men still in its evolutionary phase?

AO2 Activity

List some conclusions that could be drawn from the AO2 reasoning from the above text; try to aim for at least three different possible conclusions. Consider each of the conclusions and collect brief evidence to support each conclusion from the AO1 and AO2 material for this topic. Select the conclusion that you think is most convincing and explain why it is so. Try to contrast this with the weakest conclusion in the list, justifying your argument with clear reasoning and evidence.

WJEC / Eduqas Religious Studies for
A Level Year 2 and A2 Judaism

Key skills Theme 3DEF

This Theme has tasks that deal with specific aspects of AO2 in terms of identifying key elements of an evaluative style piece of writing, specifically counter-arguments and conclusions (both intermediate and final).

AO2 Developing skills

It is now important to consider the information that has been covered in this section; however, the information in its raw form is too extensive and so has to be processed in order to meet the requirements of the examination. This can be achieved by practising more advanced skills associated with AO2. The exercises that run throughout this book will help you to do this and prepare you for the examination. For assessment objective 2 (AO2), which involves 'critical analysis' and 'evaluation' skills, we are going to focus on different ways in which the skills can be demonstrated effectively, and also refer to how the performance of these skills is measured (see generic band descriptors for A2 [WJEC] AO2 or A Level [Eduqas] AO2).

▶ **Your task is this:** Below is a one-sided view concerning **family life as the main strength of Judaism**. It is 150 words long. You need to include this view for an evaluation; however, to just present one side of an argument or one line of reasoning is not really evaluation. Using the paragraph below, add a counter-argument or alternative line of reasoning to make the evaluation more balanced. Allow about 150 words for your counter-argument or alternative line of reasoning.

It could be argued that, rather than the family, the synagogue is the main strength of Judaism as it provides the location for all aspects of Jewish life as well as for prayer and for worship. Major life events are marked there; for example, the reading from the Torah scrolls at bar/bat mitzvah ceremonies is symbolic of the young person reaching the age when they can take personal responsibility for keeping the mitzvot. This is acknowledged and witnessed by the wider Jewish community; a community that can provide future support for the individual should it be required. And when Jews meet at the synagogue to celebrate festivals, this could be seen as providing the opportunity for them to meet with fellow believers, and thus to be reminded of the common themes which underpin Jewish identity. Further evidence for the importance of the synagogue is that it provides the venue for the community's bet midrash.

Next, think of another line of argument or reasoning that may support either argument or it may even be completely different and add this to your answer. Then ask yourself:

- Will my work, when developed, contain thorough, sustained and clear views that are supported by extensive, detailed reasoning and/or evidence?

Key skills

Analysis involves:

Identifying issues raised by the materials in the AO1, together with those identified in the AO2 section, and presents sustained and clear views, either of scholars or from a personal perspective ready for evaluation.

This means:

- That your answers are able to identify key areas of debate in relation to a particular issue
- That you can identify, and comment upon, the different lines of argument presented by others
- That your response comments on the overall effectiveness of each of these areas or arguments.

Evaluation involves:

Considering the various implications of the issues raised based upon the evidence gleaned from analysis and provides an extensive detailed argument with a clear conclusion.

This means:

- That your answer weighs up the consequences of accepting or rejecting the various and different lines of argument analysed
- That your answer arrives at a conclusion through a clear process of reasoning.

E: Judaism and migration: the challenges of being a religious and ethnic minority in Britain

T3 Significant social and historical developments in religious thought

This section covers AO1 content and skills

Background information

An initial report into the results of the 2011 census by the Institute for Jewish Policy Research indicates that 263,346 people identified themselves as Jewish on their census return forms. The census also illustrates that Britain's Jewish population is not spread evenly across the country, but rather is concentrated in a few specific areas and neighbourhoods. Perhaps one of the reasons for this phenomenon is that it is becoming frequently more difficult to maintain a Jewish lifestyle in a mainly secular society.

In an article entitled 'What is life like for Jewish people in Wales today?' journalist Huw Silk interviewed Stanley Soffa, Chairman of the South Wales Jewish Representative Council. Soffa highlighted the fact that the number of Jewish people in Wales is declining: 'A lot of the religious younger people have moved away to have more religious amenities ... People who want the religious education – the schools and universities – the social scene and restaurants have moved away ... if you want to bring up your family with a lot of Jewish schools around, with Jewish delicatessens, you can't always do it in Cardiff ... There's no religious slaughter in Wales, so if you want to buy kosher meat you have to either go to London yourself – which a lot of people do – or order it over the phone. Sainsbury's has some stuff but the choice isn't that big.' Soffa's response is indicative of a trend that means that although there are still about 2,000 Jews living in Wales, with an estimated 800 living in Cardiff (according to the 2011 census), there are certainly problems when it comes to maintaining a Jewish lifestyle.

Mark Stone, Chairman of Cardiff Reform Synagogue, accepts that there are challenges within all faith communities with declining numbers, yet does not agree that the decline is inevitable. He believes that too many leaders think that this self-fulfilling prophecy is going to happen and he does not agree with their viewpoint: 'There is so much that communities can do to reverse the trend and attract people back. Younger people cannot afford to live in the big cities, and, as such, cities like Sheffield are seeing a growth in certainly the Jewish community. And Cardiff, being a capital city, is a wonderful place to live, and we must fly the flag. Kosher food is sometimes used as a reason for not coming here, but everyone can order online anyway, so there is no problem there. We must do the right thing and make our synagogues welcoming and not stuffy. We must have a positive attitude, and if we take action to change things we will succeed.'

The converse is true, however, for areas in the UK which are home to large numbers of ultra-Orthodox Jews, whose numbers are growing at quite a rate. The fact that ultra-Orthodox Jews live in closed communities and are segregated from mainstream society may be the reason why they have been able to retain their religious lifestyle and religious practices intact; but it has come at a price – that of total segregation and the inability to assimilate.

There are certainly challenges for Jews living in Britain today; challenges that have been created by segregation and assimilation as a result of being part of a religious and ethnic minority.

Key quotes

I the LORD am your God who has set you apart from other peoples. So you shall set apart the clean beast from the unclean, the unclean bird from the clean. You shall not draw abomination upon yourselves through beast or bird or anything with which the ground is alive, which I have set apart for you to treat as unclean.
(Leviticus 20:24–25)

(Food laws) train us to master our appetites; accustom us to restrain our desires; and to avoid considering the pleasures of eating and drinking as the goal of man's existence.
(Maimonides)

Only be sure that you do not eat the blood; for the blood is the life ...
(Deuteronomy 12:23)

WJEC / Eduqas Religious Studies for A Level Year 2 and A2 Judaism

Specification content

An examination of the problems created by segregation and assimilation for Jewish communities and individuals living in Britain today with a focus on: kashrut (purity).

Key quotes

A man's table is like the altar. **(Talmud)**

A kashrut-observing Jew is brought face-to-face with his belief in the Almighty every time he lifts a fork to his mouth or puts a box of cereal in his shopping cart. To achieve that complete sense of connectedness to the Holy, an extra set of dishes seems a small price to pay. **(Robinson)**

Key terms

Chukim: commandments for which no particular reason has been given for having to keep them

Hechsher: a stamp or label certifying that a food product is kosher

Kashering: to make fit for use; to make kosher

Kashrut: religious dietary laws

Shechitah: ritual slaughter of animals as set out in Jewish law

Treifah: meaning 'torn'; food that is non-kosher

quickfire

3.21 Why does the process of kashering take place?

A hechsher

Kashrut (purity)

Kashrut is the body of Jewish law which deals with the foods that Jews can and cannot eat. Kashrut also gives rulings on how those permitted foods must be prepared and eaten. The Hebrew Bible declares that the laws of kashrut were given by God to Moses on Mount Sinai, and thus, because of their divine origin, this legislation is absolute.

Jewish food laws are examples of a class of mitzvot known as **chukim** (statutes) which are distinctive because no particular reason is given for having to keep them. Jews would say, however, that the main purpose of the food laws is to discipline the Jewish people towards holiness. They believe that it is a means by which to express the part that they have to play in the covenant relationship with God. By keeping the food laws, Jews are able to demonstrate their commitment to God at the most fundamental level. The laws of kashrut are also a way of distinguishing the Jews as the chosen people by giving them a sense of identity and belonging. Strict adherence to the law of kashrut is seen as a way of making humans 'purer', and therefore closer to God. As Deuteronomy 14:21 says: 'For you are a people consecrated to the LORD your God.' Hoffman notes: 'We see the consecrated nature of eating at many points in Jewish life. In the blessings both before and after a meal and in actions reminiscent of ancient priestly duties (for example, the washing of hands and dipping the special Sabbath bread in salt), the meal becomes a sanctified place.'

The laws concerning which animals, birds and fish may be eaten are to be found in Leviticus 11 and Deuteronomy 14. They identify certain foods as kosher; and others which are forbidden or **treifah**. According to Leviticus 11:2–3, for an animal to be kosher it must have a split hoof, and it must also chew the cud: 'These are the animals which you may eat ... anything which has a completely split hoof and chews the cud, this you may eat ...' Regarding fish, the law states that only fish that have both fins and scales can be eaten: 'Everything in the waters which has fins and scales ... you may eat' (Leviticus 11:10). As far as birds are concerned, there is no specific formula, however a list of forbidden birds is set out in Leviticus 11:13–19.

Furthermore, kosher food must be prepared in an appropriate way before consumption. Rabbinic tradition requires that an animal be slaughtered in a specific way, known as **shechitah** which involves a cut across the throat with a razor-sharp knife. Once slaughtered, the animal or bird is inspected to make sure that it is free from defects. The meat then has to be rinsed and salted so that any remaining blood is removed. This process, known as **kashering**, can be done at home, or by the butcher.

Another restriction concerning kashrut is the prohibition against cooking or eating milk and meat together: 'You shall not boil a kid in its mother's milk' (Exodus 23:19). Because of this rule, it is usual within an Orthodox Jewish household to have separate crockery, cutlery, cooking utensils and food storage and preparation areas so that the two can be kept apart. Many kosher kitchens also have two sinks so that the washing up can be done separately too. Furthermore, a period of time needs to elapse after having a meat meal before eating a dairy product.

Many Orthodox Jews keep the laws of kashrut in their entirety; however, this can pose particular problems for Jewish communities and individuals who live in Britain today. Keeping kashrut certainly has the potential to isolate and separate Jews from the wider secular society. Orthodox Jews, who observe the laws of kashrut with exact care, insist that foods be certified by a trained rabbi. In Britain, this certification is usually carried out under rabbinic supervision by KLBD, also known as the Kashrut Division of the London Beth Din. In order to overcome the problem of knowing which food products are kosher, rabbis will usually supervise the whole manufacturing process. When a product is approved, it will be awarded certification, and a symbol will be printed on the label. The symbol of kosher approval is called a **hechsher**. Some supermarkets in areas where there is a Jewish community might carry a limited line of kosher products, but it remains a problem for a Jewish person or family if they live in a non-Jewish area.

It is also often difficult, if not impossible, for Orthodox Jews to eat out in non-Jewish restaurants. In order to overcome this difficulty, however, the KLBD offers the services of a **shomer** whose job it is to supervise the kitchen of a non-Jewish establishment in order to ensure that all ingredients and methods of cooking are in accordance with the laws of kashrut. A shomer might therefore be employed for such occasions as wedding receptions or bar/bat mitzvah parties in hotels or restaurants.

However, it is usually now only within close-knit Jewish communities that kosher butchers are to be found. Such butchers are licensed by a rabbinic board, which ensures that the animals have been slaughtered and the meat prepared in the proper way. Inspectors visit the shops frequently in order to ensure that the meat is always kosher. Kosher restaurants also require certification, and their menus and kitchens will be checked to ensure that they follow the rules regarding the separation of meat and dairy products for example. Such practices, however, can lead to Jewish communities becoming segregated from mainstream society as opposed to becoming assimilated. Nevertheless, Hoffman doesn't necessarily regard segregation as a problem for Orthodox Jews: 'The Orthodox position is that the traditional halakhah is binding. What may be eaten is governed by the many regulations derived from the Bible and by the rabbinic elaborations of the biblical rules. If this entails great effort, expense, and non-assimilation into non-Jewish society, then this after all serves the purpose of all these dietary laws. They are a reminder of distinctiveness. They require discrimination, recognising that the body and food are given by God who calls for holiness in his people.'

It is clear from both the teachings of the Torah and Jewish beliefs that kosher food is a hugely important and influential part of Jewish life. However, it is an area that is open to interpretation and, as such, different groups within Judaism display differing approaches to the laws of kashrut. Many Reform Jews do not keep kashrut at all, based upon a rejection of laws that are considered to have a ritual rather than a moral basis. The Reform position was set out in the Pittsburgh Platform of 1885: 'We hold that all such Mosaic and rabbinical laws as regulate diet ... Their observance in our days is apt rather to obstruct than to further modern spiritual elevation.' As a result of this, many Reform Jews do not keep kashrut at all, whilst others have chosen to keep a degree of kashrut by avoiding some of the prohibited foods such as pork or shellfish. Some Reform Jews observe the food laws at home, but are quite comfortable in eating out in non-kosher restaurants and non-kosher homes. Such an approach, notes Hoffman, 'has evolved largely from the desire to facilitate relations with non-Jews. Certainly, eating with non-Jewish friends or in public restaurants becomes much easier.'

Reform Jews would argue that it is important to be assimilated into secular society, and, as keeping the laws of kashrut in their entirety might prevent this from occurring, there needs to be a compromise. Only in this way can Judaism survive in the modern world. This is not to be regarded as a negative thing, but rather a practicality in Britain where there is a shortage of shops and restaurants that cater for the needs of a kosher diet. Reform Jews believe that to discard these requirements does not take anything away from their faith.

AO1 Activity

Use the website of the Kosher London Beth Din (KLBD) to carry out further research about its work. After you have done your research, create the content for a webpage that provides a summary of the services that the KLBD has to offer.

T3 Significant social and historical developments in religious thought

Key quotes

... the dietary laws have the incidental consequence that Jews who wish to keep them need to live in Jewish communities where the supporting institutions of kashrut are to be found ... **(Unterman)**

Of particular importance to Reform is the distinction that is made between private and communal life. **(Hoffman)**

Key term

Shomer: meaning 'guard'; one who supervises kitchens in order to ensure that the laws of kashrut are observed

Kosher butchers are licensed by a rabbinic board.

Study tip

It is a good idea to put yourself in someone else's shoes in order to come to a better understanding of their situation. For example, have a go at applying the laws of kashrut to your own lifestyle, and note down how your eating habits might have to change as a result of the requirements.

WJEC / Eduqas Religious Studies for
A Level Year 2 and A2 Judaism

Specification content

An examination of the problems created by segregation and assimilation for Jewish communities and individuals living in Britain today with a focus on: dress.

Key quote

To the Hasid, this mode of dress proclaims him a servant of God. His clothing is a constant reminder to the outside world and to himself of his chosen religious discipline, his separateness. **(Robinson)**

Dress

An Hasidic Jew

One particular group within Judaism, Hasidic Jews, are immediately recognisable by their appearance and style of dress. Hasidic men are bearded and wear side-curls in obedience to the requirement in Leviticus 19:27 which states: 'You shall not round off the side-growth on your head, or destroy the side-growth of your beard.' They are also usually dressed in black suits with long black coats, white shirts and a large black hat worn over a small black skull cap. Some wear a round, fur hat known as a **shtreimel** on Shabbat and at other Jewish festival times. Fringes which are attached to their underclothes are also visible protruding from the waist band of their trousers.

The clothes worn by Hasidic women are also distinctive, but to a lesser extent. Modesty is required and therefore skirts are worn which cover the knees; sleeves extend over the elbows; and low necklines are not allowed. Once an Hasidic woman is married she is also required to cover her hair, therefore it is customary for a wig to be worn.

As a result of their distinctive appearance, Hasidic Jews stand out in a crowd, and their instant visibility has made them a source of ridicule and, in many cases, the victims of discriminatory, anti-Semitic action. Assimilation into secular society has been impossible for this particular group, not only because of their style of dress, but also due to the fact that, in accepting the fundamental religious beliefs of Judaism, they are required to adhere strictly to the requirements of the Jewish law which they would be unable to do in the wider society. Today, one of the largest Hasidic communities in Europe is to be found in North London. It provides all that is needed for the group to survive, thus doing away with the need for assimilation.

Key terms

Kippah: a skull cap

Shtreimel: a round, fur hat worn by Hasidic Jews

quickᖴire

3.22 Why has it been difficult for Hasidic Jews to assimilate into secular society?

Another item of clothing that is distinctive of Judaism is the **kippah**. Many Orthodox Jewish men will wear a kippah at all times; however, some Reform Jews will wear them only at the synagogue, or at special events, but not during their everyday business. Decisions about such matters have been made in light of the need to assimilate into secular society.

A kippah

AO1 Activity

Newspaper articles regarding the Hasidic community in the UK can be accessed online. Undertake some research and collate examples which can be used to illustrate how ultra-Orthodox Jews adhere to the strict requirements of the Jewish religion in modern-day Britain.

Specification content

An examination of the problems created by segregation and assimilation for Jewish communities and individuals living in Britain today with a focus on: practice of religion.

Practice of religion

The requirements of the Jewish faith to live according to the specific demands of the Torah can also make assimilation impractical within a mainly secular society. A case in point is Shabbat observance.

The home is regarded as the focus of religious activity within Judaism, and the celebration of Shabbat is centred upon the weekly Friday night meal. Orthodox Jews, wherever they live, observe the Shabbat traditions as faithfully as possible even though this can be quite challenging within a mainly non-Jewish, secular Britain. Here are some examples of the challenges which need to be overcome:

- British society and culture doesn't cater for Jewish people, and the holiness of Shabbat isn't reflected in the busy nature of a typical Saturday.

- Shabbat observance can put pressure on children. For example, it is sometimes difficult for a Jewish child, who lives in a non-Jewish area, to explain to his or her friends that they can't meet up with them on a Saturday.
- It might also be difficult for a Jewish family to get to a synagogue to celebrate Shabbat as the synagogue might be too far away for them to walk to it; and driving is not allowed on the Sabbath unless it's a case of a life or death emergency.
- Shabbat practices also mark Jews out as being different from others in society, and this can sometimes cause difficulties especially in the workplace. The requirement to be at home before sundown on a Friday night can be a particular problem especially during the winter months. A request to leave work early in order to be home in time for the start of Shabbat can lead to discriminatory behaviour from other colleagues who might perceive unfairness in what they might consider to be special treatment for their Jewish colleague.

Observing Shabbat traditions can be challenging within a mainly secular society.

However, there is diversity within the Jewish community, and not all groups suffer from the same challenges. For Reform Jews, even though Shabbat remains a very important event, the requirements of its observance are not followed as strictly as for Orthodox Jews. For instance, Reform Jews light the candles and commence Shabbat at any time on Friday evening rather than just before the sun goes down. Neither do they observe the 39 **melachot**; defining 'work' as being the job which they do to earn money, which they refrain from doing during Shabbat. They will also drive to the synagogue, use the telephone and continue to make use of electrical appliances.

However, Jewish life is also under the threat of the influences of secular society in other ways. For Orthodox Jews the marital relationship is governed by the laws of family purity, which involve visiting the **mikveh**, and the forbidding of sexual relations during menstruation. Many Jews say that doing this every month helps to keep the marriage alive. However, to an outsider this may seem to be a very strange way to behave, and many would find it difficult to understand why this should need to be the case. Many synagogues continue to provide a facility for this ritual to continue, and this is done by means of a mikveh. The purpose of immersion in a mikveh is not physical, but spiritual cleanliness; but many in secular society are unable to understand the distinction between spiritual cleansing and personal hygiene.

There are also problems reconciling the rituals and requirements of certain Jewish rites of passage with the law of the land. Judaism prescribes that following a death, the burial of the body should take place as soon as possible. Jews consider it very disrespectful to delay a burial, except in exceptional circumstances. However, this practice is not always possible when an autopsy, requested by a coroner, has to be carried out. Although Jews will comply with this as it is a matter of law, it nevertheless highlights the fact that some legislation can affect minority religious communities.

T3 Significant social and historical developments in religious thought

Key quotes

Practising Jews work in all areas of industry, trade and professions, and are able to operate within a normal work environment while still fully observing their Judaism.
(The Employer's Guide to Judaism)

The (UK) law affords various types of aid to Jews who wish to adhere to their beliefs without suffering discrimination because of their ethnicity or religion.
(The Employer's Guide to Judaism)

Key terms

Melachot: the 39 types of work forbidden on Shabbat

Mikveh: 'a place where water has gathered'; a special pool attached to a synagogue where Jews can immerse to purify themselves

quickfire

3.23 How do many Reform Jews define 'work' in relation to the requirement to rest on Shabbat?

The requirements of the Jewish faith are sometimes at odds with the requirements of UK law.

WJEC / Eduqas Religious Studies for A Level Year 2 and A2 Judaism

Specification content

An examination of the problems created by segregation and assimilation for Jewish communities and individuals living in Britain today with a focus on: education.

Key quotes

These commandments that I give to you today are to be on your hearts. Impress them on your children. **(Deuteronomy 6:6–7)**

The Mishnah lays down a balanced educational programme: 'At five ... (should be taught) Scripture, at ten Mishnah ... at fifteen Talmud.' **(Unterman)**

Non-observant parents today are more willing to send their child to an Orthodox Jewish day school ... perhaps because they fear that the alternative may be that he or she 'marries out', takes drugs, joins a non-Jewish religious movement, or simply grows up ignorant of Jewish history and culture. **(Wright)**

There is a variety of Jewish faith schools in the UK.

Education

The education of children has been a fundamental priority for the Jewish community from earliest times. The Book of Proverbs makes its importance clear when it states: 'Train up a child in the way he should go, and when he is old he will not depart from it.' (Proverbs 22:6)

In Britain there is a variety of Jewish schools which range from ultra-Orthodox to non-Orthodox, with each having their own particular approach and ethos regarding the kind of education which they feel is most beneficial for Jewish children. The majority of Jewish schools in Britain are governed by the United Synagogue, which helps to shape the schools' values and practices. A typical Orthodox school will cover the full curriculum as found in a conventional state school, but with Jewish education occupying up to 25% of the timetable. Furthermore, religious education is integrated into each day rather than as a separate element. Jewish schools such as this cater for children who come from extremely observant families to those for whom Jewish traditions are important.

An example of a school that is not under the auspices of any denomination or synagogue is JCoSS (Jewish Community Secondary School) which describes itself as 'a pluralist Jewish learning community' that welcomes students from all denominational settings rather than prioritising one. Jewish education is treated as a compulsory core subject throughout key stages 3 and 4, and world faiths are taught as well. Kosher food is served in the cafeteria, and all Jewish festivals are observed, with early closure on Fridays to accommodate Shabbat.

Outside the Orthodox community, however, many Jewish parents do not want this type of education for their children. Their sons and daughters therefore attend non-Jewish schools, and are dependent on the synagogue for their Jewish religious education. The synagogues organise a system of supplementary Jewish studies, and the children attend class after school and on Sundays. However, this has led to many Jewish children perceiving that it is the secular schooling which really matters and as such, places their religious education in second place.

Education is invariably a source of tension within modern Judaism because, states Unterman, it is an area in which 'Jewish children are fully exposed to the ideas, attitudes, and values of the wider secular society in which they live'. He continues by noting that one solution which has been adopted by a significant minority of Jewish parents is to send their children to Jewish schools. 'This', he explains, 'is meant to cushion the effect of the gentile environment, enhance social contact with fellow Jews, limit the prospect of inter-marriage, and provide a degree of Jewish education.' It could be claimed that the provision of Jewish faith schools represents a reluctance to assimilate into mainstream society.

The provision of education within Jewish faith schools has both advantages and disadvantages:

Advantages – Children are protected from the many difficulties which they might face as a Jew in a non-faith school. The lack of kosher food facilities, for instance, or having to be withdrawn from the daily acts of collective worship: these are things that mark a child out as being different from the majority of pupils, and could lead to bullying or worse. Within a Jewish school setting the cultural needs of the child can be catered for fully. The parent can also be assured that moral and ethical instruction will be in accordance with Jewish belief. There is also less of a danger of the child being influenced by the materialistic values of the secular world. Also, single-sex schools reduce the chance of inappropriate behaviour and relationships between teenage boys and girls. There is also the fear that non-faith schools could encourage assimilation at the cost of losing one's Jewish faith.

Disadvantages – Jewish faith schools, however, can generate their own problems since they can increase the sense of alienation felt by the Jewish child by continually making them aware that they are culturally different from the wider society in which they live. Faith schools might be said to be instrumental in encouraging segregation, and many Jews would argue that it is the role of the family and the synagogue to provide the religious and moral framework for children.

The role of the Jewish Leadership Council

The JLC (Jewish Leadership Council) is a Jewish charity which brings together representatives from the major British Jewish organisations. Its aim is to support and ensure continuity in the UK of a mainstream Jewish community, so that Judaism is assured of its place within British society as a whole.

The Jewish Leadership Council

The JLC's membership organisations touch on every aspect of Jewish life in the UK, such as synagogues, social care organisations, political bodies, youth movements, community centres and charities. In doing so, they believe that bringing these different perspectives together helps the Jewish community to gain in strength and to pursue common and coherent goals: 'together we are stronger, able to draw on each other's expertise and support each other' (JLC).

An example of one of the ways in which the JLC supports its members is through creating what are known as 'external affairs managers'. They exist in four specific regions: Scotland, Manchester, Leeds and Birmingham. Each manager is based in a communal building, with the appointment being made in conjunction with communal representative councils. Their role is to carry out advocacy and networking tasks for the community which they represent, whilst working to retain the particular heritage and character of each city and region: 'The JLC is committed to enabling our Jewish communities outside of London to have their voice heard.'

The JLC also acknowledges the importance that education plays in influencing the next generation's Jewish identity. It identified the growth of Jewish schools as: 'the single largest change in the UK Jewish community over the last twenty years' and, as such, commissioned a report in 2008 which noted that schools needed help in order to shape their strategic future, thereby strengthening Jewish life in the UK. The JLC therefore provides support for school infrastructure; the recruiting and training of teachers; creating curricula and providing professional development; developing school leaders; whilst also acknowledging that: 'Every Jewish school is different, with its own ethos, goals and values. We believe that this diversity should be celebrated, and that as a community we should be proud of the options we give parents to find the best fit for their child.'

Initiatives in Jewish schools include such things as the launch of the 'Yesh va' Yesh Wohl Hebrew Programme for Secondary Schools' which develops students' ability to communicate in Hebrew. Also, Jewish Studies is taught through the 'Chumash Curriculum' which enables pupils to gain a deeper knowledge and understanding of the Torah through the use of critical and analytical thinking. And all such enterprises are undertaken with the belief that it is possible to create a generation of 'engaged, educated and enthusiastic young Jewish people' (JLC).

Study tip
Make sure that you have an accurate understanding of the terms 'assimilation' and 'segregation'.

Specification content
The role of the Jewish Leadership Council.

quickfire
3.24 What is the JLC?

Key quotes
The JLC's mission is to work, through our members, to ensure the continuity in the UK, in this and future generations, of a mainstream Jewish Community that is:
1. Vibrant and vital
2. Safe and secure
3. Assured of its place within British society
4. Proud of its Jewish identity and culture
5. Confident in its support for Israel.

And to provide a range of sustainable services for the benefit of the whole community including:
1. Health, care, welfare and well-being
2. Security
3. Education, schools and leadership development
4. Political engagement
5. Social responsibility.
(The Jewish Leadership Council)

Without compromising their missions or neglecting their core audience, organisations that serve the Jewish community should, where appropriate, find ways of ensuring that their benefits spread as widely as possible.
(The Jewish Leadership Council)

quickfire
3.25 What is the aim of the 'Chumash Curriculum'?

Key skills

Knowledge involves:

Selection of a range of (thorough) accurate and relevant information that is directly related to the specific demands of the question.

This means:

- Selecting relevant material for the question set
- Being focused in explaining and examining the material selected

Understanding involves:

Explanation that is extensive, demonstrating depth and/or breadth with excellent use of evidence and examples including (where appropriate) thorough and accurate supporting use of sacred texts, sources of wisdom and specialist language.

This means:

- Effective use of examples and supporting evidence to establish the quality of your understanding
- Ownership of your explanation that expresses personal knowledge and understanding and NOT just reproducing a chunk of text from a book that you have rehearsed and memorised.

AO1 Developing skills

It is now important to consider the information that has been covered in this section; however, the information in its raw form is too extensive and so has to be processed in order to meet the requirements of the examination. This can be achieved by practising more advanced skills associated with AO1. For assessment objective 1 (AO1), which involves demonstrating 'knowledge' and 'understanding' skills, we are going to focus on different ways in which the skills can be demonstrated effectively, and also refer to how the performance of these skills is measured (see generic band descriptors for A2 [WJEC] AO1 or A Level [Eduqas] AO1).

▶ **Your next task is this:** Below is a summary of **the role of the Jewish Leadership Council**. It is 150 words long. This time there are no highlighted points to indicate the key points to learn from this extract. Discuss which five points you think are the most important to highlight and write them down in a list.

The Jewish Leadership Council is a charity whose aim is to support the mainstream Jewish community within the UK and to assure it of its place within British society as a whole. As far as education is concerned it acknowledges the importance of Jewish schools, and provides support for initiatives which will have an impact upon the ability of Jewish children to communicate in Hebrew, for example. It also promotes a deeper understanding of the Torah through its 'Chumash Curriculum' programme for Jewish studies. However, it has a wider outreach which touches upon all aspects of Jewish life in the UK such as social care organisations, community centres and charities. In doing so, it believes that bringing these different perspectives together helps the Jewish community to gain in strength and to pursue common and coherent goals: 'together we are stronger, able to draw on each other's' expertise and support each other'.

Now make the five points into your own summary (as in Theme 1 Developing skills) trying to make the summary more personal to your style of writing. This may also involve re-ordering the points if you wish to do so.

1. ....
2. ....
3. ....
4. ....
5. ....

Issues for analysis and evaluation

The possibility of assimilation into a secular society for Jews in Britain

It has been said that Judaism is a way of life which is based upon a specific set of rituals and practices that have their foundation in the Torah. Such requirements allow a Jew to cultivate their relationship with God at all levels of daily life; however, it could well be argued that in attempting to live according to religious guidelines in a secular society, Jews are in danger of isolating themselves.

Evidence for this point of view can be offered in the form of examples which illustrate that there are certainly many challenges which have the potential to make it difficult for Jews in Britain to assimilate fully into secular society. For instance, many Orthodox Jews wish to follow the laws of kashrut in their entirety. However, in order for this to be undertaken successfully, food has to be produced, prepared and eaten in a certain way as set down in the Torah and rabbinic tradition. In order for a product to be considered kosher, for example, its production has to be supervised by a rabbi, and only when it has reached the correct standard can it be awarded certification. Likewise, animals have to be slaughtered in the correct way by a process known as shechitah which involves a cut across the throat with a razor-sharp knife. This method of slaughter has caused concern amongst animal welfare groups, and serves to show just how different Jewish practices are from similar procedures in mainstream society. Some supermarkets might sell kosher food, but only in limited amounts, and so there would be a problem for a Jewish individual or family if they live in a non-Jewish area. It is also impossible for Orthodox Jews to eat in non-Jewish restaurants or in the homes of non-Jewish people, thus limiting social contact with those outside their own particular cultural group.

Jewish education is another area which, it could be argued, encourages segregation rather than promoting assimilation. On the one hand, it is perhaps understandable that Orthodox Jews make the choice to send their children to a faith school based upon the belief that by doing so they will be protecting their son or daughter from the materialist values of the secular world. Unterman highlights this attitude by noting that Jewish education 'is meant to cushion the effect of the gentile environment, enhance social contact with fellow Jews, limit the prospect of inter-marriage, and provide a degree of Jewish education'. However, on the other hand, Jewish faith schools can generate their own problems since they can increase the sense of alienation felt by the Jewish child by continually making them aware that they are culturally different from the wider society in which they live.

There are also problems reconciling the rituals and requirements of certain Jewish rites of passage with the law of the land. Judaism prescribes that following a death the burial of the body should take place as soon as possible as Jews consider it very disrespectful to delay a burial, except in exceptional circumstances. However, this practice is not always possible when an autopsy, requested by a coroner, has to be carried out. Although Jews are obliged to comply with this as it is a matter of law, it nevertheless highlights the fact that some legislation can affect minority religious communities.

Religious dress also marks a person out as different, which can also act as a barrier to assimilation. One particular group within Judaism, Hasidic Jews, are immediately recognisable by their appearance and style of dress. Hasidic men always have a beard and side curls in obedience to Leviticus 19:27: 'You shall not round off the side-growth on your head, or destroy the side-growth of your beard.' They also wear black suits, white shirts and a large black hat. Hasidic women also stand out as different as they wear modest clothing which does not reveal their

---

T3 Significant social and historical developments in religious thought

This section covers AO2 content and skills

Specification content
The possibility of assimilation into a secular society for Jews in Britain.

Key quote
When a Jew dies, Jewish law and tradition require that the funeral and burial of the deceased take place as soon after death as possible – ideally within twenty-four hours, but certainly within forty-eight hours. The funeral and burial are held so soon after death to emphasise the Jewish belief that the soul – wherein is the spark of life – immediately returns to God who gave it. **(Dosick)**

AO2 Activity
As you read through this section try to do the following:

1. Pick out the different lines of argument that are presented in the text and identify any evidence given in support.
2. For each line of argument try to evaluate whether or not you think this is strong or weak.
3. Think of any questions you may wish to raise in response to the arguments.

This Activity will help you to start thinking critically about what you read and help you to evaluate the effectiveness of different arguments and from this develop your own observations, opinions and points of view that will help with any conclusions that you make in your answers to the AO2 questions that arise.

115

WJEC / Eduqas Religious Studies for A Level Year 2 and A2 Judaism

Key questions

How far do the requirements of the Torah and rabbinic tradition prevent Jews in Britain from assimilating into mainstream society?

What part does Jewish education play in encouraging segregation or otherwise?

What evidence is there to suggest that assimilation is possible?

Key quote

The prophet Jeremiah sent a letter to the exiles in Babylon, telling them, 'Seek the peace in the city in which you find yourself, for it is in its peace that you will find peace.' This is still true today. **(Sacks)**

Cardiff Reform Synagogue

AO2 Activity

List some conclusions that could be drawn from the AO2 reasoning from the above text; try to aim for at least three different possible conclusions. Consider each of the conclusions and collect brief evidence to support each conclusion from the AO1 and AO2 material for this topic. Select the conclusion that you think is most convincing and explain why it is so. Try to contrast this with the weakest conclusion in the list, justifying your argument with clear reasoning and evidence.

neckline, arms or legs. They also wear a wig once married to cover their hair as this is a requirement. Hasidic Jews have not tried to assimilate, and live in closed communities as it is impossible to live their particular way of life in mainstream society. However, in many cases they have become victims of discrimination as a result.

Study tip

It is vital that you are able to make thorough and accurate use of specialist language and vocabulary in context in your answers; therefore, check your spelling carefully, and ensure that you have used specialist terms in the correct way.

It is important to note, however, that not all Jews have been unsuccessful in achieving assimilation into British society. Reform Jews have always been of the opinion that it is important to be assimilated into the wider society in which one lives, and they have shown that it is possible. For example, many Reform Jews do not keep kashrut at all, based upon a rejection of laws that are considered to have a ritual rather than a moral basis. The Reform position was set out in the Pittsburgh Platform of 1885: 'We hold that all such Mosaic and rabbinical laws as regulate diet … Their observance in our days is apt rather to obstruct than to further modern spiritual elevation.' Hoffman notes that this approach 'has evolved … from the desire to facilitate relations with non-Jews'. This can be used as evidence to show that Jews are able to maintain their religious devotional lifestyle without it having any detrimental effect upon their ability to function fully in mainstream society. Furthermore, Reform Jews firmly believe that this course of action does not take anything away from their faith.

Another aspect of this issue which needs consideration is to take account of the fact that the need to assimilate into secular society is of little concern for some members of the Jewish faith at all. Hoffman points out, in reference to the laws of kashrut, that for Orthodox Jews the traditional Halakhah is binding and non-negotiable. In fact, even though living according to the laws of kashrut entails great effort and brings with it the expense of non-assimilation, it is worth it as the laws are a reminder of the distinctiveness of the Jews. Hoffman expresses this in the following way: 'They require discrimination recognising that the body and food are given by God who calls for holiness in his people.'

In conclusion, some might draw attention to the fact that total assimilation isn't required anyway due to the fact that British society embraces Jewish religious identity along with a wide variety of religions, creeds and cultures. Evidence for this is demonstrated by the fact that Jews have been living successfully in Britain for many centuries, thus indicating that their presence in the UK has not been hindered by a lack of total assimilation. Indeed, UK law affords various types of aid to Jews (as well as to other religious groups), who wish to adhere to their beliefs without suffering discrimination because of their ethnicity or religion. Take, for example, the demands of Sabbath observance concerning the need to be at home before sundown on a Friday night. A request to leave work early on that day during the dark winter months has the potential to cause problems at the workplace; however, due to laws that support the right to religious freedom, practising Jews in all areas of industry, trade and professions are able to operate within a normal work environment while still fully observing their Judaism.

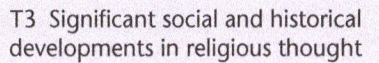

The extent to which assimilation equates to a loss of identity

Historical records tell us that Jews have lived successfully in Britain for many centuries, and the results of the 2011 UK census can be used as evidence to show that Jewish communities are still present. In spite of the fact that the question about religious affiliation on the census form was the only one that was voluntary, 263,346 people nevertheless identified themselves as Jewish on their return forms. Some might use this data as the means by which to suggest that Jews have not lost their religious identity; however, these figures do not give us a detailed insight into either the extent to which Judaism is still being practised, or into the diversity which is to be found in the Jewish community.

It could be argued that one particular branch of the Jewish faith, the Reform movement, has been successful in achieving assimilation into British society without compromising their religious identity. This achievement has come about as a result of the way in which the Reform movement has evolved in response to changes in society. The Reform position was set out in the Pittsburgh Platform of 1885 which established the principles of the movement, and which called for the following things: instead of a 'nation', Jews are to be regarded as a 'religious community' within whichever country they find themselves to be living; a rejection of laws which have a ritual rather than a moral basis; that there is no longer a need to dress in a specific way; for Jews to live in different nations is a necessary thing, as they have been chosen to spread the monotheistic truth and morality over all the earth, and to be an example to others. Hoffman notes that: 'of particular importance to Reform is the distinction that is made between private and communal life'. For example, many Reform Jews do not keep kashrut at all, whilst others have chosen to keep a degree of kashrut by avoiding some of the prohibited foods such as pork or shellfish. Some Reform Jews observe the food laws at home, but are quite comfortable in eating out in non-kosher restaurants and non-kosher homes. Such an approach, notes Hoffman, 'has evolved largely from the desire to facilitate relations with non-Jews. Certainly, eating with non-Jewish friends or in public restaurants becomes much easier.' It has also meant that Reform Jews have been able to take a full and meaningful part in mainstream British society, without the need to confine themselves within more isolated Jewish communities.

However, the attitude and practices of Reform Judaism are not widespread amongst all Jews who live in Britain today, and in direct contrast some might argue, stand the members of ultra-Orthodox groups such as the Hasidim. Many consider that Hasidic Jews have made no compromises whatsoever regarding their religious identity, and, as such, have knowingly forfeited the opportunity to achieve assimilation into mainstream British society. The Hasidim believe that the rules for life were presented by God to Moses on Mount Sinai in the form of the written and the oral Torah. Hasidic Jews hold that all of the mitzvot are relevant, and their understanding of them is that they should never lose the opportunity to keep a mitzvah. This can be seen in their distinctive personal appearance; for instance, amongst other things Hasidic men are bearded and wear side curls in obedience to the mitzvah found in Leviticus 19:27 which states: 'You shall not round off the side-growth on your head, or destroy the side-growth of your beard.' And Hasidic women are also distinctive following the requirement to dress modestly and to cover their natural hair with a wig once married. Moreover, in accepting the decision to live according to the fundamental beliefs of Judaism, they are only able to conform by living in closed communities in order to maintain the precepts of the Jewish faith according to their understanding of it. Today one of the largest Hasidic communities in Europe is to be found in North London. It provides all that is needed for the group to survive, thus guarding against a loss of identity.

T3 Significant social and historical developments in religious thought

Specification content
The extent to which assimilation equates to a loss of identity.

Key quote
Israel once was a nation but today is not a nation. It once had a set of laws that regulate diet, clothing, and the like. These no longer apply, because Israel is not now what it was then. Israel forms an integral part of Western civilisation. The reason to persist as a distinctive group was that the group has its work to do, a mission – to serve as a light to the nations. That meant, namely, to realise the messianic hope for the establishment of a kingdom of truth, justice, and peace. For that purpose Israel no longer constitutes a nation. It now forms a religious community. (Neusner)

AO2 Activity
As you read through this section try to do the following:

1. Pick out the different lines of argument that are presented in the text and identify any evidence given in support.
2. For each line of argument try to evaluate whether or not you think this is strong or weak.
3. Think of any questions you may wish to raise in response to the arguments.

This Activity will help you to start thinking critically about what you read and help you to evaluate the effectiveness of different arguments and from this develop your own observations, opinions and points of view that will help with any conclusions that you make in your answers to the AO2 questions that arise.

Key quote

An atheist, anti-religious Jew who was born of a Jewish mother would still be considered halakhically Jewish, and therefore accepted as such by his fellow Jews. (Unterman)

Key questions

What evidence is there which might be used to suggest that, for some Jewish groups, assimilation would be regarded as a total loss of identity?

Is there a means by which it is possible for Jews to maintain their Jewish identity as well as achieving assimilation?

How much of an effect does the lack of clarity regarding what makes a person Jewish have upon this issue?

AO2 Activity

List some conclusions that could be drawn from the AO2 reasoning from the above text; try to aim for at least three different possible conclusions. Consider each of the conclusions and collect brief evidence to support each conclusion from the AO1 and AO2 material for this topic. Select the conclusion that you think is most convincing and explain why it is so. Try to contrast this with the weakest conclusion in the list, justifying your argument with clear reasoning and evidence.

An alternative argument could be to suggest that there is a middle way that falls somewhere between the extremes of Hasidism on the one hand, and the liberalism of Reform Judaism on the other. Evidence of this can be seen in the way in which some Orthodox Jews have managed to achieve a balance between maintaining a life lived according to the mitzvot, whilst still being able to live and work in conventional society. Orthodox Jews tend to live in close proximity to their local synagogue, thus creating a community of like-minded neighbours. However, this does not mean that they have cut themselves off totally from wider British society. The Jewish community provides the benefits of both spiritual and practical support: spiritual in the sense of providing the basis for worship; practical in the sense of creating a community of schools, shops, societies that can allow Jews to live according to the mitzvot. For example, in order to live according to the laws of kashrut, food has to be produced, prepared and eaten in a certain way as set down in the Torah and rabbinic tradition. The slaughter of animals for meat has to be done in a particular way by a process known as shechitah, which in turn means that there is the need for a kosher butcher who has been certified by a rabbi.

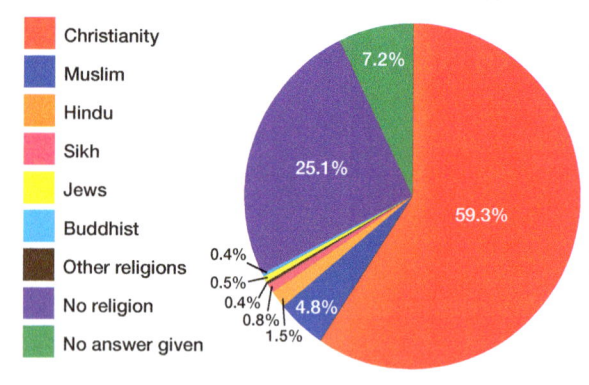

Pie chart: Christianity 59.3%, Muslim 4.8%, Hindu 1.5%, Sikh 0.8%, Jews 0.4%, Buddhist 0.5%, Other religions 0.4%, No religion 25.1%, No answer given 7.2%. Source: Data from the ONS 2011 Census

263,346 people identified themselves as being Jewish on the 2011 census of England and Wales.

Study tip

Make sure that you are familiar with the meaning of the term 'the extent to which'. It is usually used to indicate the degree to which something happens or is likely to happen.

However, evidence of a decline in Jewish communities in some parts of Britain can be used to support the suggestion that it is not always easy for Jews to retain their religious identity. Evidence for this assertion can be offered in the form of examples that illustrate the compromises that sometimes need to be made. In an article entitled 'What is life like for Jewish people in Wales today?' journalist Huw Silk highlights the fact that the number of Jewish people in Wales is declining. His interviewee, Stanley Soffa, states that: 'A lot of the religious younger people have moved away to have more religious amenities ... People who want the religious education – the schools and universities – the social scene and restaurants have moved away ... if you want to bring up your family with a lot of Jewish schools around, with Jewish delicatessens, you can't always do it in Cardiff ...' This trend, it could be suggested, shows a move towards greater segregation rather than assimilation; with many Jews putting an emphasis on retaining their religious identity at the expense of remaining a member of the mainstream community in which they were born.

In conclusion, we also need to note that when dealing with issues surrounding Jewish identity there is no clear-cut way by which to define Jewishness. For some it is linked to biological origin, with the requirement that one has to have been born to a Jewish mother; for others it is a national identity. However, even within these categories it is possible to be biologically Jewish but without religious, community or national affiliation. Without a clear definition, it can be difficult to judge the extent to which assimilation equates to a loss of identity.

AO2 Developing skills

It is now important to consider the information that has been covered in this section; however, the information in its raw form is too extensive and so has to be processed in order to meet the requirements of the examination. This can be achieved by practising more advanced skills associated with AO2. For assessment objective 2 (AO2), which involves 'critical analysis' and 'evaluation' skills, we are going to focus on different ways in which the skills can be demonstrated effectively, and also refer to how the performance of these skills is measured (see generic band descriptors for A2 [WJEC] AO2 or A Level [Eduqas] AO2).

▶ **Your next task is this:** Below is an evaluation concerning **the extent to which assimilation equates to a loss of identity**. It is 150 words long. After the first paragraph there is an intermediate conclusion highlighted for you in yellow. As a group try to identify where you could add more intermediate conclusions to the rest of the passage. Have a go at doing this.

Unlike Reform Jews, the practices of Ultra-Orthodox Jews provide evidence that they are not prepared to make compromises whatsoever regarding their religious identity, and, as such, have forfeited the opportunity to achieve assimilation into mainstream British society. Their decision has been based upon the belief that the rules for life were presented by God to Moses on Mount Sinai in the form of the written and the oral Torah. Hasidic Jews therefore hold that all of the mitzvot are relevant, and their understanding of them is that they should never lose the opportunity to keep a mitzvah. In accepting the decision to live according to the fundamental beliefs of Judaism, they are only able to conform by living in closed communities. Consequently, these communities provide all that is needed for the group to survive with no concessions being made to secular society and thus guarding against a loss of identity.

When you have done this, you will see clearly that in AO2 it is helpful to include a brief summary of the arguments presented as you go through an answer and not just leave it until the end to draw a final conclusion. This way you are demonstrating that you are sustaining evaluation throughout an answer and not just repeating information learned.

T3 Significant social and historical developments in religious thought

Key skills

Analysis involves:

Identifying issues raised by the materials in the AO1, together with those identified in the AO2 section, and presents sustained and clear views, either of scholars or from a personal perspective ready for evaluation.

This means:

- That your answers are able to identify key areas of debate in relation to a particular issue
- That you can identify, and comment upon, the different lines of argument presented by others
- That your response comments on the overall effectiveness of each of these areas or arguments.

Evaluation involves:

Considering the various implications of the issues raised based upon the evidence gleaned from analysis and provides an extensive detailed argument with a clear conclusion.

This means:

- That your answer weighs up the consequences of accepting or rejecting the various and different lines of argument analysed
- That your answer arrives at a conclusion through a clear process of reasoning.

WJEC / Eduqas Religious Studies for A Level Year 2 and A2 Judaism

This section covers AO1 content and skills

F: Holocaust theology

Background information

The Holocaust is the term used to denote the murder of six million Jews by Nazi Germany during World War II. Jews refer to the event as the **Shoah**. The roots of the Holocaust, however, can be traced back to the situation in Germany at the end of World War I. As a result of the Treaty of Versailles, which was signed in June 1919, Germany had to accept responsibility for starting the war, and was forced to pay for the cost of the damage which ran into billions of pounds. Amongst other things, Germany also lost some of its territory, and had to reduce the size of its army. Germany thus entered a period of turbulence which was characterised by high unemployment. In 1933 the National Socialist German Workers' Party (Nazi party) was elected to power, and Adolf Hitler became Chancellor of the country.

Cohn-Sherbok explains that the ideology of the Nazi party was based on German nationalism, anti-capitalism, and anti-Semitism. According to Hitler, the Jews were responsible for Germany's defeat in World War I as well as the economic and cultural decline which followed. In his autobiographical book, 'Mein Kampf', Hitler makes no secret of his animosity towards Jews. For him, Jews could never be considered true Germans because they were racially and religiously distinct: '(Jews were) not Germans of a special religion, but a people in themselves … Wherever I went, I began to see Jews, and the more I saw, the more sharply they became distinguished in my eyes from the rest of humanity.' (Hitler)

During the next few years Jews were gradually stripped of their position in society by being eliminated from the civil service, the legal and medical professions and cultural and educational institutions. Eventually laws were passed which relegated Jews to the position of second-class citizens. Their businesses were closed, and they were forbidden to share public spaces such as parks and libraries with non-Jews, in the hope that this treatment would force them to leave Germany. In November 1938, however, the Nazi party organised what Cohn-Sherbok describes as 'an onslaught against the Jewish population in which Jews were murdered and Jewish property was destroyed. This event, known as **Kristallnacht**, was a prelude to the Holocaust which brought about a new stage in modern Jewish history.'

Key terms

Kristallnacht: German attack on Jewish property which took place on 9–10 November 1938; also known as The Night of the Broken Glass

Shoah: meaning 'catastrophe'; term used to refer to the murder of six million Jews by the Nazis during World War II

Key quote

At 3 a.m. on 10 November 1938 was unleashed a barrage of Nazi ferocity as had no equal hitherto in Germany, or very likely anywhere else in the world since savagery began. Jewish buildings were smashed into and contents demolished or looted. **(Buffum)**

The destruction of Kristallnacht

With the outbreak of World War II pressure on Jews in Germany increased, and the Nazi party prepared for what was to become known as the Final Solution to the Jewish problem. At first the Jewish population was forced to live in **ghettos**, until finally they were rounded up and sent to death camps. In 1942 Auschwitz became the central extermination centre where Jews and members of other minority groups were sent to their deaths in the gas chamber. It has been estimated that by the end of the war in 1945, about six million Jews had been killed.

The traditional Jewish understanding of suffering

The traditional Jewish understanding of suffering is that it is a form of **retribution**. This is made clear in the terms of the covenant relationship that God made with the Jewish people. In accepting the terms of the covenant, the Jews were beholden to keep its requirements. If, however, they failed in their duty, they would be punished by God. An illustration of this concept is to be found in the Book of Jeremiah.

Jeremiah prophesied that idolatry and disloyalty to God would be punished, and yet that the Jews would not be fully outcast from the grace of God. During this time, Babylon took control of Jerusalem and Jeremiah witnessed the destruction of the First Temple in 586 BCE as well as the exile of the Jewish people. He had prophesied that the Jews would be scattered from their homeland and that they would suffer persecution: 'Then the word of the LORD came to Jeremiah: "… I am delivering this city into the hands of the Chaldeans and of King Nebuchadnezzar of Babylon, and he shall capture it … for the people of Israel and Judah have done nothing but evil in My sight since their youth; the people of Israel have done nothing but vex Me by their conduct …"' (Jeremiah 32:26–30)

However, Jeremiah also prophesied that God would protect the Jews from total destruction and that they would one day return to their promised land: 'See, I will gather them from all the lands to which I have banished them in My anger and wrath, and in great rage; and I will bring them back to this place and let them dwell secure. They shall be My people, and I will be their God.' (Jeremiah 32: 37–38)

The same theme, that the privilege of being the people of God carries with it the consequences of weightier and more certain judgement, is to be found in the Book of Amos: 'Hear this word, O people of Israel, that the LORD has spoken concerning you, concerning the whole family that I brought up from the land of Egypt: You alone have I singled out of all the families of the earth – that is why I will call you to account for all your iniquities.' (Amos 3:1–2)

However, even though persecution was not a new experience for the Jews, the enormity and uniqueness of the Holocaust brought with it many challenges. Indeed, many Jews have regarded it as being theologically unique; producing a religious dilemma that had never been encountered before and raising major issues about the nature of God:

- How is it possible to reconcile an all-knowing, all-loving, all-powerful God with the atrocities of the Holocaust?
- How can one speak, as does the Torah, of the absolute value of human life after such an act of **genocide**?
- How can there still be a covenant relationship between God and the Jewish people when so many of the world's Jews had been wiped out?

quickfire

3.26 How many Jews has it been estimated had been killed by the Nazis, by the end of World War II?

Key terms

Genocide: the deliberate killing of a whole nation or people

Ghettos: poor residential areas in which Jews were confined

Retribution: deserved punishment, especially for sin or wrongdoing

Key quote

For many contemporary Jews, the Holocaust represents the greatest impediment to understanding God … for some Jewish theologians, the Holocaust is a continuation of the sort of horrific tragedies that have punctuated different parts of Jewish history. But other thinkers look at the Holocaust and see a novel event, unprecedented even by the catastrophes that the Jewish people experienced earlier in their history. For many Jews, the classical biblical explanation that God sent this punishment because of the sins of the people is impossible to accept in the light of the death of six million innocent Jews. **(Epstein)**

quickfire

3.27 Which of the Jewish prophets proclaimed 'You alone have I singled out of all the families of the earth – that is why I will call you to account for all your iniquities'?

WJEC / Eduqas Religious Studies for
A Level Year 2 and A2 Judaism

The prophet Job

quickfire

3.28 How has Job 38:4 been interpreted in light of the Holocaust?

Specification content

Key theological responses to the Holocaust with reference to: the meaning of Richard Rubenstein's 'death of God'.

Key quotes

Two recent events in Jewish life have left an indelible mark on modern Jewish theology and will, no doubt, continue to determine its direction for some time to come. They are the destruction of the Jewish communities of Europe during the Nazi era, and the founding of an independent Jewish state in the Holy Land in 1948. **(Unterman)**

No man can really say that God is dead. How can we know that? Nevertheless, I am compelled to say that we live in the time of the 'death of God'. **(Rubenstein)**

Key terms

Beneficent: actively kind and generous

Omnipotent: all-powerful

Holocaust theology

Holocaust theology as a specific genre developed in the 1970s as an attempt to respond to the questions raised by the events of the Shoah. For example, there have been attempts to understand the deaths of the six million as a form of sacrifice; as an acting out of the Jewish role of the suffering servant of God. Others have seen, coming out of the death camps, a divine command that Jews and Judaism must survive at all costs. For the majority, however, it remains an insoluble problem. When Job in the Bible was struck down by a terrible series of disasters he demanded an explanation of God, and God's response was: 'Where were you when I laid the earth's foundations?' (Job 38:4) In other words, God's ways can never be fully known; humanity cannot hope to understand them; and the problem of the evil of the Holocaust must remain the ultimate theological mystery. Nevertheless, Jewish theologians continue to try to make sense of the Shoah.

AO1 Activity

After reading the background information on the Holocaust as well as the information regarding the traditional Jewish understanding of suffering, prepare a 30-second response from a Jewish perspective in answer to the question 'How is it possible to reconcile an all-knowing, all-loving, all-powerful God with the atrocities of the Holocaust?'

Richard Rubenstein

In his book 'After Auschwitz' Rubenstein argues that it is no longer possible to sustain a belief in a supernatural deity after the events of the Nazi era. Traditional Judaism had long believed that Jewish suffering had been justly imposed upon them by God, and yet Rubenstein had never before heard the argument being applied to the events of the modern world. He wrote: 'If one shared Rabban Johanna ben Zakai's view, one would be drawn to assert that the Jewish people had been exterminated because of their failure to comply with the Lord's commandments as these had been enjoined in the Torah.'

However, for Rubenstein, the experience of the Holocaust made this view both untenable and morally outrageous. As Cohn-Sherbok explains: 'It seemed amazing to him (Rubenstein) that Jewish theologians still subscribed to the belief in an **omnipotent**, **beneficent** God after the death camps. Traditional Jewish theology maintains that God is the ultimate actor in history – it interprets every tragedy as God's punishment for Israel's sinfulness.' However, Rubenstein was unable to see how this position could be maintained without viewing Hitler as an instrument of God's will.

Memorial to the victims of the Holocaust in Germany.

He wrote: 'The agony of European Jewry cannot be likened to the testing of Job. To see any purpose in the death camps, the traditional believer is forced to regard the most demonic, anti-human explosion of all history as a meaningful expression of God's purposes. The idea is simply too obscene for me to accept.' Rather he argues that it is no longer possible to believe in the God of the Abrahamic covenant who rewards and punishes the Jews as the chosen people. The Holocaust has demonstrated that such a belief has no foundation, and Jews today, he contends, live in the time of the death of God. In a technical sense, based on the Kabbalah, Rubenstein maintains that God had 'died' in creating the world through the process of **tzimtzum**, by retracting into a void to make space for existence.

Yet even though the idea of a supernatural God has been lost, Rubenstein does not call for atheism. Rather he claims that Jews can still find spiritual vitality through traditional Jewish observances such as the symbolic nature of sacrifice and the liturgy: 'For Rubenstein the archaic elements of religion are often the most meaningful and should be retained as a source of regeneration – this is particularly the case with the sacrificial system of ancient Israel and its embodiment into the Jewish liturgy' (Cohn-Sherbok). Rubenstein believes that the reasons for keeping the symbolic aspects of sacrifice were that sacrifice reminds people of moral failure; requires them to acknowledge guilt; and ultimately leads them to seek forgiveness. It focuses the attention of the community on the fact that the people have assembled to share their failures and to resolve to live better lives. After having experienced mass murder, it is important for the Jewish community to recognise the value of the Jewish tradition which has managed to control the darker aspects of human nature.

In a later book, 'Approaches to Auschwitz', Rubenstein re-evaluates his concept of God, however, as a result of his coming into contact with the civilisations and religions of Asia. As Cohn-Sherbok explains: 'In mysticism Rubenstein found a God whom he could affirm after the Holocaust – this view has replaced his earlier emphasis on the coldness and silence of the cosmos.' Rubenstein thereafter expresses a belief in a God who is **immanent** rather than **transcendent**. According to this view, God is the Holy Nothingness, and as such, the foundation and source of everything. However, Rubenstein explains that: 'To speak of God as the Holy Nothingness is not to suggest that he is a void. On the contrary, he is an indivisible **plenum** so rich that all existence derives from his very being. Why then use the term Nothingness? Use of the term rests in part upon a very ancient observation that all definition of finite entities involves negation.'

Death in the concentration camps was followed by the resurrection of the Jewish people in their ancestral home. In the crisis of the Holocaust, Jews discovered that they were totally alone; nevertheless, by their own efforts they renewed Jewish existence in Zion. And thus the Jews turned to the God who is manifested in and through nature rather than to the God of Jewish history.

Key quote

Perhaps the best available metaphor for the conception of God as the Holy Nothingness is that God is the ocean and we are the waves. In some sense each wave has its moment in which it is distinguishable as a somewhat separate entity. Nevertheless, no wave is entirely distinct from the ocean which is its substantial ground. **(Rubenstein)**

Nevertheless, Rubenstein's views are not without criticisms. In the first instance, he has been criticised for taking a very extreme view by denying the existence of God. On the one hand, whilst he *has* expressed the lack of belief felt by many Jews following the Holocaust, on the other, he has failed to offer any hope whatsoever for those religious Jews who were struggling to make sense of the Shoah in religious terms. By denying the traditional Jewish belief in God, it could be claimed

T3 Significant social and historical developments in religious thought

Key terms

Immanent: referring to a Supreme Being who is permanently present

Plenum: a space completely filled with matter

Transcendent: existing outside the material or created world and independent of it

Tzimtzum: contraction; the way in which God makes space for humankind to make its own choices

Key quotes

When I say we live in the time of the death of God, I mean that the thread uniting God and Man, heaven and earth, has been broken. We stand in a cold, silent, unfeeling cosmos, unaided by any purposeful power beyond our own resources. After Auschwitz what else can a Jew say about God? … The time of the death of God does not mean the end of all gods. It means the demise of the God who was the ultimate actor in history. **(Rubenstein)**

I believe there is a conception of God … which remains meaningful after the death of the God-who-acts-in-history. It is a very old conception of God with deep roots in both Western and Oriental mysticism. According to this conception, God is spoken of as the Holy Nothingness. When God is thus designated, he is conceived of as the ground and source of all existence. **(Rubenstein)**

that Rubenstein has failed to produce a viable **theodicy** for those who have remained loyal to the faith of Israel.

Another difficulty is that Rubenstein places great emphasis upon the concept of sacrifice as a means by which to limit the destructiveness of people in times of stress. 'Yet arguably' states Cohn-Sherbok, 'the preservation of mere words about the sacrificial without the actual deed is an insufficient vehicle for channelling the demonic side of human nature.'

Furthermore, whilst promoting the 'death of God' philosophy, Rubenstein repeatedly claims that he is not promoting atheism. In his book, 'Approaches to Auschwitz' he instead suggests a Holy Nothingness which is a concept that is very far removed from the traditional Jewish understanding of God.

And finally, in relation to Jewish practice, Rubenstein proposes that many traditional conventions within the faith, such as Bar mitzvah and keeping kashrut, continue to have a spiritual significance in contemporary society. And yet it could be argued that if Jews cease to believe in God as creator, sustainer and saviour, it is unlikely that they will feel the need to carry out such practices that are meant to glorify the divinity.

Elie Wiesel

As a Holocaust survivor, Elie Wiesel had first-hand experience of the suffering that occurred in the death camps. As a result of his experience therefore it is not surprising, claims Cohn-Sherbok, that he has not attempted to provide a positive theological response to the Shoah. Indeed, his work depicts despair, and for this reason Wiesel has come to be recognised as a spokesman for religious protest. His first three novels, entitled 'Night', 'Dawn', and 'The Accident' portray what Solomon describes as a 'narrative exegesis' of the Shoah.

Hoffman describes how Wiesel 'depicts the Jewish tragedy as a **paradigm** of the universal human experience. Using biblical and Hasidic (his own background in Hungary) tales, his novels have four main interwoven themes: witness, silence, laughter, and dialogue. However, the theology which comes through his stories imposes no systematic structure. It is rather full of great tension and has thus enabled people to talk more honestly about their experience of the Holocaust and its impact on faith.'

His first novel, 'Night' takes the form of an autobiographical memoir which maps his transition from a youthful devout Jew, well-versed in the Talmud and Kabbalah, to one who comes to doubt the justice of a God who can allow millions to die in the Holocaust without attempting to save them. He wrote of the last festival he celebrated at home before he experienced Auschwitz: it was Passover. However, he asks, how does one read the story of Passover after Auschwitz? How does one celebrate a festival where God intervenes in suffering when you have experienced the Holocaust where no such intervention was forthcoming?

The erosion of his faith began shortly after his incarceration in Auschwitz when he began to question God. He wrote: 'Some talked of God, of His mysterious ways, of the sins of the Jewish people and of their future deliverance. But I had ceased to pray. How I sympathised with Job! I did not deny God's existence but I doubted His Absolute justice.' And his despair increased as he came to realise just how out of place was the Jewish liturgy that praised God in the face of the events of the death camps. Why should Jews continue to pray when God does not reward them?

There was one event in particular, however, which marked the total destruction of Wiesel's faith in the God of his childhood, and it occurred when he witnessed the hanging of two adults and a child at the hands of the Nazi guards. He wrote: 'Behind me, I heard the ... man asking: "Where is God now?" and I heard a voice within me answer him: "Where is He? Here He is – He is hanging on this gallows ..."'

Auschwitz

Specification content

Key theological responses to the Holocaust with reference to: Elie Wiesel's 'The Trial of God'.

Key quotes

Wiesel speaks for the millions of murdered Jews and for the silent survivors. **(Hoffman)**

In an essay on belief, Wiesel refers to his childhood certainty that the world was intelligible in terms of God's providential intervention in human affairs ... But, he says, an abyss separates him from the child he once was. **(Hoffman)**

quickfire

3.29 What are the names of Wiesel's first three novels?

Key terms

Paradigm: a framework, model or pattern

Theodicy: an argument justifying or exonerating God; a term used in relation to the existence of evil and suffering

Furthermore, at the New Year service Wiesel refused to praise God in a world in which mass murder was taking place: 'This day I had ceased to plead. I was no longer capable of lamentation. On the contrary, I felt very strong. I was the accuser, God the accused.' (Wiesel)

On Yom Kippur he decided not to fast, stating: 'There was no longer any reason why I should fast. I no longer accepted God's silence. As I swallowed my bowl of soup, I saw in the gesture an act of rebellion and protest against him. And I nibbled my crust of bread. In the depths of my heart, I felt a great void.' The void of which he wrote represented his loss of faith, and 'the recognition that God had betrayed His chosen people, leaving them to die in the elaborate machinery of the camps'. (Cohn-Sherbok)

In Wiesel's second book, 'Dawn', he examines how establishment of the State of Israel represents a rejection of God as it came about without God's authorisation. He thus projected the concept that in order to be independent and self-reliant, Jews have to relinquish their dependence upon God, and effectively take on the role of God themselves. Once again, an execution scene in the book symbolises the execution of God.

In 'The Accident', Wiesel projects the image of God as a malicious, cruel deity; a God who uses humans purely for amusement and pleasure: 'Man prefers to blame himself for all possible sins and crimes rather than come to the conclusion that God is capable of the most flagrant injustice. I still blush every time I think of the way God makes fun of human beings, his favourite toys.' (Wiesel)

Cohn-Sherbok notes that Wiesel has not provided a religious explanation for the events of the Holocaust. 'Instead' he suggests, 'in these three novels he has depicted a Godless world in which there is no possibility for human redemption'.

However, it is evident that Wiesel's opinion changes, and we see in his later works what some have considered to be a call for a new start in which there is no longer anger towards God. This concept is expressed in a musical work called 'Ani Maamin' in which he now presents God as a compassionate being who weeps with the people in their distress and rejoices in the faith of those who have remained loyal despite their suffering.

In 'The Trial of God' Wiesel demonstrates his personal worries and beliefs about God, but refuses to let go and become an atheist. Nevertheless, in this play, great anger is expressed against God; God is put on trial and found to be guilty. Yet, once pronounced guilty, the judges arise and say, 'let us pray'. Cohn-Sherbok writes: 'In this play, protest is the only legitimate response to human suffering. Like Job, Wiesel is bewildered by God's apparent indifference, and he castigates Him for His lack of interest in the fate of His faithful servants ... Yet atheism is no alternative for Wiesel; instead he – through the characters in this play – engages in dialogue.'

Wiesel's approach to the Holocaust carries with it the strength of him having experienced it first-hand. This, it could be argued, gives him an insight into the Holocaust which is more developed than those of other theological writers who did not. However, there are occasions where his theology appears to contradict itself, and Cohn-Sherbok sets out some instances of these. For example, Wiesel argues that God is indifferent to suffering, and yet he is unable to abandon God completely. He maintains that God exists, and in his protests, we can discern a longing for the God of the Bible who is Lord of Jewish history.

Also, in some of his writings God appears to be on the side of violence and destruction, and yet in 'Ani Maamin' God is portrayed as a compassionate comforter; shedding tears of sorrow when the Jewish people are crushed, and being touched by the faith of those who remain true to the faith. If God had the power to save the Jews from destruction and did not do so then God is indeed cruel beyond measure. Furthermore, if God weeps at the destruction, but does nothing

Key quotes

Why should I bless His name? The Eternal, Lord of the Universe, the all-powerful and terrible was silent. What had I to thank Him for? (Wiesel)

I was the accuser, God the accused. My eyes were open and I was alone – terribly alone in a world without God and without man. (Wiesel)

Wiesel the survivor refuses to let God go, but is at odds with Him, anxious to point out that the flames of Auschwitz have destroyed the traditional belief in a benevolent God who is concerned with the Jewish people. (Cohn-Sherbok)

Key quote

The events of the years 1933–1945 seemed unparalleled in mankind's history … Many Jews were stunned into silence, some into the religious rebellion of Job. God has allowed to happen what has happened; where is God? Slowly, attempts were made to emerge from the grip of the nightmare to find both a logical and a religious response. **(Maybaum)**

Specification content

Key theological responses to the Holocaust with reference to: Ignaz Maybaum's view of Israel as the 'suffering servant', and the Holocaust as 'vicarious atonement'.

Key quotes

After the third churban … the Jewish diaspora is no longer limited to Ashkenazi and Sephardi regions, but has become a world-diaspora … The Middle Ages have come to an end. **(Maybaum)**

Yet it was our sickness that he was bearing,
Our suffering that he endured. **(Isaiah 53:4)**

Indeed, My servant shall prosper, Be exalted and raised to great heights. **(Isaiah 52:13)**

Key terms

Ashkenazi: referring to Jews from central or Eastern Europe

Churban: referring to an event of total destruction

Remnant: what is left of a community following a catastrophe

Sephardi: referring to Jews from the Iberian Peninsula

---

then, as Cohn-Sherbok pronounces: 'He must be exceedingly feeble not to do something about it.'

A final contradiction is that Wiesel maintains his commitment to a Jewish way of life despite his conviction that modern man is in a religious void. Nevertheless, Wiesel seeks to find meaning through love of Judaism and loyalty to the Jewish community. 'Yet without a religious basis' argues Cohn-Sherbok, 'it is difficult to understand how such allegiance can be sustained.' Furthermore, he concludes: 'Wiesel's theology of protest is thus not only inconsistent, but also devoid of any clear basis for a dedication to the Jewish heritage and Jewish existence.'

Ignaz Maybaum

In 'The Face of God after Auschwitz' Maybaum sets out his belief that the six million Jews who died in the death camps had been chosen by God as sacrificial victims in order to bring about God's intentions for the modern world. The suffering of the Jews was the suffering of God's faithful servants for the sake of humanity.

In order to explain the horrors of the holocaust Maybaum claimed that the Jewish world has experienced three major disasters which he refers to using the term '**churban**': 'The first churban, the destruction of Jerusalem at the hand of Nebuchadnezzar, the second churban, the destruction of Jerusalem in the year 70 by Rome, and the third churban, the destruction suffered by Jewry in the years 1933–1945, these catastrophes are "a small moment", "a little wrath", measured against the eternal love which God showers on his people.' (Maybaum)

He continues by elucidating that after every churban, the Jewish people made what he called 'a decisive progress', further claiming that as a result of each churban 'mankind progressed with us'. Thus, after the first churban, the Jews became the people of the diaspora, proving their ability to survive without attachment to a specific land. Cohn-Sherbok comments: 'For the first time in history there was a nation without land which nevertheless believed it had a holy mission.'

After the loss of the Temple, Maybaum claims: 'We made worship dependent on the spoken word alone.' The Temple had been the centre of sacrifice for the Jewish people, but after its destruction there emerged the establishment of the synagogue. Instead of sacrifice, a new form of worship developed in which prayer took precedence, and where worship was founded upon the spoken word. For Maybaum, this enabled the Jews to make spiritual progress which subsequently enlightened human awareness.

When considering the third churban, the Holocaust, Maybaum looked to personal experience. He wrote: 'My mother died in Theresienstadt, my two sisters and other relatives died in Auschwitz. Can I bring myself to conceive any kind of progress coming as a result of the third churban?' For Maybaum, even though six million Jews had perished, two thirds of the Jewish community in Eastern Europe survived. 'We are the **Remnant**,' he claimed, 'and of this we must speak with the Halleluyah of the redeemed at the Red Sea.' Through this creative act of destruction, the Jews once again escaped from slavery to freedom, but, as the surviving Remnant they must bring about changes within the Jewish community. They must become better

In this book Maybaum set out his belief that the suffering of the Jews was the suffering of God's faithful servant for the sake of humanity.

Jews than they were before the third churban; a community that is more devoted to God: 'Let the churban change you into Jews who are aware that justice and mercy and truth are holy attributes of God and the foundation of human life ... Blot out the idea that a Jewish generation is permitted to remain after the churban what it was before the churban.' (Maybaum)

Even Hitler had a role in God's providential plan. Maybaum explains: 'Thus Hitler came. He ... did what the progressive should have done but failed to do, he destroyed the Middle Ages, but did so by destroying the old Europe ... Hitler was an instrument, in itself unworthy and contemptible. But God used this instrument to cleanse, to purify, to punish a sinful world; the six million Jews, they died an innocent death; they died because of the sins of others.' The Jews became the 'suffering servant' of the Book of Isaiah; suffering collectively for the sins of the world; dying a vicarious death for the sins of humanity.

The third churban brought to an end the medieval structure of Jewish society which had existed in Europe for centuries, and in which Jews had been marginalised, and held responsible for the death of Christ. Progress in a post-Holocaust world brought with it the acceptance of the Jews as part of Western civilisation and democracy. As Cohn-Sherbok describes it: 'The remnant of the Jewish nation – the survivors of the third churban – have become increasingly Westernised, and with the rise of Western civilisation the Jew will arise too. Out of the depths into which the catastrophe of our time plunged the Jewish people, there is hope for the future.'

Maybaum's theology displays a number of strengths in that it takes away the notion that the Holocaust was a punishment for the sins of the Jewish people as well as offering a reason for the suffering of the Jews in the Holocaust. It also explains why some Jews died and others survived by reason of the Remnant. Maybaum also makes reference to the Torah frequently in his argument, which means that his opinions are held in high esteem by some Jewish scholars. However, as Cohn-Sherbok notes: 'While Maybaum appears to follow the doctrine of omnipotence to its seemingly logical conclusion (God must be the cause of the Holocaust, He did not defend his attributes of love and justice), for most Jews it is impossible to believe in a God who would be the source of the terrors of the death camps.' It doesn't make sense that God entered into a covenant relationship with the Jewish people only to kill them. Furthermore, Maybaum claims that Hitler was an instrument of God; yet if God is omnipotent there would have been no need to murder six million Jews in order to bring about a new era in human history.

Critics have also encountered a difficulty with Maybaum's use of Christian ideas in order to explain Jewish suffering, in that he presents the Jews in the death camps as being Christ-like in dying for the sins of humankind. Christ died voluntarily, which was clearly not the case for the six million Jews who perished.

The concept of churban is also a non-Jewish idea, and furthermore, it is not clear what spiritual progress (if any) has been made since the Holocaust. Cohn-Sherbok also identifies complications connected with Maybaum's vision of Jewish progress. Today, those Jews who have adopted the ideals of Western society have largely abandoned their Jewish heritage and traditions in the process.

A final issue arises from Maybaum's idea of the Jewish community as God's 'suffering servant' in that through emancipation, Jews should able to live wherever they want, thus bringing God's kingdom to all places. However, the formation of the State of Israel negates this. Cohn-Sherbok concludes: 'Thus Maybaum's interpretation of divine theodicy fails to provide an adequate answer to the question why an all-powerful and all-good God could have allowed His chosen people to perish at the hands of the Nazis.'

Key quote

The martyr dies to give us, the Remnant, an atoned future, a new day, wonderful like every morning in which God renews his creation. (Maybaum)

quickfire

3.30 What is a 'churban'?

WJEC / Eduqas Religious Studies for A Level Year 2 and A2 Judaism

Specification content

Key theological responses to the Holocaust with reference to: Eliezer Berkovitz and 'the hiding of the divine face' and 'free will'.

Eliezer Berkovitz

In 'Faith After the Holocaust', Eliezer Berkovitz, the Orthodox theologian, argues that religious belief is still possible following the atrocities of the death camps. Berkovitz claimed that Jews have a right to reason, and even to wrestle with God rather than simply to stand by and accept the horror of the Holocaust in silence. Indeed, this was not a new concept within Judaism as Abraham wrestled with God over the fate of Sodom and Gomorrah; and Job struggled with God over the misfortunes that befell him.

Berkovitz addresses the problem that God seems to have been absent from the experience of the faithful during the Holocaust by referring to biblical tradition; and in particular the verse from Isaiah 45:15: 'Truly you are a God who hides Himself, O God of Israel the Saviour.' Berkovitz talks of 'the hiding of the face' in that when suffering occurs, God 'hides his face' from human evil. Why does God do this? Rabbinic tradition maintains that God's hiding his face is not due to indifference or callousness, rather it is due to the need for God to give space in order for people to be able to develop as moral beings. God did not will that one person be righteous and another evil: instead God created the possibility for each person to be a moral agent. As Cohn-Sherbok explains: 'This means that freedom of choice is a necessity and man's freedom must not be restricted even by God Himself.'

This particular justification of evil is known as the free will defence, and Berkovitz makes very particular use of it in relation to the experiences of the Jewish people. God must 'absent himself from history' he writes, and not intervene even when this freedom is grossly misused. Hence the Holocaust should be understood as a manifestation of evil; a tragedy inflicted on the Jewish people by the Nazis. Yet divine intervention did not occur because God had bestowed free will on human beings at the time of creation.

Berkovitz rejects the notion that the Holocaust was administered as a punishment even though the phrase 'Because of our sins' is the explanation offered for God's hiding his face in some biblical passages. For example, in Deuteronomy 31:17–18 God declares: 'Then My anger will flare up against them, and I will abandon them and hide My face from them ... Yet I will keep My face hidden on that day, because of all the evil they have done in turning to other gods.'

Hoffman proposes that like most Orthodox thinkers Berkovitz does not believe that the Holocaust was unique, except in the 'objective magnitude of its humanity'. He insists that it be seen in the context of history as a whole, and the distinctive history of the Jewish people in particular. He draws upon another biblical notion, that of Israel as a suffering servant as found in the Book of Isaiah. The servant suffers not for his wrongs, but for those of other people, and his suffering is somehow part of God's purpose for the world.

Berkovitz also appeals to the Book of Job as offering an example of someone suffering great injustice, and yet who continues to believe in the providence of God. Critics, however, have judged this to be a poor comparison as Job lived to tell his tale, accompanied by the restoration of his health and happiness. This is in stark contrast to the six million who died at the hands of the Nazis, for whom all potential for moral growth was exterminated.

However, for Berkovitz, the very fact that the Jews have continued to survive throughout times of suffering bears witness to the fact that God is present even though he is hidden. The silence of Auschwitz is perhaps the most horrifying manifestation of God hiding his face, but those Jews who retained their faith glimpsed God's abiding presence in the death camps: '... although the Jews in Europe who knew well what had happened to many of their brethren and what was awaiting them should they, too, be caught, many of them did not depart from

Key quotes

Rouse yourself; why do you sleep, O Lord?
Awaken, do not reject us forever!
Why do You hide Your face, ignoring our affliction and distress? **(Psalm 44:23–24)**

He created evil by creating the possibility for evil; He made peace by creating the possibility for it. He had to create the possibility for evil, if He was to create the possibility for its opposite, peace, goodness, love. **(Berkovitz)**

The hiding God is present; though man is unaware of him. He is present in the hiddenness. **(Berkovitz)**

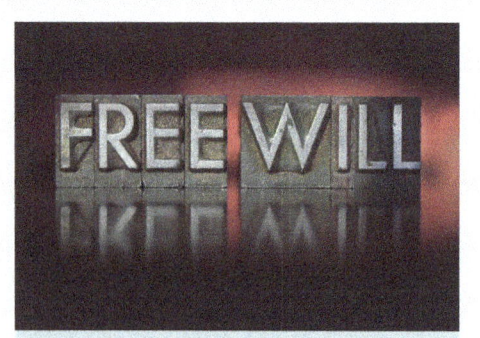

Berkovitz makes use of the free will defence in his theology.

their customary ways. In numerous places in the ghettos one could see through the windows Jews studying, or wearing tallit and tefillin, praying the daily services ... it was as if Jews had ceased being afraid.' (Berkovitz)

Berkovitz himself conceded that there is no rational explanation for the Holocaust: 'The inexplicable will not be explained, yet it will become a positive influence in the formulation of what is to be acknowledged. The sorrow will stay, but it will become blessed with the promise of another day for Israel to continue on its eternal course with a new dignity and a new self-assurance. Thus, perhaps, in the awful misery of man will be revealed to us the awesome mystery of God.'

For some, Berkovitz is the most significant writer to oppose Rubenstein's theodicy. However, notes Hoffman, such is his determination to counter Rubenstein's radicalism that his theological argument is sometimes contrived. Nonetheless, his conservatism has enabled him to give, writes Katz, 'one of the most theologically and Jewish convincing "responses" of all those who have taken part in the discussion'. Indeed, Berkovitz's theological approach has much strength. For example, he provides hope for surviving Jews that God did not abandon them completely. He also stays close to traditional Jewish theological ideas, and as a result his argument does not end in a call to atheism. It is also significant that he justifies the establishment of a Jewish State where God's presence is revealed in contemporary society: 'Because of Israel the Jew knows that history is messianism, that God's guidance – however impenetrably wrapped in mystery – is never absent from the life of the nations.' (Berkovitz)

However, his interpretation of the Holocaust also throws up a number of problems. Cohn-Sherbok believes that a major difficulty with Berkovitz's interpretation of the Holocaust lies in his argument based upon free will. If God is indeed **omniscient**, omnipotent and all-good, then God could have created a world in which there was human freedom without evil. Surely a limitation on human free will would be preferable to the Holocaust. Neither does Berkovitz's argument for free will take account of suffering which is due to natural causes (e.g. disease).

A further problem relates to the belief that God withdraws from history; a concept that appears to contradict the Torah where God is described as an abiding presence in the history of the chosen people. For example, the Hebrew slaves were freed from Egypt by divine intervention; they were saved at the Red Sea by God's actions; they were given commandments to help them live properly at Mount Sinai. This traditional understanding of God as Redeemer and Saviour opposes Berkovitz's claim that God is present but withdrawn.

According to Berkovitz, God's presence in history is displayed through the experiences of Jewish people. Yet Cohn-Sherbok argues that while the survival of the Jews after the Holocaust is astonishing, it does not logically follow that their existence alone testifies to God's abiding presence.

Study tip

Make sure that you are familiar with the details of the free will defence so that you are able to demonstrate thorough, accurate and relevant knowledge and understanding of it in relation to Berkovitz's theology.

Key quotes

Natural evil in the world is not a direct consequence of free will; thus Berkovitz's defence fails to explain every element of human suffering. (Cohn-Sherbok)

(It is) to Berkovitz's credit that he has formulated several important theological theses ... (by pointing us) in the direction of important truths that need further reflection and development. (Katz)

Key term
Omniscient: all-knowing

WJEC / Eduqas Religious Studies for A Level Year 2 and A2 Judaism

Specification content

Key theological responses to the Holocaust with reference to: Emil Fackenheim's proposal of the Holocaust as a new revelation experience of God by way of a 614th commandment.

Key terms

Buber: referring to Martin Buber, a prominent twentieth-century Jewish philosopher

Posthumous: occurring after a person's death

Transcendental: going beyond usual human knowledge or experience

Key quote

In contemporary society, a number of Jewish theologians have stressed the theme of Jewish survival in their reflections upon the Holocaust. The Jewish philosopher Emil Fackenheim, for example, argues that God issued the 614th commandment. **(Cohn-Sherbok)**

A memorial monument at Yad Vashem – Israel's official memorial to the victims of the Holocaust.

Emil Fackenheim

In 'Jewish Faith and the Holocaust' Fackenheim wrote: 'The ultimate question is: where was God at Auschwitz? For years I sought refuge in **Buber**'s image of an eclipse of God. This image, still meaningful in other respects, no longer seems to me applicable to Auschwitz. Most assuredly no redeeming voice is heard from Auschwitz, nor ever will be heard. However, a commanding Voice is being heard, and has, however faintly, been heard from the start.'

Fackenheim argues that God was present in the death camps, and out of the ashes of Auschwitz was issued the 614th commandment: 'Jews are forbidden to hand Hitler **posthumous** victories. They are commanded to survive as Jews lest the Jewish people perish. They are commanded to remember victims of Auschwitz lest their memory perish. They are forbidden to despair of man and his world, and to escape into either cynicism or otherworldliness, lest they cooperate in delivering the world over to the forces of Auschwitz. Finally, they are forbidden to despair of the God of Israel, lest Judaism perish.' (Fackenheim)

Fackenheim rejects the notion that the Holocaust was a punishment for the sins of the Jewish people, as well as rejecting the quest to find a reason or explanation for the event. Cohn-Sherbok explains: 'Those who seek to explain the horrors of the Nazi period believe they can categorise these events in various theological frameworks such as sin and punishment. For Fackenheim, however, these solutions do not take into account their full terror. What is required instead is a sensitive awareness of the enormity of this catastrophe.'

Instead, Fackenheim urges the Jewish people to continue to believe despite the magnitude of the events of the Holocaust. God, he argued, is always present in Jewish history. We do not, and cannot understand what God was doing at Auschwitz, but we must insist that God was there. Furthermore, Fackenheim believes that God revealed a further commandment: the 614th commandment. The Commanding Voice of Auschwitz decrees that Jews are under a sacred obligation to survive. Indeed, after the atrocities of the death camps, Jewish existence itself is a holy act.

Jews are also forbidden to despair of redemption or to become cynical about the world as a result of the events of the Nazi period; they are also required to continue to work for a more humane society. Katz explains that Fackenheim's theodicy invests the Jewish will for survival with **transcendental** significance: precisely because others would eradicate Jews from the earth, Jews are commanded to resist annihilation. 'Paradoxically, Hitler makes Judaism after Auschwitz a necessity. To say "no" to Hitler is to say "yes" to the God of Sinai; to say "no" to the God of Sinai is to say "yes" to Hitler.' (Katz)

Unterman further notes that the duty of survival also entails retelling the story of Nazi atrocities to a world that would prefer to forget, and for the religious Jew it further involves what he describes as 'a posture of protest against God in the name of God's own values for what has been allowed to happen'. In confronting God such a stance would result in taking issue with God. For example, it would not be unusual for them to exclaim: 'You have abandoned the covenant? We shall not abandon it! You no longer want Jews to survive? We shall survive, as better, more faithful Jews! You have destroyed all grounds for hope? We shall obey the commandment to hope which you yourself have given!' (Fackenheim)

Key quote

But the Commanding Voice of Auschwitz demands that Jews accept their condition, face up to its contradictions, and struggle for Jewish survival. The Jew of today can endure, he (Fackenheim) writes, because he must endure and he must endure because he is commanded to endure. **(Cohn-Sherbok)**

As far as the secular Jew is concerned, they too must not forsake the Jewish tradition. The Commanding Voice of Auschwitz demands Jewish unity. Fackenheim wrote: 'I think the authentic Jew of today is beginning to hear the 614th commandment. And he hears it whether, as *agnostic*, he hears no more, or whether, as believer, he hears the voice of the *metzaveh* in the mitzvah. Moreover, it may well be the case that the authentic Jewish agnostic and the authentic Jewish believer are closer today than at any previous time.'

Katz, however, questions Fackenheim's assertion regarding the nature of the Commanding Voice of Auschwitz, and asks what exactly is meant by the term 'commandment'? In the older Jewish tradition, it meant that God actually 'spoke' to the people of Israel, and yet Fackenheim rejected this literal meaning. It would therefore appear that 'commanded' has only analogical or metaphorical sense in this case. Cohn-Sherbok further queries that if God was in fact present in the death camps and issued a command to the Jewish community, then it must have been heard by someone there who could afterwards testify to such a religious experience. However, he contends, there is no evidence that anybody actually received such a command, even including Fackenheim himself.

Furthermore, regarding the commandment entreating that the Jews survive as Jews; this is a tradition that is long-held in the Orthodox branch of the Jewish faith: 'Throughout the biblical and rabbinic tradition, the conviction that Jewish survival is of cardinal importance is repeatedly expressed – in various ways the 613 commandments enshrine this belief. Thus there was no need for a further revelation in addition to what took place at Mount Sinai.' (Cohn-Sherbok)

And for many, the very fact that Fackenheim doesn't offer up a solution to the issue of Jewish suffering during the Nazi period is also problematic. Indeed, instead of offering up a reason, Fackenheim insists that such questioning must not take place. And finally, poses Katz: 'Is it appropriate that Hitler gains such prominence in Jewish theology, that Judaism survives primarily to spite his dark memory?'

T3 Significant social and historical developments in religious thought

Key terms
Agnostic: someone who believes that nothing is known, or can be known, of the existence or nature of God

Metzaveh: the commander

Key quote
Has the like of this happened in your days or in the days of your fathers? Tell your children about it, and let your children tell theirs, and their children the next generation!
(Joel 1:2–3)

AO1 Activity
After reading through each of the key theological responses, close the book and write down some key phrases and/or words relating to each theologian.

Study tip
Researching the biographical details of each of the five theologians will give you a greater insight into their chosen standpoints regarding the Holocaust.

Judaism has survived beyond the Holocaust.

Key skills

Knowledge involves:

Selection of a range of (thorough) accurate and relevant information that is directly related to the specific demands of the question.

This means:

- Selecting relevant material for the question set
- Being focused in explaining and examining the material selected.

Understanding involves:

Explanation that is extensive, demonstrating depth and/or breadth with excellent use of evidence and examples including (where appropriate) thorough and accurate supporting use of sacred texts, sources of wisdom and specialist language.

This means:

- Effective use of examples and supporting evidence to establish the quality of your understanding
- Ownership of your explanation that expresses personal knowledge and understanding and NOT just reproducing a chunk of text from a book that you have rehearsed and memorised.

AO1 Developing skills

It is now important to consider the information that has been covered in this section; however, the information in its raw form is too extensive and so has to be processed in order to meet the requirements of the examination. This can be achieved by practising more advanced skills associated with AO1. For assessment objective 1 (AO1), which involves demonstrating 'knowledge' and 'understanding' skills, we are going to focus on different ways in which the skills can be demonstrated effectively, and also refer to how the performance of these skills is measured (see generic band descriptors for A2 [WJEC] AO1 or A Level [Eduqas] AO1).

▶ **Your final task for this theme is:** Below is a summary of **Elie Wiesel's theological response to the Holocaust**. It is 150 words long. This time there are no highlighted points to indicate the key points to learn from this extract. Discuss which five points you think are the most important to highlight and write them down in a list.

Elie Wiesel had first-hand experience of the Holocaust, and, as a result, has been a major spokesperson for religious protest. In his novels he voices despair, revolt and anger at God, as well as portraying the erosion of his faith. Though others have tried to describe God's activity during the Holocaust as God 'hiding his face', Wiesel states that God has died and that Jews must take up a stance of defiance against the God who has failed them. Cohn-Sherbok notes that Wiesel has not provided a religious explanation for the events of the Holocaust. 'Instead' he suggests that: '... he has depicted a Godless world in which there is no possibility for human redemption.' In 'The Trial of God' Wiesel demonstrates his personal worries and beliefs about God, but refuses to let go and become an atheist. Instead, through the characters in this play, he engages in dialogue.

Now make the five points into your own summary (as in Theme 1 Developing skills) trying to make the summary more personal to your style of writing. This may also involve re-ordering the points if you wish to do so. In addition to this, try to add some quotations and references to develop your summary.

The result will be a fairly lengthy answer and so you could then check it against the band descriptors for A2 (WJEC) or A Level (Eduqas) and in particular have a look at the demands described in the higher band descriptors towards which you should be aspiring. Ask yourself:

- Does my work demonstrate thorough, accurate and relevant knowledge and understanding of religion and belief?
- Is my work coherent (consistent or make logical sense), clear and well organised?
- Will my work, when developed, be an extensive and relevant response which is specific to the focus of the task?
- Does my work have extensive depth and/or suitable breadth and have excellent use of evidence and examples?
- If appropriate to the task, does my response have thorough and accurate reference to sacred texts and sources of wisdom?
- Are there any insightful connections to be made with other elements of my course?
- Will my answer, when developed and extended to match what is expected in an examination answer, have an extensive range of views of scholars/schools of thought?
- When used, is specialist language and vocabulary both thorough and accurate?

Issues for analysis and evaluation

The success of Holocaust theologies in addressing the challenges raised by the Holocaust

The Jews are no strangers to persecution; however, the enormity and uniqueness of the Holocaust brought with it many challenges. At the heart of the issue is the philosophical debate surrounding what is known as the 'Problem of Evil and Suffering'. According to Jewish belief, God is omniscient, omnipotent and **omnibenevolent**. However, the Holocaust displayed unprecedented levels of evil and suffering for the Jews at the hands of the Nazi regime. If, therefore, as Jews believe, there is an overall meaning and purpose for them as part of the covenant relationship with God; that everything that happens is known to and under the absolute control of God; then the implication must be that the God of Sinai is responsible for the suffering and cruelty that was dealt out to the Jews in the death camps. Furthermore, how can one speak, as does the Torah, of the absolute value of human life after such an act of genocide? Indeed, how can there still be a covenant relationship between God and the Jewish people when so many of the world's Jews had been wiped out?

Such questions recognise that there is a need to explain the Holocaust, and there are several theologians who have tried to make both spiritual and practical sense of the suffering of the Jewish people. Richard Rubenstein, for instance, rejected the possibility of a loving God who simultaneously punishes, and wrote of living in the time of the 'death of God' thereby rejecting the traditional Jewish view of suffering as a just imposition as a result of failing to comply with the commandments as set down in the Torah. However, Rubenstein's views are not without criticism. For example, in the first instance he has been criticised for taking a very extreme view by denying the existence of God. On the one hand, he *has* expressed the lack of belief felt by many Jews following the Holocaust; on the other, he has failed to offer any hope whatsoever for those religious Jews who were struggling to make sense of the Shoah in religious terms. By denying the traditional Jewish belief in God, it could be claimed that Rubenstein has failed to produce a viable theodicy for those who have remained loyal to the faith of Israel.

For some, Eliezer Berkovitz is the most significant writer to oppose Rubenstein's theodicy, and yet therein, claims Hoffman, lies his weakness. Such is his determination to counter Rubenstein's radicalism that his theological argument is sometimes contrived and throws up a number of problems. For example, his interpretation of the Holocaust lies in his argument based upon free will. If God is indeed omniscient, omnipotent and all-good, then God could have created a world in which there was human freedom without evil. Surely a limitation on human free will would be preferable to the Holocaust. Nevertheless, Berkovitz's conservatism has enabled him to give, writes Katz, 'one of the most theologically and Jewish convincing "responses" of all those who have taken part in the discussion.' Indeed, Berkovitz's theological approach has much strength. For example, he provides hope for surviving Jews that God did not abandon them completely. He also stays close to traditional Jewish theological ideas, and as a result his argument does not end in a call to atheism. It is also significant that he justifies the establishment of a Jewish State where God's presence is revealed in contemporary society.

Emil Fackenheim's proposal that God was present in the death camps and that out of the ashes of Auschwitz was issued the 614th commandment presents what some consider to be a new revelatory experience of God that steers away from the focus on survival. Fackenheim also rejects the notion that the Holocaust was a punishment for the sins of the Jewish people, as well as rejecting the quest to

---

T3 Significant social and historical developments in religious thought

This section covers AO2 content and skills

Specification content
The success of Holocaust theologies in addressing the challenges raised by the Holocaust.

Key quote
Either God wants to abolish evil, and cannot; or he can, but does not want to. If he wants to, but cannot, he is impotent. If he can, but does not want to, he is wicked. If God can abolish evil, and God really wants to do it, why is there evil in the world? (Epicurus)

Key term
Omnibenevolent: having absolute goodness

AO2 Activity
As you read through this section try to do the following:

1. Pick out the different lines of argument that are presented in the text and identify any evidence given in support.
2. For each line of argument try to evaluate whether or not you think this is strong or weak.
3. Think of any questions you may wish to raise in response to the arguments.

This Activity will help you to start thinking critically about what you read and help you to evaluate the effectiveness of different arguments and from this develop your own observations, opinions and points of view that will help with any conclusions that you make in your answers to the AO2 questions that arise.

WJEC / Eduqas Religious Studies for A Level Year 2 and A2 Judaism

Key questions

To what extent is there a need to find an explanation for the Holocaust?

Are some theological responses to the Holocaust more successful than others?

Is it possible to come to a definitive answer in addressing the challenges raised by the Holocaust?

Key quote

If God was present in the nightmare of the Holocaust, what purpose could be served by His deafening silence? Surely in some manner God could have revealed Himself to His chosen people without violating human freedom. Instead hundreds of thousands of Jews went to their deaths believing that there is neither justice nor a judge in the universe. **(Cohn-Sherbok)**

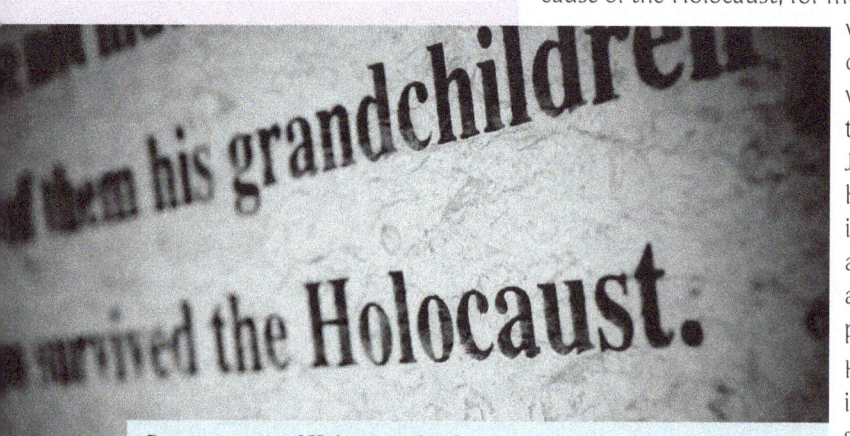

Some aspects of Holocaust theology provide hope for surviving Jews.

AO2 Activity

List some conclusions that could be drawn from the AO2 reasoning from the above text; try to aim for at least three different possible conclusions. Consider each of the conclusions and collect brief evidence to support each conclusion from the AO1 and AO2 material for this topic. Select the conclusion that you think is most convincing and explain why it is so. Try to contrast this with the weakest conclusion in the list, justifying your argument with clear reasoning and evidence.

---

find a reason or explanation for the event. However, for many, the very fact that Fackenheim doesn't offer up a solution to the problem of Jewish suffering during the Nazi period remains problematic. Indeed, instead of offering up a reason, Fackenheim insists that such questioning must not take place. This has led Katz to question: 'Is it appropriate that Hitler gains such prominence in Jewish theology, that Judaism survives primarily to spite his dark memory?'

Study tip

The 'Problem of Evil and Suffering' can be summed up by reference to what is known as the 'inconsistent triad'. An understanding of the details of this particular concept would help in your assessment of the challenges posed by the Holocaust.

Some might claim that Ignaz Maybaum's theology has been more successful than that of other theologians based upon the fact that he makes reference to the Torah frequently in his argument, which means that his opinions are held in high esteem by some Jewish scholars. His view of Israel as the 'suffering servant' has also done away with the notion that the Holocaust was a punishment for the sins of the Jewish people. It also offers an explanation as to why some Jews died and others survived by reason of the Remnant. However, critics have encountered difficulties which call into question the success of his theodicy in addressing the challenges of the Holocaust. For example, whilst Maybaum appears to follow the doctrine of omnipotence to its seemingly logical conclusion that God must be the cause of the Holocaust; for most Jews it remains impossible to believe in a God who would be the source of the terrors of the death camp. Furthermore, Maybaum claims that Hitler was an instrument of God; yet if God is omnipotent there would have been no need to murder six million Jews in order to bring about a new era in human history. Cohn-Sherbok concludes: 'Thus Maybaum's interpretation of divine theodicy fails to provide an adequate answer to the question why an all-powerful and all-good God could have allowed His chosen people to perish at the hands of the Nazis.'

However, not all responses to the Holocaust were intended to be abstract deliberations as can be seen in Elie Wiesel's personal reaction, which has its foundation in his first-hand experience of Auschwitz. This, it could be argued, gives him an insight into the Holocaust which is more developed than those of other theological writers who did not. Moreover, to consider it as being either a success or failure is really an artificial exercise. Notwithstanding, there are occasions where his theology appears to contradict itself, and Cohn-Sherbok sets out some instances of these. For example, Wiesel argues that God is indifferent to suffering, and yet he is unable to abandon God completely. Also, in some of his writings God appears to be on the side of violence and destruction, and yet in 'Ani Maamin' God is portrayed as a compassionate comforter; shedding tears of sorrow when the Jewish people are crushed, and being touched by the faith of those who remain true to the faith.

In the light of the theological deliberations and suggestions that have been considered, it is probably correct to say that these theodicies throw up more questions than answers. However, this does not mean that responses should not be made, as some might argue that a response to such a dreadful occurrence such as the Holocaust is imperative and dignified, no matter how weak. Perhaps it is fitting to conclude with words of Wiesel, who said: 'There is no answer to Auschwitz.' Yet, he continues: 'There is a response ... Never Again!'

Whether or not any Holocaust theology is legitimate

The traditional understanding of suffering within Judaism is that it is a form of retribution. This concept is made clear in the terms of the covenant relationship that God made with the Jewish people at Mount Sinai. The Mosaic covenant was a conditional covenant that reinforced the covenant God had given to Abraham; however, at Sinai, the Jews were told what they were required to do as their side of the agreement. In accepting the terms of the covenant, the Jews were beholden to keep its requirements. Failure in their duty, however, would lead to punishment by God. Thus the privilege of being God's chosen people carries with it the consequence of weighty and certain punishment should they fail in their responsibility. As the prophet Amos proclaimed: 'Hear this word, O people of Israel, that the LORD has spoken concerning you, concerning the whole family that I brought up from the land of Egypt: You alone have I singled out of all the families of the earth – that is why I will call you to account for all your iniquities.' An illustration of this concept can be found in the Book of Jeremiah when the prophet forewarned that idolatry and disloyalty to God would be punished. During this particular period in history, Jerusalem was taken under the control of the Babylonians, the Temple was destroyed, and the Jewish people were taken into exile. Some might therefore deduce from this that suffering in whatever form should come as no surprise to the Jews as it is an expected outcome following disobedience to God. A logical response to this viewpoint would thus render any theological questioning of the Holocaust as illegitimate.

However, others have argued that even though persecution was not a new experience for the Jews, the enormity and uniqueness of the Holocaust brought with it a different set of challenges which deserve consideration. Indeed, many Jews have regarded the Shoah as representing something that is both historically and theologically unique, and which has produced a religious dilemma that had never been encountered before. For instance, the quantity of those killed – six million – represents the intention to wipe out a complete nation. Coupled with this is the debate surrounding what is known as the 'Problem of Evil and Suffering'. According to Jewish belief, God is omniscient, omnipotent and omnibenevolent. However, the Holocaust displayed unprecedented levels of evil and suffering for the Jews at the hands of the Nazi regime. If therefore, as Jews believe, there is an overall meaning and purpose for them as part of the covenant relationship with God; that everything that happens is known to and under the absolute control of God; then the implication must be that the God of Sinai is responsible for the suffering and cruelty that was dealt out to the Jews in the death camps. Furthermore, how can one speak, as does the Torah, of the absolute value of human life after such an act of genocide? Indeed, how can there still be a covenant relationship between God and the Jewish people when so many of the world's Jews had been wiped out? When Job in the Bible was struck down by a terrible series of disasters, he demanded an explanation of God, and God's response was: 'Where were you when I laid the earth's foundations?' (Job 38:4) In other words, God's ways can never be fully known; humanity cannot hope to understand them; and the problem of the evil of the Holocaust must remain the ultimate theological mystery. Nevertheless, Jewish theologians believe that it is both necessary and legitimate to try to make sense of the Shoah. As Epstein wrote: 'But other thinkers look at the Holocaust and see a novel event, unprecedented even by the catastrophes that the Jewish people experienced earlier in their history. For many Jews, the classical biblical explanation that God sent this punishment because of the sins of the people is impossible to accept in the light of the death of six million innocent Jews.'

Some might argue that, as Eliezer Berkovitz claims, Jews have a right to reason and even wrestle with God rather than simply to stand by and accept the horror

Specification content
Whether or not any Holocaust theology is legitimate.

Key quote
The earlier catastrophes were great but not beyond belief and thus lived on in the memory of the generations until the time was ripe for a response. Our catastrophe, in contrast, is beyond belief and becomes ever more so with the passage of time. (Fackenheim)

AO2 Activity
As you read through this section try to do the following:

1. Pick out the different lines of argument that are presented in the text and identify any evidence given in support.
2. For each line of argument try to evaluate whether or not you think this is strong or weak.
3. Think of any questions you may wish to raise in response to the arguments.

This Activity will help you to start thinking critically about what you read and help you to evaluate the effectiveness of different arguments and from this develop your own observations, opinions and points of view that will help with any conclusions that you make in your answers to the AO2 questions that arise.

Key quote

Elie Wiesel, the Holocaust survivor ... suggests that after the death of so many Jews, we are all entitled to ask God six million questions. The human task, he suggests, is not to understand God but to question.
(Epstein)

Key questions

Is the traditional Jewish concept of suffering as a result of disobedience to God adequate as an explanation for the Holocaust?

Is it ever legitimate to question God?

To what extent is Holocaust theology of value?

References from the Torah are to be found in Holocaust theology.

AO2 Activity

List some conclusions that could be drawn from the AO2 reasoning from the above text; try to aim for at least three different possible conclusions. Consider each of the conclusions and collect brief evidence to support each conclusion from the AO1 and AO2 material for this topic. Select the conclusion that you think is most convincing and explain why it is so. Try to contrast this with the weakest conclusion in the list, justifying your argument with clear reasoning and evidence.

---

of the Holocaust without question. Evidence which provides justification for this approach can be found in the Torah when Abraham wrestled with God over the fate of the cities of Sodom and Gomorrah; and when Job struggled with God over the misfortunes that had befallen him. Such altercations show that what the Holocaust theologians were doing in questioning God's motives (or lack of them) regarding the Shoah was not a new concept in Judaism at all. In addition, just as neither Abraham's nor Job's actions brought about the end of their relationships with God, so Berkovitz contends, religious belief is still possible following the atrocities of the death camps.

Study tip

It is important for AO2 that you demonstrate confident and perceptive analysis of the nature of connections between the various elements of the approaches studied. Ask yourself, 'have I made legitimate/logical links in my answer?' Such critical analysis will help you develop your evaluation skills.

Furthermore, certain concepts connected with God and the Shoah are also highlighted through Holocaust theology by reference to scripture. For example, Berkovitz addresses the problem that God seems to have been absent from the experience of the faithful during the Holocaust by referring to biblical tradition; and in particular the verse from Isaiah 45:15: 'Truly you are a God who hides Himself, O God of Israel the Saviour.' Berkovitz talks of 'the hiding of the face' in that when suffering occurs, God 'hides his face' from human evil. Rabbinic tradition maintains that God hiding his face is not due to indifference or callousness, rather it is due to the need for God to give space in order for people to be able to develop as moral beings.

Another factor which lends weight to the legitimacy of Holocaust theology is associated with the experiences of the Holocaust theologians. Elie Wiesel's approach, as a case in point, carries with it the strength of him having experienced the Holocaust first-hand. This, it could be argued, gives him an insight which is more developed than those of other theological scholars who did not. In his play, 'The Trial of God', Wiesel demonstrates his personal worries and beliefs about God as a result of his ordeal during the Holocaust. Great anger is expressed about God; God is put on trial and found to be guilty. Yet, as Cohn-Sherbok writes: 'In this play protest is the only legitimate response to human suffering.'

To conclude, notwithstanding the many criticism that have been levelled at the Holocaust theologians for their seeming failure to reach a concordance regarding the reason for the Holocaust, this does not necessarily mean that their responses lack legitimacy. Some might indeed argue that a response to such a dreadful occurrence such as the Holocaust is imperative, and dignified no matter how weak. Also, if it provides hope for the future then surely its legitimacy is enhanced. Fackenheim, for instance proposes a theodicy which urges the Jewish people to continue to believe despite the magnitude of the events of the Holocaust. Furthermore, his belief that God revealed in a new 614th commandment the decree that Jews are under a sacred obligation to survive offers great hope for the future of the faith. Indeed, after the atrocities of the death camps, Jewish existence itself is a holy act.

AO2 Developing skills

It is now important to consider the information that has been covered in this section; however, the information in its raw form is too extensive and so has to be processed in order to meet the requirements of the examination. This can be achieved by practising more advanced skills associated with AO2. For assessment objective 2 (AO2), which involves 'critical analysis' and 'evaluation' skills, we are going to focus on different ways in which the skills can be demonstrated effectively, and also refer to how the performance of these skills is measured (see generic band descriptors for A2 [WJEC] AO2 or A Level [Eduqas] AO2).

▶ **Your final task for this theme is:** Below are listed **three basic conclusions drawn from an evaluation of whether or not any Holocaust theology is legitimate**. Your task is to develop each of these conclusions by identifying briefly the strengths (referring briefly to some reasons underlying it) but also an awareness of challenges made to it (these may be weaknesses depending upon your view).

1. Holocaust theology is not legitimate as it brings into question the traditional understanding of suffering within Judaism.

2. The enormity and theological uniqueness of the Holocaust brought with it a completely different set of challenges which deserve consideration.

3. Many aspects of Holocaust theology are grounded in the Jewish scriptures and rabbinic tradition, thus rendering those particular theodicies legitimate.

The result should be three very competent paragraphs that could form a final conclusion of any evaluation.

When you have completed the task, refer to the band descriptors for A2 (WJEC) or A Level (Eduqas) and in particular have a look at the demands described in the higher band descriptors towards which you should be aspiring. Ask yourself:

- Is my answer a confident critical analysis and perceptive evaluation of the issue?

- Is my answer a response that successfully identifies and thoroughly addresses the issues raised by the question set?

T3 Significant social and historical developments in religious thought

Key skills

Analysis involves:

Identifying issues raised by the materials in the AO1, together with those identified in the AO2 section, and presents sustained and clear views, either of scholars or from a personal perspective ready for evaluation.

This means:

- That your answers are able to identify key areas of debate in relation to a particular issue

- That you can identify, and comment upon, the different lines of argument presented by others

- That your response comments on the overall effectiveness of each of these areas or arguments.

Evaluation involves:

Considering the various implications of the issues raised based upon the evidence gleaned from analysis and provides an extensive detailed argument with a clear conclusion.

This means:

- That your answer weighs up the consequences of accepting or rejecting the various and different lines of argument analysed

- That your answer arrives at a conclusion through a clear process of reasoning.

T4 Religious practices that shape religious identity

This section covers AO1 content and skills

Specification content
Baal Shem Tov; miraculous healing; charismatic approach to worship.

D: Beliefs and practices distinctive of Hasidic Judaism

The Baal Shem Tov

The Hasidic movement within Judaism as we know it today has its roots in a powerful religious movement which swept through the Jewish communities of Eastern Europe in the eighteenth century. It began in Poland; a country where the Jewish community had suffered from numerous periods of persecution as a result of the nation's failing economy. The Jews were regarded as **scapegoats** and, as a result, many found themselves trapped in poverty whilst also suffering from religious oppression. Moreover, the traditional form of Judaism at that time was highly intellectual, lacking in emotion, and impossible to access if one were not trained in the Hebrew language. It is not surprising, therefore, that many Polish Jews became disillusioned with rabbinic Judaism, and, claims Cohn-Sherbok: 'through Hasidism sought individual salvation by means of religious pietism'.

Israel ben Eliezer (1700–1760)

The founder of this movement was Israel ben Eliezer (1700–1760) who was an itinerant preacher and healer. He was known by his followers as the **Baal Shem Tov** (or **Besht**), meaning 'Master of the Good Name'. Satlow claims that ben Eliezer was by far the most famous individual to emerge from a tradition of Jewish **shamanism** which was practised in Poland at that time. He goes on to explain that such shaman: 'asserted that they had access to divine powers, which they could harness for the benefit of their clients. To do this … they primarily used manipulations of the divine names, drawing on the … notion … that to know the true name of something is also to gain power over it.' Hence the title 'Master of the Good Name'.

Key quote

After his father's death, when the Besht was growing up, the Jews of his community were good to him because they had dearly loved his father. They sent him to a teacher for his education and he was an excellent student and made speedy progress. However, after studying for a few days, he regularly used to run away from school. They used to search for him and would find him sitting by himself in a forest. They thought he behaved like this because he had no one to look after him and was an orphan and had to make his own way. They used to bring him back to his teacher but the same thing would happen again. He ran away to the woods to be by himself. Eventually they gave up. They lost interest and no longer sent him to the teacher. So the boy grew up in very unusual circumstances. **(Cohn-Sherbok)**

Key terms

Baal Shem Tov: meaning 'Master of the Good Name' (i.e. the name of God)

Besht: an abbreviated form of the title 'Baal Shem Tov'

Scapegoat: a person or group that is made to bear the blame for something that is not of their doing

Shamanism: relating to those who act as intermediaries between the natural and supernatural worlds; those believed to have special powers, such as healing

quickfire

4.1 Who was known as the Baal Shem Tov or Besht?

Satlow continues by noting that despite the existence of a vast amount of **hagiographical** literature that arose after his death, we do not possess much historical knowledge of the Baal Shem Tov's actual life. It is believed that he was orphaned at a young age, and had an unusual childhood before becoming a great scholar and mystic. However, unlike most other Jewish shaman of the time he also belonged to a group of **pious** Jews whose members were known as Hasidim. Satlow explains: 'At that time to be a Hasid, literally "pious", meant to be part of a small and local **ascetic** and mystical group ... who sought personal contact with the divine. Leading one such group of Hasidim must also have added prestige and authority to (ben) Israel's reputation as a baal shem, one who then applied his powers for the good of the entire community.'

However, the Baal Shem Tov did not conform to the normal pattern of Hasidic behaviour. He prayed not only for his benefit, or solely for his clients, but also for the whole Jewish community: 'For him to be a Hasid meant to utilise one's connection to the divine for the good of the entire community; the people Israel became his client.' (Satlow)

Furthermore, the Baal Shem Tov did not withdraw from the world, but urged participation. The legends about him depict a charismatic man who attracted huge crowds with his message that the presence of God can be found in all creation. It is also reported that he was able to use the name of God to perform miraculous acts of healing, and this is why the people called him the Baal Shem Tov. Cohn-Sherbok retells one of the legends about him: 'Although those who were ill often visited him, he would not receive them at first. Then one day they brought a madman (or it may have been a woman) to see him. That night it was shown to him that he had passed his thirty-sixth year. He checked in the morning and found that this was correct. Then he saw the mad person and healed him ... From then on people journeyed to see him from far and wide.'

The Baal Shem Tov preached to all Jews that one did not have to be a Hebrew scholar to live in the presence of God. He did not reject the Jewish faith, but rather brought to it a new emphasis based upon the concepts of sincerity and love. As Satlow puts it: 'More than the study of sacred texts or even the punctilious observance of halakhah, God requires sincere intention.' Thus the Baal Shem Tov placed great value upon **devekut**, and talked about being 'attached' to God, with a heart that is 'on fire' with the love of God. Close gives an analogy in exemplification of this particular concept when he writes: 'An important illustration is that of the small child whose love for its father is readily apparent, even though he cannot express himself clearly in words. Thus the simple faith of the good but unlearned Jew is infinitely more precious to God than Torah knowledge; sincerity always superior to scholarship.

Hasidic Jews dancing

Key terms

Ascetic: a person whose life is characterised by self-discipline and abstention from indulgence

Devekut: devotion to God; clinging on to God; having God permanently in the mind

Hagiographical: relating to writings about the lives of holy/religious people which represent them in an idealistic way

Pious: religiously sincere

quickfire

4.2 What does the word Hasid mean?

Key quotes

He (the Baal Shem Tov) decided to live in the area of Galicia and he taught there. He could not always gather together ten men for a service in his house, but he invited a smaller number and prayed with them. He wore the very coarsest clothes and, in his poverty, his toes stuck out of the holes of his shoes. Nonetheless, he always had a ritual bath before he prayed, even on the coldest winter day, and he prayed with such concentration that sweat fell from him in great beads. **(Cohn-Sherbok)**

God loves all Jews without distinction; the greatest Torah genius and scholar and the most simple Jew are loved equally by God. **(Baal Shem Tov)**

Key quotes

If a person is attached to God then he is truly alive. **(Baal Shem Tov)**

The Besht used to say: No child is born except as a result of joy and pleasure. In the same way, if a man wants his prayers to be heard, he must offer them up with joy and pleasure. **(Aaron of Apt)**

Specification content

The opposition of the Mitnagdim.

Key quote

The path to God for the Hasid did not run through long and arduous training in the Talmud but through his own heart. Their emerging ritual practices helped them to form a unique and distinctive community, fostering a feeling of closeness within the people of Israel. **(Satlow)**

Key terms

Anachronistic: to attribute something to a historical period in which it did not exist

Excommunication: to exclude a person/group from membership of their community

Mitnagdim: meaning 'opponents'

Vilna Gaon: a renowned rabbinic scholar; the spiritual leader of Vilna

---

All people, no matter how poor or humble their origins, no matter how socially despised they may be, have ready access to God if they truly wish to serve Him.'

Under the Baal Shem Tov's charismatic leadership a great revival took place amongst the masses who were inspired to worship God and to keep the commandments in a simple but joyous way through laughing, dancing and singing their praises to God. The new Hasidic movement was thus characterised by extreme intensity of belief, and enthusiasm in worship. However, Satlow believes that it is **anachronistic** to see ben Eliezer as the founder of what would be transformed into modern-day Hasidism. Rather, he proposes, it was his disciples who created the distinctive movement based upon the Baal Shem Tov's teachings and practice.

AO1 Activity

Write down what you consider to be five key points about the Baal Shem Tov. Share your points with a study partner and explain why you have made these choices.

This practises the AO1 skill of presenting accurate and relevant knowledge and understanding.

The opposition of the Mitnagdim

The Hasidic movement rapidly gained in momentum and spread throughout Eastern Europe; however, its emphasis upon sincerity of the heart rather than Jewish scholarship raised concerns amongst Orthodox Jews who found Hasidism revolutionary and religiously liberal. Indeed, before his death in 1760, the Baal Shem Tov had incurred the wrath of the **Vilna Gaon** and some of the most important scholars in traditional Judaism. The opponents of Hasidism, or the **Mitnagdim** as they came to be known, denounced Hasidism as heretical. Robinson explains: 'Clearly, on some level the Mitnagdim saw this anti-intellectualism as a direct threat. How could unlettered peasants possibly engage in serious study of sacred texts?' Furthermore, the Mitnagdim were appalled by the behaviour observed during worship: '… men turning cartwheels and shaking uncontrollably in their prayers, singing and shouting and clapping their hands.' (Robinson)

The Vilna Gaon

In 1772 the Vilna Gaon issued a ban of **excommunication** against the Hasidim. However, the Hasidic leader, Rabbi Dov Baer, showed great self-control in the face of such action and forbade his followers from entering into a bitter dispute with the Mitnagdim.

Key quote

When Rabbi Dov Baer heard this (about the ban of excommunication), he quoted the Law to his disciples: Our enemies follow the commandment, 'You shall remove evil from your midst' (Deuteronomy 21:21). We will follow another commandment: 'You shall not take revenge or bear malice' (Leviticus 19:18). Rabbi Dov Baer summarised the teachings of the Hasidim in two maxims: Love God and love man. He forbade his followers from indulging in bitter arguments. **(Bloch)**

However, relationships between the two groups subsequently deteriorated and there followed a succession of bans of excommunication. By the end of the eighteenth century the Orthodox Jewish community of Vilna had denounced the Hasidim to the Russian government which resulted in the imprisonment of several leaders. Nonetheless, the Hasidic movement was eventually granted recognition within Russia and Austria, and another unforeseen consequence of such persecution was that it made the Hasidic movement stronger in the face of such opposition.

Study tip
Make sure that you have a thorough and accurate understanding of the specialist language and vocabulary which has been encountered in this section so far. Ask yourself if you are confident in using terms such as Baal Shem Tov, Besht, Mitnagdim and Vilna Gaon in an accurate way.

quickfire
4.3 Which Jewish leader issued a ban of excommunication against the Hasidim?

Key quote
People think that they pray to God. But this is not the case. For prayer itself is of the very essence of God.
(Rabbi Pinhas of Korzec)

Key quote
As a result of our sins, wicked and worthless men known as the Hasidim have left the Jewish fold and have set up their own places of worship. As everyone knows, they conduct their services in a mad and unseemly fashion, following different rituals which do not conform to the teachings of our holy Law … The exaggerations and miracle tales which are described in their books are clear and obvious lies and … there is even a move to disregard the obligations of the Law of Moses … the following are the protective measures agreed at our meeting:

1. We order a fast and public prayer to be kept on 25 Tevet of this year …
2. Every effort should be made to end the prayer meetings of the heretics.
3. Careful watch should be kept to ensure that no one studies their literature …
4. The validity of the ordinances proclaimed in Brody and Vilna are confirmed …
5. The animals killed by their ritual slaughters may not be eaten. It is to be regarded as carrion …
6. No one is to shelter any member of the Hasidim …
7. No member of the Hasidim may bring a suit in a Jewish court, nor hold a position as Cantor, Rabbi or, as goes without saying, as teacher of children …
8. All information, both good and bad, about the Hasidim must be brought to the attention of the court.

(Ban of excommunication 1786)

Hasidism emphasises praying with kavvanah.

Adoption of new prayer rite

The emphasis which the Baal Shem Tov placed upon devekut and attachment to God brought about a shift in the focus of worship among the Hasidim. At the very heart of this desire to serve God is the longing to return to a state of oneness with the divine. Indeed, it is prayer, by its very nature, which lends itself most readily to achieving attachment to God: 'The Baal Shem Tov … was told by heaven that all his spiritual attainments derive not from any claim to scholarship … but from the great devotion with which he prayed' (Green and Holtz). Hasidism thus teaches that all of life is an extension of the hour of prayer, and that prayer itself is the focal point around which one's entire day is centred.

Specification content
Adoption of new prayer rite.

WJEC / Eduqas Religious Studies for A Level Year 2 and A2 Judaism

Key terms

Kavvanah: literal meaning is 'intention'; used to denote a state of mental concentration and devotion at prayer

Nigunim: meaning 'melodies'

Nusach Sefard: the name for various forms of the Jewish prayer book

Key quotes

The Besht used to say: Do not laugh at a man who gestures as he prays fervently. He gestures in order to keep himself from distracting thoughts which intrude upon him and threaten to drown his prayer. You would not laugh at a drowning man who gestures in the water in order to save himself. **(Aaron of Apt)**

The Besht used to say: Sometimes a man becomes intoxicated with ecstasy when rejoicing over the law. He feels the love of God burning within him and the words of prayer come rushing out of his mouth. He must pray quickly to keep pace with them all. **(Aaron of Apt)**

Specification content
Modified liturgy.

quickfire

4.4 How do nigunim act as an aid to worship?

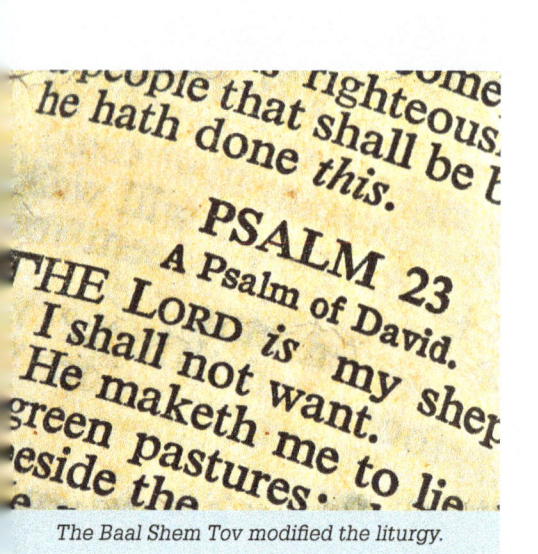

The Baal Shem Tov modified the liturgy.

Prayers are to be said with **kavvanah**, meaning concentration or proper intention. Indeed the Baal Shem Tov taught that one should say to oneself before beginning to pray that one would be willing to die through powerful concentration in prayer. De Lange notes that the early Hasidim found the requirement to pray at fixed times every day an obstacle to concentration in prayer; therefore they did away with fixed times and encouraged people to pray when they felt ready to do so with kavvanah. As Bahya Ibn Pakuda, a medieval writer puts it: 'Prayer without kavvanah is like a body without a soul.' This change in practice, however, brought further criticism from their opponents.

Hasidic prayer is characterised by great joy and can be accompanied by dancing, violent movements of the body, and even the turning of cartwheels. Indeed, the Baal Shem Tov was said to tremble so greatly in his prayer that bits of grain in a nearby barrel were seen to join him in his trembling. Other tales recounted in Hasidic lore tell of a disciple who, when he touched the Baal Shem Tov's clothing, was so seized with tremors that he had to pray for relief. Green and Holtz also tell of one of his followers who was so overcome by ecstasy while preparing for prayer in the mikveh, that he ran from the bathhouse to the adjoining synagogue and danced on the tables without realising that he was not fully dressed.

Hasidic prayer is also characterised by a distinctive accompaniment of wordless melodies called **nigunim** that represent the overall mood of the prayer. The Baal Shem Tov taught that the nigunim provide a musical path to God that transcends the limitations of language. And indeed, many nigunim are attributed to the Baal Shem Tov himself.

The Hasidim believe that every human activity is capable of being a holy act and therefore it is possible to worship God without ceasing. By means of devekut, and proper use of prayer, it is possible for a person to see the divine as it is manifest in creation. As the Baal Shem Tov proclaimed: 'Know that God's presence is with you; that you are looking directly at your Creator and your Creator at you … In Him are rooted all powers, both good and harmful: His flowing life is everywhere. Only Him do I trust! Only Him do I fear.'

Modified liturgy

The Baal Shem Tov modified the liturgy and is said to have been responsible for introducing two innovations to the Friday services: the recitation of Psalm 107 before the afternoon service, as a prelude to the Sabbath, and Psalm 23 just before the end of the evening service.

The Hasidim also adopted a new prayer rite and prayed according to one of the variations of the prayer book tradition known as '**Nusach Sefard**', a blend of Ashkenazi and Sephardic liturgies based on the Kabbalistic innovations of Rabbi Isaac Luria. This change was brought about due to the emphasis that was being placed upon the practical application of Kabbalistic concepts and ideas that had been subsumed into daily ritual of the Hasidic Jews.

A further modification was the introduction of the practice of reciting the Psalms and prayers in Ashkenazi Hebrew. This refers to the Yiddish dialects of the places from which most Hasidism originally came.

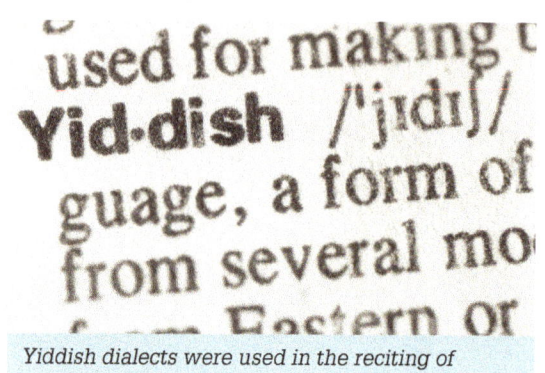

Yiddish dialects were used in the reciting of Psalms and prayers.

The influence of the rebbe

Key quote
Dov Baer used to explain that the tzaddik is like the seed of the world. When a seed is planted, it draws nourishment from the earth and brings forth fruit. Similarly, the tzaddik draws forth the holy sparks from every soul and brings them heavenwards as an offering to the Creator. **(Rabbi Baruch)**

Towards the middle of the eighteenth century a new feature of the Hasidic movement became established in the form of a new kind of leader. The rebbe (or **tzaddik**) as he was called, was considered to have attained the highest level of devekut, and as such, was spiritually superior to ordinary people. Cohn-Sherbok describes the role of rebbe: 'The goal of the tzaddik was to elevate the souls of his flock to the divine light; his tasks included pleading to God for his people, immersing himself in their everyday affairs, and counselling and strengthening them. As an authoritarian figure the tzaddik was seen by his followers as possessing miraculous power to ascend to the divine realm. In this context devekut to God involved cleaving to the tzaddik.'

Key quote
He (the rebbe) serves not only as a spiritual advisor but counsels his charges in material matters too, everything from choosing a bride to making investments. **(Robinson)**

Furthermore, the role of rebbe became a hereditary one, with fathers passing on their position to their sons or sons-in-law, thus resulting in the creation of dynasties. Intriguingly, however, says Robinson, the Baal Shem Tov did not pass on his own position to his son (even though he was a rabbi), but rather to Dov Baer, probably out of recognition for the latter's brilliance.

Key quote
The tzaddik had to be knowledgeable in the traditions – the legal and mystical traditions and the traditions of Hasidic lore and interpretation. He did not have to be learned, though it was desirable, because he could always have experts as part of his entourage. For instance, frequently a tzaddik had a rabbi, i.e. an expert in Jewish law …

1. The tzaddik had to set an example of piety. He had to be observant. He had to pray with fervour. Devekut had to be visible in him …

2. The tzaddik was expected to teach, to preach and often to train disciples. He could not be a hermit.

3. Most important, the tzaddik had to understand his power and to use it. His powers were exceptional: he could command charity, he could make marriages, he could direct lives, some could perform miracles, he could determine penances, and so on … His powers were extraordinary, but so were his responsibilities. He was expected to give advice as a counsellor, as a political leader, and as a spiritual leader. He was expected to take upon himself the burdens of his flock – their problems of sustenance, family strife, even of doubt and perplexity. If the Hasid had faith in the tzaddik, the tzaddik had to bear the burden of that faith … The tzaddik was man's representative to God, with the whole burden of Jewish life and history upon his shoulders. He was Moses on the mountain. **(Blumenthal)**

T4 Religious practices that shape religious identity

Specification content
Influence of the rebbe.

The Lubavitcher Rebbe

quickfire
4.5 What is an alternative term for 'rebbe'?

Key term
Tzaddik: meaning 'righteous one'; another term for rebbe

Within Hasidic communities the rebbe is a figure of absolute authority and power. He acts as a spiritual guide or mentor, and his rulings on religious matters are definitive. Two practices which are characteristic of the role of the rebbe are **Kvitel** and leading a **Tish**. The Kvitel is a piece of paper on which an Hasidic Jew will have written a prayer request. This will be brought to a private audience with the rebbe for him to read and then to pray on behalf of the petitioner.

The Tish is an occasion at which the rebbe will make his meal into a public event. Such events are usually held on the Sabbath and other major Jewish festivals, and involve a great deal of ceremony. At the Tish it is usual for the rebbe to be served a large portion of food from which he will take and devour a small amount, with the rest of the food being divided amongst the assembled devotees. Hasidic Jews consider this food to have been blessed by the rebbe, and thus they believe that it has spiritual or even healing powers. During the Tish there is usually the singing of hymns and joyous dancing. The rebbe will also deliver a sermon and pronounce blessings upon those who have presented themselves at the meal.

The rebbe is held in such high regard within his community that many of his disciples take special care to observe the way in which he acts. Even seemingly minute actions such as the way in which he eats, drinks, or wears his hat are liable to be imitated amongst his followers. Indeed, there is a famous story about a Hasid who travelled hundreds of miles to worship with a particular rebbe; when asked why, he said, 'I wanted to see how he ties his shoes' (Robinson). Also, Hasidic Jews will often visit the grave of a rebbe who has passed away, particularly on the anniversary of the death.

Key terms

Kvitel: a note containing a petitionary prayer which is given to a rebbe

Tish: meaning 'table'; a gathering of Hasidim around a rebbe's table

AO1 Activity

Create a 'job description' for the role of rebbe. Include the duties which are to be undertaken as well as the personal skills which are required.

Hasidic beliefs and practices

The Hasidim believe that the rules for life were presented by God to Moses on Mount Sinai in the form of the Written and the Oral Torah. Hasidic Jews hold that all of the mitzvot are relevant, and their understanding of them is that they should never let the opportunity to keep a mitzvah be lost. Cohn-Sherbok highlights their particular approach when he writes: 'Unwilling to confront the overwhelming evidence that the Torah was composed at different times in the history of ancient Israel, Hasidic Jews proclaim – without providing a justification for their view – that God revealed the Torah in its entirety to Moses on Mount Sinai and that therefore the prescriptions contained in Scripture are authoritative. Moreover, Hasidic writers piously accept cosmological doctrines without acknowledging that these theories conflict with scientific investigations into the origins of the universe.'

Rigid obedience to the mitzvah is required at all times, and allows Hasidic Jews to fulfil their duty to God through personal religious devotion. Through living a life of piety, the Hasid achieves Jewish identity, clear direction in religious life and the fulfilment of their sense of duty; all of which are a cause for great joy. As the Kotzker Rebbe said: 'Joyfulness is the outcome of holiness'. Hasidic Jews consider the world to be a source of true pleasure for humankind because it was created by God, and they therefore believe that people have a duty to be joyful because it is a way of acknowledging that the world is full of God's divine glory. Hence, Hasidic synagogues continue to be lively places, where worship is accompanied by joyous singing, music and dance.

Specification content

Life of piety; emphasis on worship rather than traditional study.

Key quote

Everything must be done for the sake of Heaven.
(The Kotzker Rebbe)

There is also a greater emphasis on religious experience through worship in Hasidism rather than through traditional study; and this is considered to hold equal importance with observation of the mitzvot. This has led to the development of a mystical tradition known as the Kabbalah. Its teachings are believed to have been transmitted through the generations back to Moses, and teach in a philosophical way how God relates to the world.

The classical text of Kabbalah is the **Zohar**. The Zohar explains the Torah by use of mystical insights. Brian Close explains that: 'Its thought rests on a complex view of the creation and continued existence of the universe and humankind through the mediation of the Torah and the commandments.' He goes on to say that the notion is that every mitzvah reveals a truth about the upper world, and every Jewish practice has cosmic significance 'since human thoughts and actions communicate themselves to the heavenly realms for evil or for good. Thus humankind is given its own part in the process of spiritual perfection.'

The obligation of an Hasidic Jew is the continual practice of devekut whereby God must be kept constantly in the mind; and every thought and action should be an expression of attachment to the Creator. Hasidic Jews place great emphasis upon the belief that God is everywhere in the universe, and that every human activity is considered to be a holy act, thus allowing a person to worship God continuously as they go about their daily life. It follows, therefore, that Hasidism places a very high value upon ethical and pious behaviour as set out in the mitzvot. This is a means of allowing the individual to achieve closeness to God, but also to set an example to the world of that which is required by the God who entered into a covenant relationship with the Jewish people at Mount Sinai. Furthermore, the emphasis upon spiritual purity means that the practice of regular mikveh use amongst Hasidic men is common, and many immerse themselves daily in the ritual bath before attending morning prayer.

Hasidic Jews tend to live in closed, tight-knit communities as it would be difficult to live according to the requirements of their faith in mainstream society. As such, membership to the group is by birth, and matrilineal descent is the means by which a child is recognised as being Jewish. Great emphasis is placed upon the family with many Hasidic Jews marrying as soon as they are legally able to do so, and Hasidic Jews usually have large families as the practice of contraception is not promoted unless there is a serious medical reason for its use. And with such a high birth rate the Hasidic community is flourishing, having a higher growth rate than other Jewish groups.

Key quote

Their rigorous laws of modesty (derived from the Law Codes), for instance, forbid a man to be alone with any woman except his wife. Even mildly intimate behaviour (such as holding hands) with your wife is considered immodest when other people are present. To ask any other woman even to shake hands is immodest. A refusal of an Ultra-Orthodox man to shake hands with a woman might be construed as rudeness or rejection by anyone not used to this degree and manner of observance, but it is in no way personal and, as explained, would pertain with any woman except his wife. **(Hoffman)**

Key quotes

The whole earth is full of His glory. **(Isaiah 6:3)**

(The Baal Shem Tov) was a mystic ... he emphasised the hidden truths over the revealed aspects of Torah. **(Weiner)**

Key term

Zohar: the classical text of Kabbalah; a mystical interpretation of the Torah

> **Key term**
>
> **Haskalah:** the period of Jewish enlightenment which began in the 18th century

> **Key quote**
>
> Great leaders create leaders. That was the (Lubavitcher) Rebbe's greatness. Not only did he lead, he was a source of leadership in others. **(Sacks)**

Hasidism retained its particular identity even during the Enlightenment (**Haskalah**), which was a period in the eighteenth century when many Jews were looking for a way in which to be brought into the mainstream of European society and culture through a reform of traditional Jewish education and practice. Close explains: 'During the Middle Ages a number of important advances had been achieved in fostering the traditional Jewish education: readings from the prayer book, the weekly portion of Scripture, study of the Talmud and even of selected passages from the rabbinic commentaries. What the child now required … was an education that broke through his or her Talmudic horizons and introduced the broader fields of European culture, thus enabling the child to be integrated into the society and state in which he or she lived. Of particular importance was the adoption of the local vernacular in place of Yiddish.' Cohn-Sherbok claims that this led to a 'post-Enlightenment world in which Jewry is no longer unified by a cohesive religious system. Instead the Jewish people have fragmented into a wide range of subgroups espousing competing interpretations of the tradition.' Against this background, however, Hasidic Judaism has remained constant, and has been acknowledged by some as being responsible for preserving Talmudic study and traditional values during the Enlightenment and to the present day.

As has been seen, the Hasidim once faced great opposition from the more traditional Orthodox Jews in the early days of its development. However, in recent times there has been greater accord: 'Although they follow different liturgies and support their separate institutions, they are united in their abhorrence of the more liberal interpretations of Judaism. Today the Hasidim are equally diligent students of the law. They remain determined proponents of the doctrine of the divine origin of the Torah and are Orthodox in every sense of the word. Jonathan Sacks the former Chief Rabbi of Great Britain and the British Commonwealth, for example, openly acknowledges his spiritual debt to the Lubavitcher Hasidim and sees them as an important and distinctive segment of the Jewish community.' (Cohn-Sherbok)

> **Key quote**
>
> There have been many great Jewish leaders in history. Some left a permanent mark on the Jewish mind by their contributions to Torah and the poetry and prose of the Jewish soul. Some created new communities, others revived flagging ones; some shaped the entire tenor of a region. But it would be hard to name an individual who, in his lifetime, transformed virtually every Jewish community in the world as well as created communities in place where none existed before. That is a measure of the achievement of the Lubavitcher Rebbe. He was not just a great leader – he was a unique one. **(Sacks)**

Study tip

You will be close to revision now so try using the techniques of exam preparation found in the Developing skills sections as a way of directing and focusing your revision.

AO1 Developing skills

It is now important to consider the information that has been covered in this section; however, the information in its raw form is too extensive and so has to be processed in order to meet the requirements of the examination. This can be achieved by practising more advanced skills associated with AO1. The exercises that run throughout this book will help you to do this and prepare you for the examination. For assessment objective 1 (AO1), which involves demonstrating 'knowledge' and 'understanding' skills, we are going to focus on different ways in which the skills can be demonstrated effectively, and also refer to how the performance of these skills is measured (see generic band descriptors for A2 [WJEC] AO1 or A Level [Eduqas] AO1).

▶ **Your new task is this:** you will have to write a response under timed conditions to a question requiring **an examination or explanation of beliefs and practices distinctive of Hasidic Judaism**. This exercise is best done as a small group at first.

1. Begin with a list of indicative content, as you may have done in the previous textbook in the series. It does not need to be in any particular order at first, although as you practise this you will see more order in your lists that reflects your understanding.

2. Develop the list by using one or two relevant quotations. Now add some references to scholars and/or religious writings.

3. Then write out your plan, under timed conditions, remembering the principles of explaining with evidence and/or examples.

When you have completed the task, refer to the band descriptors for A2 (WJEC) or A Level (Eduqas) and in particular have a look at the demands described in the higher band descriptors towards which you should be aspiring. Ask yourself:

- Does my work demonstrate thorough, accurate and relevant knowledge and understanding of religion and belief?
- Is my work coherent (consistent or make logical sense), clear and well organised?
- Will my work, when developed, be an extensive and relevant response which is specific to the focus of the task?
- Does my work have extensive depth and/or suitable breadth and have excellent use of evidence and examples?
- If appropriate to the task, does my response have thorough and accurate reference to sacred texts and sources of wisdom?
- Are there any insightful connections to be made with other elements of my course?
- Will my answer, when developed and extended to match what is expected in an examination answer, have an extensive range of views of scholars/schools of thought?
- When used, is specialist language and vocabulary both thorough and accurate?

T4 Religious practices that shape religious identity

Key skills Theme 4 DEF
The fourth theme has tasks that consolidate your AO1 skills and focus these skills for examination preparation.

Key skills
Knowledge involves:

Selection of a range of (thorough) accurate and relevant information that is directly related to the specific demands of the question.

This means:

- Selecting relevant material for the question set
- Being focused in explaining and examining the material selected.

Understanding involves:

Explanation that is extensive, demonstrating depth and/or breadth with excellent use of evidence and examples including (where appropriate) thorough and accurate supporting use of sacred texts, sources of wisdom and specialist language.

This means:

- Effective use of examples and supporting evidence to establish the quality of your understanding
- Ownership of your explanation that expresses personal knowledge and understanding and NOT just reproducing a chunk of text from a book that you have rehearsed and memorised.

WJEC / Eduqas Religious Studies for A Level Year 2 and A2 Judaism

This section covers AO2 content and skills

Specification content

Whether Hasidism contributed to the survival of Judaism.

Key quote

The teachings of Baal Shem had a tremendous impact on the masses. Here was worship which invested men and women with pride, giving purpose to their lives; worship which was enjoyable. It was, moreover, essentially practical – for true worship, according to the Baal Shem Tov, relates to every sphere of human life, even eating. **(Close)**

AO2 Activity

As you read through this section try to do the following:

1. Pick out the different lines of argument that are presented in the text and identify any evidence given in support.
2. For each line of argument try to evaluate whether or not you think this is strong or weak.
3. Think of any questions you may wish to raise in response to the arguments.

This Activity will help you to start thinking critically about what you read and help you to evaluate the effectiveness of different arguments and from this develop your own observations, opinions and points of view that will help with any conclusions that you make in your answers to the AO2 questions that arise.

Issues for analysis and evaluation

Whether Hasidism contributed to the survival of Judaism

It cannot be denied that the Hasidic movement within Judaism as we know it today has its roots in a powerful religious movement which swept through the Jewish communities of Eastern Europe in the eighteenth century. During this period in Polish history, the country's economy was falling apart, and one of the consequences of this was the social and religious oppression of the Jews. Many Jews became trapped in dire poverty, and organised religion offered very little in the way of help or consolation. The traditional form of Jewish worship at this time was through the study of the Torah. It was highly intellectual, lacking in emotion, and impossible to access if one were not trained in the Hebrew language. Nevertheless, the Jewish religion has survived into the 21st century, and some would contend that the revivalist nature of the Hasidic movement has in some way contributed to its continued existence.

In order to provide evidence for this particular stance, some would argue that it is important to consider the significance of the Baal Shem Tov; the man considered by many to be the founder of the Hasidic movement. By all accounts the Baal Shem Tov had a tremendous impact upon the people. He was a charismatic leader, and brought with him a form of worship which was enjoyable, practical, and which gave purpose to life. It was marked by extreme intensity of belief and enthusiasm in prayer and worship. Moreover, it brought a new approach to Judaism which appealed to the Jewish majority who were not schooled in the Hebrew of the Torah, nor educated in the Talmud. His message that: 'God loves all Jews without distinction; the greatest Torah genius and scholar and the most simple Jew are loved equally by God' was to rejuvenate the Jewish faith by allowing the less educated to be able to worship in a simple manner with no need for scholarly study. It could be argued that without his influence, the Jewish religion might very well have died out had it been left under the control of the scholarly elite.

It is also of note that Hasidism retained its own particular identity during the period of the Enlightenment when many other Jewish groups were looking for a way in which to be accepted into mainstream European society through a reform of traditional Jewish education and practice. This quest led in part to the end of a unified Judaism and resulted in a wide range of subgroups that held different, and in some cases, competing interpretations of Jewish tradition. Against this background, however, Hasidic Judaism remained constant, and has been acknowledged by some as being responsible for preserving Talmudic study and traditional values during the Enlightenment and up to the present day. It could therefore be maintained that Hasidism had a key role in ensuring the survival of the core tenets of the Jewish faith. Indeed, some regard it to be the truest form of Judaism with its closed, tight-knit communities providing the means by which to preserve the heritage of the faith. Furthermore, its emphasis upon matriarchal lineage has made it almost impossible for 'outsiders' to become part of the group, and thus dilute the tradition.

Study tip

It is important to note that it is not necessary to come to an absolute agreement or disagreement with the statement in question in your conclusion. A good summing-up will frequently consider a variety of factors.

It cannot be ignored, however, that Hasidism is not without its critics, and it could be claimed that it has merely enabled a specific form of Judaism to survive which is not truly representative of the more mainstream Orthodoxy. Evidence for this can be seen in the early days of the movement when the Hasidic emphasis upon sincerity of the heart rather than Jewish scholarship raised concerns amongst Orthodox Jews who found Hasidism revolutionary and religiously liberal. As Robinson points out, the Mitnagdim saw this anti-intellectualism as a direct threat to the Jewish faith. And opponents were further appalled by the behaviour they observed during Hasidic worship with men shaking uncontrollably, dancing, singing and even turning cartwheels. Moreover, the emphasis upon the Zohar which is evident within Hasidism could be perceived as shifting the focus away from traditional Torah and Talmudic study. Indeed, perhaps it is the Mitnagdim who should be given some of the credit for enabling Judaism to survive based upon their determination to preserve tradition.

There are others who might take a different view from this and claim, for example, that there are other groups within Judaism which have also had an important part to play in the survival of the Jewish faith. Reform Judaism is a case in point. The Reform belief that the Jewish religion needed to be reinterpreted and reformed in the light of Western thought, values and culture could also have been responsible for the survival of the Jewish religion. Furthermore, it is evident that such action has also enabled many Reform Jews to fare much better in Britain today due to the adaptations that were made and which were based upon the terms of the Pittsburgh Platform. It could be asserted that the Reform definition of Jews as a 'religious community' rather than a 'nation', as well as a rejection of laws which have a ritual rather than a moral basis, has enabled them to assimilate into whichever country they have found themselves to be living. They may make an outward token of their Jewishness, for example by male Jews wearing a skullcap in public as a sign of their religious identity, but they are not required to eat kosher food or keep the strict rules of the Sabbath such as not driving from one place to another on that day. It is likely that they face the least challenges of living as a Jew in Britain, and as a result have helped the Jewish faith to survive.

In conclusion, it is perhaps only right to acknowledge that the survival of the Jewish religion has not come about due to one isolated event or as a result of the actions of one particular group within it. Nevertheless, some would say that Hasidism did make a significant contribution to the survival of Judaism at a time in history when its decline could very well have brought about an end to the Jewish faith in Europe. And to follow this line of argument to its logical conclusion, it could be suggested that without Hasidism, the Reform movement would never have been given the chance to do what it did in reinterpreting the terms of the covenant to fit a more modern lifestyle.

And what of Hasidism today? The group which once faced great opposition from more traditional Orthodox groups is now itself regarded as one of the major movements of the faith. Cohn-Sherbok deduces that: 'Although they (different groups within Judaism) follow different liturgies and support their separate institutions, they are united in their abhorrence of the more liberal interpretations of Judaism. Today the Hasidim are equally diligent students of the law. They remain determined proponents of the doctrine of the divine origin of the Torah and are Orthodox in every sense of the word. Jonathan Sacks the former Chief Rabbi of Great Britain and the British Commonwealth ... openly acknowledges his spiritual debt to the Hasidim and sees them as an important and distinctive segment of the Jewish community.'

T4 Religious practices that shape religious identity

Key quote

Today, there are Hasidic communities in the United States, Israel and elsewhere. Like the Orthodox they accept the fundamental religious beliefs of the tradition and strictly follow Jewish law. Throughout the Jewish world they are regarded with respect, and constitute an important and distinctive segment of the Jewish community. **(Cohn-Sherbok)**

Key questions

To what extent has Hasidism been significant regarding the survival of Judaism?

Is Hasidism truly representative of traditional Jewish Orthodoxy?

What other things could be said to have contributed to the survival of Judaism?

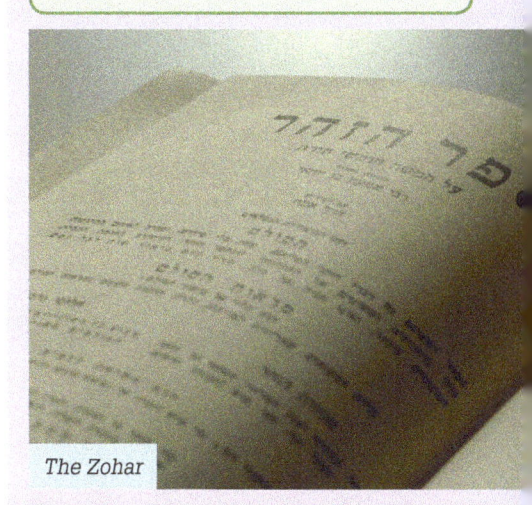

The Zohar

AO2 Activity

List some conclusions that could be drawn from the AO2 reasoning from the above text; try to aim for at least three different possible conclusions. Consider each of the conclusions and collect brief evidence to support each conclusion from the AO1 and AO2 material for this topic. Select the conclusion that you think is most convincing and explain why it is so. Try to contrast this with the weakest conclusion in the list, justifying your argument with clear reasoning and evidence.

WJEC / Eduqas Religious Studies for A Level Year 2 and A2 Judaism

Specification content
The extent to which Hasidism divides Judaism.

The extent to which Hasidism divides Judaism

When the Hasidic movement emerged in the eighteenth century and swept through the Jewish communities of Eastern Europe, it was immediately regarded as dangerous and ultimately heretical by the leaders and rabbinic authorities of traditional Judaism at that time. However, some would argue that its inception was not aimed at bringing about a deliberate divide within Judaism; and in order to provide evidence for this claim, it is important to consider the historical background whence it came. Hasidism was first established in Poland, a country whose economy was in sharp decline at that time. One of the consequences of this situation was that it led to the social and religious oppression of the resident Jewish community. Many Jews became trapped in dire poverty, and organised religion offered very little in the way of help or consolation. The traditional form of Jewish worship at this time was through the study of the Torah. It was highly intellectual, lacking in emotion, and impossible to access if one were not trained in the Hebrew language.

It is also significant that there emerged at the same time, a charismatic leader called Israel ben Eliezer. He was an itinerant preacher and healer, and is considered by many to be the founder of the Hasidic movement. Hasidic lore tells of a man who had a tremendous impact upon the people; a man who brought with him a new form of worship marked by extreme intensity of belief and enthusiasm in prayer and worship. He was known by his followers as the Baal Shem Tov, and his new approach to Judaism gained a much wider appeal amongst the Jewish majority who were not schooled in the Hebrew of the Torah, nor educated in the Talmud. It could reasonably be claimed that Hasidism did indeed bring about a major division in Judaism in its early years, and evidence for this can be seen in some of its practices.

One of the most obvious ways in which Hasidism differed from traditional Judaism was the manner in which its adherents worshipped. Opponents of the movement were appalled by the behaviour they observed, with men trembling uncontrollably, dancing, singing and even turning cartwheels. Moreover, the emphasis upon sincerity of the heart rather than Jewish scholarship raised concerns amongst Orthodox Jews who perceived Hasidism to be revolutionary and religiously liberal. Furthermore, another new feature of the Hasidic movement led to the establishment of a new kind of leader. The rebbe as he was called, was considered to have attained the highest level of devekut, and, as such, was spiritually superior to ordinary people. As Cohn-Sherbok explains: 'In this context devekut to God involved cleaving to the tzaddik.' Thus the authority which had traditionally been held within Jewish communities by the rabbis; men trained in the study of the Torah and Talmud, had now been usurped by a figure who claimed the miraculous power of ascent into the divine realm.

There was certainly no room for compromise or conciliation, and the division between the two movements is clearly illustrated by the action of the Vilna Gaon, who in 1772 issued a ban of excommunication against the Hasidim claiming: 'As a result of our sins, wicked and worthless men known as the Hasidim have left the Jewish fold and have set up their own places of worship. As everyone knows, they conduct their services in a mad and unseemly fashion, following different rituals which do not conform to the teachings of our holy Law ... The exaggerations and miracle tales which are described in their books are clear and obvious lies and ... there is even a move to disregard the obligations of the Law of Moses ...'

Study tip

It is important for AO2 that you include the views of scholars and/or schools of thought when formulating your response to a particular contention. It is a good idea therefore to note down any interesting comments that you come across during your research.

Key quote

By the 1740s he (the Baal Shem Tov) attracted a considerable number of disciples who passed on his teaching. After his death, Dov Baer became the leader of this sect and Hasidism spread to southern Poland, the Ukraine and Lithuania. The growth of this movement engendered considerable hostility on the part of rabbinic authorities, and by the end of the century the Jewish religious establishment of Vilna denounced Hasidism to the Russian government. **(Cohn-Sherbok)**

AO2 Activity

As you read through this section try to do the following:

1. Pick out the different lines of argument that are presented in the text and identify any evidence given in support.
2. For each line of argument try to evaluate whether or not you think this is strong or weak.
3. Think of any questions you may wish to raise in response to the arguments.

This Activity will help you to start thinking critically about what you read and help you to evaluate the effectiveness of different arguments and from this develop your own observations, opinions and points of view that will help with any conclusions that you make in your answers to the AO2 questions that arise.

Key quote

Unlike the major branches of modern Judaism ... adherents of Pluralistic Judaism would be actively encouraged to make up their minds about religious belief and practice. It might be objected that such extreme liberalism would simply result in chaos – such criticism, however, fails to acknowledge the state of religious diversity already existent within Jewish society. (Cohn-Sherbok)

There are others who take a different view from this and point to the fact that Hasidism is not the only group that has broken away from traditional, mainstream Orthodoxy. In point of fact, divisions have occurred at various times throughout the history of the Jewish religion. Proponents of this argument look to the period within Jewish history which is known as the Enlightenment in order to illustrate this particular line of reasoning. During the Enlightenment, many Jews began looking for a way in which to become members of mainstream European society and culture through a reform of traditional Jewish education and practice. Such a quest also resulted in a break from traditional Jewish education that was based upon readings from the prayer book, the weekly portion of Scripture, study of the Talmud, and even of selected passages from the rabbinic commentaries. What a child now needed was a broader education which would allow integration into the society and state in which he or she lived. Cohn-Sherbok claims that this led to a 'post-Enlightenment world in which Jewry is no longer unified by a cohesive religious system. Instead the Jewish people have fragmented into a wide range of subgroups espousing competing interpretations of the tradition.'

Others, however, might claim that division within Judaism should not necessarily be considered as a negative thing. It cannot be denied that in its early history, Hasidism did indeed bring about a split between itself and traditional Judaism. And yet, is it justifiable to criticise the movement when evidence demonstrates that it led to a resurgence in faith amongst the less educated European Jews at a time when the Jewish religion might very well have died out had it been left under the control of the scholarly elite? Furthermore, Reform Judaism could also be considered to have been divisive, based upon its reinterpretation of the covenant relationship. However, in the same way as Hasidism brought vitality back to the faith in eighteenth-century Europe, it could be claimed that Reform Judaism too was reacting to a situation which, once resolved, has enabled its members to live as Jews whilst also being able to assimilate into contemporary society.

In conclusion, it is important to acknowledge that, as Cohn-Sherbok states: 'No longer is Jewry united by a unified system of belief and practice. Instead, a wide variety of Jewish groupings has emerged, each with a different ideology and philosophy of Judaism.' Thus Hasidism takes its place alongside other groups who have sought to make Judaism meaningful and relevant for contemporary society. From radical and revolutionary beginnings, it has also come to be recognised by some as representative of the truest form of Judaism due to its emphasis upon the preservation of Talmudic studies and traditional values during the Enlightenment.

And what of the future? Cohn-Sherbok is of the opinion that the evolutionary process will continue in light of the demands of the modern age. Thus the search continues to seek to provide a basis for Jewish existence in contemporary society. And Cohn-Sherbok proposes that what is now needed is: '...a new interpretation of Judaism that acknowledges the depth of Jewish diversity and embraces the various and diverse forms of modern Judaism.' Thus the major Jewish groups – Orthodox, Hasidism, Reform, Conservative – will, in the future, experience further diverse forms of Judaism. Diversity which Cohn-Sherbok refers to as Pluralistic Judaism: a form of the faith which will allow all individuals the right to select those features from the Jewish heritage that they find spiritually meaningful.

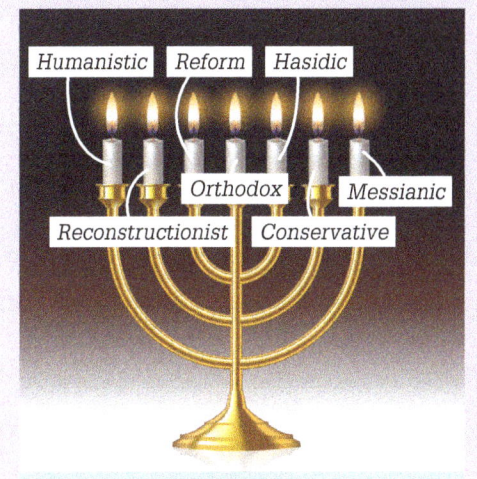

T4 Religious practices that shape religious identity

Some of the different denominations to be found within Judaism.

Key questions

Has Hasidism ever posed a significant threat to Jewish unity?

Can any one group within Judaism be considered to be totally responsible for the divisions within the faith?

What are some of the reasons for the diversity which is to be found within Judaism, and can they be justified?

AO2 Activity

List some conclusions that could be drawn from the AO2 reasoning from the above text; try to aim for at least three different possible conclusions. Consider each of the conclusions and collect brief evidence to support each conclusion from the AO1 and AO2 material for this topic. Select the conclusion that you think is most convincing and explain why it is so. Try to contrast this with the weakest conclusion in the list, justifying your argument with clear reasoning and evidence.

WJEC / Eduqas Religious Studies for
A Level Year 2 and A2 Judaism

> **Key skills Theme 4 DEF**
>
> The fourth theme has tasks that consolidate your AO2 skills and focus these skills for examination preparation.

AO2 Developing skills

It is now important to consider the information that has been covered in this section; however, the information in its raw form is too extensive and so has to be processed in order to meet the requirements of the examination. This can be achieved by practising more advanced skills associated with AO2. The exercises that run throughout this book will help you to do this and prepare you for the examination. For assessment objective 2 (AO2), which involves 'critical analysis' and 'evaluation' skills, we are going to focus on different ways in which the skills can be demonstrated effectively, and also refer to how the performance of these skills is measured (see generic band descriptors for A2 [WJEC] AO2 or A Level [Eduqas] AO2).

▶ **Your new task is this:** you will have to write a response under timed conditions to a question requiring an **evaluation of the extent to which Hasidism divides Judaism**. This exercise is best done as a small group at first.

1. Begin with a list of indicative arguments or lines of reasoning, as you may have done in the previous textbook in the series. It does not need to be in any particular order at first, although as you practise this you will see more order in your lists, in particular by way of links and connections between arguments.

2. Develop the list by using one or two relevant quotations. Now add some references to scholars and/or religious writings.

3. Then write out your plan, under timed conditions, remembering the principles of evaluating with support from extensive, detailed reasoning and/or evidence.

When you have completed the task, refer to the band descriptors for A2 (WJEC) or A Level (Eduqas) and in particular have a look at the demands described in the higher band descriptors towards which you should be aspiring. Ask yourself:

- Is my answer a confident critical analysis and perceptive evaluation of the issue?
- Is my answer a response that successfully identifies and thoroughly addresses the issues raised by the question set?
- Does my work show an excellent standard of coherence, clarity and organisation?
- Will my work, when developed, contain thorough, sustained and clear views that are supported by extensive, detailed reasoning and/or evidence?
- Are the views of scholars/schools of thought used extensively, appropriately and in context?
- Does my answer convey a confident and perceptive analysis of the nature of any possible connections with other elements of my course?
- When used, is specialist language and vocabulary both thorough and accurate?

Key skills

Analysis involves:

Identifying issues raised by the materials in the AO1, together with those identified in the AO2 section, and presents sustained and clear views, either of scholars or from a personal perspective ready for evaluation.

This means:

- That your answers are able to identify key areas of debate in relation to a particular issue
- That you can identify, and comment upon, the different lines of argument presented by others
- That your response comments on the overall effectiveness of each of these areas or arguments.

Evaluation involves:

Considering the various implications of the issues raised based upon the evidence gleaned from analysis and provides an extensive detailed argument with a clear conclusion.

This means:

- That your answer weighs up the consequences of accepting or rejecting the various and different lines of argument analysed
- That your answer arrives at a conclusion through a clear process of reasoning.

E: Philosophical understandings of the nature of God and religious experience found in Kabbalah

Esotericism: meditation, visual aids, art and magic

> **AO1 Activity**
>
> As you work through this section make a list of the names of all scholars and schools of thought that you come across. When you have done so, write a brief summary alongside each one so that you have a useful aid for your revision.

Kabbalah is the name given to the mystic tradition that is to be found within Judaism; its purpose being to experience the divine nature and presence of God. The term Kabbalah also refers to a body of mystical teaching. Alexander suggests that there are three general characteristics of Jewish mysticism:

1. The aim of the mystic is to achieve personal and intimate communion with God, either through ecstatic experience, or through contemplation as in the Kabbalah. However, it is important to note that within Judaism there is a consciousness of the 'otherness' of God, and the gap which divides a person from their Creator. As a result of this, Jewish mystics do not describe their mystical experience as becoming one with God.

2. The path to communion with God is not through reason or intellect; it does not proceed by way of logical argument or rational proof. Rather, it is **esoteric** in nature, using powerful, emotive symbols and imagery, which appeal more to the imagination. This is particularly evident in the Kabbalah.

3. The mystics are concerned with 'secrets', 'mysteries' and 'hidden things'; seeking to penetrate below the surface of things to discover hidden truths and striving to experience what Alexander describes as 'a world of unity and ultimate reality'.

Joseph Dan proposes that it was during the thirteenth century when particular groups of Jewish esoterics and mystics emerged in Spain, France and Italy, who claimed to be in possession of a secret tradition concerning the meaning of scriptures and other ancient texts. They initially described themselves using terms such as 'those in the know' and 'those who know the secret wisdom' until the terms 'Kabbalah' and '**Kabbalists**' became the dominant designation for them. As Dan explains: 'The term "Kabbalah" in this context means an additional layer of tradition, one that does not replace anything in the usual … tradition but adds to it an esoteric stratum.' Furthermore, the Kabbalists claimed that this secret tradition was given to Moses directly from God on Mount Sinai and was subsequently transmitted in secret through the following generations by oral communication from father to son; teacher to pupil.

Study tip

An understanding of the characteristics of mysticism would be of help to you in this section, therefore it would be a good idea to refer to your philosophy of religion notes on the nature of religious experience.

T4 Religious practices that shape religious identity

This section covers AO1 content and skills

Specification content
Esotericism: meditation, visual aids, art and magic.

Key terms
Esoteric: secret or mysterious; likely to be understood by a small number of people who have special knowledge

Kabbalists: followers of Kabbalah

quickfire
4.6 What is the meaning of the term 'Kabbalah'?

Key quotes
The Kabbalah, according to the kabbalists, is never new; it can be newly discovered or newly received, but essentially it is millennia-old divine truth. **(Dan)**

One should not discuss … the Creation unless there are two besides him, nor the Divine Chariot with one individual, unless he was a wise man and had much knowledge of his own. **(Mishnah Hagiga 2:1)**

Ezekiel's vision of the celestial chariot

Key quotes

In all known periods of the development of this mystical tradition, Jewish mystics were in possession of, and apparently practised, a wide variety of mystical techniques … all of them included a deep involvement of the mystic, who was expected to invest considerable effort in order to attain his religious goal. **(Idel)**

In the Kabbalah of Abraham Abulafia and his school, devekut is fundamentally rooted in the combinations and permutations of the names of God. In Abulafia's concept of language, we learn that language is perceived as the universe itself; it reveals the structure of the Divine names of God; it reveals the structure of the laws of reality; and each letter of the Hebrew alphabet is in itself an entire world …The Hebrew language is not a human creation but a Divine emanation and a result of Divine revelation. **(Shokek)**

Jewish esotericism has its foundation in a statement found in the Mishnah (Hagiga 2:1), which declares that it is forbidden to discuss two sections from the scriptures in public, and further warns of the danger of studying them even in small groups. The first concerns the chapters of Genesis that describe creation, and the second relates to the chapters of the Book of Ezekiel which describe the prophet's vision of the celestial chariot. 'Thus, these chapters and subjects were separated from the body of Jewish traditional expounding and speculation, and relegated to a separate realm, which was regarded as spiritually – and sometimes even physically – dangerous.' (Dan)

There is a famous Talmudic story concerning four sages which outlines the dangers and expertise required for the practice of Kabbalah. Rabbis Azzai, Ben Zoma, Elisha ben Abuyah and Akiva entered a pardes (a royal garden). Azzai died as a result of the experience; Ben Zoma went mad; Elisha ben Abuyah destroyed the plants and only one, Akiva, entered in peace and departed in peace.

It is not entirely clear what the entrance to pardes actually signifies, but Dan explains that it was understood to represent a profound religious experience of entering the divine realm and suggesting some kind of meeting with God. The parable warns of the problems and the dangers that lie in following the mystical tradition as, of the four who entered pardes, only one who entered came out at peace: Azzai was totally intoxicated by the experience to such an extent that he lost the will to stay in the world; Ben Zoma went mad because he could not absorb what he saw; Elisha ben Abuyah saw a vision of an angel seated in God's presence and came to the conclusion that there must be two authorities in Heaven. His response was to cut the plants down in an attempt to cut apart that which was not meant to be separate, thus deserting the truth of God's oneness. Akiva, however, was the only one who did not demand to understand the mysteries he witnessed, or to use his own interpretation of what he had experienced.

Kabbalah places great emphasis upon the practice of meditation as the foremost method of achieving a true understanding of hidden truths as it is considered to be the means by which a person can take control of their mind, and achieve a state of consciousness in which they can achieve greater spiritual insight.

A significant exponent of meditation within Kabbalah was Abraham Abulafia who was active in Spain in the thirteenth century. He taught that our awareness of hidden things is hindered by the thoughts, feelings and sensory perceptions that fill up our minds on a daily basis. The goal of meditation for Abulafia was therefore to free the soul by removing the obstacles that constrict it. His method of meditation is focused upon the letters of the Hebrew alphabet and/or the names of God. As Matt explains: 'Here there is no concrete, particular meaning, no distraction, just the music of pure thought. As the highest form of this method of meditation, Abulafia recommends "jumping" or "skipping," a type of free association between various combinations of letters guided by fairly lax rules. Thereby, consciousness expands.'

In preparation for meditation, Abulafia also highlighted the need to set oneself apart from others in order to avoid distraction; to undertake specific breathing exercises; and to wear clean garments.

Visual aids to meditation can also be employed, an example of which being the names of God presented in a particular format. Such an aid would be used with the goal of connecting with God, or even ascending to an even higher level.

The Hebrew alphabet

A further example presented by Idel, is the enactment of kavvanah through the visualisation of colours as part of prayer. This technique began in the late thirteenth and early fourteenth centuries and is connected with a Spanish Kabbalist who is known as Rabbi David. Rabbi David said: 'We are not allowed to visualise the ten **Sefirot** … Therefore, you should always visualise that colour which is (attributed to the **Sefirah**) … afterward you shall draw down by your visualisation the efflux from the "depth of the river" to the worlds down to us – and this is the true (way), received [in an esoteric manner] by oral tradition.' Idel concludes: 'Therefore we can surmise that the process of visualisation enabled the ascent of the Kabbalist's imaginative faculty to a higher ontological level, and only afterward could he attract the divine efflux downward.' The teachings of Kabbalah can also be viewed as a kind of Jewish art, which takes place in the privacy of the devotee's mind whilst meditating.

Within Kabbalah, tefillin also take on a greater significance as aids to worship. Freeman explains that at the time of creation, only seven of the ten Sefirot descended within seven days and generated our world. The first three, however, those of the mind, stayed in heaven. He continues by explaining that people's bodies are not generally synchronised with their minds and thus neither are their hearts or their actions. Consequently, tefillin is all about healing the rift. By putting on tefillin, an individual does their part by connecting the mind and heart with the leather straps and black boxes with scrolls inside. The effect, he claims reverberates throughout the cosmos: 'Heaven connects to earth, spiritual to physical, Creator to creation. Everything starts getting into harmony with its essence and inner purpose.' (Freeman)

The mitzvot are also a focus for meditation as they represent the contact point between a person and God. Unterman explains that in rabbinic Judaism the mitzvot proper are preceded by a benediction: 'who has made us holy through His mitzvot and commanded us to …'. However, the mystics introduced a further short prayer of meditation which was recited before the usual benediction. The aim of these meditations was to bring out the mystical meaning of the mitzvah about to be performed, the angels or divine names specific to it, and its consequences for the higher levels of reality. For example: 'For the sake of the unification of the Holy One, blessed be He and His Shekinah, in awe and devotion I am prepared and ready to perform mitzvah (named here) to the full command of my Creator.'

References to magic are also evident within a small number of ancient esoteric treatises. For example, the treatise entitled 'The Sword of Moses' lists hundreds of what Dan calls magical incantations and procedures which are linked to such things as medical remedies, love potions and even walking on water. Magic is also the subject of another treatise, 'The Book of Secrets'. However, it is the concept of the **golem** which stands as one of the most noteworthy examples of the use of magic within Kabbalah. The golem is a figure brought to life by magical means. The Talmud (Sanhedrin 38b) says that Adam was originally created from dust as a golem before receiving his soul.

The Sefer Yezirah contains the instructions for the creation of a golem. The procedure is a long and complicated one involving the recitation of incantations, and the mixing of soil and water. The figure created will usually only be used as a mental image; one that can be used as the means by which a person can transport themselves into the divine realm. However, sometimes it might be transferred into clay form. Dan claims that: 'the phenomenon of the golem contributed meaningfully to the portrayal of the Kabbalah as an esoteric, mysterious, and powerful compendium of ancient magic. … The life force of the golem is the Hebrew alphabet, the secret name of God inserted under his tongue, or the word "truth", one of God's names engraved on his forehead … The legend of the golem conformed to, and strengthened the image of the Kabbalah as doctrine that could bring great benefits, but one that also includes some sinister, dangerous elements.'

Key terms

Golem: an artificially created human being brought to life by Kabbalistic rites

Sefirah: emanation (singular)

Sefirot: emanations (plural)

The golem in clay form

WJEC / Eduqas Religious Studies for A Level Year 2 and A2 Judaism

Specification content
Role of the Zohar.

quickfire

4.7 What does the word 'Zohar' mean?

Key quotes

(The Zohar's) thought rests on a complex view of the creation and continued existence of the universe and humankind through the mediation of the Torah and the commandments. **(Close)**

When God resolved to create the world, He looked into the Torah, into its every creative world, and fashioned the world accordingly; for all the worlds and all the actions of the world are contained in the Torah. **(Zohar)**

Open my eyes, that I may perceive the wonders of Your teaching. **(Psalm 119:18)**

With roots stretching back to the Bible and nurtured throughout Jewish history, the Kabbalah began to grow and flourish with the publication of the Zohar. **(Dosick)**

Moses de Leon

Role of the Zohar

The Zohar (meaning 'radiance' or 'splendour') is the classical text of the Kabbalah. It is written in a form of the Aramaic language which was common in Israel during the period 539 BCE–70CE, and takes the form of a midrash, presenting mystical teachings on the five books of the Torah. It is made up of three volumes; the first covering the Zohar on Genesis; the second on Exodus; the third on the remaining books of the Torah. There also exist additional volumes such as a collection known as the 'New Zohar', for example, which contains a compilation of later materials covering other biblical books such as the Song of Songs and Lamentations.

The teachings found within the Zohar emphasise that the Torah contains what Dosick describes as: 'higher truths in addition to the literal meaning of the text; that the highest goal of a human being is to reach for and understand the innermost secrets of existence; and that every human act has a ripple effect on the entire universe.' Rabbi Simeon bar Yochai said that the stories of the Torah are only the Torah's outer clothing. He remarked that people are prone to make judgements about others they meet based upon their outer garments, and that they regard the clothes as if they tell us all that needs to be known about the wearer. In the same way he described the Torah as a body which is clothed in earthly tales. However, those who are wise will not take the words of the Torah at face value, but will attempt to find out what lies beneath, and go in search of a deeper understanding. The Zohar is thus considered to be a text that caters for those who seek to find a deeper meaning to life including the purpose of creation and the nature of one's relationship with God and the world.

The Zohar covers many themes such as the nature of God; the creation of the world; the relationship of God to the world through the ten Sefirot; the mysteries of the divine names; the nature of good and evil; the nature and destiny of the soul; redemption; the importance of the Torah; the Messiah; holidays; and the mitzvot.

Authorship of the Zohar has been attributed to Moses de Leon, a Kabbalist who lived in Spain at the end of the thirteenth century. De Leon claimed that the Zohar was a copy of an ancient mystical document which recorded the teachings of Rabbi Simeon bar Yochai (who lived in the second century). However, its link to Rabbi Simeon has been impossible to verify. Unterman tells of the attempts to authenticate it by Rabbi Isaac of Acre, a contemporary of Moses de Leon, who has left a long account of his efforts to verify the antiquity of the Zoharic text:

'One of the views which R. Isaac came across was that Moses de Leon only ascribed the work to the great sage R. Simeon bar Yochai in order to charge more for his copies of the manuscript. In fact, however, he wrote it himself through the possession of a "magical writing name", i.e. a technique of automatic writing where the author composes under the influence of an angelic or heavenly force. Moses de Leon swore an oath to R. Isaac that he had the original, ancient, manuscript in his house and invited him to come and see it. Unfortunately, Moses died before the offer could be taken up.' (Unterman)

Furthermore, as Unterman explains, Rabbi Isaac reported 'in the name of Moses de Leon's widow, that the Zohar was composed by Moses de Leon himself'. It is now generally agreed among modern scholars that the Zohar was written by Moses de Leon.

Notwithstanding the debate regarding its provenance, the Zohar is regarded by many as a sacred book, with De Lange noting that some North African synagogues contain two holy arks, one for the Torah and another for the Zohar. It also had a big influence in Hasidism, and it is said that the Baal Shem Tov always carried a copy with him. Extracts from the Zohar are to be found in contemporary Jewish prayer books even amongst non-Orthodox groups; however, it has not been fully accepted in mainstream Judaism. The Jewish Encyclopaedia explains why: '… the Zohar was censured by many rabbis because it propagated many superstitious beliefs, and produced a host of mystical dreamers, whose over-excited imaginations peopled the world with spirits, demons, and all kinds of good and bad influences'.

The focus on the experience of God and trying to penetrate God's essence: En Sof (infinite)

Abraham Heschel, a Jewish theologian, explains that the main purpose of mysticism for Judaism is that God is very real, and thus the desire of the mystic is 'to feel and enjoy Him; not only to obey but to approach Him … They want to taste the whole wheat of spirit before it is ground by the millstones of reason. They would rather be overwhelmed by the symbols of the inconceivable than wield the definitions of the superficial.'

'What, then, is the mystic doctrine of God in Judaism?' asks Neusner. Heschel answers that question in the following way: 'Mystic intuition occurs at an outpost of the mind, dangerously detached from the main substance of the intellect.' He continues by explaining that the world is charged with God's presence and that every object within it offers a sign of the Deity's qualities. He continues: 'To the Kabbalist, God is not a concept, a generalisation, but a most specific reality; his thinking about Him full of forceful directness.' However, such is the nature of God that the Kabbalist acknowledges 'that He is beyond the grasp of the human mind and inaccessible to meditation. He is the **En Sof**, the infinite, "the most Hidden of all Hidden".'

However, if this is so, how can En Sof ever be revealed to human beings? Robinson says that the holy texts are one aspect of God's revelation, and that the Sefirot are another. He further explains that God can be experienced in many forms through Sefirot which act as filters between a person and God: 'Another translation of Sefirot is "channels"; … that allow us to focus on and hear the "radio signals" of the All Powerful mixed in among the static of everyday life. The emanations, then, are the ways in which God is able to interact with the sensual world, the world we inhabit.' (Robinson)

Key quote

The En Sof has granted us manifestations of His hidden life: He had descended to become the universe; He has revealed Himself to become the Lord of Israel. The ways in which the infinite assumes the form of the finite existence are called Sefirot. These are various aspects or forms of Divine action, spheres of Divine emanation. They are, as it were, the garments in which the Hidden God reveals Himself and acts in the universe, the channels through which His light is issued forth. **(Heschel)**

Specification content
The focus on the experience of God and trying to penetrate God's essence: En Sof (infinite).

Key term
En Sof: meaning 'infinite'; a term used in Jewish Kabbalism to refer to God

Key quote
When you contemplate the Creator, realise that his encampment exists beyond, infinitely beyond, and so, too, in front of you and behind you, east and west, north and south, above and below, infinitely everywhere. Be aware that God fashioned everything and is within everything. There is nothing else. **(Kabbalah – translated by Matt)**

Specification content

The focus on the experience of God and trying to penetrate God's essence: Sefirot (emanations).

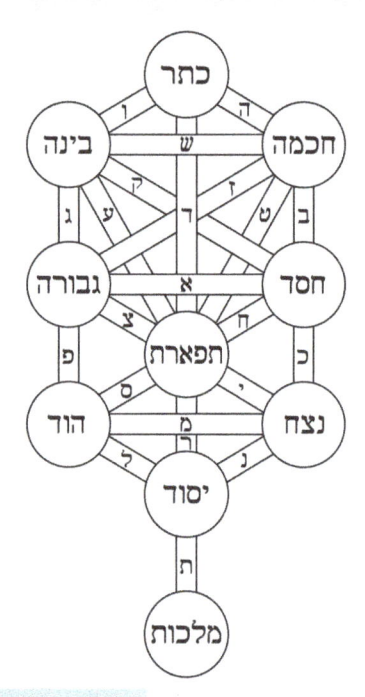

The Tree of Life

Key quote

Keter represents the first stirrings of Will within the Godhead, a primal impulse that precedes even thought but which is essential for any action to take place. It is also called Ayin/Nothingness, for it was out of the infinite void that the Almighty created. When a Jew seeks a oneness with God through ecstatic prayer or meditation, it is to this state of Nothingness, the annihilation of all ego, that she aspires. **(Robinson)**

The focus on the experience of God and trying to penetrate God's essence: Sefirot (emanations)

Key quote

We are not allowed to visualise the ten Sefirot ... Therefore, you should always visualise the colour (attributed to the Sefirah) ... **(David)**

There are ten Sefirot, each linked in a complex figure that some have called the 'Tree of Life'. Each Sefirah is identified with a part of the body, one of the names of God, and, for the majority, a colour. They are:

1. Keter (Crown)
2. Hokhmah (Wisdom)
3. Binah (Understanding)
4. Hesed (Loving kindness)
5. Gevurah (Power)
6. Tiferet (Beauty)
7. Netzakh (Victory)
8. Hod (Splendour)
9. Yesod (Foundation)
10. Malkhut (Sovereignty)

Each of the attributes of God are highly interdependent, with each one linked to several others. It is claimed that by coming to an understanding of their interrelationship, one can understand, albeit on a limited scale, the process of Creation itself.

'How many are the things You have made, O Lord ... the earth is full of your creations.' (Psalm 104:24)

Keter (Crown) is the first emanation from En Sof and represents the first stirring of the will of God to create the universe. Moshe Miller describes Keter as 'the generator and activator of all the other sefirot', and uses the following analogy in order to explain its nature more clearly: 'If a person has a will to do something he begins to invent ways in which to achieve his goal. Once he has discovered a theoretical method he starts to plan out how to achieve this in reality. From there he initiates activity. As long as he has not yet achieved his desire, his will drives him onwards until he does so. Similarly Keter contains within it the ultimate goal which it seeks to attain.'

Robinson notes that the name of God associated with Keter is 'Ehyeh' which is what God says to Moses when he asks who speaks to him from the bush which flamed but did not burn: 'And God said to Moses, "Ehyeh-Asher-Ehyeh".' Tigay translates this phrase as 'I will be what I will be', meaning 'My nature will become evident from my actions'. In relation to the human body, Keter is positioned above the head, and has no colour assigned to it.

Hokhmah (Wisdom) is the first Sefirah to be actually generated, and which Miller describes as the 'life-force of all Creation'. As Psalm 104:24 declares: 'How many are the things You have made, O Lord; You have made them all with wisdom (Hokhmah); the earth is full of your creations.' Robinson likens Hokhmah to the sperm which will impregnate Binah (the third Sefirah) as the first step in the process of creation. In relation to the human body, Hokhmah is associated with the right side of the brain, and its colour is blue.

Binah (Understanding) originates from Hokhmah, and it is because of this relationship, explains Green, that 'they are often treated by Kabbalists as the primal pair, the ancestral Abba and Imma, Father and Mother, the deepest polarities of male and female within the divine (and human) self'. Robinson further describes Binah as representing 'the point at which Divine inspiration begins to take on a definite form'.

Binah brings understanding to Hokhmah, in which all the creative processes are potentially contained. Whereas Hokhmah is the sperm, Binah is the womb, and thus the further seven Sefirot are given life.

Binah is associated with the name of God that is **Elohim**, and is situated to the left of the brain in the 'Tree of Life'. Its related colour is green.

The three highest Sefirot (Keter, Hokhmah and Binah) are considered to be beyond human understanding, representing as they do the most primal and mystical level of the divine world. Green describes the seven following Sefirot as emerging in sequence: 'Under the influence of Neoplatonism, the Kabbalists came to describe the Sefirot as emerging in sequence ... this sequence does not have to be one of time, as the Sefirot constitute the inner life of Y-H-V-H, where time does not mean what it does to us. The sequence is rather one of an intrinsic logic, each stage a response to that which comes "before" it.'

Hesed (Loving kindness) represents the grace or love of God which calls for the response of love from the human soul in return. Green further explains: 'This gift of love is beyond measure and without limit; the boundless compassion of Keter is now transposed into a love for each specific form and creature that is ever to emerge.'

Hesed is associated with the name of God that is **El**, and its position on the 'Tree of life' coincides with the right arm. Its related colour is white.

Gevurah (Power) is paired with Hesed and the two, acting in union, maintain an important balance in the world between justice and mercy. Robinson explains that without Gevurah, the world would be so overwhelmed by God's love that it would be reabsorbed into the Divine; and without Hesed, God's judgement would be let loose bringing destruction upon the world. As Green puts it: 'Too much love and there is no judgement, none of the moral demand that is so essential to the fabric of Judaism. But too much power or judgement is even worse.' The Zohar refers to the force of evil by using the term '**Sitra Akhra**' indicating that too much Gevurah is its source.

Gevurah represents the left arm of the Sefirot in human form, and its colour is red. As with Binah, Gevurah is associated with Elohim as the name of God.

Tiferet (Beauty) holds a position within the centre (the torso) of the 'Tree of Life' and provides a further balance between Hesed and Gevurah, joining as it does the extremes of left and right. Green describes it as the central beam in God's construction of the universe, and draws attention to one of the instructions for the building of the Tabernacle found in Exodus 26:28 which states: 'The centre bar halfway up the planks shall run from end to end.' The emphasis upon stability is thus emphasised in relation to the proper running of the universe, and Tiferet can be seen to be the unifying force between the upper nine Sefirot. Robinson also points out that Tiferet is often associated with the Written Torah, and its colour is purple.

Netzakh (Victory), Hod (Splendour) and Yesod (Foundation) form a second group of supporting Sefirot. Green describes them as the channels 'through which the higher energies pass on their way into the tenth Sefirah, Malkhut or Shekinah, the source of all life for the lower worlds'. Robinson describes Netzakh and Hod as more earthly versions of Hesed and Gevurah with Netzakh representing God's active grace and benevolence in the world, whilst Hod denotes the manner in which God's judgement is meted out on earth. Netzakh corresponds to the right leg and Hod to the left. They are associated with the names **YHVH Tsva'ot** and **Elohim Tsva'ot** in relation to God's epithets.

Yesod's position in the middle of the 'Tree of Life' is representative of the joining together of all the cosmic forces: 'the flow of all the energies above now united again in a single place' (Green). Robinson further explains that Yesod is the means

Key quotes

As Hokhmah emerges, it brings forth its own mate, called Binah ... Hokhmah and Binah are two sefirot that are inseparably linked to one another; each is inconceivable to us without the other. Hokhmah is too fine and subtle to be detected without its reflections or reverberations in Binah. The mirrored halls of Binah would be dark and unknowable without the light of Hokhmah. **(Green)**

Binah ... is the point at which the flash of intuition is refined into a conscious thought. **(Robinson)**

quickfire

4.8 Which are the three highest Sefirot?

Key terms

El: name for God denoting might, strength and power

Elohim: one of the many names for God that are found in the Jewish scriptures

Elohim Tsva'ot: meaning 'God of Hosts'

Sitra Akhra: meaning 'other side' and referring to the opposite of holiness

YHVH Tsva'ot: meaning 'Lord of Hosts'

by which Tiferet, the male principle of the Divine, impregnates Malkhut, the female embodiment of the Divine: 'Yesod is the way in which Divine Creativity and Fertility are visited upon all creation.' (Robinson)

Yesod corresponds to the following names of God: **El Hai** and **El Shaddai**, and its colour is orange.

Malkhut represents both God's sovereignty and divine presence (shekinah) in the world. Shekinah is not a word that is used in the Torah but is to be found in rabbinic tradition. It denotes a profound relationship between God and each individual, and is the feminine aspect of God. Some rabbis teach that the shekinah is the part of God that is in exile along with the Jewish people. Other rabbis say that the shekinah permeates the world in the same way that the soul permeates the body; just as the soul sustains the body, the shekinah sustains the world.

Malkhut usually correlates to the feet, and is associated with the name Adonai. Its colours are either blue or black.

The focus on the experience of God and trying to penetrate God's essence: Devekut (clinging on)

Devekut is a fundamental concept of Kabbalah and is regarded as being the primary goal of the mystic. Its meaning within Kabbalah denotes the concept of 'clinging on', which signifies achieving communion with God; a state in which all other thoughts, senses and experiences are cast aside.

It is evident that devekut was the primary goal in early Kabbalah, and this is apparent through the writings of a thirteenth-century Jewish scholar known as Isaac the Blind who is reported to have said: 'The essence of the service of the enlightened and of those who contemplate His name is "cling to Him". This is in reference to Deuteronomy 13:4 which states: "Follow none but the Lord your God, and revere none but Him; observe His commandments alone, and heed only His orders; worship none but Him, and hold fast (or cling) to Him".' The concept of devekut is also to be found in other scriptural texts such as in Deuteronomy 11:22: 'If, then, you faithfully keep all this Instruction that I command you, loving the Lord your God, walking in all His ways, and holding fast to Him …'

Devekut – the highest step on a spiritual ladder

The Jewish Virtual Library explains that devekut is usually described as the highest step on a spiritual ladder, which can only be reached after the believer has mastered the attitudes of fear of God, love of God, for example, and which is achieved mainly during times of prayer or meditation before prayer, through using the right intention (kavvanah). The aspect in the divine world to which the mystic prays when aspiring to reach the state of devekut is usually the Shekinah. However, to continue with the analogy of devekut as a spiritual ladder, it is possible for a person to climb from one Sefirah to another, and in doing so to raise one's soul from one point to the next in mystic contemplation: 'As the various portions and words of prayer and the various deeds that the commandments require correspond to different parts and powers in the divine world, so does the soul rise with the works and deeds towards the Sefirah to which it is intended. Thus the mystic may achieve devekut with the higher Sefirot, such as yesod (the ninth), tiferet (the sixth), Gevurah (fifth), and hesed (fourth) in the divine ladder.' (Jewish Virtual Library)

Key terms
El Hai: meaning 'The Living God'
El Shaddai: meaning 'God Almighty'

Specification content
The focus on the experience of God and trying to penetrate God's essence: Devekut (clinging on).

Key quote
(En Sof) manifests everything from potential to actuality … It is He that arranges the Sefirot in their pattern … each one in its proper place in the sequence, but in Him there is no order. He created everything with Binah, and nothing created Him. He is an architect (and He) designed everything with Tiferet, but He has no design nor an architect. He fashioned everything with Malkhut but nothing fashioned Him. Since He is within these ten Sefirot, He created, designed, and fashioned everything through them. (In the ten Sefirot) He established His unity so that they (the Sefirot) would recognise Him. **(Zohar)**

quickfire
4.9 Give two examples from the Book of Deuteronomy which refer to the concept of devekut.

Usually the Kabbalists emphasise that such communion with God through prayer is transitory in nature, and it is only after death that a believer can hope that their soul will achieve a permanent state of devekut with God. Such a union, however, will not be achieved until the redemption after the coming of the Messiah, when all just Jews will live together eternally in the state of devekut.

The Jewish Virtual Library also notes that there is a connection between being in a state of devekut and prophecy, which is the outcome of such union between a person and God: 'The fathers of the nation, Moses, and the prophets were described as people who achieved a lasting state of devekut. When devekut is achieved, "The Holy Spirit" comes into contact with the mystic and gives him superhuman spiritual abilities.' (Jewish Virtual Library)

The focus on the experience of God and trying to penetrate God's essence: Tikkun (repair)

Key quote

When God chose the Jewish nation and they heard the Revelation at Sinai, it became their task to restore the world. (Robinson)

Tikkun is a term which means 'repair' or '**reparation**', and is one of the key concepts to be found in Kabbalah. Robinson tells us that a twentieth-century Jewish scholar named Gershom Scholem argued that its significance grew as a result of the ideology that was devised by Isaac Luria and his followers who questioned the existence of evil in the world.

Robinson explains that two of the key concepts in Lurianic Kabbalah are the 'contraction' (tzimtzum) and the 'shattering of the vessels'. Luria puts forward a story of creation in which En Sof had to bring into being an empty space in which Creation could occur in order to allow for free will to exist. After the contraction, a stream of divine light flowed from God into the empty space in the shape of the Sefirot and Adam Kadman, the first man: 'The light flowed from Adam Kadman, out of his eyes, nose, mouth, creating the vessels that were eternal shapes of the sefirot. But the vessels were too fragile to contain such a powerful – Divine – light. The upper three vessels were damaged, the lower seven were shattered and fell. Thus the **tehiru** became divided into the upper and lower worlds, a product of the shattering. And so evil came into the world, through a violent separation between those elements that had taken part in the act of creation and others that had wilfully resisted, contributing to the shattering of the vessels. The elements that had fought against the creation were the emerging powers of evil, but because they opposed creation they lack the power to survive; they need access to the Divine light, and continue to exist in the world only to the extent that they gather the holy sparks that fell when the shattering took place.' (Robinson)

And so it was that when Adam failed to bring about redemption due to his sinfulness, the responsibility was duly placed upon the shoulders of the Jewish people. As Robinson puts it: 'The responsibility on the Jewish people is a collective one; under Luria's terms, the Jewish people should be seen as a fighting army under siege. No days off, no respite, a hard battle to live by the Commandments and to repair the world. If one falters, others must take up his burden. Consequently, Lurianic thinking combines a radical understanding of God and Creation with a profoundly conservative attitude toward Jewish observance. But it also reanimates the daily routine of observing the mitzvot, giving them a new and more intense significance than ever before.'

> **Specification content**
> The focus on the experience of God and trying to penetrate God's essence: Tikkun (repair).

Key quotes

God is everywhere, even within the human being. The proper response to God's presence is devekut, practices that lead to one's 'cleaving' to the divine. (Satlow)

Isaac of Acre describes devekut as 'pouring a jug of water into a flowing spring, so that all becomes one', yet he warns his reader not to sink in the ocean of the highest sefirah: 'The endeavour should be to contemplate but to escape drowning ... Your soul shall indeed see the divine light and cleave to it while dwelling in her palace.' (Matt)

quickfire

4.10 Who described devekut as 'pouring a jug of water into a flowing spring, so that all becomes one'?

Key terms

Reparation: the act of making good

Tehiru: the surge of infinite energy and light

Tikkun: meaning 'repair'; the restoration of cosmic harmony

The goal of Kabbalah, Luria claims, was to advance the tikkun so that the damage caused by the shattering can be undone: 'For Luria and his followers, tikkun had a very specific meaning. Every time that a human performs a mitzvah, she raises one of the holy sparks out of the forces of evil and restores it to the upper world. Conversely, every time that a human sins, a divine spark plunges down. The day will come, if all do their part, when the entire remaining supply of Divine Light will be restored to the upper world; without access to the Divine Light, evil will be unable to survive and will crumble away to dust.' (Robinson)

Performing a mitzvah

The concept of tikkun occurs very frequently in the Zohar and it is evident that it is through prayer and ritual that Jews can contribute to the reversal of the shattering of the vessels. When every individual has fulfilled their own tikkun, the world will attain a state of cosmic harmony and the messianic age will dawn. One passage from the Zohar describes the act of prayer as a process involving four different grades of tikkun: 'The first tikkun is the restoration of oneself, self-perfection; the second tikkun is the restoration of this world; the third tikkun is the restoration of the world above throughout all the hosts of heaven; the fourth tikkun is the restoration of the holy name through the mystery of the holy chariots, and the mystery of all the worlds above and below with the proper kind of restoration.' In other words, explains Tishby, the worshipper, the physical world, the world of angels and the system of Sefirot can all be restored by the power of human prayer. However, first the worshipper must approach prayer through careful preparation: 'The tikkun of the worshipper is accomplished by his purifying himself of earthly desires, by fulfilling religious precepts before praying, and through the sanctification of prayer and kavvanah.' (Tishby)

Tishby continues by identifying the following specific prayers which are to be recited:

- The Hallelujah Psalms and the prayer 'Blessed be He who spoke' stimulate the forces of nature and all created beings to praise and glorify God. This can bring about the accomplishment of the tikkun of this world.
- 'Creator of ministering spirits' can bring about the restoration of the intermediate world and the angels.
- The central prayers of the Jewish faith, the Shema and the Amidah, are linked to the tikkun of the system of Sefirot.

However, the restoration of the lower and upper worlds will only be accomplished when the prayer that is directed toward them reaches its goal. As the Zohar states: 'All the words that a man utters through his mouth in that prayer ascend aloft, and split atmospheres and firmaments until they reach the place that they reach, and they form themselves into a crown upon the king's head, and a crown is made from them.'

AO1 Activity

Using an online quiz-maker website, create an interactive quiz on Kabbalah which can be used as part of your revision programme.

Study tip

An extensive range of scholarly views/schools of thought is to be found in this section, and your ability to convey a variety of opinions/theories accurately and concisely would distinguish a high-level answer from one that is simply vague or general.

Key quote

Ethical behaviour, following the mitzvot, no matter how seemingly trivial, takes on a new, cosmic significance. Forget to say the blessing over bread? You have contributed to universal evil. Put up a mezuzah on the door of your new house? You have helped to redeem the whole world. **(Robinson)**

AO1 Developing skills

It is now important to consider the information that has been covered in this section; however, the information in its raw form is too extensive and so has to be processed in order to meet the requirements of the examination. This can be achieved by practising more advanced skills associated with AO1. For assessment objective 1 (AO1), which involves demonstrating 'knowledge' and 'understanding' skills, we are going to focus on different ways in which the skills can be demonstrated effectively, and also refer to how the performance of these skills is measured (see generic band descriptors for A2 [WJEC] AO1 or A Level [Eduqas] AO1).

▶ **Your new task is this:** you will have to write a response under timed conditions to a question requiring **an examination or explanation of the focus on the experience of God and trying to penetrate God's essence: En Sof (Infinite); Sefirot (emanations); Devekut (clinging on); and Tikkun (repair)**. This exercise can either be done as a group or independently.

1. Begin with a list of indicative content, as you may have done in the previous textbook in the series. This may be discussed as a group or done independently. It does not need to be in any particular order at first, although as you practise this you will see more order in your lists that reflects your understanding.
2. Develop the list by using one or two relevant quotations. Now add some references to scholars and/or religious writings.
3. Then write out your plan, under timed conditions, remembering the principles of explaining with evidence and/or examples. Then ask someone else to read your answer and see if they can then help you improve it in any way.
4. Collaborative marking helps a learner appreciate alternative perspectives and possibly things that may have been missed. It also helps highlight the strengths of another that one can learn from. With this in mind, it is good to swap and compare answers in order to improve your own.

When you have completed the task, refer to the band descriptors for A2 (WJEC) or A Level (Eduqas) and in particular have a look at the demands described in the higher band descriptors towards which you should be aspiring. Ask yourself:

- Does my work demonstrate thorough, accurate and relevant knowledge and understanding of religion and belief?
- Is my work coherent (consistent or make logical sense), clear and well organised?
- Will my work, when developed, be an extensive and relevant response which is specific to the focus of the task?
- Does my work have extensive depth and/or suitable breadth and have excellent use of evidence and examples?
- If appropriate to the task, does my response have thorough and accurate reference to sacred texts and sources of wisdom?
- Are there any insightful connections to be made with other elements of my course?
- Will my answer, when developed and extended to match what is expected in an examination answer, have an extensive range of views of scholars/schools of thought?
- When used, is specialist language and vocabulary both thorough and accurate?

Key skills

Knowledge involves:

Selection of a range of (thorough) accurate and relevant information that is directly related to the specific demands of the question.

This means:

- Selecting relevant material for the question set
- Be focused in explaining and examining the material selected.

Understanding involves:

Explanation that is extensive, demonstrating depth and/or breadth with excellent use of evidence and examples including (where appropriate) thorough and accurate supporting use of sacred texts, sources of wisdom and specialist language.

This means:

- Effective use of examples and supporting evidence to establish the quality of your understanding
- Ownership of your explanation that expresses personal knowledge and understanding and NOT just a chunk of text from a book that you have rehearsed and memorised.

WJEC / Eduqas Religious Studies for A Level Year 2 and A2 Judaism

This section covers AO2 content and skills

Specification content
The possibility of a personal mystical union with God in Judaism.

Issues for analysis and evaluation

The possibility of a personal mystical union with God in Judaism

The existence of a mystic tradition within Judaism known as Kabbalah is indicative of a belief that it is possible to experience the divine nature and presence of God. However, as Alexander suggests, this path to God is not through reason or intellect by way of logical argument or rational proof. Rather, it is esoteric in nature, using powerful, emotive symbols and imagery, which appeal more to the imagination. Furthermore, the esoteric nature of this particular movement means that it is concerned with secrets, mysteries and the discovery of hidden truths in an attempt to experience what Alexander describes as 'a world of unity and ultimate reality'.

It can also be argued that this secret tradition was given by God to Moses on Mount Sinai and has been subsequently transmitted down through the generations ever since in secret by oral communication between father and son and teacher to pupil. Indeed, it has been asserted that Jewish esotericism has its foundation in the Mishnah, in a statement which declares that it is forbidden to discuss two sections from the scriptures in public, and further warns of the danger of studying them even in small groups. The two such sections relate to the chapters of Genesis that describe creation and the chapters of the Book of Ezekiel which describe the prophet's vision of the celestial chariot.

An important point for consideration here, however, is what Kabbalah means by 'experiencing' God. Alexander notes that it is important to understand that within Judaism there is a consciousness of the 'otherness' of God, and the gap which divides a person from their Creator. As a result of this, Jewish mystics do not usually describe their mystical experience as becoming one with God.

Kabbalists nevertheless maintain that that there are several ways of achieving personal communion with God. For instance, one method involves interpreting the traditional teachings of Judaism in a symbolic way that involves highly specialised practices that are not available to everyone. One of the characteristics of Kabbalah is its emphasis upon the practice of meditation, which it regards as being the foremost method of achieving a true understanding of hidden truths. Through meditation a practitioner can take control of their mind in order to reach a state of consciousness in which they can achieve greater spiritual insight.

In addition, Kabbalah also possesses the Zohar which is considered to be the classical text of the mystical tradition, containing as it does what Dosick describes as 'higher truths in addition to the literal meaning of the text; that the highest goal of a human being is to reach for and understand the innermost secrets of existence; and that every human act has a ripple effect on the entire universe'. It is thus considered to be the text that caters for those who wish to experience the divine nature and presence of God.

Other aspects of Kabbalah also support the possibility of achieving closeness to God, and the concept of En Sof is one such example. Even though Kabbalists acknowledge that God is beyond the grasp of the human mind, one aspect of divine revelation is through the Sefirot which act as filters between a person and God. As Robinson explains: 'they allow us to focus on and hear the "radio signals" of the All Powerful mixed in among the static of everyday life. The emanations, then, are the ways in which God is able to interact with the sensual world, the world we inhabit.'

Devekut is also a fundamental concept of Kabbalah which is regarded as being the primary goal of the mystic. It denotes the notion of 'clinging on', which signifies achieving communion with God in a state in which all other thoughts, senses and experiences are cast aside. Evidence for its veracity as a concept has

Key quote

Torah in the Zohar is not conceived as a text, as an object, or as material, but as a living divine presence, engaged in a mutual relationship with the person who studies her. More than that, in the Zoharic consciousness Torah is compared to a beloved who carries on with her lovers a mutual and dynamic courtship. (Hellner-Eshed)

AO2 Activity

As you read through this section try to do the following:

1. Pick out the different lines of argument that are presented in the text and identify any evidence given in support.
2. For each line of argument try to evaluate whether or not you think this is strong or weak.
3. Think of any questions you may wish to raise in response to the arguments.

This Activity will help you to start thinking critically about what you read and help you to evaluate the effectiveness of different arguments and from this develop your own observations, opinions and points of view that will help with any conclusions that you make in your answers to the AO2 questions that arise.

been linked to scriptural evidence such as that found in Deuteronomy 13:4 which states: 'Follow none but the Lord your God, and revere none but Him; observe His commandments alone, and heed only His orders; worship none but Him, and hold fast (or cling) to Him.'

Moreover, Tikkun, the esoteric, actual spiritual force of repair, also suggests that communion with God is possible through prayer and the fulfilment of religious precepts, thus bringing about the completion of all God's creation.

Study tip

Make sure that you have a clear understanding of the relationship between Kabbalah and the beliefs and practices of traditional Judaism.

Furthermore, through visual and magical means, some individuals have even claimed to have had a 'mystical union' with God. Evidence for this can be found in a school of early Jewish mysticism known as Merkavah mysticism. The aim of this contemplative system was to be a 'merkavah rider' and free oneself from the bonds of physical existence in order to ascend to the heavenly realms. Followers of this tradition were not content to be commentators on the biblical text; they sought to experience it for themselves. Tradition has it that it was possible for some particularly pious individuals to ascend into the divine realm and return to earth to convey the secrets that they had discovered.

There are others who might take a different view from this and claim that traditional Judaism sees its focus as being on Torah and Talmudic studies, which are very different from Kabbalah, and which do not involve any such experience with God. This is because God is considered to be transcendent, 'other', Holy and 'set apart' from humanity and the realms of experience. Taking up this point, Afterman argues that: 'In contrast, the Talmud and Mishnah created a religion that did not allow or demand the human to spiritually love God and practically denied the possibility to actually "cleave" to Him. The rabbis rather emphasised the communal and physical aspects of the religious life.'

Further to this point, there is the argument that Judaism is already grounded in an experience of God, for example through **kavod** in the Biblical narrative and shekinah in rabbinic literature. These two particular concepts may be mystical in nature; however, it could be argued that such experience is not specifically one of union with God, but more a sense of the 'other'.

As far as the Zohar is concerned, the doubts that exist regarding its authorship have meant that it has not been accepted in mainstream Judaism in spite of the fact that extracts from it are to be found in some contemporary Jewish prayer books. Criticism of it lies in the fact that many rabbis perceived it to be the source of superstitious beliefs, and a text that: 'produced a host of mystical dreamers, whose over-excited imaginations peopled the world with spirits, demons, and all kinds of good and bad influences'. (The Jewish Encyclopedia)

In conclusion, it is also important to consider the fact that many scholars regard the ideal of contemplative or mystical communion with God as a medieval innovation, and therefore a relatively late development within Judaism. Also, it has been argued that the practices of Kabbalah are too far removed from traditional Judaism in the eyes of many in the Jewish tradition today, and that even the claims for 'mystical union' with God represent a distortion of the original teachings of Kabbalah.

Key quote

In ancient forms of Jewish mysticism … mysticism is about empowerment and knowledge – but no mystic or angel integrates himself into God Himself!
(Afterman)

T4 Religious practices that shape religious identity

Kavod is used to express the energy that is encountered in moments of awe such as at the revelation on Mount Sinai

Key questions

To what extent does Kabbalah maintain that it is possible to achieve personal mystical unity with God?

What evidence does Kabbalah present to suggest it is possible to experience the divine nature and presence of God?

Is Kabbalah truly representative of traditional Jewish thought?

Key term

Kavod: literally means 'heavy' or 'weighty', but often denotes honour or glory. It attempts to describe the experience of standing in the presence of God

AO2 Activity

List some conclusions that could be drawn from the AO2 reasoning from the above text; try to aim for at least three different possible conclusions. Consider each of the conclusions and collect brief evidence to support each conclusion from the AO1 and AO2 material for this topic. Select the conclusion that you think is most convincing and explain why it is so. Try to contrast this with the weakest conclusion in the list, justifying your argument with clear reasoning and evidence.

WJEC / Eduqas Religious Studies for A Level Year 2 and A2 Judaism

Specification content
The value of aids to worship in Kabbalah.

The value of aids to worship in Kabbalah

Moshe Idel claims that in all known periods of the development of Kabbalah its followers were in possession of, and practised, a wide variety of mystical techniques which acted as aids to worship. This, he claimed, included the deep involvement of each practitioner, who invested considerable effort in order to attain their religious goal. Some might claim therefore that this suggests that aids to worship have an important part to play in Kabbalah, and that they act as the means by which a person can come to experience the divine nature and presence of God. Furthermore, the fact that the path to God within this particular mystic tradition is esoteric in nature might lead one to expect that symbolism and imagery of some kind needs to be present in order to act as a focus for worship, especially in ways which appeal to the imagination.

For example, to the Kabbalist, God is not a concept but a specific reality. However, such is God's nature that Kabbalists acknowledge that God is beyond the grasp of the human mind. Within the mystic tradition God is described as En Sof, the infinite, or as Herschel claims, 'the most Hidden of all Hidden'. A problem thus presents itself in that if God is hidden from mankind, how can En Sof ever be revealed to humans? Kabbalah presents a solution via an aid to understanding which has come to be known as the Tree of Life. Its value as an aid to worship in Kabbalah is significant as it presents, in diagrammatical format, ten Sefirot which are considered to be the ten attributes through which God is manifested. The Tree of Life describes the different stages along a path to awareness of God: 'The roots connect the Tree to the all-encompassing Reality Beyond Being, and the Tree portrays the flow of Life that finally manifests itself as everyday world reality.' (Falcon and Blatner)

The practice of meditation could also be considered by some to be of value as an aid to worship in Kabbalah, as great emphasis is placed upon it as the foremost method of achieving a true understanding of hidden truths. Meditation is considered to be the means by which a person can take control of their mind, and achieve a state of consciousness in which they can achieve greater spiritual insight. Abulafia, a medieval exponent of meditation within Kabbalah, stressed its importance as the means by which to free the soul by removing the obstacles that constrict it. He taught that a person's awareness of hidden things is hindered by the thoughts, feelings and sensory perceptions that fill up the mind on a daily basis. Kabbalists also make use of the Hebrew alphabet in conjunction with the names of God for the purpose of meditative training as a further means of emptying the mind so as to concentrate on divine matters. As Cohn-Sherbok notes: 'By engaging in the combination of letters and names, the mystic was able to empty his mind so as to concentrate on divine matters. Through such experiences the kabbalists believed they could attempt to conduct the soul to a state of the highest rapture in which divine reality was disclosed.' In addition, the Hebrew letters continue to act as an important aid to worship, with meditation upon them still a common practice amongst followers of Kabbalah who claim that such contemplation can lead to deeper levels of spiritual experience than is usually encountered through traditional forms of Jewish worship.

Key quote

One must therefore familiarise oneself with the ways of the Torah and know the purpose of the Holy Names. He should be expert in them, and when he needs to request something from God, he should concentrate on the Name designated to handle that question. If he does so, then not only will his request be granted, but he will be loved in the heavens and beloved in the world; he will inherit both this world and the next. **(Rabbi Gikatila)**

AO2 Activity

As you read through this section try to do the following:

1. Pick out the different lines of argument that are presented in the text and identify any evidence given in support.
2. For each line of argument try to evaluate whether or not you think this is strong or weak.
3. Think of any questions you may wish to raise in response to the arguments.

This Activity will help you to start thinking critically about what you read and help you to evaluate the effectiveness of different arguments and from this develop your own observations, opinions and points of view that will help with any conclusions that you make in your answers to the AO2 questions that arise.

Meditation is a means of achieving a true understanding of hidden truths.

Study tip

Your ability to reflect accurately the views of different groups within Judaism as part of your analysis and evaluation would distinguish a high-level answer from one that is vague or general.

It is interesting to note that there are certain aids to worship that are common to both the mystical tradition and to those who follow a more traditional Jewish path. Such an example is the use of tefillin, which are worn as a direct commandment from God which can be found in the first paragraph of the Shema: 'Tie them as symbols on your hands and bind them on your foreheads' (Deuteronomy 6:8). Joseph Caro taught that the box worn on the head acts as a reminder to serve God with the mind; whilst the one which is wound around the weaker arm pointing to the heart serves as a reminder to serve God with the heart. However, some might suggest that within Kabbalah, the tefillin have a greater significance as aids to worship as they act to heal the rift between mind and action. Freeman highlights this concept when he explains that by putting on tefillin, an individual does their part by connecting the mind and heart with the leather straps and black boxes with scrolls inside. The effect, he claims reverberates throughout the cosmos: 'Heaven connects to earth, spiritual to physical, Creator to creation. Everything starts getting into harmony with its essence and inner purpose.' (Freeman)

A similar comparison might also be made concerning the significance of the mitzvot. Within Kabbalah the mitzvot act as a focus for meditation as they represent the contact point between a person and God. In rabbinic Judaism the mitzvot proper are preceded by a benediction: 'who has made us holy through His mitzvot and commanded us to ...'. However, within the mystic tradition is a further short prayer of meditation which precedes the usual benediction. For example: 'For the sake of the unification of the Holy One, blessed be He and His Shekinah, in awe and devotion I am prepared and ready to perform mitzvah (named here) to the full command of my Creator.' It could therefore be claimed that this particular aid to worship is of value as it provides the means by which the worshipper can achieve an understanding of the mystical meaning of the mitzvah which is about to be performed.

However, there are others who might take a different view from this, and claim that not all aids to worship that are to be found in Kabbalah are of value. The use of magic is one such example, with the concept of the golem in particular used as evidence for this viewpoint. As Dan explains: 'the phenomenon of the golem contributed meaningfully to the portrayal of the Kabbalah as an esoteric, mysterious, and powerful compendium of ancient magic. ... The life force of the golem is the Hebrew alphabet, the secret name of God inserted under his tongue, or the word "truth", one of God's names engraved on his forehead ... The legend of the golem conformed to, and strengthened the image of the Kabbalah as doctrine that could bring great benefits, but one that also includes some sinister, dangerous elements.' However, in its defence, this aspect of Kabbalah is not something that is practised by the average Kabbalist. Indeed there are stories within the mystic tradition itself that contain warnings against the pursuit of such action.

Ultimately it could be said that one's opinion regarding the value of aids to worship in Kabbalah is wholly dependent upon whether or not one considers Kabbalah to be a credible tradition within Judaism. And there are even differences of opinion on this matter within the wider Jewish community with some dismissing it as nonsense, whilst others, as in the Hasidic community, for example, accepting mysticism as an important part of its tradition.

T4 Religious practices that shape religious identity

Key questions

What evidence is there to suggest that aids to worship are of value in Kabbalah?

To what extent is there common ground between the aids to worship which are found in Kabbalah compared with those found in mainstream Judaism?

Is Kabbalah truly representative of traditional Jewish thought?

Key quote

Here is the strong foundation which I deliver to you that you should know it and engrave it upon your heart: the Holy Name, the whole of the Torah, the sacred Scriptures and all the prophetic books; these are all full of divine names and tremendous things. Join one to the other. Depict them to yourself. Test them, try them, combine them ... First begin by combining the letters of the name YHVH. Gaze at all its combinations. Elevate it. Turn it over like a wheel ... Do not set it aside except when you observe that it is becoming too much for you because of the confused movements in your imagination. (Abulafia)

AO2 Activity

List some conclusions that could be drawn from the AO2 reasoning from the above text; try to aim for at least three different possible conclusions. Consider each of the conclusions and collect brief evidence to support each conclusion from the AO1 and AO2 material for this topic. Select the conclusion that you think is most convincing and explain why it is so. Try to contrast this with the weakest conclusion in the list, justifying your argument with clear reasoning and evidence.

WJEC / Eduqas Religious Studies for A Level Year 2 and A2 Judaism

Key skills

Analysis involves:

Identifying issues raised by the materials in the AO1, together with those identified in the AO2 section, and presents sustained and clear views, either of scholars or from a personal perspective ready for evaluation.

This means:

- That your answers are able to identify key areas of debate in relation to a particular issue
- That you can identify, and comment upon, the different lines of argument presented by others
- That your response comments on the overall effectiveness of each of these areas or arguments.

Evaluation involves:

Considering the various implications of the issues raised based upon the evidence gleaned from analysis and provides an extensive detailed argument with a clear conclusion.

This means:

- That your answer weighs up the consequences of accepting or rejecting the various and different lines of argument analysed
- That your answer arrives at a conclusion through a clear process of reasoning.

AO2 Developing skills

It is now important to consider the information that has been covered in this section; however, the information in its raw form is too extensive and so has to be processed in order to meet the requirements of the examination. This can be achieved by practising more advanced skills associated with AO2. For assessment objective 2 (AO2), which involves 'critical analysis' and 'evaluation' skills, we are going to focus on different ways in which the skills can be demonstrated effectively, and also refer to how the performance of these skills is measured (see generic band descriptors for A2 [WJEC] AO2 or A Level [Eduqas] AO2).

▶ **Your new task is this:** you will have to write a response under timed conditions to a question requiring **an evaluation of the possibility of a personal mystical union with God in Judaism**. This exercise can either be done as a group or independently.

1. Begin with a list of indicative arguments or lines of reasoning, as you may have done in the previous textbook in the series. It does not need to be in any particular order at first, although as you practise this you will see more order in your lists, in particular by way of links and connections between arguments.

2. Develop the list by using one or two relevant quotations. Now add some references to scholars and/or religious writings.

3. Then write out your plan, under timed conditions, remembering the principles of explaining with evidence and/or examples. Then ask someone else to read your answer and see if they can then help you improve it in any way.

4. Collaborative marking helps a learner appreciate alternative perspectives and possibly things that may have been missed. It also helps highlight the strengths of another that one can learn from. With this in mind, it is good to swap and compare answers in order to improve your own.

When you have completed the task, refer to the band descriptors for A2 (WJEC) or A Level (Eduqas) and in particular have a look at the demands described in the higher band descriptors towards which you should be aspiring. Ask yourself:

- Is my answer a confident critical analysis and perceptive evaluation of the issue?
- Is my answer a response that successfully identifies and thoroughly addresses the issues raised by the question set?
- Does my work show an excellent standard of coherence, clarity and organisation?
- Will my work, when developed, contain thorough, sustained and clear views that are supported by extensive, detailed reasoning and/or evidence?
- Are the views of scholars/schools of thought used extensively, appropriately and in context?
- Does my answer convey a confident and perceptive analysis of the nature of any possible connections with other elements of my course?
- When used, is specialist language and vocabulary both thorough and accurate?

F: Ethical debate within Judaism about embryo research

Background information

Key quote

How does Jewish law go to work in relating to very modern issues, many of which are obviously the result of spectacular advances in medicine that are of very recent times? … How can we find principles enshrined in those early sources that have relevance and application in the highly complex questions that arise from these dramatic advances in medicine? **(Jakobovits)**

The advances in medical science which have occurred over the past fifty years have brought about developments which would once have been thought impossible. For example, the expertise to carry out organ transplants has prolonged the life of people who would otherwise have died. However, such developments have not been made without serious consideration for the ethical issues that have arisen as a result of new technology and practices. This has led to the establishment of **bioethics** which is concerned with the study of ethical issues that arise as a result of new advancements brought about in biology and medicine. Moreover, as Ellenson notes, when seeking solutions which are considered to be morally and ethically correct: '… many turn to religious tradition for direction and guidance … (asking) the ethical authorities of their tradition to put forth principles that will guide judgements and to articulate reasons that will provide warrants for legitimate action'.

As far as Jewish medical ethics has been concerned, it has been predominantly characterised across all denominations by use of the Halakhic tradition. This method of seeking a suitable ethical standpoint is one in which precedents from rabbinic literature are sought in order that principles for new situations can be prescribed. As Newman explains, this process involves three steps: '(1) identifying precedents from classical Jewish literature, (2) adducing principles from these texts, and (3) applying these principles to new sets of facts.'

However, this has not prevented genuine differences of opinion from emerging. As Ellenson points out: 'Adherence to a common methodology does not preclude pluralism within the system. Authorities within any system of law can read precedents either stringently or leniently. They can assert that one set of precedents or values contained in the canon of a tradition is relevant to the matter at hand, while another group may assert that such precedents either have no bearing or have been completely misread. Affirmation of a common methodology in no way ensures a single … outcome.'

Study tip

Although it isn't necessary to have a detailed scientific or technical knowledge of the scientific procedures that are covered in this part of the specification, it is important that you understand the basic principles behind each one.

T4 Religious practices that shape religious identity

This section covers AO1 content and skills

Key term

Bioethics: the study of ethical issues that have arisen as a result of new advances in medical and biological research

Key quote

For over a millennium, rabbis have employed responsa to apply the ideas derived from the sacred texts of Judaism to the problems of a contemporary situation. Viewed in this way, Jewish medical ethics evidence the same methodological concerns and qualities that one would discover in any legal process. **(Ellenson)**

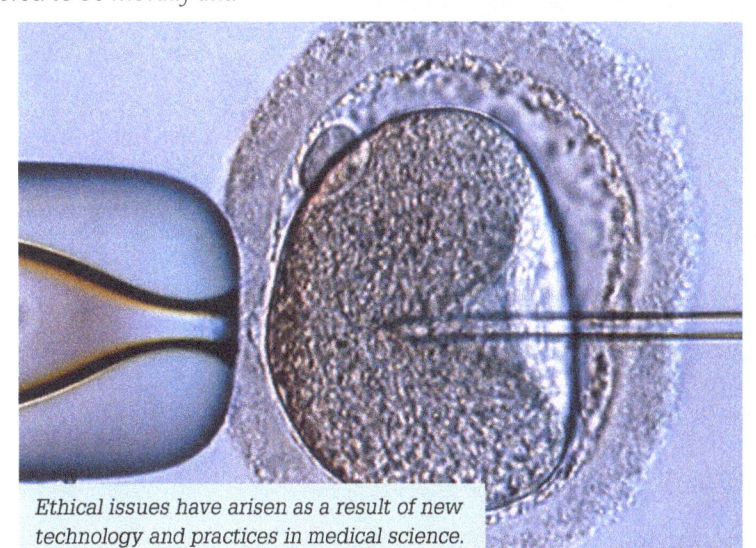

Ethical issues have arisen as a result of new technology and practices in medical science.

Halakhic tradition guides Jews when making ethical decisions.

169

WJEC / Eduqas Religious Studies for A Level Year 2 and A2 Judaism

Specification content

Jewish contributions to the debate about embryo research with particular reference to: the relationship between stem-cell research and pikuach nefesh (the sanctity of life).

quickfire

4.11 What are stem cells?

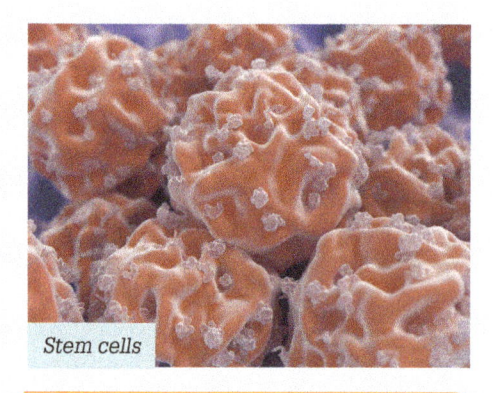

Stem cells

Key term

Pikuach nefesh: the sanctity of life

Jewish contributions to the debate about embryo research with particular reference to: the relationship between stem-cell research and pikuach nefesh (the sanctity of life)

During the latter part of the twentieth century scientific research into cell biology led to the discovery of stem cells. Stem cells are special types of cells that have the potential to grow into any type of cell found in the body. Such is their nature that they can be used to replace cells that are damaged or diseased, leading researchers to believe that they have the potential to cure many diseases such as heart disease and Parkinson's disease. Stem cell technology could also be used to repair damaged immune systems and rebuild bones and cartilage amongst other things.

Stem cells are to be found in embryos, although Pauline Yearwood explains that they can come from many other sources too, such as from umbilical cords, bone marrow, tissues and fat from adult humans. However, it is the stem cells from embryos that medical research has shown to have the greatest potential of all. It is possible to remove stem cells from human embryos that are a few days old, for example from unused embryos that have been left over from fertility treatment and which would be destroyed anyway. Yet herein lies the crux of an ethical dilemma: 'The stem cells most likely to be of scientific value come from discarded embryos. Is it ethical to use them?' (Yearwood)

In order to address this dilemma, many Jewish ethicists have referred to one of the core principles of the Jewish religion: **pikuach nefesh**. Pikuach nefesh is the principle that the saving, protecting, and preservation of life is of utmost importance, and it has its basis in the Torah: '... Do not do anything that endangers your neighbour's life' (Leviticus 19:16). Judaism teaches that all life comes from God; therefore, it is considered to be the gift of God, and to do anything which might take away or shorten that life is looked upon as murder.

Indeed, pikuach nefesh is such a core precept within Judaism that it overrides any other religious teaching. For example, if the life of a person is in danger, any mitzvot may be ignored in order to save them. The Talmud emphasises this principle by reference to Leviticus 18:5: 'you shall therefore keep my statutes ... which if a man does, he shall live by them'. The rabbis added to this: 'That he shall live by them, and not that he shall die by them' (Babylonian Talmud).

However, the decision regarding the use of stem cells from embryos is not as clear-cut as it may seem regardless of the application of the principle of pikuach nefesh. Daniel Eisenberg, an expert in traditional Jewish approaches to medical ethics, looks to the Halakhic perspective on such research and asks: 'what could the possible objections to such research be?' His response is discussed in an article entitled 'Stem Cell Research in Jewish Law'.

Firstly, he considers the practice of in vitro fertilisation (IVF) which has been accepted by most rabbinic authorities on the grounds that as long as the husband's sperm is used then it is permissible as a means of fulfilling the mitzvah of procreation. However, this medical process led to new questions relating to the status of the spare embryos that are not implanted; one of which is whether it is right to destroy pre-embryos. To answer this question Eisenberg looks to the approach to abortion in Jewish law and says that there is reason to argue that prior to forty days gestation the foetus lacks what he calls 'humanity,' and is not considered to be an actual person, and therefore it is possible to extrapolate that destruction of such a foetus is not forbidden by Jewish law.

This leads to the next question: may a very early embryo be sacrificed for stem cells? There is broad (although not unanimous) Halakhic agreement that stem-cell research is permitted on spare embryos: if the pre-embryo is to be destroyed then it might as well be used for research purposes and life-saving work. Indeed, Rabbi Moshe David

Tendler, in testimony for the National Bioethics Advisory Commission, argued strongly in favour of the use of pre-embryos for stem-cell research.

Rabbi Elliot Dorff concurs with this opinion by arguing that embryos which stay outside the womb have no chance to become children, and therefore it is a mitzvah to use these embryos for research: 'It's not only permitted, there is a Jewish mandate to do so.' (Dorff)

A further issue that Eisenberg identifies is whether it is permissible to fertilise ova specifically to create an embryo for stem cells or not. He notes that this is a complex issue and concludes that most rabbinic authorities would not favour such action: 'The mere existence of already created pre-embryos creates a need to decide the halakhic ramifications of their destruction. We therefore may decide that such research is permitted **bedieved** (**ex post facto**), once the pre-embryos exist. However, since there are **poskim** who forbid abortion even within the first forty days, it is much harder to argue **lichatchila** (**a priori**) that creation of pre-embryos with the intention of destroying them is permitted.' (Eisenberg)

Dorff, however, claims that creating an embryo specifically to be a source of stem cells is permissible, but less morally justifiable. Rabbi Aaron Mackler, whilst supporting stem-cell research, is wary of using anything other than embryos taken from fertility clinics which have already been created for the purpose of in vitro fertilisation.

Eisenberg concludes by emphasising that the principle of life is a strongly held Torah ideal and asks 'should we ban stem-cell research on embryonic cells as a dangerous encroachment on the sanctity of life?' He refers once more to Tendler who stated: 'Jewish law consists of biblical and rabbinic legislation. A good deal of rabbinic law consists of erecting fences to protect biblical law ... But a fence that prevents the cure of fatal diseases must not be erected, for then the loss is greater than the benefit. In the Judeo-biblical legislative tradition, a fence that causes pain and suffering is dismantled. Even biblical law is superseded by the duty to save lives, except for the three cardinal sins of adultery, idolatry and murder ... Life-saving abortion is a categorical imperative in Jewish biblical law. Mastery of nature for the benefit of those suffering from vital organ failure is an obligation. Human embryonic stem-cell research holds that promise ...'

Key terms

a priori: prior to experience; based on knowledge that proceeds from theoretical deduction

Bedieved: done after the fact

Blastocyst: a very early stage of a mammalian embryo which is formed before implantation into the uterus

ex post facto: with retrospective action

Lichatchila: done in the best way possible

Poskim: a Jewish legal scholar whose job it is to decide Halakhah in cases where previous authorities are inconclusive or where no precedent exists

Key quote

... there are two prerequisites for the moral status of the embryo as a human being: implantation and forty days of gestational development. The proposition that humanhood begins at zygote formation, even in vitro, is without basis in biblical moral theology. (Tendler)

Jewish contributions to the debate about embryo research with particular reference to: somatic cell nuclear transfer (SCNT)

Somatic cell nuclear transfer (SCNT) is the technique by which the nucleus of a body cell (a soma) is transferred to an egg that has had its own nucleus removed. Once inside the egg, various treatments are given to the ovum to encourage cell division, and the fertilised egg is allowed to develop to a very early point known as the **blastocyst** stage. At this stage, a culture of embryonic stem cells (ESCs) can be created from the inner mass of the blastocyst. The blastocyst has almost 100% identical DNA to the original organism.

SCNT as a technology has been used in the field of reproductive cloning, the most famous example being that of Dolly the sheep who was successfully cloned in 1996. However, the process is also used for the production of human embryos which are used for the collection of stem cells. The purpose of collecting stem cells in this way is so that they can be used in research, and also for regenerative medicine. This application is known as therapeutic cloning.

Specification content

Jewish contributions to the debate about embryo research with particular reference to: somatic cell nuclear transfer (SCNT).

Dolly the sheep

Key quote

Our bodies belong to God ... God ... can and does impose conditions on our use of our bodies. Among those is the requirement that we seek to preserve human life and health (pikuach nefesh). As a corollary to this, we have a duty to seek to develop new cures for human diseases. (Dorff)

Key quotes

The Jewish tradition accepts both natural and artificial means to overcome illness. Physicians are the agents and partners of God in the ongoing act of healing. Thus the mere fact that human beings created a specific therapy rather than finding it in nature does not impugn its legitimacy. On the contrary, we have a duty to God to develop and use any therapies that can aid us in taking care of our bodies, which ultimately belong to God. **(Dorff)**

We stand on the cusp of a new era today because an explosion of genetic knowledge in recent years has provided us the ability to pursue certain health and wellness advantages even before pregnancy has begun. **(Popovsky)**

quickfire

4.12 Which Jewish scholar claimed that the practice of healing is a mitzvah?

Specification content

Jewish contributions to the debate about embryo research with particular reference to: pre-implantation embryo research.

quickfire

4.13 What does the acronym PGS stand for?

quickfire

4.14 Which inherited condition is especially prevalent within some Jewish communities?

Stem-cell research, using stem cells that have been collected by SCNT, has the potential to find new and effective treatments for Parkinson's disease (a progressive neurological condition), as well as for many other conditions. Reform Jews believe that the moral imperative to pursue stem-cell research is clear: 'Our tradition requires that we use all available knowledge to heal the ill, and "when one delays in doing so, it is as if he has shed blood".' (Shulchan Arukh)

Dorff links stem-cell research to the concept of responsible dominion over nature. He notes that: 'we are God's "partners in the ongoing act of creation" when we improve the human lot in life'. Tendler adds further emphasis to this concept when he claims that God has given humans a 'positive commandment' to 'master the world'. Such a commandment has been interpreted as including the obligation to find methods by which to bring about healing. Many Jews believe that God has given humankind the knowledge by which we can develop new treatments for diseases and illnesses that cause suffering. Such action also allows us to act on the principle of Tikkun Olam.

Most Jewish ethicists approve of therapeutic cloning; for instance, the Union for Reform Jews in the USA made the following resolution to support: 'research using somatic gene therapy; ... research using somatic cell nuclear transfer (SCNT) technology for therapeutic cloning; ... support efforts by the scientific community to develop regulations and monitor those using SCNT technologies.'

The reasoning behind this resolution is based, once again, on the concept of pikuach nefesh. If preserving life and promoting health are amongst the most important values then it follows that Jews should take advantage of medical advances. An article from ReformJudaism.org makes reference to one of the teachings of Nachmanides, a thirteenth-century Jewish scholar, who claimed that the practice of healing is not merely a profession but a mitzvah, and thus a righteous obligation. A responsum from the CCAR (Central Conference of American Rabbis) applies Nachmanides' principle to human stem-cell research: 'If we define the administration of life-saving medical therapy as pikuach nefesh, we should not forget that physicians could not save lives were it not for the extensive scientific research upon which our contemporary practice of medicine is based. Since research into human stem-cells partakes of the mitzvah of healing, surely our society ought to support it.'

Jewish contributions to the debate about embryo research with particular reference to: pre-implantation embryo research

Pre-implantation embryo research has resulted in a technology called pre-implantation genetic screening (PGS). PGS is used in cases where a person or a family has a serious genetic condition that is likely to be passed on from one generation to the next. PGS allows for the screening of embryos during IVF so that only healthy embryos are placed back in the womb.

One such inherited condition is Tay-Sachs disease, which although rare, is especially prevalent in Jewish communities of Ashkenazi descent. Tay-Sachs causes progressive damage to the nervous system and is usually fatal. Many Jews already support pre-implantation screening of embryos for Tay-Sachs on the basis that as long as this technology is used to prevent disease and suffering then it is justified and seen as following the principle of pikuach nefesh.

Dr Sherman Silber believes that PGS represents no moral or ethical risk because at that point in time the soul has not yet entered the embryo. Embryo research to promote life is therefore acceptable and also must be regarded as an obligation: '... the early embryo does not yet have a soul and is not yet a person. Nonetheless it cannot be just discarded for no reason, because it is a step toward the commandment "be fruitful and multiply". But it would not be considered murder to utilise an early embryo for research that might eventually save lives.' (Silber)

Indeed, the concept of inherited disorders and heredity in general is to be found in a number of Judaism's classical sources. Wright points out that there is a ruling in the Talmud that a man may not marry a woman whose family members suffer from epilepsy or leprosy, on the grounds that these diseases may pass to any children. She also cites Genesis 31:10 in which Jacob is aware of the transmission of characteristics from animal parents to their offspring.

However, the use of genetic technology is not without its issues and most Jews are opposed to the selection of embryos in order to produce a child of a particular gender, for example; or one who would have certain traits such as hair colour, height or other qualities. On one level, this is understandable in view of the experiences of the Jews during the Holocaust when the Nazis used their knowledge of genetics to try to create what they considered to be a superior race.

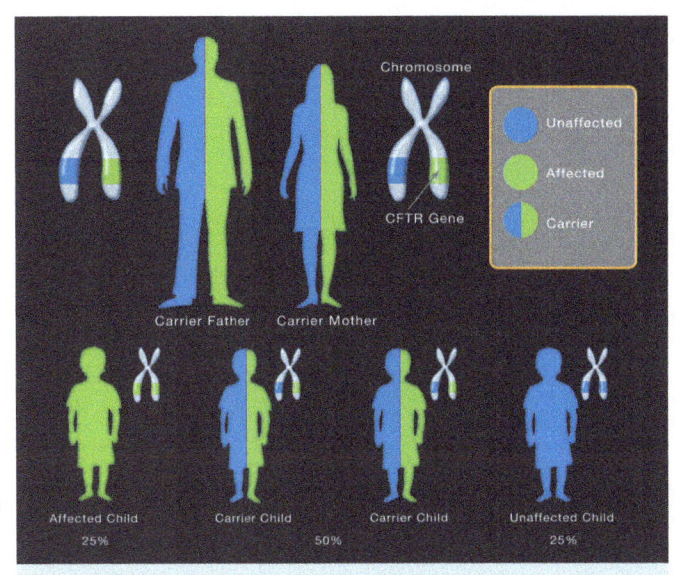

In his book on *Biomedical Ethics and Jewish Law* (published in 2001), Dr Fred Rosner draws together some of the issues that are pertinent to genetic therapy and genetic engineering for both now and in the future. Regarding gene surgery or genetic manipulation, he refers to Rabbi Azriel Rosenfeld who argues that genes are sub-microscopic particles and as no process invisible to the naked eye is forbidden in Jewish law, in theory such treatment cannot be considered to be ritually unclean. In addition, a priest only declares ritually unclean that which his eyes can see.

Another argument which lends itself to permitting gene surgery or manipulation, claims Rosner, is the fact that a sperm or ovum or even the fertilised zygote is not a person. This is because under Jewish law such status is only conferred upon a foetus implanted in the mother's womb. He also argues that any surgery performed on a live human being must certainly be permitted on a sperm or ovum or fertilised zygote. For example, if a surgical cure for haemophilia, Tay-Sachs disease or Huntingdon's disease were possible, it must surely be permissible to cure or prevent these diseases by gene surgery.

However, Rosner also offers an opposing argument from Rabbi Moshe Hershler who questions the ethics of experimenting with gene therapy to try and save the life of a child with Tay-Sachs disease if the unsuccessful outcome of the experimentation would lead to the shortening of the child's life. He also notes that Hershler: 'is of the opinion that gene therapy and genetic engineering may be prohibited because "he who changes the (Divine) arrangement of creation is lacking in faith (in the Creator)", and he (Hershler) cites as support for his view the prohibition against mating diverse kinds of animals, sowing together diverse kinds of seeds, and wearing garments made of wool and linen.' (Leviticus 19:19)

Hershler's line of reasoning, however, is rejected by Rabbis Auerbach and Neuwirth who contend that genetic engineering is not comparable to the grafting of diverse types of animals or seed: 'The main purposes of gene therapy are to cure disease, restore health, and prolong life, all goals within the physicians' Divine licence to heal. Gene grafting is no different than an "organ graft" such as a kidney or corneal implant, which nearly all rabbis consider permissible.' (Rosner)

Serious genetic conditions can be passed on from one generation to the next.

AO1 Activity

Write a short paragraph for each of the following concepts which illustrates the part each plays in the ethical debate within Judaism about embryo research: (a) Halakhah (b) Pikuach nefesh (c) Soul (d) Tikkun Olam.

Key quotes

Using genetic technology for therapeutic purposes is acceptable, but many related issues have yet to be addressed. **(Rosner)**

One must weigh the Jewish imperative to pursue good health against a number of harms that may follow from the expanded use of PGS technology, including increased medical risk to the mother, the destruction of embryos and possible emotional harm to the child born from this procedure. **(Popovsky)**

You shall not let your cattle mate with a different kind; you shall not sow your field with two kinds of seed; you shall not put on cloth from a mixture of two kinds of material. **(Leviticus 19:19)**

… a man should not marry a woman from a family of epileptics or from a family of lepers, as these diseases might be hereditary. **(Babylonian Talmud)**

Once, at the mating time of the flocks, I had a dream in which I saw that the he-goats mating with the flock were streaked, speckled and mottled. **(Genesis 31:10)**

A comparison of the views proposed by Rabbi J. David Bleich and Rabbi Moshe David Tendler

Rabbi J. David Bleich

Rabbi J. David Bleich is Professor of Jewish Law and Ethics at Yeshiva University, New York. Bleich is generally opposed to the destruction of pre-embryos and their use in stem-cell research due to his belief that such a course of action is tantamount to killing the embryo. There exists a debate amongst Jewish scholars as to whether the soul enters the embryo at the moment of fertilisation or forty days later.

Bleich is also opposed to the use of stem cells which have been sourced from aborted foetuses explaining that if government funding were made available for such a practice then it might put pressure on some women who were wavering over whether or not to have an abortion to go ahead with the procedure. He said: 'When you have government funding, and you have people talking to the mother about the fact that her baby could help humanity, that does become a motivating force (in causing her to have an abortion).' He therefore recommended against foetal tissue research for this reason.

However, Bleich does not rule out the process entirely as he considers the use of embryos created via **parthenogenesis** to be acceptable. Using this process, scientists are able to expose unfertilised eggs to chemicals that induce division so that they multiply into fledgling embryos. Such embryos are not able to survive, even if returned to the womb and because they are not viable from the moment of inception, their destruction does not constitute the destruction of a foetus or of a potential human.

For the same reason Bleich is also not opposed to the use of embryos, fertilised in vitro, that are non-viable due to abnormalities which have become apparent. Such embryos are routinely discarded as it is highly unlikely that they would survive if transferred to a woman's uterus. Scientists have shown that extracted cells from non-viable embryos have developed, and thus stem cells can be grown in a laboratory.

Rabbi Moshe David Tendler

Rabbi Moshe David Tendler is an American rabbi and noted expert in Jewish medical ethics. Tendler calls stem-cell research 'the hope of mankind', and argues strongly in favour of the use of pre-embryos for stem-cell research.

Tendler believes that the soul doesn't enter the embryo at conception, but only after forty days have passed, and for this reason he doesn't consider the destruction of an embryo as homicide: 'The Judeo-biblical tradition does not grant moral status to an embryo before forty days of gestation ... After forty days – the time of "quickening" recognised in common law – the implanted embryo is considered to have humanhood, and its destruction is considered an act of homicide. Thus, there are two prerequisites for the moral status of the embryo as a human being: implantation and forty days of gestational development. The proposition that humanhood begins at zygote formation, even in vitro, is without basis in biblical development.' (Tendler)

Specification content

A comparison of the views proposed by Rabbi J. David Bleich and Rabbi Moshe David Tendler.

There exists a debate amongst Jewish scholars as to when ensoulment occurs.

Key term

Parthenogenesis: the development of a germ cell without fertilisation

Key quote

The only hope we have of understanding what's going on in the whole field of oncology, of cancer work, now resides in the stem-cell research. **(Tendler)**

Furthermore, he makes a strong case for stem-cell research and therapy based upon the Jewish obligation to save life wherever possible: 'In stem-cell research and therapy, the moral obligation to save human life, the paramount ethical principle in biblical law, supersedes any concern for lowering the barrier to abortion by making the sin less heinous. Likewise, the expressed concern that this research facilitates human cloning is without merit. First, no reputable research facility is interested in cloning a human, which is not even a distant goal … Second, those on the leading edge of stem-cell research know that the greater contribution to human welfare will come from replacement of damaged cells and organs by fresh stem cell products, not from cloning. Financial reward and acclaim from the scientific community will come from such therapeutic successes, not from cloning.' (Tendler)

Furthermore, although Tendler accepts that an important part of Jewish law consists of what is known as 'building a fence around the law' in order to keep people as far away from sinning as possible, he sums up the issue of protective enactment again with the words: 'Jewish law consists of biblical and rabbinic legislation. A good deal of rabbinic law consists of erecting fences to protect biblical law … But a fence that prevents the cure of fatal diseases must not be erected, for then the loss is greater than the benefit. In the Judeo-biblical legislative tradition, a fence that causes pain and suffering is dismantled. Even biblical law is superseded by the duty to save lives … Mastery of nature for the benefit of those suffering from vital organ failure is an obligation. Human embryonic stem-cell research holds that promise …'

Key quote

… even if pre-embryos may be destroyed, should we enact preventative laws barring stem-cell research that requires the destruction of potential lives to avoid cheapening life by treating the process of creating humans as another scientific process, stripped of its miraculous underpinnings? **(Eisenberg)**

Study tip

There are a number of websites which offer more detailed information about the status of stem-cell research in the UK. For instance, the websites of the Human Fertilisation and Embryology Authority and the Medical Research Council provide a good source of information on some of the latest procedures and treatments.

The views and work of Professor Clare Blackburn

Clare Blackburn is Professor of Tissue Stem Cell Biology at the MRC (Medical Research Council) Centre for Regenerative Medicine at the University of Edinburgh. Blackburn and her team are especially interested in how stem cells in the developing and mature **thymus** are controlled. The thymus plays a key role in our immune system; however, it degenerates with age and becomes less effective; it can also be damaged by certain medical treatments. Stem-cell research has been fundamental in the search for a way in which to replace a lost or damaged thymus.

Professor Clare Blackburn

Specification content
The views and work of Professor Clare Blackburn.

Key quote
Regenerative medicine … seeks to repair or replace damaged or diseased human cells or tissue to restore normal function, which holds the promise of revolutionary patient care in the 21st century … Promoting stem-cell research and regenerative medicine is a priority for the MRC and the UK government. **(MRC)**

Key quote

By directly reprogramming cells we've managed to produce an artificial cell type that, when transplanted, can form a fully organised and functional organ. This is an important first step towards the goal of generating a clinically useful artificial thymus in the lab. **(Blackburn)**

Blackburn and her research group first identified and characterised the specific stem cell population from which the thymus develops. They next turned their focus to the mechanisms that build and maintain the thymus, and those responsible for age-related thymus degeneration. Blackburn explains that their overwhelming goal is to develop improved cell replacement for boosting thymus function.

Key term
Thymus: a gland which plays an important role in the development of the immune system which is located near the heart

Key quote

The thymus is one of the first organs to degenerate in normal healthy individuals. As we age, it becomes smaller and less effective, making us more susceptible to infection and less able to benefit from vaccination. By the age of 70, the thymus is around a tenth of the size of an adolescent's. (MRC)

quickfire

4.15 How might Blackburn's research findings ultimately be of benefit to elderly people?

In 2014 the MRC website announced that Blackburn and her team had succeeded in growing, for the first time, a fully functioning organ from lab-created cells; an accomplishment which: 'heralds the possibility of not only helping those with thymus disorders, but also boosting immunity against infections in the elderly'. (MRC)

After many years of studying how the thymus is formed in the embryo, Blackburn's team made a significant breakthrough when they were able to grow a fully functioning thymus from scratch in a mouse by transplanting cells that were originally created in a laboratory.

> 'To create the thymus gland, Clare and colleagues took cells called fibroblasts from a mouse embryo and exposed them to high levels of a protein called FOXN1, which is known to guide formation of the thymus inside the developing embryo. FOXN1 was able to "reprogram" the fibroblasts to become a completely different type of cell called thymus epithelial cells. The team mixed these so-called induced thymus epithelial cells ... with other thymus cells. Next they grafted them on to the kidneys of genetically identical mice ... Incredibly, this was all that was needed for the cells to develop into a well-formed organ with the same structure as a healthy thymus.' (MRC)

'It was very exciting', said Blackburn. 'We hadn't really expected it would work. But not only did we make a functioning thymus, but we were amazed to see that it was properly organised and had all of the right cell types inside – without us doing anything overt to make that happen except for kicking off the differentiation program of this key type of thymus cell.'

The MRC report continues by explaining that the research team showed that their reprogrammed cells were able to produce different types of T cells from immature blood cells in the lab. If this procedure could be made to work in people then it could be used to help patients in need of a T cell boost. The technology could be used, for example, in the treatment of leukaemia patients who have undergone a bone marrow transplant and who need a functioning thymus in order to rebuild the immune system once the transplant has been received. However, it is envisaged that elderly people will make up the largest group of those who would benefit most greatly from this research, as the technology could be used to boost the function of the thymus in order to provide greater immunity against infection.

Key quote

... elderly people aren't as good at responding to new strains of virus or completely new infections. So if we could boost the function of the thymus in old age, either by transplanting a new one or regenerating the old one, it could help elderly people to fight off new infections such as seasonal flu. **(Blackburn)**

The technique so far has only been tested on mice, and therefore the next step is to repeat the process using human cells. Blackburn's long-term aim is to use the procedure to provide replacement organs for people with weakened immune systems.

AO1 Activity

Review the contents of this final section of the specification, and create a mind map which displays the major ethical issues that need to be addressed in connection with embryo research.

AO1 Developing skills

It is now important to consider the information that has been covered in this section; however, the information in its raw form is too extensive and so has to be processed in order to meet the requirements of the examination. This can be achieved by practising more advanced skills associated with AO1. For assessment objective 1 (AO1), which involves demonstrating 'knowledge' and 'understanding' skills, we are going to focus on different ways in which the skills can be demonstrated effectively, and also refer to how the performance of these skills is measured (see generic band descriptors for A2 [WJEC] AO1 or A Level [Eduqas] AO1).

▶ **Your new task is this:** It is impossible to cover all essays in the time allowed by the course; however, it is a good exercise to develop detailed plans that can be utilised under timed conditions. As a last exercise:

1. Create some ideal plans by using what we have done so far in the Theme 4 Developing skills sections.

2. This time stop at the planning stage and exchange plans with a study partner.

3. Check each other's plans carefully. Talk through any omissions or extras that could be included, not forgetting to challenge any irrelevant materials.

4. Remember, collaborative learning is very important for revision. It not only helps to consolidate understanding of the work and appreciation of the skills involved, it is also motivational and a means of providing more confidence in one's learning. Although the examination is sat alone, revising as a pair or small group is invaluable.

When you have completed each plan, as a pair or small group refer to the band descriptors for A2 (WJEC) or A Level (Eduqas) and in particular have a look at the demands described in the higher band descriptors towards which you should be aspiring. Ask yourself:

- Does my work demonstrate thorough, accurate and relevant knowledge and understanding of religion and belief?

- Is my work coherent (consistent or make logical sense), clear and well organised?

- Will my work, when developed, be an extensive and relevant response which is specific to the focus of the task?

- Does my work have extensive depth and/or suitable breadth and have excellent use of evidence and examples?

- If appropriate to the task, does my response have thorough and accurate reference to sacred texts and sources of wisdom?

- Are there any insightful connections to be made with other elements of my course?

- Will my answer, when developed and extended to match what is expected in an examination answer, have an extensive range of views of scholars/schools of thought?

- When used, is specialist language and vocabulary both thorough and accurate?

Key skills

Knowledge involves:

Selection of a range of (thorough) accurate and relevant information that is directly related to the specific demands of the question.

This means:

- Selecting relevant material for the question set

- Be focused in explaining and examining the material selected.

Understanding involves:

Explanation that is extensive, demonstrating depth and/or breadth with excellent use of evidence and examples including (where appropriate) thorough and accurate supporting use of sacred texts, sources of wisdom and specialist language.

This means:

- Effective use of examples and supporting evidence to establish the quality of your understanding

- Ownership of your explanation that expresses personal knowledge and understanding and NOT just a chunk of text from a book that you have rehearsed and memorised.

WJEC / Eduqas Religious Studies for A Level Year 2 and A2 Judaism

This section covers AO2 content and skills

Specification content
The effectiveness of Jewish ethical teachings as a guide for living for Jews today.

Issues for analysis and evaluation

The effectiveness of Jewish ethical teachings as a guide for living for Jews today

For many Jews, the Torah remains the starting point when any new question or issue arises within Judaism. However, the pace of change regarding progress made in medical science over recent decades has been so brisk and astounding, that it is bound to raise questions regarding the effectiveness of Jewish ethical teachings in dealing with such developments. How does one stay true to the responsibilities of the covenant which was established at Sinai in a world which now bears very little resemblance to those times?

Some would argue that Jewish ethical teachings *are* effective as a guide for Jews in contemporary society as they remain true to the principles of the covenant by use of the Halakhic tradition. The practice of seeking a suitable ethical standpoint by this method involves the following process: firstly, precedents from classical Jewish literature and rabbinic tradition are identified; secondly, principles are adduced from these texts; thirdly, these principles are applied to new sets of facts. Such principles are considered to be morally and ethically correct as they represent a direct line of transmission between the revelation at Mount Sinai to the present day. As such, the Halakhic tradition allows Jews to apply precepts to current situations whilst retaining the veracity of covenant responsibility. As Ellenson notes: '... many turn to religious tradition for direction and guidance ... (asking) the ethical authorities of their tradition to put forth principles that will guide judgements and to articulate reasons that will provide warrants for legitimate action'.

Key quote

... (traditional and liberal Jews) share two fundamental perspectives: that Jewish ethics must draw substantively on traditional Jewish teaching, since this is what ultimately distinguishes it from other systems of ethical thought and practice, and that traditional Jewish teaching is not self-evidently relevant to modern circumstances but must be appropriated and interpreted if it is to provide authentic moral guidance to modern Jews. **(Dorff and Newman)**

An illustration of this particular assertion is the way in which Halakhic guidance has been used to bring about a ruling concerning pre-implantation embryo research. Wright identifies a number of classical Jewish sources that deal with the concept of heredity. For example, in Genesis, we read that Jacob is aware of the transmission of characteristics from animal parents to offspring; and the Talmud presents a ruling that a man may not marry a woman whose family members suffer from epilepsy or leprosy on the grounds that these diseases may be passed on to their children. Wright explains that the consideration of such teachings has brought about the acceptance of pre-implantation genetic screening amongst many Jewish groups, especially in the case of screening for Tay-Sachs disease which is prevalent within Ashkenazi Jewry. When the UK government gave permission for the regulated cloning of embryos, a statement from the Office of the Chief Rabbi stated that: 'the spirit of Jewish law welcomes any technological advances which have the potential of enhancing human life'.

AO2 Activity

As you read through this section try to do the following:

1. Pick out the different lines of argument that are presented in the text and identify any evidence given in support.
2. For each line of argument try to evaluate whether or not you think this is strong or weak.
3. Think of any questions you may wish to raise in response to the arguments.

This Activity will help you to start thinking critically about what you read and help you to evaluate the effectiveness of different arguments and from this develop your own observations, opinions and points of view that will help with any conclusions that you make in your answers to the AO2 questions that arise.

Furthermore, some would argue that by virtue of the fact that Jewish ethical teachings are based upon the principle of pikuach nefesh, they are justified in claiming that Jewish ethical teachings are effective as a guide for living for Jews today for the following reason: the obligation to save, protect and preserve life is so important that Jews have a duty to do what they can to heal the sick and to prevent disease. If stem-cell research can bring about remedies that are not currently available elsewhere, then many Jews support it. Moreover, Jews consider that they are acting in partnership with God in what Dorff calls 'the ongoing act of creation' when working to improve human life by use of stem-cell research. If God, as Jews believe, has given humankind the knowledge to develop new treatments for diseases and illnesses that cause suffering then it is only right and proper that such scholarship be used to bring about healing. Such action also finds its basis in the principle of Tikkun Olam where the goal of repairing the world is enacted through the search for, and application of, new medical technologies which can bring about cures for diseases as well as by introducing preventative measures.

However, it is at this point that a cautionary note needs to be introduced, as some take the view that certain Jewish ethical teachings are not wholeheartedly accepted amongst all Jews. This may lead some to conclude therefore that not all Jewish ethical teachings are effective for contemporary society. Solomon, for instance, notes that not everyone is convinced that the Halakhic process is sound and refers to Gordis who suggests that some rulings of the Orthodox tradition (particularly objections to a particular practice) do not arise from genuine Halakhic argument, but from an underlying disapproval. He gives the example of rulings on artificial insemination by a donor as coming from what he describes as: 'revulsion at the notion of a married woman being impregnated by another man's sperm'. Dorff is also aware of this issue, contending that the Orthodox position is dominated by rules and precedents: 'which they misapply or arbitrarily extrapolate because they do not allow sufficiently for the differences between the times in which the precedents were set and the radically different medical situation of our time'. (Solomon)

Study tip

An awareness and understanding of different ethical theories would be of help to you in this section; therefore, it would be a good idea to refer to your notes on religious ethics as a reminder.

There also exist notable differences of opinion between leading contemporary Jewish ethicists such as Bleich and Tendler. Bleich, for instance, is generally opposed to the destruction of pre-embryos and their use in stem-cell research due to his belief that such a course of action is tantamount to killing the embryo. Tendler, on the other hand, considers stem-cell research to be 'the hope of mankind' and argues strongly in favour of the use of pre-embryos for stem-cell research. He bases his viewpoint on the belief that the soul doesn't enter the embryo at conception, but only after forty days have passed, and for this reason he doesn't consider the destruction of an embryo as homicide. When faced with such disparity, some might be of the opinion that Jewish ethical teachings are not effective as a guide as there are too many examples of principles which are diverse in nature.

However, such is the nature of rabbinic tradition that this difference of opinion would not be considered unusual within the faith, and, as Wright indicates: 'The number and availability of new genetic techniques is likely to increase in the future ... as would be expected, given the diversity of Judaism in the modern era, a range of halakhic and extra-halakhic factors come into play in debates surrounding genetic science.'

Perhaps, in conclusion, it is only right to remind ourselves that the current advances in medical science have raised questions and issues that could never have been envisaged at the time when the Jewish law was formulated. Nevertheless, as Solomon notes, many thousands of rabbinic responsa have now been published as a result of the challenges faced by contemporary medical technology. Furthermore, Jewish ethical teaching is being applied in some hospitals in Jerusalem which are allowing Halakhic rulings to be put to the test. Solomon also observes that: 'academic institutions such as Ben Gurion University ... have chairs in Jewish Medical Ethics; rabbinic organisations such as the Rabbinical Council of America issue regular updates on medical Halakhah; and books and articles on the ethics and Halakhah of medicine are authored by experts from all Jewish denominations.' Such evidence must surely be indicative of the fact that Jewish ethical teachings *are* effective as a means by which to guide Jews as they make important medical decisions in contemporary society.

Key quote

(Dorff's) own preference ... is for a three-stage approach. First, the Jewish conceptual and legal sources must be studied in their historical contexts. On this basis, one can identify the relevant differences between our own situation and that in which the texts were formulated. Then and only then can one apply the sources to the contemporary issue, using not only purely legal reasoning but 'theological deliberations concerning our nature as human beings created by, and in the image of, God'. (Solomon)

T4 Religious practices that shape religious identity

Key questions

How far is it possible to retain the spirit of Jewish law when faced with technological advances in the world of medicine?

What evidence is there to suggest that Jewish ethical teachings are able to provide guidance in contemporary society?

Do you consider that the Halakhic tradition can provide guidance even though differences of opinion are evident within the system?

Tay-Sachs is an inherited disorder which is evident within some Jewish communities.

AO2 Activity

List some conclusions that could be drawn from the AO2 reasoning from the above text; try to aim for at least three different possible conclusions. Consider each of the conclusions and collect brief evidence to support each conclusion from the AO1 and AO2 material for this topic. Select the conclusion that you think is most convincing and explain why it is so. Try to contrast this with the weakest conclusion in the list, justifying your argument with clear reasoning and evidence.

Specification content

The extent to which pikuach nefesh is compatible with embryo research.

The extent to which pikuach nefesh is compatible with embryo research

The pace of change regarding progress made in medical science since the latter part of the twentieth century to the present day has been incredibly rapid, particularly in the field of embryo research. Scientific research, especially in the domain of cell biology, has led to the discovery of stem cells. Such is the nature of stem cells that researchers believe that they have the potential to cure many diseases which, at present, are a danger to human life. Any new medical technology is bound to raise questions within Judaism regarding the ethical status of such procedures, and one way in which many Jewish ethicists have addressed the dilemma is to apply what is considered to be one of the core principles of the Jewish faith: pikuach nefesh.

At a basic level, it would first appear that pikuach nefesh is entirely compatible with embryo research: Judaism teaches that all life comes from God; therefore, it is considered to be the gift of God, and to do anything which might take away or shorten that life is looked upon as murder. It follows therefore, that if a new medical procedure is identified that can lead to the improvement of, or saving of a life then it should be accepted wholeheartedly. This concept has its basis in the Torah: '... Do not do anything that endangers your neighbour's life' (Leviticus 19:16). Indeed, pikuach nefesh has such status in Judaism that it overrides any other religious teaching: 'Our theological predisposition is not only to welcome, but to aggressively pursue new technologies that improve our lives and our world ... The preservation of human life, pikuach nefesh, is paramount in Jewish law, and all biblical and rabbinic prohibitions – except murder, illicit sexual relations and idolatry – are suspended to facilitate its preservation.' (Reichman)

However, the decision regarding the use of stem cells from embryos is not as clear-cut as it may seem regardless of the application of the principle of pikuach nefesh. As Yearwood points out: 'The stem cells most likely to be of scientific value come from discarded embryos. Is it ethical to use them?'

There are a number of responses to this question which illustrate that the answer is not straightforward. Eisenberg asks: 'what could the possible objections to such research be?' Although the practice of in vitro fertilisation is accepted by most rabbinic authorities (as long as the husband's sperm is used), this has led to further questions regarding the status of the spare embryos that are not implanted; one of which is whether it is right to destroy pre-embryos or not. Eisenberg refers to the approach to abortion in Jewish law and says that there is reason to argue that prior to forty days gestation the foetus lacks what he calls 'humanity', and is not considered to be an actual person, and therefore it is possible to extrapolate that destruction of such a foetus is not forbidden by Jewish law.

This leads to the next question: may a very early embryo be sacrificed for stem cells? There is broad Halakhic agreement that stem-cell research is permitted on spare embryos: if the pre-embryo is to be destroyed then it might as well be used for research purposes and life-saving work in accordance with the principle of pikuach nefesh. Indeed, evidence in favour of this stance was given by Rabbi Tendler in a testimony for the National Bioethics Advisory Commission. Furthermore, Dorff concurs with this opinion by arguing that embryos which stay outside the womb have no chance to become children, and therefore it is a mitzvah to use these embryos for research: 'It's not only permitted, there is a Jewish mandate to do so.'

Key quote

How can we account for the primacy of pikuach nefesh ...? There are two interlinked answers to this question. Of course, in saving a human life, we are saving one who was made in the image of God. But the Talmud offers another answer, in the tractate Sanhedrin: 'The reason that Adam was created alone is to teach you that whoever destroys a single human being is considered by the Torah as if he had destroyed the entire world; and whoever keeps a single human alive is considered by the Torah as if he had kept the entire world alive.' **(Robinson)**

AO2 Activity

As you read through this section try to do the following:

1. Pick out the different lines of argument that are presented in the text and identify any evidence given in support.
2. For each line of argument try to evaluate whether or not you think this is strong or weak.
3. Think of any questions you may wish to raise in response to the arguments.

This Activity will help you to start thinking critically about what you read and help you to evaluate the effectiveness of different arguments and from this develop your own observations, opinions and points of view that will help with any conclusions that you make in your answers to the AO2 questions that arise.

Study tip

This particular section of the specification allows for a variety of scholarly views to be used. It would be a good idea to create a list of relevant quotations which can be used in order to illustrate a variety of viewpoints.

A further aspect of this argument is to consider whether pikuach nefesh extends as far as to allowing the creation of embryos specifically as a source of stem cells. Dorff considers it to be permissible, but less morally justifiable; whilst Mackler is wary of using anything other than embryos taken from fertility clinics which have already been created for the purpose of in vitro fertilisation. Tendler, on the other hand, warns against being too ready to erect fences to protect biblical law by claiming that: 'a fence that prevents the cure of fatal diseases must not be erected, for then the loss is greater than the benefit'. Indeed, some would claim that the strong value placed on the sanctity of human life should be used to encourage embryo research: to regard it as a mandate rather than a request.

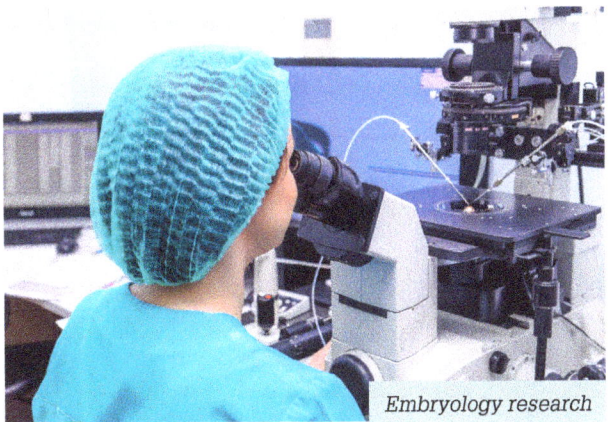

Key quote

Medical research, after all, partakes of the mitzvah to preserve human life, which our tradition teaches is the highest of all moral duties. Thus, the large supply of 'excess' embryos that exist in fertility clinics constitutes a resource of life-saving potential, and Jewish tradition … allows and encourages us to use these embryos for the purposes of human stem-cell research. (Washofsky)

Some issues have been raised, however, regarding the use of somatic cell nuclear transfer (SCNT). This process has been used in the field of reproductive cloning; however, it is also used for the production of human embryos which are used for the collection of stem cells. The purpose of collecting stem cells in this way is so that they can be used in research, and also for regenerative medicine. This application is known as therapeutic cloning. Most Jewish ethicists approve of therapeutic cloning, which has the potential to find new and effective treatments for Parkinson's disease as well as for many other debilitating and life-threatening conditions. For instance, the Union for Reform Jews in the USA passed a resolution supporting research using somatic gene therapy, basing its reasoning on the principle of pikuach nefesh. This acceptance is echoed in a response from the CCAR which states: 'If we define the administration of life-saving medical therapy as pikuach nefesh, we should not forget that physicians could not save lives were it not for the extensive scientific research upon which our contemporary practice of medicine is based. Since research into human stem-cells partakes of the mitzvah of healing, surely our society ought to support it.'

Embryology research

The possibility of cloning humans, however, remains at odds with many in the Jewish tradition, although there are differences of opinion even within this field of embryo research. Some view creation as an ongoing process which allows for human participation, thus allowing for reproductive cloning if it were to bring about the means by which life could be improved and preserved. Tendler, however, dismisses human cloning for the time being by indicating that: '… those on the leading edge of stem-cell research know that the greater contribution to human welfare will come from replacement of damaged cells and organs by fresh stem-cell products, not from cloning.' Added to this are concerns that creating humans through cloning could bring about unforeseen future suffering in the form of psychological distress, thus negating the principle of pikuach nefesh entirely.

At the present time, it would appear that the majority Jewish position is generally that pikuach nefesh is compatible with embryo research. However, what of the future? As Wright points out, the number and availability of new genetic techniques is likely to increase, with the introduction of properly functioning genes to correct the effect of defective ones in future. It therefore appears that the debate regarding the compatibility between pikuach nefesh and embryo research will continue. 'But it seems likely that ways will be found for religious Jews of all denominations to gain positive benefit from research and interventions that are carefully and responsibly undertaken.' (Wright)

Key questions

What justification does the principle of pikuach nefesh provide for embryo research?

What issues exist for Jews concerning the status of using embryos for stem-cell research?

To what extent does pikuach nefesh cover all aspects of current embryo research?

AO2 Activity

List some conclusions that could be drawn from the AO2 reasoning from the above text; try to aim for at least three different possible conclusions. Consider each of the conclusions and collect brief evidence to support each conclusion from the AO1 and AO2 material for this topic. Select the conclusion that you think is most convincing and explain why it is so. Try to contrast this with the weakest conclusion in the list, justifying your argument with clear reasoning and evidence.

Key skills

Analysis involves:

Identifying issues raised by the materials in the AO1, together with those identified in the AO2 section, and presents sustained and clear views, either of scholars or from a personal perspective ready for evaluation.

This means:

- That your answers are able to identify key areas of debate in relation to a particular issue
- That you can identify, and comment upon, the different lines of argument presented by others
- That your response comments on the overall effectiveness of each of these areas or arguments.

Evaluation involves:

Considering the various implications of the issues raised based upon the evidence gleaned from analysis and provides an extensive detailed argument with a clear conclusion.

This means:

- That your answer weighs up the consequences of accepting or rejecting the various and different lines of argument analysed
- That your answer arrives at a conclusion through a clear process of reasoning.

AO2 Developing skills

It is now important to consider the information that has been covered in this section; however, the information in its raw form is too extensive and so has to be processed in order to meet the requirements of the examination. This can be achieved by practising more advanced skills associated with AO2. For assessment objective 2 (AO2), which involves 'critical analysis' and 'evaluation' skills, we are going to focus on different ways in which the skills can be demonstrated effectively, and also refer to how the performance of these skills is measured (see generic band descriptors for A2 [WJEC] AO2 or A Level [Eduqas] AO2).

▶ **Your new task is this:** It is impossible to cover all essays in the time allowed by the course; however, it is a good exercise to develop detailed plans that can be utilised under timed conditions. As a last exercise:

1. Create some ideal plans by using what we have done so far in the Theme 4 Developing skills sections.

2. This time stop at the planning stage and exchange plans with a study partner.

3. Check each other's plans carefully. Talk through any omissions or extras that could be included, not forgetting to challenge any irrelevant materials.

4. Remember, collaborative learning is very important for revision. It not only helps to consolidate understanding of the work and appreciation of the skills involved, it is also motivational and a means of providing more confidence in one's learning. Although the examination is sat alone, revising as a pair or small group is invaluable.

When you have completed the task, refer to the band descriptors for A2 (WJEC) or A Level (Eduqas) and in particular have a look at the demands described in the higher band descriptors towards which you should be aspiring. Ask yourself:

- Is my answer a confident critical analysis and perceptive evaluation of the issue?

- Is my answer a response that successfully identifies and thoroughly addresses the issues raised by the question set?

- Does my work show an excellent standard of coherence, clarity and organisation?

- Will my work, when developed, contain thorough, sustained and clear views that are supported by extensive, detailed reasoning and/or evidence?

- Are the views of scholars/schools of thought used extensively, appropriately and in context?

- Does my answer convey a confident and perceptive analysis of the nature of any possible connections with other elements of my course?

- When used, is specialist language and vocabulary both thorough and accurate?

Questions and answers

Theme 1: DEF

AO1 answer: *An answer examining the nature of the Mishnah: content, style and importance for study in Judaism*

A weaker answer

Hoffman says that 'The Mishnah's essential message is that the Jewish people, in spite of the absence of the Temple, retains its sanctity.' [1] The Mishnah is a collection of lessons, quotations and legal rulings that were put together by Judah Ha-Nasi. It is written in Hebrew and has six sections: women, holidays and festivals are three of the sections. [2]

The Mishnah is important because it gives guidelines which explain how the mitzvot should be interpreted. The guidelines are known as Halakhah. The Mishnah presents details of debates which have been held by Jewish scholars, and provides a judgement so that Jews know how to carry out the mitzvot in everyday life. [3]

Some scholars have said that the Gemara is more important than the Mishnah, and this is because it has more content and gives a much clearer understanding of how to live according to the mitzvot. The Gemara also makes links between what is written in the biblical texts which the Mishnah doesn't do. However, the Gemara wouldn't exist if it wasn't for the Mishnah, and so maybe it isn't as important after all. [4]

In conclusion, the Mishnah is important as it is one of two texts which make up the Talmud. As Dosick says: 'Rabbinic Judaism has served Judaism well … by applying ongoing principles … to meet new and potentially threatening situations.' [5]

Commentary

1. A scholarly quotation has been used, but it stands alone as there is no connection between it and that which follows.
2. There are some correct facts here, but it is vital to be able to name and offer a description of *all* of the six sections.
3. This is a good, basic, explanation of the Mishnah; however, it needs an example in order to illustrate the nature of the debates and/or judgements made.
4. This is a digression from the question set. There *is* a link between the Mishnah and the Gemara, but the question requires attention to be paid to the Mishnah alone. Furthermore, the content of this paragraph is more suited to an AO2 answer.
5. The final paragraph adds very little to the response. A perfectly acceptable scholarly quotation has been learned, but unfortunately has merely been tagged on to the end of the answer with no effectiveness.

Summative comment

Overall, this response is superficial and misses many key opportunities for development. A limited range of scholarly views has been used, but they have not been used accurately or effectively.

AO2 answer: *An answer evaluating whether or not Midrash is an imprecise science*

Excerpt from a strong answer

In the first instance, Satlow's description of Midrash as 'a rule-driven form of interpretation' might lead some to argue that this very definition promotes Midrash as a precise skill or technique that is capable of bringing about some kind of systematic observation. Indeed, the fact that Midrash presents a method that has been accepted, and which holds an important position within the canon of Jewish sacred texts could be used as evidence for this particular contention. [1]

However, others might focus on the fact that Midrash, as a method of interpretation, is bound to leave itself open to a variety of opinions, and thus is not as precise as it could be. Evidence for this can be offered by drawing attention to the fact that collections of midrashim often contain two or more rabbinical opinions on the same subject which provide no precise conclusion as to which of the arguments is the most significant. Evidence for this can be taken from a debate in the Jerusalem Talmud over the question of what is the most important verse in the Torah. One rabbi claims it is 'You shall love your neighbour as yourself', based upon the key precept of self and self-interest; whilst another says that 'When God created man, He made him in the likeness of God' which uses the image of God as the key principle of human existence. [2]

Another line of argument might take account of the fact that there are two distinct elements within the Midrash: Halakhah and Aggadah. It could be argued that Halakhah, for instance, shows evidence of greater precision in its interpretation of that which is considered to be the word of God. For example, the clear practice within Orthodox Judaism of wearing tefillin boxes on the arm and forehead has arisen from the interpretation of the verses from Deuteronomy 6 that state: 'These commandments that I give you today are to be on your hearts … Tie them as symbols on your hands and bind them on your foreheads.' [3]

By contrast, however, Midrash Aggadah might not be regarded as being as precise in its method. Robinson, for instance, notes that it is not a conventional method of literary interpretation. Indeed, some aggadic passages discuss issues such as angels and demons, and contain legends from the lives of rabbis, or biblical figures such as Abraham. However, such stories were never meant to be taken at face value, and are seen as offering the means by which to make a moral or ethical point … **4**

Commentary

1. A relevant and appropriate scholarly viewpoint has been used to very good effect as part of the opening argument.
2. The second paragraph provides a clear counter-argument through an alternative interpretation of the role of Midrash, backed up by relevant evidence.
3. A detailed analysis of the structure of the Midrash adds greater depth to the argument.
4. This paragraph shows the complexity of the issue, and, if the student continues in the same manner and arrives at a conclusion that summarises and supports their overall point of view, then this will be a very strong response.

Summative comment

This answer displays well-developed responses to specific arguments using a number of examples to support key points. It is coherent and well organised, and moves smoothly from one point to the next. Views of scholars/schools of thought and specialist vocabulary have been used appropriately throughout.

Theme 3: ABC

AO1 answer: *An answer examining the origins of Religious Zionism*

A strong answer

Religious Zionism relates to the belief that the city of Zion will once again become the city of God where Jews will once again take up residence. Zion is one of the biblical names for Jerusalem. It is also synonymous with the Land of Israel, the place that God promised the Jews as part of the covenant relationship made with Abraham: 'I will give to you and to your descendants after you … all the land of Canaan, for an everlasting possession.' (Genesis 17:7–8).

After many years of wandering in the wilderness after their escape from slavery in Egypt, the Jews finally established themselves in the land that God had promised them. King David made Jerusalem his capital city, and it became the centre for worship. The name Zion came about due to the fact that one of the hills upon which the city was built was Mount Zion. Eventually the name came to signify the whole land. However, when the Jews were sent into exile in Babylon, they longed to return to the land which God had given them. As Psalm 137 tells us: 'By the rivers of Babylon, there we sat, sat and wept, as we thought of Zion.'

Hope remained that the Holy Land would once again be restored to them, and there is evidence of this in the Book of Amos which says: '"I will restore my people Israel. They shall rebuild ruined cities and inhabit them… I will plant them upon their soil, nevermore to be uprooted from the soil I have given them," says the LORD your God.' Zion is so significant within Judaism that the beliefs which have developed around it have become known as 'Zion theology'. **1**

The prophecies of Isaiah speak of Zion as the 'glorious crown' which will be 'renowned on earth', meaning that Zion will not only be significant for the Jews but that it will become a light to all nations: 'And nations shall walk by your light.' It will be the place on earth where there will be peace and justice under God's rule. The prophet Jeremiah also emphasises the importance of Zion. He speaks of repentance being followed by the restoration of the Jewish nation where the leaders will be God's choice, and as such will be just and fair at all times. **2**

The connection between Jews and the Land of Israel is also evident in the liturgy. For example, the Amidah contains references to the return to Jerusalem, such as in the words, 'To Jerusalem, your city, return in mercy and dwell in it as you have promised.' Furthermore at Passover, the seder meal ends with the words 'Next year may we be in Jerusalem; next year may we be free.' **3**

It has been argued that Religious Zionism, with its emphasis upon a return to the Land of Israel is the true origin of Zionism. However, Hoffman indicates that it now means something different and has taken on a political identity. 'The whole weight of the biblical promise, with the collective hope of ingathering, lies behind the Jewish association with Israel, the land. "The Holy Land" is one to which you make aliyah, the term used generally now of "immigration" to Israel. But any line of continuity with what is now understood as Zionism in terms of Israel, the State, is not a straight one.' **4**

Commentary

1. A very good introduction that shows an accurate understanding of 'Zion' and its significance for Judaism. Very good use has also been made of relevant, supporting quotations from biblical texts.
2. The answer continues to show a thorough knowledge and understanding of the issue by making reference to further examples from the biblical text.
3. There are more effective uses of examples to illustrate the importance of Zion.
4. The conclusion presents an insightful comment from a scholarly source which indicates depth of knowledge regarding the wider debate relating to Zionism.

Summative comment

This answer has a good structure and displays many excellent characteristics which include relevant quotations from sacred texts, as well as a reference to a scholarly opinion. Specialist language has also been used accurately. If anything is lacking then more extensive use of scholarly viewpoints would have improved it further.

AO2 answer: *An answer evaluating whether or not Zionism is specifically a Jewish movement*

A weaker answer

Zionism is a political movement which was started by Theodore Herzl at the end of the nineteenth century. However, Herzl was not a practising Jew, which means that Zionism is not specifically a Jewish movement. **1**

Zionism does not have to be linked to the Jewish religion because it came about due to anti-Semitism and the need to create a state where all Jews could live their lives based upon the teachings of the Torah. **2**

Orthodox Jews do not believe that Zionism has anything to do with Judaism. This is because they believe that only God can bring about the return of the Jewish people to the Promised Land. Reform Jews are also against Zionism because they don't believe in the need to return to the Promised Land. **3**

On the other hand, the Bible is full of quotations which say that the Jews will be able to return to the Promised Land at some time in the future. For example, Amos the prophet spoke about it in his book. **4**

In conclusion, it could be suggested that even if Zionism is not specifically a Jewish movement, it has helped religious Jews to live together as part of one nation. **5**

Commentary

1. A weak introduction which lacks detailed analysis, and which does not allow for an alternative point of view.
2. This statement is inaccurate and also contradictory: on the one hand stating that Zionism doesn't need to be linked to Judaism; whilst on the other saying that it would provide the means by which Jews could live according to God's laws as set down in the Torah.
3. The statements presented here are valid, although they need further development. For instance, Orthodox Jews believe that the return to Zion must be preceded by messianic redemption; and for Reform Jews, the Pittsburgh Platform suggests that it is a necessary thing for Jews to be dispersed across the world in order to spread the truth of God to all nations.
4. This is true, but there is no evidence of evaluation or critical analysis, and neither is there a relevant scriptural quotation.
5. A weak conclusion, which, as in other parts of the answer, suffers from lack of development.

Summative comment

The answer shows that there is confusion regarding the different understandings of the term Zionism. A limited number of issues have been identified and partially addressed, but points have been presented without depth of discussion. The answer also lacks relevant scriptural evidence as well as scholarly viewpoints.

Theme 3: DEF

AO1 answer: *An answer examining the role of the family and the Jewish home as foundational for Jewish principles*

A weaker answer

The home is important to Jews as lots of festivals are celebrated there by having meals and building a sukkah, for example. Jews also put a mezuzah on the front door when they move in to remind them of God every time they go inside. **1**

The family is also important to Jews as it is the place where the parents teach the children how to live as Jews. The Talmud gives instructions about how this should be done. One of the Ten Commandments says that children in Jewish families have to honour their parents, meaning that they should always listen to them and do as they are told. **2**

Parents have different roles in the family and it's not just about religion. For example, Jewish parents must make sure that their children learn how to survive in life and be able to get a good job. The Talmud says that Jewish children who do not learn a trade will become robbers in later life. **3**

In conclusion, we can see that the role of the family and the Jewish home are important as foundational for Jewish principles. **4**

Commentary

1. The facts are correct but they need further development. For instance, why is the home significant within the Jewish faith? How do the various festivals provide the opportunity for worship in the home? Also, a discussion of the ceremony of chanukat habayit, and a scriptural reference to Deuteronomy 6:4–9 should have been included.
2. The statements are correct, but there is no development. The Talmud and the Ten Commandments have been mentioned, but there are no accompanying quotations.

3. The Talmud has been used as evidence here, but the actual quotation has not been cited. Furthermore, the meaning of the quotation which has been alluded to has not been understood fully.
4. This merely reiterates the theme of the question with nothing new to add, and has no depth of meaning.

Summative comment

This response lacks scriptural and scholarly sources as well as extensive use of specialist language. Furthermore, it lacks development, and does not deal with both the home and family in a balanced way.

AO2 answer: *An answer evaluating the possibility of assimilation into secular society for Jews in Britain*

An excerpt from a strong answer

Some would argue that there are certainly challenges for Jews living in Britain today which have the potential to make it difficult for them to assimilate fully into secular society. For instance, having to live according to the specific demands of the Torah can be a challenge. An example which can be used in evidence of this is that many Orthodox Jews wish to follow the laws of kashrut in their entirety. However, in order for this to be undertaken successfully, food has to be produced, prepared and eaten in a certain way … It is also impossible for Orthodox Jews to eat in non-Jewish restaurants or in the homes of non-Jewish people, thus limiting social contact with those outside their own particular cultural group … **1**

Jewish schools might also be said to encourage segregation rather than assimilation. This could have the negative effect of highlighting the cultural differences between the Jewish children and those who attend non-faith schools. However, for Orthodox Jews, providing a school based on the values of the religion would be seen as a way of protecting their children from the materialistic values of the secular world. **2** Unterman highlights this argument when he claims that a Jewish education 'cushions the effect of the gentile environment, enhances social contact with fellow Jews, limits the prospect of inter-marriage'. **3**

However, not all Jews have the same view. Reform Jews would argue that it is important to be assimilated into secular society, and they have shown that this is possible. For example, many Reform Jews do not keep kashrut at all, whilst others keep the food laws at home, but are comfortable eating out in non-kosher restaurants and homes. Hoffman notes that this approach 'has evolved … from the desire to facilitate relations with non-Jews'. This can be used as evidence to show that Judaism can survive in a secular society, where there is compromise. Furthermore, Reform Jews firmly believe that this course of action does not take anything away from their faith. **4**

To conclude, some might argue that segregation rather than assimilation isn't actually a problem for Orthodox Jews at all. As Hoffman points out (in reference to the laws of kashrut), for Orthodox Jews the traditional Halakhah is binding: '… if it entails great effort, expense and non-assimilation into non-Jewish society, then this after all serves the purpose of all these dietary laws. They are a reminder of distinctiveness. They require discrimination recognising that the body and food are given by God who calls for holiness in his people.' And such is the nature of Britain as a multi-cultural society, that there is a place for such a way of life even within a nation that is mainly secular. **5**

Commentary

1. This is a good evaluative style introducing a particular line of argument with a clear example and evidence to prove it. Furthermore, use of the phrase 'which have the potential to make it difficult …' does not prevent a strong presentation of counter-arguments.
2. Further evidence is offered which serves to illustrate the potential of specific Jewish practices leading to segregation rather than assimilation. However, the candidate also identifies a Jewish viewpoint from the Orthodox tradition which shows perception.
3. The view of a key scholar is used appropriately and in context.
4. A counter-argument is introduced which displays an understanding of the diverse views that are to be found within the Jewish faith. A further scholarly reference is also used in context.
5. The conclusion demonstrates that lack of assimilation for Orthodox Jews should not necessarily be regarded as a problem. It also places the whole debate within the context of British society.

Summative comment

A confident critical analysis and perceptive evaluation of the issue has been displayed, with the key arguments resting solidly on relevant examples which are accompanied by detailed reasoning. The views of scholars have been used extensively, and have served to support the claims which have been made.

Theme 4: DEF

AO1 Answer: *An answer examining the influence of the rebbe*

A weaker answer

The rebbe was a new kind of leader in the Jewish religion, and they still exist today in some Jewish communities. **1** The rebbe should not be confused with a rabbi. The word rabbi means 'my master', and a rabbi is the spiritual head of a Jewish community. Modern rabbis play a very important part in the Jewish community. For example, they lead the prayers in the synagogue and also carry out weddings and funerals. They also study the Torah and teach Hebrew. There are also rabbis who are involved with checking that food is prepared according to the kosher food laws as set out in the Torah. **2**

The rebbe is more spiritual in nature than an ordinary rabbi. He is considered to be closer to God with the ability to approach the God on behalf of the people. It is also believed that rebbes have miraculous powers such as the power to heal people who are ill. A person usually becomes a rebbe because their father was one. **3**

The rebbe has a big influence in his community, and has many followers who watch him carefully and copy what he does. The rebbe also has an influence on his community by preaching, and teaching his followers. **4**

In summary, the rebbe is an important figure of authority, the most important in Jewish history considered to be the Baal Shem Tov who founded the Hasidic group within Judaism. He taught that it is more important to live a spiritual life through simple faith than to be a scholar of the Torah. He also taught that people should be attached to God. **5**

Commentary

1. The statements are accurate, but there needs to be more detail, for example, when did the role of rebbe become established? In which kind of Jewish communities are they to be found?
2. This is a classic digression from the focus of the question. The question is about the influence of the rebbe, and here we have a detailed explanation of the role of the rabbi.
3. This is correct, although it would be good to see more specialised language here such as 'tzaddik' and 'devekut' as well as a scholarly definition of the role of rebbe.
4. This is accurate, but needs further development through use of illustration. For example, many followers of a rebbe will watch how he dresses, eats and acts for instance, and will imitate his ways.
5. The influence of the Baal Shem Tov has been placed in the conclusion almost as an aside.

Summative comment

This is an example of an answer that could easily be developed further in order to achieve a higher level. However, the issues that have been identified lack depth. For instance, there are no scholarly viewpoints or quotations, and specialist vocabulary has not been used.

AO2 answer: *An answer evaluating whether Hasidism contributed to the survival of Judaism*

A strong answer

In the first instance, it is important to note that many would agree that Hasidism has certainly had an impact upon the survival of Judaism. However, the extent of its impact and whether or not it can be said to have been the sole contributor to the survival of the Jewish faith needs to be considered in greater depth. **1**

When considering whether Hasidism has contributed to the survival of Judaism or not, some would suggest that it is important to place the development of the movement within an historical context. It arose as a religious movement in the eighteenth century in Eastern Europe at a time when there was hardship and the economy was in decline. Unfortunately for the Jews, as the minority group they began to suffer from discrimination and oppression. However, due to the significance of a man known as the Baal Shem Tov, the Jewish religion underwent a dramatic rejuvenation. He brought about a new form of worship which was marked by extreme intensity of belief and enthusiasm in prayer and worship. This was in contrast to the traditional form of Jewish worship which was based upon study of the Torah, and was therefore not accessible for the majority who were not trained in Hebrew. Evidence for this can be found in the words of the Baal Shem Tov himself who preached that: 'God loves all Jews without distinction; the greatest Torah genius ... and the most simple Jew are equally loved by God.' Some have argued that without his influence, and the subsequent development of the Hasidic movement, the Jewish religion might have died out if left under the control of the minority of Torah scholars. **2**

Furthermore, it is also important to note that Hasidism has remained constant up to the present day, even during the period known as the Enlightenment when other Jewish groups sought acceptance into mainstream European society through reform of traditional Jewish education and practice. It is ironic therefore that a group which at first made a stand against the traditional practices of its time, should now be acknowledged as being responsible for the preservation of the core principles of the Jewish faith. In addition, Hasidism also places great emphasis upon matriarchal lineage which has meant that its traditions have not been diluted by outsiders. Each of these things might be used to argue for its importance in ensuring the survival of Judaism. [3]

However, in opposition to the view that Hasidism has been the sole contributor to the survival of Judaism, evidence can be offered which shows that there are other Jewish groups who have also played their part. Some might suggest, for example, that Reform Judaism has also been significant due to its emphasis on reinterpreting beliefs and practices in order to ensure that the faith remains relevant at any time in history. Furthermore, it could be argued that Reform Jews have managed to retain their religious identity as well as achieving assimilation into British society. The adaptations made by Reform Jews are based upon the terms of the Pittsburgh Platform which defines Jews as a 'religious community' rather than as a nation. For example, a Reform Jew may wear a kippah as a sign of religious identity, but might not keep kosher outside the home. As a result of this flexibility, it is more likely that they face fewer challenges living as Jews in a mainly secular society, and a consequence of this approach is that it has helped the Jewish faith to survive. [4]

In conclusion, it is important to note that Hasidism is not without its critics, with some claiming that it has merely allowed a specific form of Judaism to survive which is in no way considered to be conventional. In its early days, for example, it was opposed by the Mitnagdim who, Robinson points out, considered the group to be a direct threat to the Jewish faith. Perhaps therefore the Mitnagdim should also be given some credit for the survival of Judaism, based upon their determination to preserve tradition. [5]

Commentary

1. A brief, but relevant introduction which highlights the focus for analysis and evaluation that is to follow.
2. An excellent line of argument which is perceptive in its evaluation, and which makes accurate use of a significant quotation.
3. Other reasons are offered with explanations which illustrate good analytical skills.
4. A clear counter-argument has been introduced through an opposing line of reasoning, giving clear evidence, explanation and examples to support there being other Jewish groups who have contributed to the survival of Judaism.
5. A good summary which responds well to the focus of the question.

Summative comment

An excellent answer which presents a confident critical analysis and perceptive evaluation of the issue. The use of scholars has been used appropriately and in context. An interesting conclusion introduces a further alternative viewpoint which suggests that the debate is much more complex.

Quickfire answers

Theme 1 DEF

1.1 Mishnah and Gemara.

1.2 Halakhah refers to the complete body of rules and practices that Orthodox Jews are bound to follow: the rules and regulations by which a Jew 'walks' through life.

1.3 Seeds (Zeraim); holidays (Moed); women (Nashim); damages (Nezikin); holy things (Kodashim); purity (Tohorot).

1.4 The Jerusalem Talmud and the Babylonian Talmud.

1.5 It represents an unbroken chain of tradition that reaches back to the transmission of the Oral Torah to Moses at Mount Sinai, and provides a comprehensive, written version of Jewish Oral law.

It has enabled guidelines in the form of Halakhah to be created, thus ensuring that the mitzvot that were transmitted from God to Moses can be interpreted correctly in order to remain relevant no matter how times and society have changed over the millennia.

1.6 The purpose of midrash is to seek truth in scripture, and use it to address present-day issues which have no precedent in the Torah.

1.7 Peshat, remez, derash, and sod.

1.8 Halakhah is the legal rulings and the reasoning behind them that govern Jewish practice. Aggadah is anything found in rabbinic writings that isn't about legal discussions and decisions, and comprises a wide-ranging collection of legends, parables, folklore and stories that add depth of understanding and meaning to the Jewish experience.

1.9 The name given to the rabbinical method of interpreting the legal topics contained in scripture.

1.10 They act in an advisory role and are not considered to be binding or obligatory. Final decisions are made by individuals or communities who take into account all the factors that are relevant to them at a particular time and place, and then they choose accordingly.

1.11 Peshat, the 'plain' or 'literal' sense meaning of a passage.

1.12 Thirteen Principles of Faith.

1.13 To update the law of the Talmud and to make it clear and concise for the Jews of the time. He wanted to take the Tanakh, the two Talmuds and midrashic literature, and to condense them into something that almost anyone could read.

1.14 'In the beginning of God's creation of the heavens and the earth, the earth was unformed and void, darkness was on the face of the deep, and the spirit of God hovered over the face of the waters.'

1.15 'Ex nihilo' means (of creation) out of nothing; 'de novo' means (creation) from pre-existing matter.

Theme 3 ABC

3.1 Amos, Isaiah, Jeremiah.

3.2 The 1870s.

3.3 Der Judenstaat.

3.4 1948

3.5 The Law of Return.

3.6 God drew three drops of water and three drops of fire from the celestial Torah, and from them made the world.

3.7 People lack both the comprehension to describe God's true nature as well as the language with which to express it.

3.8 Sefer Yezirah or Book of Creation.

3.9 6,000 years or thereabouts.

3:10 Midrash Genesis Rabbah 3:7; Talmud Chaggiga 13b–14a; Midrash Psalms 90:4.

3.11 Hamburg.

3.12 The United States of America.

3.13 'Liberationist thought' is a term that is used to describe the movement which attempts to address the problems of poverty and injustice in the world; and social action is at its heart.

3.14 Religious pluralism is the view that no one religion can claim to be the sole and exclusive source of truth.

3.15 Alenu.

Theme 3 DEF

3.16 Affixing a mezuzah to the doorpost of the house.

3.17 Ezekiel.

3.18 Lighting Shabbat candles; taking challah; and keeping the laws of ritual purity.

3.19 It has allowed women to take a more active part in worship and education through membership of small worship groups that are based upon the principle of equality, and which are led by lay people rather than a rabbi.

189

3.20 'Standing Again at Sinai – Judaism from a feminine perspective' by Judith Plaskow.

3.21 The purpose of kashering is to make sure that no blood remains in butchered meat. This is in accordance with Deuteronomy 12:23 which states: 'Only be sure that you do not eat the blood; for the blood is the life ...'

3.22 Hasidic Jews are required to adhere strictly to the requirements of the Jewish law which they would be unable to do in the wider society.

3.23 They define 'work' as being the job which they do to earn money, and which they refrain from doing during Shabbat.

3.24 The JLC (Jewish Leadership Council) is a Jewish charity which brings together representatives from the major British Jewish organisations. Its aim is to support and ensure continuity in the UK of a mainstream Jewish community, so that Judaism is assured of its place within British society.

3.25 Its aim is to enable pupils to gain a deeper knowledge and understanding of the Torah through the use of critical and analytical thinking.

3.26 Six million.

3.27 Amos.

3.28 God's ways can never be fully known; humanity cannot hope to understand them; and the problem of the evil of the Holocaust must remain the ultimate theological mystery.

3.29 'Night', 'Dawn', and 'The Accident'.

3.30 An event of total destruction.

Theme 4 DEF

4.1 Israel ben Eliezer.

4.2 Pious.

4.3 The Vilna Gaon.

4.4 By providing a musical path to God that transcends the limitations of language.

4.5 Tzaddik.

4.6 The name given to the mystic tradition that is to be found within Judaism that aims to experience the divine nature and presence of God.

4.7 'Radiance' or 'splendour'.

4.8 Keter, Hokhmah and Binah.

4.9 Deuteronomy 13:4: 'Follow none but the Lord your God, and revere none but Him; observe His commandments alone, and heed only His orders; worship none but Him, and hold fast (or cling) to Him.'

Deuteronomy 11:22: 'If, then, you faithfully keep all this Instruction that I command you, loving the Lord your God, walking in all His ways, and holding fast to Him ...'

4.10 Isaac of Acre.

4.11 Stem cells are special types of cells that have the potential to grow into any type of cell found in the body.

4.12 Nachmanides.

4.13 Pre-implantation genetic screening.

4.14 Tay-Sachs disease.

4.15 The technology could be used to boost the function of the thymus in order to provide greater immunity against infection.

Glossary

a priori: prior to experience; based on knowledge that proceeds from theoretical deduction

Acronym: a word made from the first letters of other words

Adonai: meaning 'Lord'

Aggadah: all non-legal rabbinic literature, e.g. stories, legends, extracts from sermons

Aggadot: plural of Aggadah

Agnostic: someone who believes that nothing is known, or can be known, of the existence or nature of God

Agunah: meaning 'chained' and referring to a woman whose husband is missing but not known to be dead

Alenu: the prayer that marks the end of all three daily prayer services at the synagogue

Aliyah: meaning 'ascent' or 'going up'; also used in the sense of 'immigration' to the Land of Israel

Allegorical: relating to a story or picture, for example, which can be interpreted to reveal a hidden meaning usually moral or spiritual in nature

Alms: donations of food, money, etc., for the poor

Amidah: the name of a daily prayer

Amoraim: rabbinic interpreters of the third and fourth century whose discussions are recorded in the Talmud

Anachronistic: to attribute something to a historical period in which it did not exist

Ani Ma'amin: a poetic form of Maimonides' 'Thirteen Principles of Faith' which is recited every day after morning prayers at the synagogue

Anthropomorphise: to attribute human form/behaviour/characteristics to God

Anti-Semitism: hostility to and/or discrimination against Jews

Aramaic: a language used in the Near East from the 6th century BCE

Arboreal: denoting an animal that lives mainly in trees

Aristotelianism: a school or tradition of ancient Greek philosophy that takes its defining inspiration from the work of the philosopher Aristotle

Ascetic: a person whose life is characterised by self-discipline and abstention from indulgence

Ashkenazi: referring to Jews from central or Eastern Europe

Assimilated: to have become part of a larger group especially when they are of a different race or culture

Baal Shem Tov: meaning 'Master of the Good Name' (i.e. the name of God)

Bar mitzvah: 'son of the commandment'; the coming of age ceremony for a Jewish boy at 13 years of age

Bat mitzvah: 'daughter of the commandment'; the coming of age ceremony for a Jewish girl at 12 years of age

BCE: Before the Common Era

Bedieved: done after the fact

Beneficent: actively kind and generous

Berakhot: blessings

Bereshith: literal meaning 'at the head of' or 'in the beginning (of)'

Besht: an abbreviated form of the title 'Baal Shem Tov'

Bet din: meaning 'house of judgement'; a rabbinical court

Bet midrash: house of study

Bioethics: the study of ethical issues that have arisen as a result of new advances in medical and biological research

Birkat Hamazon: blessing said after a meal

Blastocyst: a very early stage of a mammalian embryo which is formed before implantation into the uterus

Brit milah: circumcision

Buber: referring to Martin Buber, a prominent twentieth-century Jewish philosopher

CE: referring to the Common Era; the period beginning with the traditional birth year of Jesus

Celestial: relating to heaven

Challah: a special loaf of bread used on Shabbat and festivals

Chanukat habayit: the ceremony of dedication for a new Jewish home

Chukim: commandments for which no particular reason has been given for having to keep them

Chumash: a printed text containing the Five Books of Moses

Churban: referring to an event of total destruction

Civil rights: the rights of all citizens to political, social and religious freedom and equality

Codifying: arranging laws or rules into a systematic code

Consecration: making something sacred; setting it apart for holy use

Corporeal: having a bodily form

Cosmogony: a theory regarding the origins of the universe

Cosmology: use of evidence of, and within, the universe to prove the existence of God

De novo: (creation) from pre-existing matter

Decalogue: the Ten Commandments

Der Judenstaat: meaning 'The Jewish State'; a pamphlet written by Herzl in 1896

Devekut: devotion to God; clinging on to God; having God permanently in the mind

Diaspora: the term used to denote the Jews who live outside Israel

Didactic: intending to teach or instruct

El Hai: meaning 'The Living God'

El Shaddai: meaning 'God Almighty'

El: name for God denoting might, strength and power

Elohim Tsva'ot: meaning 'God of Hosts'

Elohim: one of the many names for God that are found in the Jewish scriptures

Emanation: something that issues or proceeds from something else

Empiric: based on experimental, observation or experience rather than on theory

En Sof: meaning 'infinite'; a term used in Jewish Kabbalism to refer to God

Eretz Hakodesh: meaning 'The Holy Land'

Eretz Yisrael: meaning 'Land of Israel'

Esoteric: secret or mysterious; likely to be understood by a small number of people who have special knowledge

Ethical monotheism: God is the source of one standard of morality and requires that people act decently toward each other

Ethical: to live according to a set of moral principles

Ex nihilo: (of creation) out of nothing

ex post facto: with retrospective action

Excommunication: to exclude a person/group from membership of their community

Exegesis: a critical explanation of a text, especially of scripture

Existential: relating to human existence

Gaon: meaning 'pride', 'genius', or 'outstanding scholar'

Gemara: a rabbinical commentary on the Mishnah

Gematria: numerology

Gemilut hasadim: 'the giving of loving kindness'; doing good deeds

Genocide: the deliberate killing of a whole nation or people

Gentile: the term used for a person who is not a Jew

Geonim: name given to the heads of the two Babylonian academies in Sura and Pumbedita, which exercised great authority over the Jewish world in the seventh and eighth centuries

Get: a document of divorce

Gezerot: prohibitions against behaviour that seemingly break the mitzvot or could lead to transgressions

Ghettos: poor residential areas in which Jews were confined

Golem: an artificially created human being brought to life by Kabbalistic rites

Haggadah: means 'telling', the text recited at the Seder meal

Hagiographical: relating to writings about the lives of holy/religious people which represent them in an idealistic way

Halakhah: literal meaning: 'the path that one walks'; Jewish law

Halakhic: relating to Jewish law; from 'halakhah' meaning 'the path that one walks'

Halakhot: laws

Haredi: meaning 'fearful'; a member of a Jewish group characterised by strict adherence to the traditional form of Jewish law, and rejection of modern secular culture

Haredim: plural form of Haredi

Hasidim: literally means 'the pious one'; an ultra-orthodox wing of Judaism

Haskalah: the period of Jewish enlightenment which began in the 18th century

Havdalah: a ceremony performed at the end of Shabbat and festivals

Havruta: a study partner (for Talmudic study)

Havurah: meaning 'fellowship' or 'companionship'

Hechsher: a stamp or label certifying that a food product is kosher

Herem: ban; excommunication

Heresy: belief or opinion contrary to the authorised teachings of the faith

Holocaust: the term used to denote the murder of nearly 6 million Jews by Germany between 1933 and 1945

Homiletical: relating to 'homily'; a sermon

Homily: a sermon

Hovovei Zion: meaning 'lovers of Zion'; organisations established with the aim of supporting Jewish settlement in the Land of Israel

Imitatio dei: meaning 'imitation of God'

Immanent: referring to a Supreme Being who is permanently present

Israel: used in this particular context as a term for the Jewish people

Kabbalah: Jewish mystical tradition

Kabbalists: followers of Kabbalah

Kashering: to make fit for use; to make kosher

Kashrut: religious dietary laws

Glossary

Kavod: literally means 'heavy' or 'weighty', but often denotes honour or glory. It attempts to describe the experience of standing in the presence of God

Kavvanah: literal meaning is 'intention'; used to denote a state of mental concentration and devotion at prayer

Ketubah: marriage contract

Kibbutz: a communal settlement

Kibbutzim: plural form of kibbutz

Kiddush: a ceremony of prayer and blessing over wine to sanctify Shabbat and Jewish festivals

Kiddush: the ceremony of blessing recited over wine that welcomes in the Sabbath in a Jewish home

Kippah: a skull cap

Kippot: plural of 'kippah', a skull cap

Knesset: the Parliament of modern Israel

Kodashim: 'holy things'; 5th of the six orders of the Mishnah

Kosher: food which a Jew is permitted to eat; food prepared in accordance with Jewish dietary laws

Kristallnacht: German attack on Jewish property which took place on 9–10 November 1938; also known as The Night of the Broken Glass

Kvitel: a note containing a petitionary prayer which is given to a rebbe

Laymen: people who do not hold religious office; i.e. in the Jewish faith, people who are not rabbis

Lichatchila: done in the best way possible

Liturgy: the set form of words or ritual used in worship

Lurianic Kabbalah: a school of Kabbalah named after Rabbi Isaac Luria who developed it

Megillot: the five scrolls that are read on special holidays. They are Song of Songs, Ruth, Lamentations, Ecclesiastes and the book of Esther

Mekhilta: meaning 'rules of interpretation'; the name given to a particular collection of midrashim

Melachot: the 39 types of work forbidden on Shabbat

Menorah: a seven-branched candelabrum

Merkavah: meaning 'chariot'; a school of early Jewish mysticism, drawn from the Book of Ezekiel, signifying a mystical vision of divinity

Messianic: relating to the Messiah, the 'anointed one'; one who will usher in a new era for humanity, which will be established under the rule of God

Metaphor: a thing regarded as representative or symbolic of something else

Metzaveh: the commander

Mezuzah: a small parchment scroll fixed to the right-hand doorpost of every room in a Jewish house (except bathroom and toilet)

Midrash Rabbah: meaning 'The Great Midrash'; the name given to a particular collection of midrashim

Midrash: meaning 'to inquire' (from the Hebrew word 'darash'); referring to the literature developed in classical Judaism that attempts to interpret Jewish Scriptures

Midrashim: plural of midrash

Mikdash me'at: meaning 'a small sanctuary/temple'

Mikveh: 'a place where water has gathered'; a special pool attached to a synagogue where Jews can immerse to purify themselves

Minyan: a group of ten males over the age of 13 required before an act of communal prayer can take place

Minyanim: plural of 'minyan'

Mishnah: meaning 'a teaching that is repeated'; a collection of oral laws

Mishnayot: a paragraph

Mishneh Torah: meaning 'Repetition of the Torah'

Mitnagdim: meaning 'opponents'

Mitzvah: commandment

Mitzvot: commandments

Moed: 'holy times' or 'holidays'; 2nd of the six orders of the Mishnah

Nashim: 'women'; 3rd of the six orders of the Mishnah

Nationalism: a movement which seeks to preserve a nation's culture

Nezikin: 'damages'; 4th of the six orders of the Mishnah

Nigunim: meaning 'melodies'

Notarikon: from a Greek word meaning 'shorthand writer'

Nusach Sefard: the name for various forms of the Jewish prayer book

Omnibenevolent: having absolute goodness

Omnipotent: all-powerful

Omniscient: all-knowing

Oral Torah: God-given instructions for living, transmitted by word of mouth

Ordain: to appoint as a rabbi

Palaeontology: the branch of science concerned with fossil animals and plants

Parable: a story used to illustrate a moral or spiritual lesson

Paradigm: a framework, model or pattern

Parthenogenesis: the development of a germ cell without fertilisation

Particularism: the doctrine that God has chosen to have a relationship with one particular group (in this case, the Jews) rather than a relationship which is open to everyone

Perek: chapter of the Mishnah

Philologist: a person who studies literary texts

Piety: being religiously sincere

Pikuach nefesh: the sanctity of life

Pious: religiously sincere

Plenum: a space completely filled with matter

Pluralistic: relating to 'pluralism', the existence of variety within a group

Plurality: a large number or variety

Pogroms: the organised persecutions or massacres of Jews

Poskim: a Jewish legal scholar whose job it is to decide Halakhah in cases where previous authorities are inconclusive or where no precedent exists

Posthumous: occurring after a person's death

Progressive Revelation: the concept that old laws of the Bible are no longer applicable in modern society in which new ethical, moral and spiritual values have been 'revealed'

Prophet: a person chosen to express the will of God

Rabbinical: relating to rabbis

Rambam: an acronym for Rabbi Moses ben Maimon

Rashi: an acronym for Rabbi Solomon ben Isaac

Rebbe: the title given to the spiritual leader of Hasidic Jewish communities

Redaction: to edit a text

Redemption: the act of being saved

Remnant: what is left of a community following a catastrophe

Reparation: the act of making good

Responsa: answers to questions on Halakhah given by Jewish scholars on topics addressed to them

Retribution: deserved punishment, especially for sin or wrongdoing

Rosh Chodesh: meaning 'head of the month'; the first day of the month, marked by the birth of the new moon

Sage: someone of great wisdom and knowledge

Sanhedrin: Supreme rabbinical court

Scapegoat: a person or group that is made to bear the blame for something that is not of their doing

Secular: relating to things which are not religious

Sedarim: orders

Seder Olam: meaning 'order (or chronology) of the world;' a text that contains a chronology of the Jewish people from the creation of the universe to the construction of the Second Temple in Jerusalem

Seder: the ritual service and ceremonial dinner which takes place in the Jewish home at Passover

Sefer Yezirah: Book of Creation; an early cosmological text

Sefirah: emanation (singular)

Sefirot: emanations (plural)

Sephardi: referring to Jews from the Iberian Peninsula

Shabbat: the seventh day of the week; the day of rest according to the Ten Commandments

Shabbatot: plural of Shabbat

Shamanism: relating to those who act as intermediaries between the natural and supernatural worlds; those believed to have special powers, such as healing

Shechitah: ritual slaughter of animals as set out in Jewish law

Shekinah: means 'dwelling' or 'settling' and denotes the divine presence of God in the world

Shiva: the seven-day period following burial

Shoah: meaning 'catastrophe'; term used to refer to the murder of six million Jews by the Nazis during World War II

Shomer: meaning 'guard'; one who supervises kitchens in order to ensure that the laws of kashrut are observed

Shtreimel: a round, fur hat worn by Hasidic Jews

Shul: a term used for synagogue

Shulchan Arukh: the Code of Jewish Law

Sifra: 'book'

Sifrei: 'books'

Sitra Akhra: meaning 'other side' and referring to the opposite of holiness

Sukkah: A 'booth' or 'hut'

Sukkot: meaning 'booths' or 'huts'; the name of the festival commemorating the wandering of the Jews during their time in the wilderness

Tabernacle: the portable sanctuary in which the Jews housed the Ark of the Covenant

Taking challah: when making challah, a small piece of dough is separated and either burned or disposed of in a respectful way in accordance with the command in Numbers 15:18–21

Talmud: 'teaching' or 'study': the work of the collected scholars as a running commentary to the Mishnah

Talmud Bavli: The Babylonian Talmud

Talmud Yerushalmi: The Jerusalem Talmud

Tanakh: Hebrew name for the Bible

Tannaim: 'teachers' or 'repeaters'; term given to the contributors of the Mishnah

Tefillin: two small leather boxes with compartments that contain passages from the Torah

Tehiru: the surge of infinite energy and light

Theodicy: an argument justifying or exonerating God; a term used in relation to the existence of evil and suffering

Glossary

Theology: the study of God, religious belief and revelation

Thymus: a gland which plays an important role in the development of the immune system which is located near the heart

Tikkun: meaning 'repair'; the restoration of cosmic harmony

Tikkun Olam: meaning 'repair of the world'; used in relation to social action and the pursuit of social justice

Tish: meaning 'table'; a gathering of Hasidim around a rebbe's table

Tithe: the giving of a tenth of one's income, after taxes have been taken, to charity

Tohorot: 'purity'; 6th of the six orders of the Mishnah

Torah: means 'instruction' or 'teaching' and refers to the first five books of the Jewish scriptures; it can also refer to the whole of Jewish teaching

Tractate: a volume of the Talmud

Transcendent: existing outside the material or created world and independent of it

Transcendental: going beyond usual human knowledge or experience

Treifah: meaning 'torn'; food that is non-kosher

Tzaddik: meaning 'righteous one'; another term for rebbe

Tzedakah: 'charity'; literal meaning is 'justice' or 'righteousness'

Tzimtzum: contraction; the way in which God makes space for humankind to make its own choices

Universal: relating to all people, and not just to one particular group

Vilna Gaon: a renowned rabbinic scholar; the spiritual leader of Vilna

Yeshiva: a Jewish academy for Talmudic study

YHVH Tsva'ot: meaning 'Lord of Hosts'

Yigdal: meaning 'magnify'; a synagogue hymn containing the Thirteen Principles of Faith

Zeraim: 'seeds'; 1st of the six orders of the Mishnah

Zion: one of the names for Jerusalem; also used as a name for all of Israel

Zohar: the classical text of Kabbalah; a mystical interpretation of the Torah

Index

613 mitzvot 25, 31, 33, 38
a priori 171
acronym 22, 24, 36, 38
Adonai 40, 93, 160
Aggadah/Aggadot 9, 22–29, 31–34
    ethical/didactic 25, 28–29, 31–32
    and Halakhah 22–28, 31–32
Aggadic midrashim *see* Midrash Aggadah
agnostic 131
agunah 97, 104
Alenu 81, 83, 86
Aliyah 50, 55
allegorical 23, 69, 76
alms 46, 83
Amidah 10, 20, 49, 162
Amoraim 9
anachronistic 140
Ani Ma'amin 64
anthropomorphise 66
anti-Semitism 50–52, 54, 57, 59, 61, 110, 120
Aramaic 8–9, 11, 15, 20, 156
Aristotelianism 39–41, 44–45
art 155
ascetic 139
Ashkenazi 126, 142, 172, 178
assimilation 50, 52, 57, 59, 61, 78, 107, 109–110, 112, 115–118, 149, 151
Baal Shem Tov 138–143, 145, 148, 150, 157
Babylon/Babylonia 9, 11–13, 49, 92, 116, 121, 135
    exile 49, 92, 116, 121, 135
Babylonian Talmud 10–14, 17, 135, 170, 173
    difference from Jerusalem Talmud 11–14
bar mitzvah 94, 102–103, 109, 124
bat mitzvah 94, 102–103, 109
BCE, definition of 7
bedieved 171
beneficent God 122
Berakhot 8, 12
Bereshith 40, 64
Berkovitz, Eliezer 128–129, 133, 135–136
Besht *see* Baal Shem Tov
bet din 98
bet midrash 103
bioethics 169, 171, 180
Birkat Hamazon 93
Blackburn, Professor Clare 175–176
blastocyst 171
Brit Milah 97, 105
Buber, Martin 130
CE, definition of 6
celestial 64, 154, 164
challah 96

chanukat habayit 92
charity 24, 46, 81, 88, 113
chukim 107–108
Chumash 36, 43, 93, 113
churban 126–127
civil rights 78
clothing 27, 56, 79, 110, 115, 117
codifying 7, 17
consecration 92, 102, 108
corporeal 40, 66
cosmogony 64
cosmology 39, 67–68, 74, 76, 144
creation 40–41, 64–71, 73–76, 81, 128, 145, 153–156, 158, 160–161, 164–165, 167
    challenge of science 64–71, 73–76
de Leon, Moses 156
Decalogue 24
Der Judenstaat 52
derash 22, 24, 36–37, 43
devekut 139, 141–143, 145, 150, 154, 160–161, 164
diaspora 61, 126
didactic 25, 28, 31
divorce 8, 54, 60, 62, 95, 97–98, 104–105
dress *see* clothing
education 53, 107, 112–113, 115, 118
El 159
El Hai 160
El Shaddai 160
Elohim 159
Elohim Tsva'ot 159
emanation 41, 65–67, 154–155, 157–158, 164
embryo research debate 169–176, 178–181
empirical 69, 73
En Sof 157–158, 160–161, 164, 166
Eretz Hakodesh 48
Eretz Yisrael 48
esoteric 153–155, 164–167
ethical 28–29, 31–32, 34, 39, 44–45, 79–81, 87, 89, 103–104, 112, 145, 162, 169–176, 178–181
ethical monotheism 79–80, 89
'Ethics of the Fathers' 6, 17, 19, 65
evolution 69–70, 73–76
ex nihilo 41, 64–66
ex post facto 171
excommunication 78, 140–141, 150
exegesis 22, 36, 40, 43, 99, 124
existential 83
Exodus 17, 22, 24, 26, 37, 40, 84, 86, 94, 102, 108, 156, 159
Fackenheim, Emil 130–131, 133–136
family, role of 92–97, 102–103
feminism 95–100, 104–105
First Zionist Conference 52

Index

free will 66, 128–129, 133, 161
Gemara 6, 9–13, 18–20, 22
gematria 24
gemilut hasadim 81, 88
Genesis 1 22, 29, 40–41, 64–66
genocide 121, 133, 135
Gentile 83, 86–87, 112, 115
Geonim/Gaon 13, 66, 140, 150
get 97; *also see* divorce
gezerot 26, 31
ghettos 121, 129
God, characteristics of 122–123, 127, 129, 133–135, 165
golem 155, 167
Guide for the Perplexed 38–41, 46, 65, 68, 74, 76
Haggadah 93
hagiographical 139
Halakhah 7–9, 12–14, 17–18, 22–28, 31–34, 38–39, 44–45, 56, 95, 97, 104–105, 109, 116, 139, 171, 179
    and the 613 mitzvot 25, 31, 33
    and Aggadah 22–28, 31–32
    Orthodox views, revealed will of God 26–27
    Reform views, revealed will of God 27–28
Halakhic 12, 18, 19, 26–28, 32–34, 38–39, 44–45, 84, 87, 98, 118, 169–171, 178–180
Halakhot 12
Haredi/Haredim 56–57, 60, 62, 103
Hasidic Judaism 13, 95, 110, 115–117, 124, 138–146, 148–151, 167
    beliefs and practices 144–146
    men and women, roles of 95
Hasidim 13, 117, 139–142, 144, 146, 149–150
Haskalah 146
havdalah 17–18
havruta 15
Havurah 97
Hebrew language 8, 15, 22–24, 36, 40, 53–54, 64, 67, 78, 81, 103, 113, 138, 142, 148, 150, 154–155, 166–167
Hebrew Scriptures 43–44, 82, 88–89
hechsher 108
herem 78
heresy 13, 78
Herzl, Theodor 51–54, 59–61
Hitler, Adolf 120, 122, 127, 130–131, 134
Holocaust 54–55, 120–131, 133–136, 173
    theology 120–131, 133–136
homiletical/homily 22, 24
Hovovei Zion 51
imitatio dei 15
immanent God 123
interfaith dialogue 83–84, 87
Israel, State of 53–57, 60–62, 125, 127
Jerusalem
    biblical names for 48, 59, 61
    Temple, destruction of 7, 17, 26, 32, 121, 135
Jerusalem Talmud 10–14, 17, 33
    difference from Babylonian Talmud 11–14

Jewish Leadership Council (JLC) 113
Kabbalah 24, 66, 123–124, 145, 153–156, 160–162, 164–167
Kabbalists 66, 70, 142, 153, 155–160, 164, 166–167
kashering 108
kashrut 107–109, 115–118, 124
kavvanah 141–142, 155, 160, 162
ketubah 95, 97–98
kibbutz 53
kibbutzism 53
kiddush 17, 93
kippah/kippot 27, 110
Knesset 55, 60
Kodashim 8–9
kosher 26, 95, 102, 105, 107–109, 112, 115, 117–118, 149
Kristallnacht 120
Kvitel 144
Law of Moses 97, 141, 150
laymen 78
Leviticus 22, 26, 28, 33, 37, 83, 89, 94, 102, 107–108, 110, 115, 117, 140, 170, 173, 180
liberationist thought 80–81
lichatchila 171
liturgy 49, 59, 61, 64, 79, 83, 86, 96–100, 105, 123–124, 142
    modified 142
Lurianic Kabbalah 66
magic 39, 155, 165, 167
Maimonides (Rabbi Moses ben Maimon) 13, 23, 26, 33, 38–41, 43–46, 64–66, 68–69, 74, 76, 107
Maybaum, Ignaz 126–127, 134
meditation 154–155, 157–158, 160, 164, 166–167
Megillot 22
Mekhilta 22
melachot 11
menorah 93
Merkavah 67, 165
messianic redemption 56, 60, 62
metaphor 23, 33, 68–69, 74, 76, 123, 131
metzaveh 131
mezuzah 26, 33, 92, 162
Mitnagdim 140–141, 149
Midrash Aggadah 28–29, 32–34
Midrash Genesis 71, 75
Midrash Halakhah 26, 31–33
Midrash Konen 64
Midrash Psalms 71, 75
Midrash Rabbah 22–23
Midrash/Midrashim 22–26, 28–29, 31–34. 36–40, 43–46, 64, 71, 75, 156
    approaches of scholars to 36–40, 43–46
    imprecise science 33–34
Midrashic method 22–25
midrashim 22
migration 107
mikdash me'at 92–93, 102
mikveh 111, 142, 145
minyan/minyanim 94–99, 104

Mishnah 6–12, 14, 17–20, 22, 29, 31, 38, 45, 87, 112, 153–154, 164–165
    and Gemara 9–10, 18–20
    importance of 14–15, 17–20
    structure and development of 6–14
mishnayot 8
Mishneh Torah 38–39, 44–46
mitzvah 9, 18, 70, 90, 94–95, 102–103, 109, 117, 124, 131, 144–145, 155, 162, 167, 170–172, 180–181
mitzvot 7–8, 14, 19, 25–27, 31, 33, 38, 54, 56, 59–60, 62, 66, 76, 79, 81, 88, 93–95, 102–103, 108, 117–118, 144–145, 155–156, 161–162, 167, 170
Moed 8–9
Moses 6, 14, 17, 19, 25–27, 31–32, 36, 38–39, 41, 43, 46, 48, 65, 68, 78, 84, 86, 97, 108, 117, 141, 143–145, 150, 153, 155, 158, 161, 164
mystic tradition see Kabbalah
mystic union with God 164–165
Nashim 8, 100
nationalism 50–51, 54, 60, 120
Nazis 120–122, 124, 127–128, 130–131, 133–135
Nezikin 8
nigunim 142
notarikon 24
Nusach Sefard 142
omnibenevolent God 133, 135
omnipotent God 122, 127, 129, 133–135
omniscient God 129, 133, 135
Oral Torah 6, 14, 17, 19, 26, 31, 82, 117, 144
ordain 56, 97, 100, 105
Orthodox Judaism 7, 13, 25–27, 32–33, 44–45, 60, 62, 69, 73, 83–84, 86, 95–97, 104, 107–112, 115–116, 118, 140–141, 146, 149–150
    attitudes towards other religions 83–84, 86–87
    men and women, roles of 95–97
    views of Halakhah as revealed will of God 26–27
palaeontology 70
parable 23–25, 29, 31, 154
paradigm 124
parthenogenesis 174
particularism 84, 86
partnership minyanim 98–99
Passover 50, 93, 97, 124
perek 8
persecution 38, 50–51, 121, 133, 135, 138, 141
Peshat 22–23, 33, 36–37, 40, 43
philologist 36, 43, 53
piety/pious 13, 56, 60, 62, 78, 139, 143–145, 165
pikuach nefesh 170–172, 178, 180–181
Pittsburgh Platform 27, 62, 79–84, 86–90, 109, 116–117, 149
Plaskow, Judith 96–97, 99–100, 105
plenum 123
pluralism/pluralistic 27, 78, 82–83, 86–87, 99, 112, 151, 169
plurality 40, 66
pogroms 51
poskim 171
posthumous 130

prayer 10, 12, 20, 25–26, 38, 45, 50, 64, 78–79, 81, 83, 87, 93–100, 103, 105, 126, 140–142, 144–146, 148, 150–151, 155, 157–158, 160, 162, 165, 167
prayer rite 141–142
pre-implantation embryo research/genetic screening 172–173, 178
Progressive Revelation 79
prophet 6, 13, 17, 19, 24, 38, 49, 59, 61, 81, 89, 93, 116, 122, 135, 154, 161, 164, 167
rabbinical 6–7, 15, 26–27, 33, 38, 80, 98, 100, 109, 116, 179
Rambam 38; also see Maimonides
Rashi (Rabbi Solomon ben Isaac) 36–37, 40, 43–44, 46
Rebbe 13–14, 143–144, 146, 150
redaction of the Mishnah 7, 11
Reform Judaism 15, 27–28, 78–80, 82–84, 86–90, 95–96, 98, 104, 117–118, 149, 151
    attitude towards other religions 82–84, 86–87
    development of 78–79
    men and women, roles of 95–97
    and pluralism 27, 78, 82–83, 86–87
    views of Halakhah as revealed will of God 27–28
remez 22–23
Remnant 126–127, 134
reparation 161
responsa 27–28, 32, 38, 169, 179
retribution 121, 135
Rosh Chodesh 96–97
Rosh Hashanah 93, 103
Rubenstein, Richard 122–124, 129, 133
sage 6–7, 9–12, 17–20, 22–23, 25–26, 31, 33, 39, 46, 65, 81, 90, 92, 102, 154, 156
Sanhedrin 7, 11–12, 22, 155, 180
scapegoats 138
schools see education
science, challenge of 64–71, 73–76
secular 23, 54, 56–57, 59–60, 62, 78, 98, 102–105, 107–112, 115–116, 131
    society 107–112, 115–116
secularisation 48–57
sedarim 8
Seder 93, 99
Seder Olam 71
Sefer Yezirah 67, 155
Sefirah/Sefirot 155, 158–162, 164, 166
Sephardi 126, 142
Shabbat/Shabbatot 14, 17–18, 26, 28, 54, 60, 62, 93, 95–96, 102–103, 105, 110–112
shamanism 138
shechitah 108, 115, 118
Shekinah 50, 155, 159–160, 165, 167
Sitra Akhra 159
shiva 94
Shoa 120, 122–124, 133, 135–136
shomer 109
shtreimel 110
shul 96
Shulchan Arukh 28, 172

Index

Sifra/Sifrei 22
sod 22, 24–25, 33
somatic cell nuclear transfer (SCNT) 171–172, 181
stem-cell research 170–172, 174–175, 178–181
suffering, traditional Jewish understanding of 121
Sukkah 12, 93
Sukkot 12, 93
Tabernacle 92, 102, 159
taking challah 96
Talmud 6, 9–15, 17–20, 22–23, 25, 27, 33–34, 36–39, 43–46, 69, 71, 75–76, 79, 81, 83, 92, 94, 97–98, 102, 104–105, 108, 112, 124, 140, 146, 148–151, 154–155, 165, 170, 173, 178, 180
    importance 14–15
Talmud Bavli 10, 12; *also see* Babylonian Talmud
Talmud Yerushalmi 12–13
Tanakh 24, 28, 32, 34, 39, 45–46, 93–94, 102
Tannaim 7–8, 17
tefillin 23, 26, 33–34, 96, 104, 129, 155, 167
tehiru 161
Tendler, Rabbi Moshe David 171–172, 174–175, 179–181
theodicy 124, 127, 129–130, 133–134, 136
theology 13, 40, 49, 61, 64, 79, 99, 120–129, 131, 134–136, 171
Thirteen Principles of Faith 38, 45, 64
thymus 175–176
tikkun 80–81, 88–89, 161–162, 165, 172, 178
Tikkun Olam 80–81, 88–89, 172, 178
Tish 144
tithe 81
Tohorot 8–9
Torah 6, 8–9, 12, 14–15, 17–20, 22–23, 25–27, 31–34, 36–40, 43–46, 48, 54, 56, 59–62, 64, 68–71, 73–76, 78–79, 81–84, 86, 88–90, 92–93, 95–99, 103–104, 109–110, 113, 115, 117–118, 121–122, 127, 129, 133–136, 139, 144–146, 148–150, 156–157, 159–160, 164–167, 170–171, 178, 180
tractate 6, 8, 11–12, 14, 180
transcendent God 123, 165
transcendental 130
treifah 108
tzaddik 143, 150
tzedakah 81, 88, 90
tzimtzum 123, 161
universal 52, 60–62, 80, 84, 86–87, 103, 124, 162
universe, age of 71, 75
Vilna Gaon 140, 150
Wales, Jews living in 107
Wenig, Margaret 100
Wiesel, Elie 124–126, 134, 136
women, role of 95–100, 104–105
yeshiva 15, 18, 20, 97, 174
YHVH Tsva'ot 159
Yigdal 38, 45
Zeraim 8, 12
Zion 48–57, 59–62, 123

Zionism 48–57, 59–62
    Labour 53–54
    political 51–52, 54, 59, 61–62
    Religious, origins of 48–50
    secular 54, 56–57, 60, 62
Zionist Movement 51–56, 59–60, 62
Zohar 145, 149, 156–157, 159–160, 162, 164–165